The Big Screen Comedies of Mel Brooks

The Big Screen Comedies of Mel Brooks

Robert Alan Crick

McFarland & Company, Inc., Publishers
Jefferson, North Carolina, and London

Library of Congress Cataloguing-in-Publication Data

Crick, Robert Alan.
The big screen comedies of Mel Brooks / Robert Alan Crick.
p.   cm.
Includes bibliographical references and index.

ISBN 0-7864-1033-7 (illustrated case : 50# alkaline paper)

1. Brooks, Mel.   I. Title.
PN2287.B695C75   2002   792.7'028'092 — dc21   2002008952

British Library cataloguing data are available

Manufactured in the United States of America

Cover photograph: Kenneth Mars, Gene Wilder and Zero Mostel
in the 1968 Mel Brooks film *The Producers* (Photofest)

McFarland & Company, Inc., Publishers
Box 611, Jefferson, North Carolina 28640
www.mcfarlandpub.com

Table of Contents

Introduction

How on earth — or even on planet Spaceball for that matter — does one even begin to adequately evaluate the big-screen comedy of writer-director Mel Brooks? Easily one of the funniest men the movies have ever produced, Brooks possesses the wondrous power to leave fans convulsed with laughter, to lift the spirit, to unburden the soul, and with knockout hits like *The Producers, Blazing Saddles,* and *Young Frankenstein* he has done just that many times over. When Brooks' talents — honed to such razor-sharp comic excellence in the days of *Your Show of Shows, Get Smart,* and "The 2,000 Year Old Man" — really hit their targets dead-on, when his extraordinary skills as film farceur really show themselves at their top-of-the-heap, good-as-it-gets mirth-making best, the keyboard falls silent as the writer fumbles for just the right adjective to describe him. *Hilarious? Delightful? Uproarious? Side-splitting?* At times like these, when Brooks is on a full-fledged, all-out, no-holds-barred comic roll, the ever-reliable Mr. Webster mysteriously fails us, Monsieur Roget, that most dependable of Frenchmen, falls inexplicably flat.

At the same time, however, Brooks' films further defy analysis because, to Brooks lovers' never-ending frustration, they also have an unsettling tendency to turn out so much like the jokes that comprise them: peculiarly hit-or-miss endeavors, one minute shoot-the-moon brilliant, the next falling so far short of his own best work the disappointment as fans leave the theater hangs heavy as lead in the popcorn-scented air. *Young Frankenstein,* one of Brooks' all-time finest, carries with it such timeless magic just *mentioning* it brings back floods of happy memories — of top-hatted corpse-monsters tap dancing to Irving Berlin, of blind toastmasters scalding houseguests with lit candles and hot soup, of stork-legged hunchbacks with Ping Pong ball eyes — yet name a less flamboyant, more down-to-earth little comedy like *Life Stinks* and all but the most diehard fans shrug with disinterest at the whole idea. With Brooks, one never feels sure what to expect — whether the very next scene will leave him rolling in the aisles with all-out delight or just shaking his head with grim dissatisfaction, whether he'll be asking, between hysterical giggles, "What will that lunatic think of next?" or, visibly underwhelmed, simply "What was that lunatic thinking?"

Of course, Brooks might just as easily ask moviegoers the same question, mightn't he? In a medium where the Stallones and Schwarzeneggers grunt, flex, and machine-gun their way to box-office godhood while vastly superior actors go barely paid and barely noticed, where obvious treasures like *It's a Wonderful Life* and *Bringing Up Baby* can't drag audiences into theaters in first release but junk-food output like *The Cannonball Run* rakes in millions, it's hardly Brooks' fault alone when fans don't always respond. Still, the fact that even the same shrewd filmmaker who won raves with pictures like *The Producers* and *Young Frankenstein* could occasionally turn out a film so many fans felt, like Princess Vespa's fiancé in *Spaceballs*, just "didn't do it" for them, reveals how wildly unpredictable Brooks' comic universe often is.

He's a curious man, Mel Brooks, as impossible to anticipate from film to film as in old *Tonight Show* and *Larry King Live* interviews, in which he's as likely to dance on tabletops or spew spit-takes as rein himself in and just quietly answer the questions. His films' tones vary widely, from the warm, old-fashioned quaintness of *The Twelve Chairs* to the gritty, sacrilegious brashness of *History of the World—Part I*, from the bend-all-rules lunacy of *Spaceballs* to the conscientious semi-sobriety of *Life Stinks*. No doubt the Motion Picture Association of America, the group issuing theater ratings to U.S. movies, found him one of its most unpredictable clients, Brooks being one of only a handful of directors ever to lens films rated, at one time or another, G, PG, PG-13, and R.

Think of it: following MPAA ratings, a Mel Brooks film festival's target audience might range all the way from the *Babe* and *Little Mermaid* crowds to fans of *Pulp Fiction* and *Natural Born Killers*!

In a sense, though, Brooks' entire career revolves around just such contradictions, both off-screen and on. His comedy absolutely steeped in Jewish overtones, Brooklyn-born comedy star Melvin Kaminsky on the one hand seems to take his faith very seriously—insert a nickel for every rabbi, Star of David, and menorah in the Brooks canon and one's piggy bank ends up quite, quite full indeed—yet he is at the same time the sort of comic who, in *History of the World—Part I*, has an impertinent Moses God-grumbling atop Mount Sinai like some street-sassy schoolboy, tortured rabbis spouting body part vulgarities in the Spanish Inquisition, and just about everyone from cavemen to French nobles behaving abominably enough to make the average churchgoer cringe, Jew and non–Jew alike. Pretty shocking stuff, some of it, fully meriting all the objections leveled at it and then some—yet just when one prepares to write off Brooks as just another trashy Hollywood smut peddler, he comes up with a gag so *Leave It to Beaver* innocent, so *Love Finds Andy Hardy* old-fashioned, so *Kukla, Fran, and Ollie* childlike, one is suddenly struck by the extraordinary impression that Mel Brooks may be just a big misunderstood teddy bear after all.

This is, remember, the same Mel Brooks who in *Young Frankenstein* has Marty Feldman's stooped-over, cane-bearing hunchback Igor, meeting Gene Wilder's Dr. Freddy Frankenstein for the first time, ask him, "Walk this way," then, dissatisfied that Freddy hasn't stooped over too, clarify, "*This* way," demonstrate precisely the tread he means, and then helpfully hand Freddy his cane as an assist. How can one possibly watch a scene this happy-go-lucky innocent, this wonderfully fourth-grade schoolyard silly and not be charmed by it? Indeed, seeing Brooks enjoy this goofy old chestnut so much he uses it again, slightly altered, in *History of the World—Part I* and *Robin Hood: Men in Tights* only verifies what we've suspected about our favorite big-screen funnyman all along: no matter how "adult" some of his gags might be, at heart Brooks is just a big silly kid, a grown man who may read Tolstoy in his spare time but probably still loves "knock, knocks," riddles, and elephant jokes every bit as much as the typical carefree ten-year-old. Brooks' brain may swirl with Shelley and Stoker and Shakespeare, but his boyish spirit is pure Bazooka Joe.

Perhaps it's partly because Brooks clearly *is* so smart so many critics are tempted to take potshots at him. His figurative mantelpiece hangs brimming with awards: Oscars for his work on Ernest Pintoff's 1963 cartoon "The Critic" and writing *The Producers*; a Grammy for his and Carl Reiner's *The 2,000 Year Old Man in the Year 2,000* album; an Emmy for co-writing the 1966 *Sid Caesar, Imogene Coca, Carl Reiner, Howard Morris Special*; three more for playing comb-needy Uncle Phil ("Firm embrace! Firm embrace!") on TV's *Mad About You*; a trio of Tonys for his and Thomas Meehan's dazzling 2001 *The Producers* smash Broadway musical adaptation—all richly respected, vastly estimable honors not just handed out like candy from a jar.

His well regarded Brooksfilms company has tackled such "thinking man's" pictures as *The Elephant Man* (1980), *The Doctor and the Devils* (1985), *The Fly* (1986), and *84 Charing Cross Road* (1987), prestige films helmed by such directoral luminaries as David Lynch and David Cronenberg and starring such top-flight talents as Anthony Hopkins, Timothy Dalton, Jonathan Pryce, Jeff Goldblum,

Geena Davis, and Mrs. Mel Brooks herself, the magnificent Anne Bancroft. We have in Brooks a man whose various movies, for all their occasional raw crudity, also include highbrow nods to Dostoevsky (*The Twelve Chairs*) and Nietzsche (*Blazing Saddles*), Darwin (*Young Frankenstein*) and Kafka (*The Producers*; *Spaceballs*), Jung (*High Anxiety*) and Sophocles (*History of the World—Part I*)—in short, a man well-read and intelligent enough he could easily win pats on the back for the sort of super-sophisticated, high-class, rapier-witted comedy associated with the likes of Billy Wilder or Preston Sturges or Ben Hecht. For some reason, though, Brooks doesn't seem much interested. Maybe it's because we've already *had* a Wilder and Hecht and Sturges, and he figures just as they found their niche, he's found his. If not Brooks, to whom *else*'s films can we go for Yiddish-spewing, Old-West Indian chiefs; for madhouse patients convinced they're cocker spaniels; for Catholic abbots who pray in pig latin?

And that, film fans, is why the movies need Mel Brooks. Excepting the far-out lunacy of the occasional *Airplane!* or *Top Secret!* or *Hot Shots!*—all of which, by the way, might never have existed in the first place without Brooks to pave the way—scenes fit perfectly well in Brooks comedies that couldn't possibly fit anywhere else. In Brooks, horses get strung up on the gallows just like the doomed badmen who ride them (*Blazing Saddles*), restaurant patrons spew spicy-food heat clouds like smokestacks (*Silent Movie*), Vikings take off helmets to reveal natural-born, bull-like horns underneath (*History of the World—Part I*). Nobody else gives fans movie scenes boasting such unbridled goofiness, and quite possibly nobody else could. *Mel* Brooks might get away with hooking up video Pong games to a hospital patient's life-support monitor as he does in *Silent Movie*, but that other Brooks, *Albert* Brooks, could never get away with — or try — anything even close to that, not in a film like *Modern Romance* or *Lost in America* or *Mother* anyway. A character in *High Anxiety* can fall to her death straddling a broom, cloaked, and cackling like the Wicked Witch from *The Wizard of Oz* and Brooks fans, by now long ago used to such improbables, accept it almost without question, but could *When Harry Met Sally* and *Sleepless in Seattle* scribe Nora Ephron succeed so effortlessly with the same joke? Or Brooks' fellow *Your Show of Shows* alumni like Larry Gelbart, or Carl Reiner, or Woody Allen, or Neil Simon? Here and there, possibly, in their more fanciful, farcical moments — Gelbart in *Neighbors*, perhaps, Reiner in *The Man with Two Brains*, Allen in *Sleeper*, Simon in *Murder By Death*— but for the most part the gags are much too broad, the jokes too no-holds-barred boundless for the sort of reality-rich, matter-of-fact universes Brooks' former colleagues prefer puttering around in.

Indeed, even though we know Brooks has read Ovid and Rostand — his 2,000 Year Old Man is an "an avid Ovid reader," and stage-acted a terrific Cyrano before getting his nose fixed — the filmmaker Brooks nevertheless pulls his allusions less often from art and literature than pop culture: Mr. Coffee; Pong; Doublemint; H & R Block; Looney Tunes; *Home Alone*; *ABC's Wild World of Sports*. Like the brainy schoolgirl who plays the fool to keep her D-minus boyfriend from feeling he's in over his head, Brooks often seems to be holding back, denying us the classiest part of himself. And from a strictly business sense, why not? Albert Brooks' and Woody Allen's movies may be more sophisticated, but they probably don't rent nearly as well on home video or, for that matter, play nearly as often on Saturday afternoon TV. How many twelve-year-olds *really* care

about renting the likes of *Defending Your Life* or *Shadows and Fog*— especially when *History of the World* — *Part I* or *Dracula: Dead and Loving It* awaits them just one shelf over?

Still, even if the money has nothing to do with it, even if all Brooks is after with movies like *Spaceballs* and *Robin Hood: Men in Tights* is just having fun, making the sort of comedies *he* likes, it's still a little irksome that a man so intellectually astute he once habitually reread *War and Peace* every few years would rather give us gags about horse droppings (*Silent Movie*), bird droppings (*High Anxiety*), and bat droppings (*Dracula: Dead and Loving It*) than make us laugh through sheer wit, sheer highbrow-crafty repartee. Brooks needn't apologize for being what he is, exactly — like the old Cole Porter song says, all the world loves a clown, and clowns don't come much funnier than Brooks — but even his fans sometimes wonder why a man this smart, this keen, this clever, would rather go for the tasteless guffaw than the refined chuckle, the shake-the-rafters horselaugh than the behind-the-napkin titter. Even Shakespeare could get pretty bawdy, we realize, even Euripedes pretty risqué, but must *Silent Movie* really include that outhouse-lewd boardroom table joke? Must *History of the World* — *Part I* really flash at us all those bare Roman buttocks? Must *Spaceballs'* Dark Helmet, so beloved by all the kiddies, really use *that* word?

Brooks himself would probably laugh at such prudery, of course — he likely had just such goody-goody squeamishness in mind scripting all those daffy "uptight Victorian" gags in *Dracula: Dead and Loving It*— but the fact remains that many film fans genuinely miss the days when *adult* meant the likes of *My Man Godfrey* and *Double Indemnity* and not *Porky's* and *Basic Instinct*; when child actors didn't mouth the same back alley obscenities as a De Niro or

Pesci or Pacino; when screenwriting Oscars were awarded to films whose "brilliant" dialogue wasn't comprised largely of the same four-letter word machine-gunned at us two and three hundred times; when animators didn't routinely sneak sex imagery inside cartoon clouds and oceans and grass. Is Meg Ryan really superior to Irene Dunne because she can say bleep-nasty words Ms. Dunne never dared to? Bruce Willis a better romantic lead than James Stewart because Mr. Stewart never bared his posterior on screen? Surely not, yet modern-day cinema would have us believe it.

However much one may agree film and TV were long too conservative about such things (on Brooks' pal Carl Reiner's *The Dick Van Dyke Show*, young marrieds Rob and Laura Petrie slept in twin beds for years), we know too that good comedy needn't always rely on the shocking and sordid. For all his affection for testing the limits of good taste, Brooks is never so creatively destitute the easy gasp-gag is the best he can do. Self-restraint may not exactly come to Brooks second-nature, but all the comic lechery in the world couldn't make *History of the World — Part I's* raunchy, rowdy "French Revolution" section one bit funnier than seeing Brooks' button-down psychiatrist Dr. Richard Thorndyke, Sinatra-style, suddenly belt out *High Anxiety's* title song like a pro in a hotel piano bar, gabbing it up with patrons between stanzas, strutting about the place as if he's been knocking 'em dead all his life. That sort of out-of-nowhere insanity is sheer comic gold, Mel Brooks at his unparalleled zany best, and he doesn't need a single cheap laugh to do it.

Come to think of it, Thorndyke's hilarious mid-movie metamorphosis from conservative professional man to celeb-style crooner reminds one quite a bit of Brooks' own Jekyll-and-Hyde inconsistencies — not just because Brooks plays Thorndyke himself on screen, but because his best work depends so often on making such farfetched matchups work. Little wonder, considering how discordant it seems for a man of his obvious intellect to script banana peel gags (*History of the World — Part I*) and pie-in-the-face jokes (*Blazing Saddles*, or *Silent Movie* — take your pick) that Brooks would declare, as he did to Bob Costas in a *Later* interview for NBC-TV in 1991, that juxtaposition is so crucial to his comedy. "I always like juxtapositions," explained Brooks. "I like a juxtaposition of texture: something smooth, hard, metallic, and gleaming juxtaposed to something soft, dirty, cottony, woolly, and with garnish on it. Juxtapositions always work."

Well, not always, perhaps, but pretty often. And it's true: Brooks' films positively brim with side-by-side absurdities, burst at the seams from oddball mismatches that win laughs just from the sheer absurdity of seeing such loon-goofy opposites placed end to end. World War II Nazis doing musical comedy in *The Producers*? That's juxtaposition. Pious-looking priests gone mad from Commandment-smashing avarice in *The Twelve Chairs*? Juxtaposition again. Cows loping about saloons and churches in *Blazing Saddles*? Reanimated corpses reading *The Wall Street Journal* in pajamas in *Young Frankenstein*? Coca-Cola cans flung like hand grenades in *Silent Movie*? Mature psychiatrists conversing in embarrassed baby talk in *High Anxiety*? Just as Brooks claims, it all boils down to just one trick: "Juxtaposition, juxtaposition, juxtaposition."

One of the first TV sketches Brooks supposedly ever wrote for what eventually became known as *Your Show of Shows* depended on such collisions of incongruities: Sid Caesar as a sort of skin-clad "street Tarzan" who battles Buicks as if they were

African lions in the "jungles" of 1950s Manhattan. Similar conceptual clashes fueled much of Brooks' and *Your Show of Shows* co-writer Carl Reiner's best "2,000 Year Old Man" recordings over the years as well. Reiner's interviewer wants to know what Brooks' Old Man thinks is mankind's all-time greatest scientific achievement. Fire, perhaps? The steam engine? The light bulb? The splitting of the atom? Not so, says the Old Man. It's Saran Wrap, he says. And the greatest medical discovery? The development of penicillin, maybe? Dr. Salk's polio vaccine? The first heart-lung machine? Not even close; it's Liquid Prell. The routines particularly thrived on linking bigger-than-life historical characters with the ridiculous and the mundane. Moses' mother and father, like parents posting their child's report card on the refrigerator, had the Ten Commandments tablets framed and hung over their mantle. King Arthur's legendary Round Table, Brooks reveals, wasn't round but oval, with extra leaves added whenever the knights came over. Joan of Arc was a real "cutie" the Old Man dated, at least until she ran off to save France. Dr. Sigmund Freud was an absolutely terrific basketball player, but nobody gives him credit for it because all he ever did was "set up the shots."

TV's *Get Smart* (1965–70), the classic spy comedy which Brooks co-created with Buck Henry, likewise depends upon such clashes of incompatibles. Its secret agent hero is an accident prone near-imbecile, yet his name is Max Smart. An early partner is Fang, a time clock-punching spy dog whose ferocious name completely belies his lazy, big dumb mutt demeanor. Max wears a telephone in his shoe — excepting one's underwear, perhaps, surely the last item of apparel anyone would want to press against his face to make a phone call. Disguised agents pop up in the most nonsensical locales, squeezed up inside baby buggies, cello cases, and cigarette machines. Even though the number of *Get Smart* episodes Brooks himself actually scripted can be counted on the fingers of one hand, his mania for comic contrasts is all over the series, his and Henry's pilot in particular (a dwarf named Mr. Big?), and when Brooks later created other shows the principle worked as well as ever, even if one couldn't prove it from the Nielsens. In his short-lived ABC Robin Hood comedy *When Things Were Rotten* (1975) twelfth-century versions of Col. Sanders roam Nottingham peddling Kensington Fried Pheasant, while on Brooks' even shorter lived NBC hotel sitcom *The Nutt House* (1989) the titular establishment's elevator operator is virtually blind.

Small surprise, then, that so much of Brooks' movie humor is based on just such head-on impacts between the expected and the unexpected, the logical and the absurd. Brooks' very first self-directed movie scene ever, in *The Producers*, contains several (Zero Mostel's greed-driven office trysts with gray-haired dowagers old enough to be his mother; sweet little old ladies who play sex-hungry contessas and meow like alleycats; etc.), and its entire premise depends on tightly juxtaposed opposites for its very existence. If Gene Wilder's mousy, fidgety Leo Bloom were just as corrupt and reckless as Mostel's Max Bialystock, *The Producers* wouldn't be even a fraction as funny, and if this unlikely twosome's big Broadway show didn't yoke together two themes at least as outrageous as Brooks' match-up of Nazis and song-and-dance, we'd simply have no film.

Brooks' juxtapositions aren't always this integral to the plot, but even when they aren't they're often astonishingly funny: money-crazed priests screaming "What a gorgeous chair!" just before smashing one to smithereens in *The Twelve Chairs*; Wild West killers virtuously heading back for toll-booth dimes instead of just riding around over empty desert in *Blazing Sad-*

dles; cigar-smoking old crones seducing young men with late-night Ovaltine in *Young Frankenstein*; *Ben Hur*–style chase scenes aboard electric wheelchairs in *Silent Movie*; rock-tied "WELCOME" messages flung through windows by neighborly violence addicts in *High Anxiety*; Leonardo Da Vinci arriving in person to paint his Last Supper "group portrait" in *History of the World — Part I*; Yiddish-spewing space trolls hawking cereal and coloring books in *Spaceballs*; passion-starved bag ladies shedding more clothes layers than overheated Arctic explorers in *Life Stinks*; terrified muscle-builder types "drowning" in barely six inches of water in *Robin Hood: Men in Tights*; ever-so-polite English madmen gobbling grasshoppers at tea in *Dracula: Dead and Loving It*. Not every piece on display in Brooks' Hall of Comic Juxtapositions is this inspired, but it's a crowded hall indeed, and when the trick really works, the comedic after-effects can be dazzling.

Rather ironically, however, mismatches of a different form — the ones appearing in reviews of his films — have haunted and hounded Mel Brooks' entire directorial career. Right from the start Brooks found critical reaction to his movies a maddening amalgam of acclaim and reproach, and he made no secret how much he detested the way reviewers would perform weird judgmental flip-flops reviewing his work, would praise him in one paragraph and then in the next, as he put it, "take it back" as if all those kind words ultimately amounted to nothing. How, Brooks wondered, could critics simultaneously like and dislike a movie in practically the same breath? How could they admit having laughed at one of his films — laughter being, presumably, the primary goal of comedy — yet still refuse to recommend it? Why couldn't they just make up their minds, take a stand, either across-the-board applaud Brooks' work or just take-no-prisoners denounce it?

Valid enough questions, certainly, all of them, but one need view only one or two Brooks films, particularly his later ones, to see why critics — and, indeed, the author of this book — find even this comic genius's very finest material so hard to appraise. For better or worse, a Mel Brooks comedy is typically a very mixed bag, and mixed bag movies earn mixed bag reviews, both from fans and critics. *History of the World — Part I* contains some of the funniest bits in the whole history of film — it's worth the ticket price just for the wacky "Inquisition" song-and-dance bit alone — but it's so erratic structurally and drags out its weakest bits for such long stretches we find it mystifying Brooks didn't fine-tune matters right off. *Spaceballs* showcases some of the slyest, sharpest satirical jabs at politics and commercialism ever committed to film, most of them neatly revolving around Brooks himself as both inept officeholder President Skroob and product-pushing hobgoblin Yogurt, yet Brooks' attractive, perfectly capable male and female leads, superb actors both, for some reason come across so run-of-the-mill bland both hero and heroine end up virtually forgotten once the story is over. Unquestionably, each of these comedies deserves credit for the parts that work — any film critic worth his thumbs owes Brooks that — but when the flashes of brilliance come stitched together this loosely, this patchwork spotty, blanket raves are hard-won.

Further contributing to these mixed responses is a fundamental confusion among both critics and audiences — at times, indeed, perhaps even within Brooks himself — as to precisely what sort of movies Brooks is making to start with. Nick Smurthwaite and Paul Gelder hit upon the problem directly when they named their 1982 book about the director *Mel Brooks and the Spoof Movie* — a terrific title, no doubt about it, but one whose accuracy depends very much on what one means by *spoof*. In its broadest sense, certainly, the description is dead-on; if spoofing somebody else's work means merely having a little harmless, good-natured fun with it without implying the one doing the spoofing could do better, that's Brooks in a nutshell. Brooks loves Hitchcock, for instance, so *High Anxiety* re-interprets the Master of Suspense's best bits, but even played for laughs the film ends up more affectionate tribute than arrogant tirade. Not for a minute does an admiring Brooks want audiences to think he's saying Hitchcock was a fool, an incompetent, some third-rate Hollywood hack. Like some giggly little boy stomping around in his father's oversized suit and hat and shoes and necktie, deep-voicing pretend business calls and chairing make-believe board meetings, Brooks isn't really making fun of Daddy, isn't mocking him; he's just having fun playing dress-up, that's all, just having a grand old time slipping into the Big Man's wardrobe. That's still spoof, all right; that's still parody — but spoof with a little *s*, parody with a small *p*.

If, on the other hand, one's definition implies lacing all that affectionate tomfoolery with a certain amount of criticism, a sort of impudent stripping bare of one's target to reveal once and for all Hollywood's emperors do indeed wear no clothes, Brooks' filmmaking resume is relatively spoof-free. *Blazing Saddles* remains the most obviously incontestable qualifier, easily fitting this latter, more demanding definition with its brazen, tough-love mockery of a genre fans swallowed whole for years. The film's title sounds absolutely perfect for a "real" frontier epic yet proves absolutely meaningless, and Brooks' blood-pumping lyrics for the film's great title song, brilliantly punctuated by frontier-violent whip-cracking and the gut-wrenching urgency of Frankie Lane's vocals, ring every bit as high-energy

melodramatic and finally just as sound-and-fury hollow. Its unorthodox hero, Cleavon Little's hip, black Sheriff Bart, manages to unmask the simple-minded shallowness of the typical Western universe just by showing up, and like the plywood village Bart builds near the end of the film, the flimsy vision of an all-white, justice-minded American West is as easily kicked over as Bart's Hollywood phony "noble, selfless hero" speech. When the film's big street fight finale bursts right off the set and into the musical shooting next door — surely one of *the* great comic masterstrokes of the cinematic twentieth century — Brooks explodes the genre's bull-roar balderdash the way no movie ever dared to before. Now *that's* Spoof with a capital *S*.

The real problem remains that surprisingly few critics of any medium have ever truly come to grips with exactly what a spoof is, let alone any of its supposed synonyms and near-synonyms. Most Brooks pictures are clearly comic *takeoffs*, but calling them sendups may be pushing it. Bending the original out of shape slightly may be enough to make a movie a takeoff, but *sendup* suggests the original wasn't exactly perfect to start with and needs some of the wind taken out of its sails. The British used to call the implied foolishness-exposing of the latter term "taking the mickey out" — a surprisingly useful expression, whatever a *mickey* is, because the implication is something the original had before (self-importance, influence, prestige) gets stripped away. If *Mad* magazine tackles TV's *M*A*S*H* and merely tweaks it a little, gives its characters silly names and dialogue and such, the program itself loses nothing, and its creators may even celebrate the ribbing as a sort of career-validating milestone. If, however, the magazine takes potshots at the series' theoretical shortcomings — way, way more Christmas episodes than the real-life Korean War had Decembers; latter-year scriptwriting that abandons the brilliantly unfettered looseness of Larry Gelbart's Robert Altman-esque originals; final seasons so movie-of-the-week serious the show makes *Schindler's List* look whimsical — then *Mad* has produced something quite different indeed.

When Bette Midler serenaded Johnny Carson with new, funny lyrics to "You Made Me Love You" for his next-to-last *Tonight Show*, reviewers praised Midler's enchanting "parody" the next day — but laughing at the changes and laughing at the original aren't quite the same. Warner Bros.' classic "The Mouse That Jack Built" cartoon likewise features mouse versions of Jack Benny, Mary Livingston, Don Wilson, and Eddie "Rochester" Anderson, but probably not one animator involved didn't count *The Jack Benny Program* among radio's all-time finest half-hours. No question this sort of thing gets called parody all the time, or spoof, or sendup, but is that all there is to it? And if so, if all one need do to parody, say, *Casablanca* is change "Casablanca" to "Basaclanca" and "Rick Blane" to "Dick Blame," then replay the same story for laughs, what's the big honor in calling someone a parodist at all? If that's all it takes, every third grade schoolkid who ever changed the names of classmates Rufus and Lizzy to "Goofus" and "Dizzy" had best hire himself a really first-rate publicist and demand his Great American Parodist Award right now.

In a 1977 review of Brooks' *High Anxiety*, *New Yorker* film critic Pauline Kael argues this very point, charging Brooks with delivering what she calls "a child's idea of satire — imitations, with a funny hat and a leer." Kael labels Brooks' stock in trade *satire*, not *parody*, but even so she still pinpoints the essence of the whole complaint: that, parody — *true* parody, with the capital *P* — perhaps requires not just mimicry but mockery. We've all tried out our John Wayne ("Howdy, pilgrim!") and Cary Grant ("Judy, Judy, Judy") since childhood, may even have gotten laughs for it, but unless we're arguing Wayne makes an unconvincing cowboy or Grant a poor excuse for a high-class ladies' man, what's the point? The laughs come from sheer recognition ("Hey, you sound just like him!"), not ridicule, and if the imitation is a particularly bad one ("*That's* who that was? You're kidding!"), the snickers come our way, not Wayne's or Grant's.

In short, even granting Brooks' "spoofs" are often deliriously funny, is it enough solely to imitate in a funny way, or must the parodist dip his pen, even lightly, in Swiftian poison, exposing the original as foolish, faulty, and ill-conceived? "All Brooks does," complains Kael, "is let us know he has seen some of the same movies we have," inform us he has seen *Stagecoach* and *Bride of Frankenstein* and *Spellbound* too and loved them, and while no doubt exists Brooks imitates John Ford, James Whale, Alfred Hitchcock, and the rest better than anyone else in the business, it's easy to see why the Pauline Kaels of the world might well have looked at each new Brooks spoof-with-a-smile and wondered if perhaps parody ought to pursue some higher goal.

In Brooks' defense, we have to acknowledge he's far from alone in all this; if Brooks, the big-screen master of "small *s*" spoofing if ever there was one, gets more credit for producing "big *P*" parody than he really deserves, the same holds true for 99.99 percent of all parodists of the TV-and-movie era. Only once in a *High Anxiety* blue moon are the parodist's theme-mangling and bad puns really out to make some sort of point, and excepting the occasional mock epic in one's old high school English lit text, even the classics are usually more takeoff than take-down.

Perhaps in the long run none of this matters much — a laugh is a laugh, after all, no matter what function it serves — but the issue at least helps explain why some reviewers find it harder to whole-heartedly sing the praises of a fun but not terribly ambitious Brooks film like *Robin Hood: Men in Tights* the same way they applaud no-doubt-about-it genre-smashers like *Blazing Saddles*. However much Brooks' Sherwood silliness may amuse with its plays on words, anachronisms, and sight gags, it's clear he loves the legend too much to really give the myth the pummeling the word *parody* seems to imply. With his Errol Flynn–ish good looks, dashing athleticism, and lofty English elegance, titular star Cary Elwes is about as close to the mark as any casting director is ever likely to get — but then, Brooks isn't doing a serious Robin Hood film, so what does it matter? Unless this Robin is substantially different from previous big-screen incarnations — gets unmasked as some egotistical, self-serving phony, perhaps, or played so Dudley Do-Right virtuous he defies belief — where's the parody in that? The film is still funny anyway, of course, and it's true Brooks every once in a while still comes up with something to give the myth a good thrashing (its opening joke, for one, in which angry peasants protest the old burning-down-the-village cliché), but in the end the posters' "The Legend Had It Coming" claim still seems more like wishful thinking than an accurate, true-to-the-picture depiction of what *Robin Hood: Men in Tights*' comedy is all about.

In fact, Brooks' growing tendency to embrace his target genres so non-critically in his later films, of making funny movies within classic genres rather than about them, may explain why the presence of non-genre ridicule in his post-'70s efforts — that is, satire — takes on so much added import. Satirizing man's faults and foibles is one of Brooks' real talents — even *The Producers* and *The Twelve Chairs*, his first two films, teem with sharp-tongued

barbs directed at everything from show biz smarm to upper-class arrogance to clerical greed — and as Brooks' genre-exploding packs less firepower than it did in his *Blazing Saddles* days, it helps his later films no end that he can still make life's blowhards and bad eggs look like fools. If Brooks admires Preston Sturges and Frank Capra too much to let fly at them in *Life Stinks*, fine, but at least let him lash out at *someone*: greedy businessmen, corrupt lawyers, unfeeling clergymen, inept physicians, whatever. If he's too fond of vampire stories to drive a stake through dear old Bram Stoker's heart, well and good, but at least have him let loose elsewhere — on Victorian prudery, British stuffiness, nineteenth-century medical incompetence, *something*. Happily, Brooks obliges handily, loading portions of his later films with a so many satirical swipes they almost — almost — make up for whatever conviction they might lack spoof-wise. No, *Spaceballs* doesn't level any serious charges against George Lucas's *Star Wars* films or sci-fi and space travel films in general, but his assaults on political recklessness and mass-market commercialism sting as sharply as anything Brooks has ever done. Even when Brooks lets his biggest and broadest topics pass him by — the structural flaws, the logic lapses, the over-reliance on cliché — he almost always attacks the smaller, sometimes subtler topics head-on.

The most common complaint about Brooks' post-'70s work has nothing to do with either satire or parody, however, but with comedy itself, plain and simple. Critics may forgive *Dracula: Dead and Loving It* for not making them laugh at the "right" targets — at Stoker's novel, at gothic romance, at Hollywood horror films — but not making them laugh often enough, at something, at anything, seems downright inexcusable. Not that anybody's counted, but movies like *Blazing Saddles* and even the leisurely old-fashioned *Young*

Frankenstein seem to squeeze in twice as many laughs as Brooks' later films, and don't think for a minute fans and critics haven't noticed. Who wouldn't feel something was lacking if, say, *Bringing Up Baby* or *The Road to Morocco* or *Duck Soup* suddenly cut out every second or third chuckle? We've seen *Dracula* played gag-free; what we want are enough big giggles to fill every last second reminiscing on the car ride home.

Brooks' early films also benefited from a dazzling array of screwball comic talent, kooky, crazy, natural-born side-splitters whose bigger-than-life wackiness meshed almost perfectly with madman Brooks' own, but for whatever reasons (Studio pressure? Star unavailability? Faulty judgment?), many of Brooks' later casts, however talented, often look bland, unfunny, mundanely run-of-the-mill. Twenty years earlier, a film like *Robin Hood: Men in Tights* might have featured such stellar cuckoos as Gene Wilder, Madeline Kahn, Cloris Leachman, Marty Feldman, Harvey Korman, and Kenneth Mars in its major and supporting roles — uproariously funny celebrities who virtually guaranteed hilarity just by showing up, and just the far-out laugh-inducers Brooks' films so sorely need. These same actors gave the cinema some extraordinarily fine serious work too, of course, and lots of it, but comedy was where they were needed most, and working with Brooks pushed them into some zany comic otherworld all their own, where Kahn's opera training twisted itself into the screwball extravagance of *Blazing Saddles*' "I'm Tired" and Mars' extraordinary play-to-the-back-row Broadway bombast turned into the raving-mad Nazi of *The Producers*. Like Sid Caesar and Imagine Coca in *Your Show of Shows*, like Don "Agent 86" Adams and Bernie "Siegfried" Kopell on *Get Smart*, Wilder, Kahn, Leachman, Feldman, and the rest of these zanies could

steal every last scene, swallow up everything in their vast comic wake. We couldn't take our eyes off them, and we were already half laughing the second they strode onto the screen.

With rare exceptions, however — mostly several dozen colorful loonies from TV's *Saturday Night Live* and Second City/*SCTV*, people like Jon Lovitz, Julia Sweeney, Eugene Levy, Martin Short, Joe Flaherty, Andrea Martin — few really big comic actors to come along after the mid–'70s bore the same distinctively quirky look and sound of the really top funnymen of just a few years before. What about the Marx Brothers, the Three Stooges, Laurel and Hardy, W.C. Fields, Bob Hope, Red Skelton, Jerry Calona, Joe E. Brown, Arthur Lake, Charlie Ruggles, Gracie Allen, Ed Wynn? All might have made glorious Brooks maniacs, but were all pretty much long gone before Brooks first stepped behind the camera. Phyllis Diller, Buddy Hackett, Lucille Ball, Jonathan Winters, Jerry Lewis, Don Knotts, Dick Van Dyke? All had been huge stars in the '60s, but it made little sense to drop, say, old-time eccentrics Howard Morris or Ronny Graham to start using them *now*.

None of this was Brooks' fault, really. He couldn't help it any more than we could that most of the really great comic personalities of film, radio, and TV were fast starting to disappear. The era of *Milton Berle, Jack Benny, Steve Allen*, and *Ed Wynn* was long behind us well before Brooks got his big chance in the director's chair, and the one-of-a-kind-colorful celebrities who so often populated it — Jackie Gleason, Art Carney, Mel Blanc, Martha Raye, Rose Marie, Morey Amsterdam, Joe Besser, Sheldon Leonard, Danny Thomas, Jimmy Durante, Danny Kaye, Gale Gordon, Bill Dana, Louis Nye — had lost most of their show-biz luster (though none of their talent) before Brooks even got started.

Stanley Kramer's 1963 film *It's a Mad Mad Mad Mad World* alone boasted a cast so fantastic its credits read like the ultimate wish list of Brooks-worthy comic giants (Phil Silvers, Sid Caesar, Milton Berle, Buddy Hackett, Jonathan Winters, Terry-Thomas, Jim Backus, Paul Ford, Jerry Lewis, Don Knotts—and that's for starters), but it's inconceivable Brooks or anyone else could have assembled an equal collection of crazies too many years after. Maybe *Sunset Blvd.*'s Norma Desmond got it wrong; maybe it really *was* the stars that got small.

Either way, it's pretty clear not just anybody who gets laughs in movies and TV is quite right for Mel Brooks. Lovable *M*A*S*H* goofballs MacLean Stevenson and Jamie Farr might fit right in, but Alan Alda? Mike Farrell? David Ogden-Stiers? *WKRP in Cincinnati*'s peerlessly nutty Richard Sanders and Gordon Jump, sure, but Gary Sandy? Jan Smithers? One imagines any number of cast members from TV's *Sgt. Bilko*, *Car 54, Where Are You?*, or *I Love Lucy* could make the switch, but how many from *Father Knows Best*, *Leave It to Beaver*, or *The Donna Reed Show*? Even granting the warmer, softer touch of these last three shows, and even their perfectly cast actors' obvious light comedy expertise, could Robert Young ever really out-zany Phil Silvers? Hugh Beaumont out-loony Joe E. Ross? Donna Reed out-kooky Lucille Ball?

Maybe so. *Gilligan's Island*'s Russell Johnson and Dawn Wells weren't meant to be as funny as Bob Denver and Alan Hale, Jr., but anyone who recalls Johnson's dead-on Cary Grant and Wells' terrific Eliza Doolittle–ish Audrey Hepburn knows the right material can bring out the inner-wacko in just about anyone. So who knows? Maybe Abbott was every bit as funny as Costello, but we just never got a chance to see it. Maybe, given the right material, Martin was just as dive-bomb crazy as Lewis. Maybe the funniest Marx Brother was Zeppo all along.

And, then again, maybe not. All typecasting aside, all the acting talent in the world can't make someone Brooks-worthy if he's not naturally pretty funny already. In the Sunday comics, Broom Hilda and Snuffy Smith could never win the same laughs drawn like Mary Worth and Steve Canyon, not even with the same gags, and in animation one can't give Porky Pig and Marge Simpson the same voices as Flash Gordon and Brenda Starr and expect their funniest bits to go over the same way. A Mel Brooks comedy works very much along these lines, and even granting that post-Golden Age pop culture hasn't exactly given the Lou Costellos and Gracie Allens much real competition, the mind reels recalling all those once-popular off-center eccentrics, many hardly seen in movies at all after the mid–'70s, who might have been absolutely fantastic in a Mel Brooks film. We've listed dozens already, but just imagine what Brooks might have done with even a few of these crazier-than-life scene-stealers: Peter Sellers, Dudley Moore, Peter Cook, Carol Burnett, Soupy Sales, Marty Allen, Rich Little, Hans Conrad, Peter Ustinov, Carol Channing, Vito Scotti, Robert Morse, Jerry Colona, Bob Hope, Tony Randall, Marty Ingels, Eva Gabor, Sammy Davis, Jr., Iris Adrian, Joe Flynn, Eileen Brennan, John Fiedler, Alice Ghostly, Wally Cox, Flip Wilson, Ronnie Schell, Charles Nelson Reilly, Shirley Booth, Foster Brooks, Sherman Hemsley, Bernard Fox, Don Rickles, Larry Storch, Tim Conway, Richard Pryor, Paul Lynde. TV's *Monty Python's Flying Circus* might have been a great spot for Brooks to go kook-shopping—a John Cleese, Eric Idle, or Michael Palin might have worked wonders for his Robin Hood film; *Rowan & Martin's Laugh-In* maybe even more so. Just imagine what Brooks might have done with the dippy-ditzy likes of Ruth Buzzi,

Arte Johnson, Jo Anne Worley, Lily Tomlin, Henry Gibson, and Alan Sues.

Sadly, though, for one reason or another over the years Brooks lost many of the best and brightest he did have. Zero Mostel, so dizzyingly frantic in *The Producers*, proved too much star for even madman Brooks to cope with, and slipped from the ranks after just one great time at bat. Gene Wilder, whose wacky genius was rarely more evident than when he and Brooks pooled their talents on film, won raves with *The Producers, Blazing Saddles*, and *Young Frankenstein*, then struck out on his own. Kenneth Mars, so sublimely off-kilter in *The Producers* and *Young Frankenstein*, disappeared from Brooks' usual gang of cutups the same time as Wilder. Dom DeLuise, who had third-billing in both *The Twelve Chairs* and *Silent Movie* and gave *Blazing Saddles'* big finale the kind of inspired comic leg-up one can't imagine coming from anyone else, kept up his association with Brooks for years afterward, but where those films had DeLuise all but spinning like a top and turning cartwheels, his roles in *Spaceballs* and *Robin Hood: Men in Tights* amounted to little more than voice-overs and sit-downs. Madeline Kahn, so deliciously vibrant in *Blazing Saddles, Young Frankenstein*, and *High Anxiety*, played a small part in *History of the World — Part I* in the early '80s, then focused her talents elsewhere the rest of her too-brief career. Harvey Korman, every bit as over-the-edge terrific with Brooks as in all those glorious TV sketches opposite Carol Burnett, did absolutely dazzling work in *Blazing Saddles* and *High Anxiety*, reappeared for the final section of *History of the World — Part I*, then didn't work with Brooks on film again until *Dracula: Dead and Loving It* nearly fifteen years later. Marty Feldman, who had enough comic genius to fill a dozen Brooks films, lived long enough to co-star in only two, *Young Frankenstein* and *Silent*

Movie. TV regular Ron Carey, cast to perfection in *High Anxiety*, played far smaller roles in the earlier *Silent Movie* and *History of the World — Part I* later on, then more or less fell out of sight altogether. Brooks' old *Your Show of Shows* buddy Howard Morris, so adorably quirky in *High Anxiety*, reappeared briefly in *History of the World — Part I*, then didn't turn up again until *Life Stinks* a decade later. Overall, by the time of 1987's *Spaceballs*, Brooks' much-beloved mid–'70s mainstays had all just about disappeared, and the loss was deeply felt.

Felt just as sharply, though, is the affection both fans and critics have for Brooks himself, both as a screen personality and human being. Those who love Brooks recognize even his best films contain their share of flaws, but they'll also defend them to the last should anyone rebuke them too far. Oh, sure, *History of the World — Part I* is vulgar, but goodness, that "Inquisition" song is great fun! Yes, *Spaceballs'* young romantic leads practically evaporate from memory and into thin air, but oh, those swipes at movie merchandising — Spaceballs: The Bedsheet, Spaceballs: The Breakfast Cereal, Spaceballs: The Coloring Book! *Life Stinks*? Not funny enough, certainly, but what a beautiful dance number in that colorful warehouse of rags! *Robin Hood: Men in Tights*? Way too much standing and sitting around, way too little action — but those songs, those songs! *Dracula: Dead and Loving It*? Too skimpy on the joke front, true, but what delightful performances from its Dr. Seward, its Harker, its Van Helsing, its Renfield! Magnificent!

The Big Screen Comedies of Mel Brooks attempts to spotlight special little moments like these, at greater length than the typical half-page or even half-column in *Entertainment Weekly, Newsweek, Variety*, or *The New York Times*. Fans long ago frustrated by the short, absurdly simplistic critiques of Brooks' films in reference books that casually capsulize his entire cinematic output in a few short paragraphs or even ignore him entirely will, one hopes, be pleased that this book makes every effort to give one of filmdom's all-time greatest comic talents his much-delayed due. In a market flooded books analyzing, over-analyzing, and over-over- analyzing pop culture from TV's *Star Trek* to *Dawson's Creek* to *The X-Files*, surely it's high time the big-screen comedy accomplishments of one of the movies' funniest men is given another look, especially considering Brooks' entire career has largely lain neglected by writers of full-length analyses since the mid–'80s, when the last truly significant books about Brooks appeared.

Even so, fans expecting a mere "puff piece" on Brooks, a book ignoring the weaknesses of Mel Brooks' lesser films and concentrating solely on his best work, are likely to find *The Big Screen Comedies of Mel Brooks* something of a disappointment. Two hundred pages of unmitigated praise and no criticism would amount to little more than a glorified press kit, a means of peddling the Mel Brooks Box Set on home video — something akin to the way the Disney marketing people often slap the word "masterpiece" or "classic" on just about everything the late Mr. Disney ever did. Not every comedy Mel Brooks ever made was a great one, and this volume will make no attempt to disguise that fact. *The Big Screen Comedies of Mel Brooks* is a book of reviews, simple as that — of considerably more expansive, more meticulously detailed reviews, granted, but a book of reviews nonetheless. Its goal isn't public relations but film criticism — essentially very much the sort of thing Gene Siskel and Roger Ebert used to do every week on TV, but taking a good deal more time to explain the motivations behind those helpful but unavoidably cryptic thumbs-ups and thumbs-downs. Thumbs

and stars and A-B-Cs are all worthwhile systems, and they work just great on TV ads and movie posters — but by themselves, alone, they can only tell us just so much.

Brooks' fans — indeed, even Mr. Brooks himself — might not be pleased with some of what *The Big Screen Comedies of Mel Brooks* has to say about all his films, any more than any of us might be to see *our* efforts judged in print. How many parents would receive an unqualified "thumbs up" for the way they've raised their children? Husbands for the way they treat their wives? Doctors for their bedside manner? Politicians for the way they govern? Teachers for the way they teach?

Probably not many. Still, the commercial arts are a special case. As individuals, we often hate the films the critics love, and often love the ones they hate, so half the fun of going to the movies is the pleasure that comes from hearing other people's appraisals and happily disagreeing with them. Reviews ultimately amount to mere matters of opinion, and when conflicting views collide, all the better. Reality — the real truth — probably lies somewhere in the middle, but to arrive at it we must first debate it a little, pull on the tug-of-war rope hard from both ends and see what happens.

What one hopes will happen here, of course, is that *The Big Screen Comedies of Mel Brooks* will start film fans talking about Mel Brooks again. If some of the reviews within seem just a tad harsh, others a tad generous, at least older fans will have something freshly Brooksian to squabble over for a change, and maybe youngsters who've never even heard of Mel Brooks will be curious enough to wander over to the local video store and discover the joys of *The Producers* or *Blazing Saddles* or *Young Frankenstein* for the first time. It's these newer, up-and-coming Brooks fans one envies most. With comedies like these, even the least of them, they're in for a real treat.

1

★ ★ ★

"I'M HYSTERICAL, AND I'M WET!"

The Producers

★ ★ ★ ★ ★

(1968)

In his New York City office, bankrupt play producer Max Bialystock (Zero Mostel), once a high-living hitmaker now reduced to defrauding love-starved old ladies, is caught in mid-swindle by nervous young accountant Leo Bloom (Gene Wilder). After the exit of one elderly conquest (Estelle Winwood), harsh, boisterous Bialystock slowly wins the trust of the baby blanket–toting Bloom, who between anxiety attacks casually observes that a recent financial discrepancy by Bialystock — raising $2,000 more than needed to fund a play that failed after one night — might have made Bialystock a millionaire had he simply duped more investors out of greater sums.

Blinded by greed, Bialystock treats the angst-ridden Bloom to a day of carefree frivolity in Central Park, convincing him to take a real risk for once and turn his offhand remark into a reality. Having actually had fun for the first time in his by-the-book, over-cautious life, Bloom joins the renamed "Bialystock & Bloom," and the search for "the worst play ever written," a sure-fire flop. Eventually, Bialystock finds it: an appalling pro–Nazi monstrosity called *Springtime for Hitler*.

Buying the play from author Franz Liebkind (Kenneth Mars), a helmet-wearing Nazi eager to reveal Hitler's "good" side, Bialystock chases old lady investors until he sells 25,000 percent of the play. "On top" again, Bialystock spends big on new offices, a limousine, and buxom Swedish secretary Ulla (Lee Meredith), who speaks no English, and while Bloom fears such lavishness will look bad in court should their scheme backfire, Bialystock is having far too much fun to care.

Further ensuring failure, Bialystock and Bloom enlist Roger DeBris (Christopher Hewett), a flamboyant dress-wearing stage director with an effeminate male secretary named Carmen Giya (Andreas Voutsinas) and virtually no talent whatsoever. Acting on DeBris' idea of making *Springtime for Hitler* a musical, Bialystock holds open auditions for a singing Führer, but it is a lost latecomer, an earring-wearing hippie named Lorenzo St. DuBois, or

15

L.S.D. (Dick Shawn) whose spaced-out "flower child" flakiness Bialystock believes is utterly guaranteed to sink the play.

Insulting a major theater critic with a bribe on opening night, Bialystock believes his plan foolproof, and when the audience is left dumbstruck by an opening number featuring tap-dancing Nazis, he and Bloom confidently celebrate in a bar across the street. In their absence, however, their worst fear is realized: L.S.D.'s hippie Hitler, so terrible it's funny, is misperceived as brilliant comedy. Even when Liebkind, furious his beloved Fuhrer is being mocked, tries to stop the play, his accent and war helmet only inspire more wild laughs. *Springtime for Hitler* is a smash!

A frantic Bloom's plan to confess to the police triggers a wild office fight with Bialystock until Liebkind storms in firing. After Liebkind's bullets and energy are exhausted, the three men plot to close the show by blowing up the theater but, after nearly getting killed in the blast, end up on trial. Bloom delivers a heartfelt speech crediting Bialystock with bringing friendship into his joyless life, and they are sent to prison. Still, having learned nothing, Bialystock and Bloom — with Liebkind on piano — are soon readying their fellow convicts for *Prisoners of Love*, another terrible stage musical for which Bialystock and Bloom are selling hundreds of nonexistent shares.

★　★　★

So much hyper-enthusiastic adulation surrounds Mel Brooks' 1968 directorial debut film *The Producers* these days, it's hard to believe the movie that won Brooks that year's Academy Award for Best Original Screenplay wasn't the same rake-in-the-money, lines-around-the-block Broadway mega-hit that fetched a record ninety-nine bucks a seat thirty-three years

later. While *The Producers'* word-of-mouth reputation as one of the funniest comedies ever made has grown steadily ever since — and surely any film about two Broadway con men stealing investments from a seemingly surefire musical flop called *Springtime for Hitler* can't help creating a buzz of some kind — the year's real stars weren't show-biz schemers Max Bialystock and Leo Bloom but Fanny Brice, HAL the computer, and Oscar Madison and Felix Ungar, as William Wyler's *Funny Girl* took 1968's biggest U.S. dollars, trailed closely by Stanley Kubrick's *2001: A Space Odyssey*, and Gene Saks' *The Odd Couple*, based on the play by Brooks' *Your Show of Shows* pal Neil Simon.

Success can't really be measured in mere financial terms, of course (though one might not want to tell cash-hungry schlockmeisters Max and Leo that), but *Bullitt* outgrossed Brooks that year too, as did *Romeo and Juliet*, *Oliver!*, *Planet of the Apes*, *Rosemary's Baby* — the list goes on. Indeed, as well regarded as it is now (and that's *highly* regarded, at least by those who don't mind Nazi jokes and "good guys" who cheat and steal), for its first several years of post-release *The Producers* remained less well known than dozens of other 1968 films, from hits to near-hits to just plain flops — *Blackbeard's Ghost*, *Chitty Chitty Bang Bang*, *The Thomas Crown Affair*, *Yellow Submarine*, *Charly*, *The Lion in Winter*, *Ice Station Zebra*, *The Boston Strangler*, *Yours, Mine and Ours*, *Speedway*, *Barbarella*, even Brooks ally Howard Morris's *With Six You Get Eggroll*. For sheer pop culture impact, 1968 was an amazing year at the movies, one in which Elvis and the Beatles were screen stars every bit as big as Rock Hudson and Charlton Heston, and space vixens and talking chimps sold candy and cola right alongside Dickens and Shakespeare.

Happily, though, thanks partly to the 2001 Broadway smash starring Nathan

Lane and Matthew Broderick, and partly because Brooks' script and stars are so funny sooner or later it was bound to get its due, *The Producers*' reputation just keeps growing, and many who for years had no idea this wildly funny little taboo-smasher even existed now name Brooks' first film in the same breath as *Blazing Saddles* or *Young Frankenstein*. They're right, too; rookie outing or not, the movie that put "When you got it, flaunt it!" in *Bartlett's Book of Familiar Quotations* is one of Brooks' best — never so break-all-rules crazy as *Blazing Saddles*, nor so expertly directed as *The Twelve Chairs* or *Young Frankenstein*, but quite possibly his most satisfying, from its wacky, irredeemably greedy title characters to the wickedly satiric lyrics of Brooks' classic main theme.

What makes *The Producers* work better than so many subsequent Brooks films makes the 2001 stage version work so beautifully as well: first, a speedier, snappier comic pace than most later Brooks movies, which, funny as they often are, rarely race ahead with the never-let-up comedic thrust propelling stars Zero Mostel and Gene Wilder here; second, a cast of actors whose presence and performances are so expressive and colorful that viewer expectations leap up just at the sight of them; and, third, a straight-from-the-heart, deep-seated affection between Mostel's Max and Wilder's Leo far less evident among the central characters in most of Brooks' later films.

Ably assisted by secretary/casting director Alfa-Betty Olsen, Brooks just keeps piling laugh upon laugh, almost as if he's still making every between-ads second count back at *Caesar's Hour* or *Get Smart*. Zero Mostel's Max in particular barely pauses for breath the entire film; as nutso Nazi playwright Franz Liebkind, actor Kenneth Mars spews his raving-mad Churchill-bashing with similar breakneck frenzy; and even Gene Wilder's mild-mannered Leo, like Mr. Peepers on pep pills, drops his measured, Clark Kent delivery for super-accelerated paroxysms in no time flat.

Still, as fast and furious as Brooks' laugh-lines come, the actors he's chosen make them seem doubly funny, either because they're such surefire comic naturals, or because, lacking Don Knotts' beanpole bugginess or Buddy Hackett's mouthful-of-marbles pudginess, they work all the harder playing it to the hilt, and bury run-of-the-mill averageness beneath comic exaggeration the likes of which softer, subtler comedies have never seen. Mostel's bucking bronco explosiveness; Wilder's Chicken Little panic attacks; Mars' zick-az-pea-zoup German; Shawn's Maynard G. Krebs beatnik cool — not every actor could get away with such cartoon-like theatrics, but Mostel, Wilder, and the rest of the cast are such gifted performers they make it all work. What's more, the fact that several of these stars, especially Wilder, would take even bigger comic risks later on makes *The Producers* seem even funnier today. In 1968, who knew *Start the Revolution Without Me*, *Blazing Saddles*, *Young Frankenstein*, *Silver Streak*, and *Stir Crazy* lay ahead? No one — but now, thanks to all that kooky, crazy nonsense, just *seeing* Wilder seems to guarantee a good time.

Finally, though, *The Producers* still ends up more than just another fast-paced showcase for a great cast. Yes, the dialogue crackles, and yes, Mostel, Wilder, and crew squeeze every last ounce of craziness out of every last scene — but then, just when the story needs some old-fashioned sentiment, Brooks does a sensational about-face and gives Max and Leo a moment of earnest, three-dimensionalized honesty and humanity that genuinely touches the heart.

Mousy accountant Leo, whose casual remarks inspire tax delinquent Max's scheme to bilk investors out of a fortune on a close-in-one-night musical in the first place, tickles us silly with his nervous nelly infantilism, yet we feel for him too, and for Max, who somehow wins our sympathy even while breaking every law in the book. When deposed stage great Max bewails his fall from top of the show-biz heap to bottom of the Broadway barrel; when a happy-for-the-first-time Leo, dancing amid fountain jets at Lincoln Center, shouts to the heavens his intention of leaving wimpy nothing-ness behind; when Leo apologizes to Max for calling him "fat," and Max, touched, replies with a hug and smile; when Leo defends Max in court and means every word — in scenes like these Brooks hits heights of characterization untapped later on, just as does his 2001 stage show when Max sings "The King of Broadway," Leo "I Wanna Be a Producer," and both "'Til Him." Not even the emotional depths hinted at by ex-noble Ippolit Vorobyaninov's final choice of begging over loneliness in 1970's *The Twelve Chairs* makes the impact of Max's cash-poor desperation or Leo's pre–Max friendlessness, though the soul-spilling speeches delivered by Freddy Frankenstein and his monstrous "son" in *Young Frankenstein* (1974) certainly come close — but why so little character development in, say, *Robin Hood: Men in Tights* (1993) or *Dracula: Dead and Loving It* (1995)? Why don't we feel we know Robin or Dracula as well as we know Max and Leo?

Perhaps part of the explanation lies in the fact that, where Brooks' Robin Hood is still mostly all-hero and his Count Dracula still mostly all-villain, anti-heroes Max and Leo defy easy categorization. Cary Elwes' Robin may fall off the odd horse or get beaned by the occasional chandelier, but he's still basically the same old Douglas Fairbanks/ Errol Flynn–type Robin Hood we've seen a hundred times, and for all his staircase falls and window collisions, Leslie

Nielsen's Count remains the same sly, regal parasite played by Bela Lugosi and Christopher Lee for years. Max and Leo, though, come to us entirely shorthand free — no tights, no arrows, no feathered caps, no tuxedos, no capes, no fangs.

Then too, Brooks' story focus in *The Producers* isn't as divided as it is in those later films. Every last scene in *The Producers* directly involves Max and Leo, who are both the film's "bad guys" and its "good guys," where Brooks' Sherwood Forest flick at times deserts Robin to fill us in on what the evil Sheriff and Prince John are up to, and his vampire comedy, like Bram Stoker's novel, devotes long stretches to Van Helsing, Seward, Jonathan Harker, Mina, Lucy, and others. No matter what happens, our pals Max and Leo are always *The Producers'* center of attention.

Then too, for all Brooks' behind-camera inexperience at the time (just one movie teaser, really, for 1963's *My Son, The Hero*), Brooks tends to pull more colorful performances out of his cast in *The Producers* than in several later films, and in many respects his very cinematic naiveté contributes as much to its comedic success as anything else. Amid swipes at Brooks' "ineptitude" and "amateurish camera angles," in fact, Pauline Kael hits upon this irony in her generally positive review in *The New Yorker*, faulting him, at least by implication, for using so many close-ups of Zero Mostel instead of either (a) pulling the camera back so Mostel's in-your-face comic vastness doesn't feel quite so rattle-the-rafters enormous; or (b) asking Mostel himself to "tone down his effects for the camera." Strictly speaking, perhaps, Kael might be right; maybe Brooks needn't go quite so far letting big, boisterous Max Bialystock fill up the screen. ("Max"— what a fitting name for such an expansive personality!) On the other hand, though, all those loving close-ups of Mostel and Gene Wilder also

Fearing for their lives, mousy accountant Leo Bloom (Gene Wilder) and money-hungry business partner Max Bialystock (Zero Mostel) find none-too-bright secretary Ulla (Lee Meredith) blissfully unconcerned about the pistol-waving lunatic shooting up their office in Mel Brooks' directorial debut film *The Producers*, a 1968 Oscar-winner securing Wilder a Best Supporting Actor nomination. The Broadway musical version won a record-smashing twelve Tonys in 2001.

help make Max and Leo such vivid, expressive personalities and make our relationship with them feel more intimate, and if at times Brooks' camera sits a few feet closer than strictly necessary, who cares? Even with its corny puns and wild costumes, the characters in *Robin Hood: Men in Tights* make nowhere near the gut-level comic impact Max and Leo do here, and it's a fair bet Brooks' shoot-from-across-the-set standoffishness in that film doesn't help.

No, whether from painstaking strategy or mere beginner's luck, Brooks' decision to keep his daffy main characters so vividly front-and-center works just beau-

tifully, as does the fact that, even when he backs off a bit and photographs his actors from across the room, Mostel and Wilder remain — very much like Broadway's Max and Leo, Nathan Lane and Matthew Broderick, forced to overplay to make up for the physical distance between theater seat and stage — so animated, so lively, we're swept up in all that brisk, infectious energy no matter where the camera is. (Wilder even earned an Oscar nomination for all that liveliness, and the only real surprise is that Mostel didn't snag one too.) Talented as Brooks' actors are in 1991's *Life Stinks*, office scenes there, as written for and played by a fairly no-nonsense Stuart Pankin, Michael Ensign, Matthew Faison, and even sitcom star Jeffrey Tambor, pale beside these, in which Mostel's Max breaks loose like the proverbial bull in a china shop, Wilder's Leo like the legendary chicken with his head cut off. Business-suited or not, these two aren't button-down; they're like two over-sugared school kids.

Maybe the fact that so many of *The Producers*' stars came to the film almost directly from the stage and standup has something to do with it: Mostel's movie career went back to 1943, but the star of Broadway's *Fiddler on the Roof* and *A Funny Thing Happened on the Way to the Forum* (both scripted by *Your Show of Shows* grads, the former by Joseph Stein, the latter by co-author Larry Gelbart) had spent the decade racking up Tony wins; Brooks had handpicked Wilder, well before his *Bonnie and Clyde* debut, after seeing him on stage with Brooks' wife Anne Bancroft; Kenneth Mars, another stage vet, made this his first movie; and between films Dick Shawn had done nightclub comedy for years. Whether from so many project-to-the-exits types all in one place, however, or Brooks' camera's aggressive homing in on every over-the-top smile and sneer, Max and Leo's dialogue comes off better than it likely could have in any other film. Even if this *isn't* Brooks' best film, having so many give-it-all-they've-got talents aboard, and their director so rabid about zeroing in on them, helps Max and Leo make a memorable impact on us in ways later, subtler acting and directing techniques never could have managed.

The personalities Brooks creates here aren't nice people, of course, Max in particular, but love or hate them, this too only adds to *The Producers*' comic impact. Their lines are so startling and their behavior so extreme they can't help making a big impression; we could no more ignore Max Bialystock than we could Groucho Marx, whose acid-tongued anti-establishment demeanor this sleazy show-biz scoundrel so often brings to mind. Seducing lovesick little old ladies for their old-age nest eggs; fawning over below-the-radar Nazis; pledging support to investors, directors, actors, and writers even while plotting to wreck their show; insulting, bullying, and then leading honest young Leo astray; dynamiting a theater; urging a gun-toting lunatic to murder a troupe-ful of actors — frankly, anyone as deceitful, insensitive, and downright ruthless as Max *deserves* the prison sentence he's dealt at the end of the film. The fellow's dangerous, literally a public menace.

Yet somehow, despite all this, Brooks and Mostel still make us *care* about this man, far enough even that when Max's rock-bottom rotten *Springtime for Hitler* musical suddenly turns surprise success, we feel the rug yanked out from under us right along with him. The fact that trusting, mild-mannered Leo likes him so much has a lot to do with it — we like Leo, and if *he* admires this grasping, greedy ne'er-do-well, surely Max has some merit — as does the fact that, for good or ill, he shows joyless, friendless Leo the best time of his unhappy life. Max is Leo's tempter, a sort of Broadway Beelzebub dangling Easy Street prosperity like forbidden fruit, but he's his savior too, rescuing him from sad-sack isolation and bookish, unloved emptiness. Who but Max Bialystock could turn a law abiding, goody-goody, milk-and-cookies type like Leo into a senior-scamming crook, could convince a fellow Jew, of all people, into helping him mount a play venerating Hitler — and go about it in such a delightfully fatherly way, enticing attention-starved, childlike Leo with outdoor hot dogs, merry-go-round rides, and helium-filled balloons?

"Little Boy Bloom" himself is a remarkably rich character too. Perhaps only

Peter Boyle's maligned, misunderstood Monster from *Young Frankenstein* arouses so much compassion in us as Gene Wilder's shy, spiritless accountant Leo Bloom, and as much as one hates to see anyone this puppy-dog amiable turn felon, with Leo, "going bad" nearly qualifies as some twisted forward step. We don't want Leo corrupted, certainly don't want to see him behind bars, but for all his integrity at the start of the film he's so beaten-by-life pathetic he's really in jail already; allying himself with Max robs him of his freedom, but it also gives him his first real taste of it. Leo is Pinocchio becoming a real boy by embracing Pleasure Island, not fleeing it, a conscience-denying Jiminy Cricket swimming to, not from, the whale Monstro, drawn toward danger because getting swallowed up by Max's powerhouse destructive energies makes him finally feel alive.

With *The Producers*, in fact, Brooks very much goes right where many of his later films go a tad wobbly: fusing comedy and character so tightly one can barely tell where one ends and the other begins. Like Brooks vet Andrew Bergman's 1979 *The In-Laws*, *The Producers* relies more on personality than gimmicks, something untrue of make-no-bones-about-it spoof films of Brooks' later years. Choreographer Alan Johnson's lavish *Springtime for Hitler* showpiece is, admittedly, what everyone recalls most, but what really makes *The Producers* soar is the way its wit comes from human nature, from people. *Springtime for Hitler* remains unforgettable, but, on film or on stage, our friends Max and Leo are the *real* show we keep coming back for, winning our sympathy in part because, putting it bluntly, we're every bit as greedy and needy as they are.

Indeed, Brooks' oft-cited observation that really good storytelling should begin with the question "What do the leading characters *want*?" has never been more dead-on than it is here. Like ex-nobleman Vorobyaninov in *The Twelve Chairs*, Max wants rich food, nice clothes—the good life the onetime theater king basked in when he could still pick a hit—and, like born-poor Bender, young pal Leo wants all these because he's never had them and thinks it's high time. The match-up isn't seamless (in *The Twelve Chairs* the elder fortune hunter is the bossy, take-charge one, and in *The Producers* the younger man also seeks friendship, not just riches), but with *The Producers* the "What do they want?" factor saturates every scene, from Max's wild cry of "I want that money!" to Leo's exuberant "I want everything I've ever seen in the movies!" Indeed, the film begins with Max in mid-swindle (sweet talking old ladies in his office for money) and ends that way too (rehearsing another would-be failure, *Prisoners of Love*, while slammer mate Leo oversells shares yet again). As the new play's song says, no one can put this pair's hearts "in jail"; greed just keeps on driving them, spurring them on toward catastrophe just as fiercely as before.

More room to develop character— Brooks always counted this among his chief reasons for leaving TV for film, and, true to his word, character truly is where he places most of his emphasis here. *The Producers* isn't just about cheating and chicanery; it's about personal growth, change, and psychological and interpersonal advancement, especially Leo's, whose very name hints at a flowering into something vibrant and new.

In his excellent study *Method in Madness: The Comic Art of Mel Brooks*, Maurice Yacowar points out that with *The Producers* Brooks creates the first of several early films lacking the traditional male-female love story we're used to and focusing instead on two distinctively Brooksian males who bridge the gap between them and become good pals. No, we're not talking homosexuality here (though that gets poked fun at too, and still more so in Brooks' 2001 musical, in which a Führer-to-be Liebkind's broken leg forces Roger DeBris on stage as a last-minute Hitler), but rather something entirely platonic, something remarkably close to brother-brother or father-son. It's the sort of thing Brooks would investigate repeatedly over the years with such relationships between characters played by Ron Moody and Frank Langella in *The Twelve Chairs*; Cleavon Little and Gene Wilder in *Blazing Saddles*; and Gene Wilder and Peter Boyle in *Young Frankenstein*—though for the last two, of course, he does include first Madeline Kahn and then Kahn and Teri Garr to explore his films' developing male-female relationships too.

We also see this fraternal/paternal element between characters played by his leads in *Silent Movie* (Brooks, Marty Feldman, Dom DeLuise); *High Anxiety* (Brooks, Ron Carey, Howard Morris); *History of the World—Part I* (Brooks, Ron Carey, and Gregory Hines); *Spaceballs* (Bill Pullman, John Candy); *Life Stinks* (Brooks, Howard Morris, Teddy Wilson); *Robin Hood: Men in Tights* (Cary Elwes, Dave Chappelle, Eric Allan Kramer, Mark Blankfield); and *Dracula: Dead and Loving It* (Brooks, Harvey Korman, Steven Weber), though more and more his work moves away from buddy-buddy friendship tales to traditional Hollywood romance. *High Anxiety*'s Dr. Thorndyke reaffirms his protégé-mentor kinship with Prof. Lilloman, for instance, and nearly adopts driver Brophy as a pet, yet Brooks also gives his hero a future bride in Madeline Kahn's Vicki. Similarly, *History of the World—Part I*'s Comicus and Jacques win Mary-Margaret Humes' Miriam and Pamela Stephenson's Mademoiselle Rimbaud, *Spaceballs*' Lone Starr weds Daphne Zuniga's Princess Vespa, *Life Stinks*' Goddard

Bolt marries Lesley Ann Warren's Molly, *Robin Hood: Men in Tights*' Robin weds Maid Marian, and *Dracula: Dead and Loving It*'s Jonathan Harker saves Amy Yasbeck's Mina from the title vampire's clutches. At this early stage, though, Brooks hasn't yet entered his *Love American Style* phase and isn't all that interested in playing matchmaker. *The Producers* is a love story all right, but only about the love of money—and, of course, the sort of parental, paternal love Papa Bialystock finally develops for new "son" Leo.

Of course Max's idea of being fatherly, as in Brooks' old *New Faces* skit "Fathers and Sons," includes teaching his "child" to steal, and such ethical perversity in the name of fame and money supplies yet another motif for Brooks to play with. In *Comedy Central: The Essential Guide to Comedy*, Christopher Claro and Julie Klam charge that in this picture "every character is completely nuts," and if that's an exaggeration it's only because it's questionable at what point eccentricity stops and unqualified madness takes over. They're not all rubber room certifiable, maybe, but quite a few of them surely could be, and, as in *High Anxiety*, in which even an expert psychiatrist like Dr. Richard Thorndyke can't step into an elevator without panicking or utter grown-up medical terms with little girls in the room, in *The Producers* the question isn't so much "Who's crazy?" but "Of all the crazies, whose craziness comes closest to passing for normal?"

Certainly one of its nearest-to-normal characters is Max, yet even here we have someone whose every act runs contrary to the sound and sensible. Here's a man turned into a shameless gigolo for doddery old women he'd never pursue if they didn't have money; who surrounds himself with no-talents, misfits, and losers, not because he imagines they're gifted but because he's sure they'll guarantee failure; who, even though actors and playhouses are his bread and butter, proposes killing his cast and then dynamites their theater; and who, like some fireman-turned-arsonist or vegetarian-turned-butcher, has completely given up on spotting hits and dedicated himself now to staging crash-and-burn flops. Max sounds rational because he's so tricky and authoritative, is the idea man — but, for all his mockery of the others' idiosyncrasies, he's no great prize himself.

Yet Max suffers none of the painfully crippling emotional neuroses plaguing poor Leo. Where shout-out-the-window extrovert Max protests life with plenty of boom and bluster, Leo is more hand-wringing weakling than arm-waving tyrant, a hysteria-prone nebbish so ill at ease he still carries a ragged old baby blanket like Linus, Charles Schulz's under-confident "Peanuts" youngster — only *this* schoolboy is thirty-something years old. Truth be told, Linus looks pretty well-adjusted compared to Leo, whose born-loser loneliness even more closely recalls Charlie Brown, and when Max starts bellowing full-blast early on, Leo works himself up into a fear-frenzy so fever-pitched Max argues this strung-out worrywart needs not a blanket but a straitjacket. We're tempted to agree — at least until we meet characters even more off-the-beam than Leo.

Ranked high among them is *Springtime for Hitler* playwright Franz Liebkind, who may well merit that straitjacket considering he storms Max's office firing off ammo late in the film. A war-helmeted screwball with a Ludwig Von Drake accent, Kenneth Mars' Liebkind reveres Hitler as devoutly as Max loves money, and for this perhaps we should hate him, but he's so tragically misguided and filled with paranoid dread (at first he's certain Max and Leo are government-sent Nazi hunters come to arrest him) we feel for him much as we do the cowardly Leo. After all, only an absolute crackbrain could write a "love letter to Hitler" like the script Liebkind sells Max and mean it. Billions of people out there to adopt as his hero, and this idiot picks *Hitler*?

The director Max hires isn't much saner, taking still further Brooks' "show business as madness" theme. Christopher Hewett's English transvestite Roger DeBris, whose last name clues us in on the kind of projects he picks, not only drools over the prospect of seeing *Springtime for Hitler* on stage but is so sociologically "out of the loop" that till now he's never connected the Third Reich with Germany. DeBris' self-absorption is so complete it seems never to occur to him either that the lady's dress and wig might strike outsiders as a bit strange, and we're pretty sure this isn't the first time he's stepped out like some padded-up Ethel Merman wannabe — nor the first time this quality-blind egotist has mistaken tawdry, tasteless, and tacky for high-class theater.

Then again, DeBris' weirdly effeminate, icily jealous assistant Carmen Giya looks even stranger, and he's not even wearing a dress. Dark, bearded, and squeezed into body-hugging, womanish black, Andreas Voutsinas' Giya suggests some gonzo mix of Satan, Andy Warhol, and Emma Peel, and the home he meticulously fusses over for DeBris seems like the perfect place for him, from racy Roman god statues to elevators so tiny guests and escort end up nose to nose. We can only guess what unconventional goings-on this place sees in the off-hours — not that we'd ever want to — but one need only look at DeBris all dolled up and Giya in his catsuit to get the idea.

Excepting maybe unrepentant Nazi Liebkind, though, Brooks' spaced-out hippie Lorenzo St. DuBois, a.k.a. L.S.D., may be the biggest loon of the bunch. A sort of cinematic forerunner to brain-fried space cadet Reverend Jim on TV's *Taxi*, Dick Shawn's L.S.D. not only strays into the

Springtime for Hitler auditions by mistake, all those years of popping and inhaling have taken such a toll he can barely recall his own name. With his flower-child hip boots, Beatle haircut, pirate earring, and soup can necklace, a less likely Hitler we've never seen, not even among the demented throng of ill-trained amateurs who turn out for Max's open cattle call. Though his singing isn't half bad, L.S.D.'s self-authored musical freakout "Love Power" sounds so like the ravings of a mental ward maniac it's as if Hitler had written it himself, and by the time he sits crumpled on the stage clutching a banana like a motherless chimp, we know Max has found his man.

Even many of Brooks' characters who aren't specifically connected to show business are a little off-balance: Max's English-deficient secretary Ulla, completely oblivious to Liebkind's Yosemite Sam gun-blasting in her boss Max's office; the muddle-brained Drunk who thinks Max's barroom toast to "Failure" is kindly directed at him; the "boyd"-bemoaning woman at Liebkind's apartment building who insists on being called a "concierge"; and the elderly "Hold Me Touch Me" Lady, who pressures a revolted Max into shockingly sexual role-playing games. None of these folks are crazy exactly, but they're all off-center in the best Mel Brooks tradition.

Delighting us scene after scene, *The Producers* revels in such idiosyncrasies. Part of the joke with L.S.D.'s singing comes from Brooks' awareness that "Love Power" sounds every bit as rambling and incoherent as countless real songs from the '60s. We'd like to think only L.S.D. could write such a bewildering Age of Aquarius mess, but goodness knows how many members of *The Producers*' original audience who laughed at his way-out clothes and music dressed and entertained themselves just like him? Brooks himself didn't write "Love Power," oddly enough (Herb Hartic

and Norman Blaoman handled the lyrics and music on this one), but the basic satiric stimulus clearly springs from Brooks, who would take similar potshots at contemporary music in *High Anxiety* with his own so-noisy-it's-fatal "If You Love Me Baby, Tell Me Loud" concoction.

"Love Power" barely scratches *The Producers*' satirical surface, though, since just about every aspect of the film makes fun of something. Max, Leo, DeBris, Giya, L.S.D, even the *Springtime for Hitler* audience — these aren't just characters but types, vehicles through which Brooks sends up the whole Broadway show-biz scene. Do unconscionable, anything-for-a-buck producers truly exist in the real world, unashamedly flattering and conning their way to the top? Entertainment industry bean-counters really engage in criminal bookkeeping, shuffling numbers to hide money they don't want others to get wind of? Behind-the-scenes director types really move in circles of pleasure-seeking, libertine oddballs? Actors really behave like zoned-out, blissed-out, substance-abusing simpletons? Theatergoers shift from outright disgust to all-embracing acclaim the instant someone tells them the offending production is tongue-in-cheek chic, in-joke ironic, and cutting-edge trendy? Yes, yes, yes, yes, and yes — at least sometimes, as Brooks well knows.

Being both Jewish and a World War II veteran, Brooks also knows all too well what Hitler did to the Jews and countless others in the 1930s and '40s, and it's here, in the way he strikes back, that Brooks' satiric brilliance really comes through. In *The Films of Mel Brooks* Neil Sinyard explains the strategy this way: "In *The Producers* ... [Brooks] holds Nazism up to ridicule in the hope that the corresponding laughter will ensure that such an obscenity can never again be taken seriously as a political philosophy." Sermonize against Hitlerism, Brooks argues, and those who hate sermons may not listen; mock it, make it the butt of a potent enough gag, and maybe we can horselaugh it out of existence. Impossible? Maybe — but then, recall that frail, funny-looking boy or girl the others teased and tormented all through grade school? After all that, what chance did *he* really have to become senior class president? What chance did *she* have to become prom queen?

Unfortunately, since not everyone recognizes satire when he sees it, such efforts run a real risk of backfiring (remember all those angry listeners who thought Randy Newman's anti-bigotry hit "Short People" was sung in earnest?), and no doubt those who feel Hitler shouldn't be joked about in *any* context find *The Producers* in bad taste, like those "regular army" military types who still resent TV's *M*A*S*H* because they just can't get past Klinger's dresses and Hawkeye's bathrobe. Still, Brooks is onto something here — what is satire for if not to discredit the cruel and unjust? — and could Hollywood find an audience for scores of "Nazis are morons!" comedies and not just an occasional few, maybe the threat of another Holocaust might die out once and for all.

What surely won't die out, though, is the vast enjoyment Brooks' self-penned *Springtime for Hitler* brings, at least for those not overly touchy about seeing comedy and Nazism played side by side. While it's true the non-singing section of Liebkind's ditzy production doesn't come off all that well on film (it can't be easy staging a first-rate depiction of a third-rate play), the actual "Springtime for Hitler" number is a comedy-lover's dream, a triumph of satiric lyrics, music, singing, dancing, and costuming. This may very well be "the best of the best" of Brooks.

On its most basic level, obviously, the sequence is a witty takeoff on all those eye-popping song-and-dance sequences made famous by Busby Berkeley and others for years, a caricature of the smile-up-a-storm spirit of all those ultra-buoyant, super-enthusiastic musicals once so popular on stage and film. The real target, though, remains Nazism, and the brilliantly preposterous image of tune-warbling, tap-dancing stormtroopers (wonderful, wonderful staging from Alan Johnson) will outlast much of Berkeley's best work. Since not everyone living there during World War II was pro–Hitler, it's too bad Germany itself takes so much guilt-by-association spillover (the song links the Nazis' rise as "springtime" for Germany too, and some of the chorus girls wear mock beer mugs and pretzels), but such is the nature of satire. An attack on American slaveholders will likely hit modern Southerners pretty hard too, whether everyone's ancestors were guilty or not.

Brooks has quite a lot of fun playing around with musical theater conventions, actually, subverting stage musical traditions not just in his big *Springtime for Hitler* mock extravaganza but with his whole story line overall. Maurice Yacowar notes how Brooks shrewdly "plays against the romantic tradition" of the genre throughout: the way Max "courts" Leo (nonsexually, of course) to win him to his side; in Max's "handsome suitor" seduction of not pretty young ingenues but way-past-their-prime old ladies for whom he has no attraction whatever; in the way Max hires a secretary solely as a sex object, one whose "mod" attire and '60s go-go dancing scarcely resemble the ladylike elegance of Ginger Rogers; in the far from customary relationship between dress-wearing Roger DeBris (is "DeBris" also a play on the Jewish word *bris*? wonders Yacowar) and his slinky, over-possessive valet. Musicals — and movies about *making* musicals, like the classic old Mickey Rooney/Judy Garland smile-a-thons for MGM — are supposed to be all lovey-dovey, wide-eyed innocence, all boy-meets-girl, everything-good-in-the-world exhilaration. Instead, Brooks gives us Broadway shows about murderous, anti–Semitic maniacs; fountain-burst fanfares cementing criminal intent; sex-starved old spinsters hoodwinked by hustlers; curvaceous hip-twisters hired for looks, not talent; and kinky kinships between manservants and men in drag.

That's plenty of weird material for a movie about an entertainment genre traditionally so inoffensive (up till then, anyway), but its very subversiveness is finally what makes the picture so distinctive. Since *Springtime for Hitler* itself lasts only a few minutes on film, *The Producers* isn't a spoof in the usual sense (it's really more a "plot picture" than a "style picture," and develops more along the lines of *Life Stinks* than *Spaceballs*), but the material both before and after Brooks' bit of mock Broadway, as Yacowar notes, sends up the great classic musical conventions too. In old MGM musicals like *Babes on Broadway* or *Girl Crazy*, perky young do-gooders Mickey Rooney and Judy Garland are forever trying to "put on a show" to benefit poor children or save some down-for-the-count schoolhouse from shutting down, and no doubt Brooks loves these kids just as much as we do. His "let's put on a show" story is bound to be less altruistic than Rooney and Garland's, though (like the "2,000 Year Old Man" Robin Hood, showman Max steals from everybody and keeps everything), and it's great fun seeing him twist the expected all out of shape. Hollywood would have us believe in virtuous heroes, not unconscionable anti-heroes; in the gentlemanly treatment of women, not the pursuit of them for sex or money; in entertainments whose creators put good taste and cultural sensitivity ahead of profit, not the other way — but in *The Producers*, "heroes" are capable of just about anything, especially where money is concerned.

Even without such social and artistic re-evaluations, though, *The Producers* makes for real can't-miss entertainment, especially with a cast this good. Reviewer Leonard Maltin once labeled *The Producers* "one of those rare films that gets funnier with each viewing," and while in a literal sense that's impossible Maltin clearly realizes how superbly character-dependent Brooks' work really is. Everyone agrees how wonderful Mostel and Wilder are in Brooks' title roles, yet their hilarious exchanges really do seem heightened once we're finally able to distance ourselves from the focus-stealing ingenuity of Brooks' whole central idea. Seeing *The Producers* for the first time, we're too caught up in Liebkind's *Springtime for Hitler* idiocy and Max's wild scheme to fully appreciate Mostel and Wilder's acting; only on the second and third runs do we spot the hundreds of brilliant little touches Mostel tosses out while running around shouting his lines — and even then, if we're not careful, we'll miss Wilder's own little extras while we're watching Mostel.

And how can anyone *help* watching Zero Mostel? We may have missed out on seeing this great human dynamo transfer his Tony-winning Tevye from *Fiddler on the Roof* from Broadway to film, but his sublimely tempestuous Max Bialystock in *The Producers* is so rich and gloriously theatrical (in a movie whose very subject matter depends on the histrionic and affected) this one movie alone very nearly makes up for it. By most accounts Mostel's assertive, hyper-dynamic personality made directing him a bit frustrating for Brooks, whose "I reserve the right to be the only psychotic on the set" comment in a *Playboy* interview later on reveals how much these two madmen had in common. This is, after all, the same Brooks who once let loose a rail-against-fate mock outburst at the 1955 Emmys when the *Phil Silvers Show* team, not Sid Caesar's, secured the Best Comedy Writing win; who twice turned on *Your Show of Shows* newcomer Howard Morris and robbed him as a joke, convincing him he suffered a split-personality disorder; who, in aviator garb, burst into a closed-door meeting screaming "Lindy made it!" at full voice at the same show.

Despite this, however, Brooks happily praised Mostel's colossal talents again and again for decades, fervently acknowledging that he couldn't have found a better Max Bialystock had he searched a thousand years. Indeed, Brooks had wanted Mostel from the start, and, all disharmony fast forgiven, even long after just couldn't say enough nice things about his comic expertise. And why not? With *The Producers* Mostel proves yet again what fans of Broadway's *A Funny Thing Happened on the Way to the Forum* and *Fiddler on the Roof*, Brooks among them, already knew: that this was a performer so much larger than life the biggest movie screen in the world wasn't big enough to hold him. At his best — and just try to imagine a greater compliment than this — he reminds one of Jackie Gleason, with whose bombastic, lucklessly enterprising Ralph Kramden of TV's *The Honeymooners* Max has so much in common. Like Gleason, Mostel is never funnier than when his explosive energy blasts through, yet we never stop loving him because we can see the humanity behind it all; Max yells a lot, and loudly, but we know he's mostly bark, not bite.

Very nearly as impressive, though, is how unbelievably funny Mostel's costar Gene Wilder is, particularly given *The Producers* was only his second film. Brooks knew early on wife Anne Bancroft's stage friend was just perfect for the lion-named, pussycat-hearted character he had in mind — he told him so before *The Producers* was fully scripted — and both Wilder and comedy fans won one of the movies' all-time lucky breaks when Brooks showed up years later to finally recruit him for real. With *The Producers* Wilder paved the way for comic triumphs from *Start the Revolution Without Me* to *Willy Wonka and the Chocolate Factory* that would keep his career bubbling along for years, and he's so fantastically funny with Brooks' Oscar-fated material behind him, the mind reels thinking what might have been had they stayed together after the twin triumphs of 1974's *Blazing Saddles* and *Young Frankenstein*. Whether scurrying around in crazy-eyed hysterics or, shell-shocked, just hugging his baby blanket and babbling incoherently, Wilder's Leo reminds one of the meek little tailor Motel from Mostel's *Fiddler on the Roof*, the one Tevye scares out of his wits with the sound of his big, booming voice alone. Even when he's knee-deep in illegalities we still can't hate him. Who could hate anyone as hapless and lonely and unhappy as Leo Bloom?

Who could hate *The Producers*' other key characters either, each lent just enough camera time to make his mark, but never so much of it we're booing him off the screen? By all logic, for instance, we should find Kenneth Mars' Franz Liebkind every bit as repellent as the Nazi armbands Jewish schemers Max and Leo don to appease him, then toss in the garbage and spit on (how's that for political commentary?), yet somehow we find him too out-of-his-head pitiable to wish ill on even if he *does* think one of history's worst madmen hung the moon. Why? Partly it's because Brooks is so careful to forge a satiric link between Hitler fanaticism and dementia, partly because Mars himself is such a quirky, far-out delight. But then Mars is *always* excellent where silly accents are concerned, really (remember his puffed-up musicologist in 1972's *What's Up Doc?*), and whether he's raving about Hitler's house-painting expertise or showing up on opening night in a tuxedo and German war helmet, Mars pushes *The Producers* to dizzy

Despite facing prison for cheating investors owed after their "surefire" flop becomes a surprise Broadway hit, soft-hearted Leo Bloom (Gene Wilder) rejects fellow schemer Max Bialystock's wild plan to have Nazi playwright Franz Liebkind (Kenneth Mars, center) kill all the actors — but agrees to help Max (Zero Mostel) dynamite the theater in *The Producers*, for which writer-director-lyricist Mel Brooks won the 1968 Best Original Screenplay Academy Award.

new heights every time he appears. Brooks was smart to use him again later — but what a shame it was only once.

Even more regrettably, Brooks never reused stage actor–director Christopher Hewett at all, despite his obvious talent and eventual celebrity status years later on TV's *Mr. Belvedere*. (Ironically, Hewett's death in August 2001 came nearly two months to the day after Broadway's Gary Beach won a Tony for the same role.) With that superb British accent and upper-crust elegance, Hewett is one of just a handful of actors who could strut about in a dress and keep right on talking as casually as if it were a three-piece suit; shallow, merit-blind di-

rector Roger DeBris seems no more aware of how peculiar he looks than he is of how laughably superficial he sounds. Not only does DeBris know next to nothing about the history of Holocaust, he "fixes" *Springtime for Hitler*'s "depressing" third act — rewrites World War II — for a more "upbeat" Nazi win! Little known to filmgoers in 1968, Hewett was a real find Brooks would have been lucky to find again.

On-screen sidekick Andreas Voutsinas has a similarly memorable turn as DeBris' live-in underling Carmen Giya. A makeup-coated weirdo with the traipse of a neutered panther, Giya is as bizarre as DeBris is depthless, and Voutsinas wrings every ounce of comedy—and oddness—he can from the part. Though physically non-threatening (he's too jealous-lover swishy for that), the character's sooty features, Joan Crawford eyebrows, and piercing eyes might terrify us if we met him after dark—he's like Lucifer dressed as *Batman*'s Julie Newmar, a *Star Trek* Klingon spiced up with a flicker of Cruella deVil—and Brooks liked Voutsinas' catty, arty approach well enough to cast Voutsinas in similar, smaller parts in *The Twelve Chairs* and *History of the World—Part I*.

Dick Shawn is pretty terrific too, his psychedelic simpleton L.S.D. (a comic extension of his beach-house swinger from 1963's *It's a Mad Mad Mad Mad World*) perfectly embodying the peace sign and Flower Power era. If the late '60s upheld dropping out, tuning in, and turning on, for L.S.D. the tuning in must have been to some all-protest song station on Mars. Shawn's fine, funny performance is marred only—and only slightly—by "Love Power's" mild overlength and the intentional awkwardness of his *Springtime for Hitler* lines, the novelty of L.S.D.'s hipbooted hippie-ness wearing off fast the longer he and his "Nazis" voice Brooks' deliberately bad dialogue onstage. The idea of a drugged-out flower child playing Hitler by way of *Hair* is just dandy, but, like the acid-trip, slacker laziness of "Love Power," it amuses just so long before *The Producers* hurts too, yet the fault isn't really Shawn's, or even Brooks' (this is *supposed* to be a lousy play, recall). Shooting a high-energy scene with a character who's ultra-mellow is like making an action movie about boredom; maybe it *can* be done, but goodness knows *how*. Either way, Shawn plays L.S.D. so dead-on it's hard to believe Brooks never reused him. This was one funny, funny man.

What's still harder to believe, though, is that Brooks could secure so many funny people for his first film, even in small roles. Lee Meredith, for instance,

is just right as Swedish secretary Ulla, agreeably paving the way for Teri Garr's Inga in *Young Frankenstein* and exhibiting some nicely Garr-like comic timing (the bit in which Ulla offers the gun-firing Liebkind coffee is priceless); eighty-five-year-old stage great Estelle Winwood (who'd live to see 101!), as Max's "Touch Me, Feel Me" wildcat, nearly steals her one scene; later *Prizzi's Honor* Oscar nominee William Hickey has a nicely goofy turn as a bar drunk; and Madelyn Cates, largely unknown, turns a potentially go-nowhere part as Liebkind's poor-but-proud "concierge" (the one who objects to his "boyds" on the roof) into a thirty-second wonder, advancing the film's respect-chasing theme even while coming off nutty. Among the others, we can't omit longtime actor Shimen Ruskin as the Jewish landlord asking God to ignore Max's "crazy" talk; John Zoller, seen fleetingly as the huffy drama critic Max slyly insults with a bribe; Brutus Peck as the hot dog vendor Max ironically accuses of trying to be a "big shot"; future *My Favorite Year* and *Maude* TV actor Bill Macy in a quick bit as the jury foreman who declares the bombers "incredibly guilty"; and Barney Martin, another beloved TV face, in a quick bit as the *Springtime for Hitler* Goring reminding L.S.D.'s ditzy Hitler that Germany shouldn't be bombed. (It's too late; L.S.D. is pretty well bombed already.)

We don't want to get carried away, of course; as terrific as it is, *The Producers* is no more perfect than any well-made film. If Dick Shawn's rib-tickling "Love Power" song loses some of its comic sheen from overlength, his play-acting segment's dead calm gets hit still harder because, in contrast to any movie director's natural instincts staging a real play, Brooks is limited not only as to where his camera *can* go but where it logically *should*. Move in too close, let us feel we too are able to roam about onstage, and *Springtime for Hitler* ends up looking just as dynamic and lively as the rest of the film. Normally that sort of thing is a plus—Brooks' idol Alfred Hitchcock always saw filmed stage plays as an opportunity to heighten the drama of a previously static original, since his camera could easily close in on the actors and props at key moments to intensify audience emotion—but suppose one desires the opposite effect? What if one needs to impress upon the viewer that he's seeing not *Dial M for Murder*, a good play, but *Springtime for Hitler*, a bad play? The play-within-the-film's dialogue really does tax our patience (if *The Producers* were *all* like this, we'd all be halfway back to the video store by now), and presumably that's the plan—but how do we know *all* this flatness is the fault of L.S.D. and DeBris and not Mel Brooks?

More troubling, though, is Brooks' big Hitler-audition scene, easily the most disappointing part of the film. Pauline Kael claimed this segment was "potentially so great that what [Brooks] does with it lets you down," and indeed it is here we sense a little of the air seeping out of what has mostly been grand, giddy fun. As in *Springtime for Hitler* (the dialogue part, not the song), we're naggingly aware we haven't heard John Morris's nifty music or Mostel and Wilder's snappy patter for some time and start shifting a little in our seats. (Were this a cartoon, this is the spot where we'd hear crickets chirp, or see a lone tumbleweed roll by.) Frankly, all these would-be Hitlers just aren't that funny, don't come across much stranger than the mad-as-a-hatter genuine article, and their presence is more unsightly than witty. Kael's right—a preposterous parade of devastatingly bad Hitlers should have been one of the funniest parts of the film—but as settled on here we're longing for a more entertaining alternative, maybe some high-speed musical montage.

But why nit-pick? We could argue that the opening music from Brooks' old *All-American* and *shinbone alley* ally John Morris is a tad too shrill, or that the extended freeze-frames drag the credits out too badly, but then we'd be overlooking how much zing and zest Brooks' lively little ditty lends the movie right off. We could complain too, as Brooks would later, that the film takes too long after *Springtime for Hitler* getting Max and Leo in jail and working on *Prisoners of Love* (like *Films in Review*'s Norman Cecil, who felt its "over-stretched" storyline "falls apart" here, by the time L.S.D. turns up on stage we're pretty well ready for the movie to be over), but we'd be forgetting all the fun seeing Max and Leo dodge bullets after their cool-cat Hitler sends Liebkind into a vengeful rage, ignoring Leo's courtroom outpouring of gratitude for Max's finally giving him reason to smile. No, *The Producers* isn't perfect, but who'd want to miss all that?

Who'd want to miss Leo's early near-nervous breakdown, either, with his classic "I'm hysterical—and I'm wet!" and his terrified screams as Max, like some ascot-wearing King Kong, leaps about him as he lies on the floor? *The Producers* must include a thousand funny lines, loony images, and crazy gestures, and while its villains-as-heroes irreverence is sure to offend some, nobody can say the film doesn't work. Even its opening credits, thanks to John Morris's spirited "Springtime for Hitler" instrumentation, and Brooks' decision to plunge us into the comedic just seconds in, seem funnier than those in later films—we've laughed a dozen times before the words "Directed by Mel Brooks" appears on-screen, and not even *Young Frankenstein* can say that—and the "Prisoners of Love"–accompanied wrap-up hits us the same way. Indeed, one can tell this is a film rich with feeling from the end credits too, which reuse Brooks' dazzling romp-at-the-fountain shot — focus on emotion — instead of some cold, soulless million-name scrawl on background black.

What a fine, funny little movie. Small wonder so few disagreed when, once the American Film Institute released its picks in June 2000 of the past century's hundred top U.S. comedies, *The Producers* came in a triumphant eleventh, topped only by *Airplane!*, *The Graduate*, *It Happened One Night*, *M*A*S*H*, *Blazing Saddles* (Brooks again), *Duck Soup*, *Annie Hall*, *Dr. Strangelove*, *Tootsie*, and *Some Like It Hot*. His faith in his talent and material happily vindicated all over again, Mel "Numbers Five and Eleven" Brooks must have grinned from ear to ear.

Besides all that, the listing boded well for Brooks' first major project of the twenty-first century: a full-blown, super-spectacular Broadway musical version of *The Producers* featuring some of the top talents of the American stage. Just imagine: Nathan Lane, a Tony-winner in Zero Mostel's old role from Larry Gelbart's *A Funny Thing Happened on the Way to the Forum*, as Max; Matthew Broderick, Tony winning star of the *How to Succeed in Business Without Really Trying* revival and so many great Neil Simon plays, as Leo; a book by Mel Brooks and *Annie*'s Thomas Meehan, a veteran of many hit Brooks-linked movies and TV shows; and music and lyrics by the great Mel Brooks himself. All Broadway was abuzz, and on June 3, 2001, *The Producers*, already the best-reviewed Broadway show in memory and recipient of a record-setting fifteen Tony nominations, rewrote the record books again, taking home every last Tony it could possibly win, with Matthew Broderick unable to share Best Actor with same-category winner Nathan Lane, and Roger Bart (Carmen Giya) and Brad Oscar (Franz Liebkind) likewise stepping aside for a Best Featured Actor win by castmate Gary Beach as Roger DeBris. Cady

Huffman (Ulla) won as Best Featured Actress; Susan Stroman as Best Director and Best Choreographer; Robin Wagner for Best Scenic Design; William Ivey Long for Best Costume Design; Peter Kaczorowski for Best Lighting Design; Doug Besterman for Best Orchestration — and creator Mel Brooks, either shared or solo, took home three: for Best Musical, Best Book, and Best Score.

At age seventy-four, Mel Brooks, winner of two Oscars, four Emmys, a Grammy, and now three Tonys, had given Broadway (and Tony acceptance speeches) its biggest laughs in ages. Even with his Best Screenplay win three decades old, public enthusiasm for Max and Leo was suddenly higher than ever, so high just about everybody wished he could blink himself into a New York theater seat for just one night. As Mel Brooks, Nathan Lane, Matthew Broderick, and crew worked and laughed themselves silly taking on Broadway for real, and video copies of the original rented like gangbusters, *The Producers*, like Franz Liebkind's ill-chosen "quick fuse," just kept on sizzling. Neither time nor quick-fuse dynamite, it seems, could keep *Springtime for Hitler* down.

CAST: Zero Mostel (Max Bialystock); Gene Wilder (Leo Bloom); Kenneth Mars (Franz Liebkind); Estelle Winwood ("Hold Me Touch Me"); Christopher Hewett (Roger DeBris); Andreas Voutsinas (Carmen Giya); Dick Shawn (L.S.D.); Lee Meredith (Ulla); Renee Taylor (Eva Braun); David Patch (Goebbels); Bill Hickey (The Drunk); Barney Martin (Goring); Shimen Ruskin (The Landlord); Frank Campanella (The Bartender); Josip Elic (Violinist); Madelyn Cates (Concierge); John Zoller (Drama Critic); Brutus Peck (Hot Dog Vendor); Ann Ives, Amelie Barleon, Elsie Kirk, Nell Harrison, Mary Love (The Ladies); Bill Macy (Jury Foreman).

CREDITS: Director: Mel Brooks; Producer: Sidney Glazier; Screenplay: Mel Brooks; Presented by: Joseph E. Levine; Assoc. Producer: Jack Grossberg; Dir. of Photog.: Joseph Coffey; Assist. Director: Michael Hertzberg;

Second Assist. Director: Martin Danzig; Editor: Ralph Rosenblum, A.C.E.; Prod. Designer: Charles Rosen; Costume Designer: Gene Coffin; Titles Design: Elinor Bunin; Music: John Morris; "Love Power" Words: Herb Hartic/Music: Norman Blaoman; "We're Prisoners of Love" Words/Music: Mel Brooks; "Springtime for Hitler" Words/Music: Mel Brooks; Music Supervisor: Felix Giglio; Choreographer: Alan Johnson; Unit Manager: Louis A. Stroller; Casting Director: Alfa-Betty Olsen; Prod. Supvr. for Embassy Pictures/Universal Marion Corp.: Robert Porter; Script Supvr.: Betty Todd; Prod. Sec.: Connie Schoenberg; Camera Operator: Edward Brown; Set Decorator: James Dalton; Gaffer: Morton Novak; Set Grip: Edward Engels; Constr.: Joseph Williams: Scenic Artist: Shelly Bartolini; Carpenter: Eli Aharoni; Prod. Sound: Willard Goodman; Makeup: Irving Buchman; Assist. Ed.: Michael Breddan; Sound Ed.: Alan Heim; Opticals: Creative Opticals, Inc.; Wardrobe: Celia Bryant; Assist. to Producer: Robert Buchman; Prints: Pathe; 1968, Embassy Pictures, Inc.; 88 minutes.

2

★ ★ ★

"HOPE FOR THE BEST, EXPECT THE WORST"

The Twelve Chairs

★ ★ ★ ★ ★ ★

(1970)

In 1927, in a tiny village of the post–Revolution Soviet Union, elderly Claudia Ivanova (Elaine Garreau) summons her priest, Father Fyodor (Dom DeLuise), and her widowed son-in-law Ippolit Vorobyaninov (Ron Moody) for a deathbed confession. Vorobyaninov, a marshal of the nobility before the Revolution ten years before, arrives just as Father Fyodor scurries off, but he does not understand the priest's quick exit until he hears Mrs. Ivanova's dying disclosure: just before being driven from her late daughter's Starograd estate during the Revolution, Mrs. Ivanova sewed her valuable jewels into one of twelve dining room chairs later seized as public property.

Craving his old life of luxury, Vorobyaninov sets off for the mansion in Starograd, where he finds the estate now an old age home and his drunken former servant Tikon (Mel Brooks) still living in its basement. He also meets — and distrusts — Tikon's new acquaintance, op-

portunistic young drifter and smooth-talking ladies' man Ostap Bender (Frank Langella), who immediately suspects Vorobyaninov of hiding some profit-driven scheme and slyly threatens to involve Soviet authorities unless he includes Bender as an equal partner. Helpless, Vorobyaninov must agree.

Learning from Tikon eleven chairs were seized by the Bureau of Housing, Vorobyaninov seeks out the twelfth, but at the mansion door he is shocked to see Father Fyodor fleeing with the chair, which the two greed-gripped rivals rip apart and find empty. Bender then meets Father Fyodor at the Bureau, spots him as a competitor, and, posing as an employee, misdirects him to a Mr. and Mrs. Bruns (David Lander, Diana Coupland) in Irkusk, Siberia — whom the priest follows to Yalta and pesters to near-madness buying a similar, valueless set of chairs.

Vorobyaninov and Bender find the real chairs in a Moscow museum and

33

watch helplessly as seven are taken away to the freight entrance. After tearing open the other four to no avail, they see six of the remaining seven loaded on a theater company truck, but while Bender inquires after the seventh, Vorobyaninov briefly spies, then loses sight of it as it is carried through a rail yard.

Finding the rest of the chairs stage troupe props, Bender passes off Vorobyaninov as an actor on the company's ship, where they rip open four chairs to no use. Forced ashore after Vorobyaninov's inept stage debut displeases producer Nikolai Sestrin (Andreas Voutsinas), Bender reduces him to posing as a fallen epileptic to beg for funds, then ruins two more chairs bought from troupe thief Sevitsky (Vlada Petric). Seeking one already sold, Vorobyaninov grabs the chair from a Finnish aerialist in mid-tightrope walk but loses it to Father Fyodor, who, after climbing a steep cliff, despairs as Voro-byaninov and Bender leave him trapped there with a torn-apart, jewel-free chair.

After walking back to Moscow, they sneak a free meal at the city's new Railway Workers' Communal House of Recreation — and locate the last chair. Returning at night, they find this one empty too — and learn the jewels, gone, were used to build the center. Enraged, Vorobyaninov attacks a night watchman and policeman, then flees with Bender, the one-time nobleman still clinging to a broken chair back until, facing humiliation or starvation, he makes his choice: again feigning epilepsy, he runs in place on the ground as Bender happily works the crowd for money.

★   ★   ★

Mel Brooks' 1970 comedy *The Twelve Chairs*, the long-neglected "middle child" born after his Oscar-winning 1968 debut movie *The Producers* but before his 1974

smash *Blazing Saddles*, tends to go completely unmentioned in most recollections of Brooks' best works, but any "Best of Brooks" list worth compiling at all should certainly clear off a little room for this, the single greatest unsung victory of Melvin "Mel Brooks" Kaminsky's early directorial career. Film students have spent entire semesters studying cinematic "art" not half so lovingly shot, scored, or scripted, and have hailed as genius movies without a tenth this much insight into the human condition while leaving the skillful, subtle excellence that is *The Twelve Chairs* almost completely ignored.

If even fans of Mel Brooks' big screen endeavors rarely so much as mention his second film, however — well, let's not be too hard on them. *Jaws* devotees don't often bring up Steven Spielberg's *The Sugarland Express*, either, or *Batman* addicts Tim Burton's *Ed Wood*, or *Psycho* enthusiasts Alfred Hitchcock's *Marnie*, yet those are all well-made movies too, and all now long overdue their place in the sun. Sometimes box office is everything, however, and while filmgoers in 1970 made a solid hit of Herbert Ross's *The Owl and the Pussycat*, flocked to Robert Altman's *M*A*S*H*, laughed aloud at Arthur Hiller's Neil Simon farce *The Out-of-Towners*, even had a grand old time lining up for Robert Butler's *The Computer Wore Tennis Shoes* over at Disney, by year's end Brooks' *The Twelve Chairs* had barely even dented the collective consciousness. To this day most people for whom just mentioning Mel Brooks is enough to call up screwball images from *Blazing Saddles* or *Young Frankenstein* remain completely unaware *The Twelve Chairs* even exists, just as most of them have absolutely no idea Brooks won an Oscar for his work on Ernest Pintoff's *The Critic* cartoon or once played a bit part in Ezio Greggio's film *Silence of the Hams*.

What a terrible shame, too. No, *The Twelve Chairs* isn't Brooks' funniest movie (come to think of it, it remained his *second* funniest only until he helmed *Blazing Saddles*), but none of his post–1970s projects enhances our appreciation of his cinematic talents the way this film does. More artfully photographed and socially self-aware than either of the two better-known Brooks films that surround it, this cunning period comedy about ordinary men driven to desperation by forbidden wealth very much deserves to be seen — not just because no study of Mel Brooks as comic-turned-moviemaker can really be complete without it, but because *The Twelve Chairs* all on its own represents Brooks at his most poetically astute and aesthetically satisfying. All those skeptics who've labeled Mel Brooks a second- or even third-rate director should take a long, hard look at *The Twelve Chairs*, whose camera placement feels exactly right so often that only finicky moviegoers, who that same year made mammoth hits out of *Love Story* and *Airport* but couldn't have cared less about Soviet priests and bureaucrats, could have denied it the success it deserved.

Brooks' highly intelligent choice of source material doesn't exactly hurt the film's visual excellence any either. Soviet authors Illya Ilf and Yevgeny Petrov's oft-filmed novel about three rivals' greedy pursuit of a fortune in pre-Revolution jewels stashed inside one of twelve dining chairs gives the director plenty of great-looking material to point his camera at, and a vista-savvy Brooks, effectively dressing up an already pretty convincing 1970 Yugoslavia to look like the 1920s U.S.S.R., makes fantastic use of just about every last frame. Yugoslav cinematographer Djordje Nikolic's exquisitely photographed open-air locales create in the viewer a real sense of having been swept away to another time and place, thus setting *The Twelve Chairs* nicely apart from, say, 1981's *History of the World — Part I*, in which too many unconvincing papier-mâché boulders and stagy-

looking palace interiors keep shattering Brooks' cinematic spell. Compare, furthermore, the teeming-with-realism, sumptuously textured "Soviet" communities here with the front-shot only, sitcom-phony facade meant to pass for a burning village in *Robin Hood: Men in Tights*, and — well, frankly there is no comparison. Brooks' hasn't just apathetically approximated 1927 Soviet village life with *The Twelve Chairs*; he's recaptured it, painter-like, or at least comes as close to it as anyone in 1970 could without access to an H.G. Wells time machine and a carte blanche permit from Brezhnev to shoot anywhere on Cold War Soviet soil he jolly well pleased.

We can tell *The Twelve Chairs* breaks new ground for Brooks pretty much right off, even if many of *The Producers'* surface elements are still there. Again we're given a down-on-his-luck, self-serving anti-hero as lead, played this time by stage great Ron Moody; another little old lady (Elaine Garreau), a dying, gem-hoarding mother-in-law, not an unrelated geriatric man-chaser this go-around, whose fragile emotional neediness the protagonist is less concerned with than in profiting off her naiveté; and soon not one but two Leo Bloom–ish outsiders (Dom DeLuise as the expiring woman's priest; Frank Langella as a wily street youth) whose outward virtue goes right out the window once the dollar signs (ruble signs?) start dancing. This outing, however, Brooks' money-hungry Max Bialystock figure isn't the least bit eager for an ally, and of the two Bloom substitutes, Moody's character builds up a full-blown hatred for the one (DeLuise's priest, who wants the gems solely for himself) and only the most reluctant of unions with the other (Langella's wily young stranger). The characterizations of the film's two business partners are vastly different from those in *The Producers* as well, with Moody's bungling, babe-in-the-

woods artlessness a far cry from Bialystock's fox-crafty slickness, and Langella's
commanding young desperado, unlike
Bloom, already so worldly-wise and tricky
he could teach even Max Bialystock a thing
or two.

It's really *The Twelve Chairs*' opening
credits that tell us we're seeing a new Mel
Brooks at work, though. Revealing an eye
for the picturesque rarely seen in him before or since, Brooks underscores the film's
superb theme music (the tune comes from
Johannes Brahms, given a fine "peasant
Russia" feel by John Morris) with quaint,
almost nineteenth-century images of real-

life Yugoslavian locals going about their
daily routines, scene after scene of "Soviet"
men, women, children, and animals somehow looking both serenely unhurried and
hustle-bustle busy at the same time. With
these brief, lovingly photographed Alan
Heim–edited snippets, Brooks leaps well
beyond his stagy TV sketch comedy roots
and gracefully enters the realm of true cinematic art, captures with almost documentary candor the spirit of a simpler
time. One gets the sense that behind these
handbarrows real exchanges get made, that
we're seeing real townspeople who live in
real houses and sit down together as real

In post–Revolution Starograd, drunken Soviet menial Tikon (Mel Brooks) reveals all he knows
of the whereabouts of a dozen missing dining room chairs to his greedy former master Ippolit
Vorobyaninov (Ron Moody) and Vorobyaninov's opportunistic young accomplice Ostap Bender (Frank Langella), both eager to get their hands on the one chair housing a fortune in jewels, in Brooks' second time out as director, 1970's *The Twelve Chairs*.

families to real meals. Teeming with horse-carts and pushcarts, boot peddlers and fruit peddlers, sheep and cattle, piglets and geese, these scenes feel like some exquisite cross between Tolstoy and Dickens, populated by whole streets-ful of lively Soviet Micawbers and Copperfields and Cratchits and Twists—fitting, it turns out now, given the presence of at least two screen Fagins, *Oliver!*'s Ron Moody and *Oliver & Co.*'s Dom DeLuise.

Brooks shows real affection for these people too, the actual, off-screen Russians no doubt because his own parents were born among them, their spirited Yugoslav stand-ins because he came to cherish their warmth and hospitality filming them—yet none of this prevents his depicting their shortcomings as well as their strengths. *The Twelve Chairs* finds laughs in greed, egotism, selfishness, corruption, malice, cruelty—traits as common to simple Russian peasants as to anyone else in Brooks' works, from the dollar-hugging show biz cheats of *The Producers* and *Silent Movie* to the wallet-squeezing hospital quacks of *High Anxiety*, from the billionaire status seekers of *Life Stinks* to the pocket-lining political opportunists of *Blazing Saddles*, *History of the World—Part I*, or *Robin Hood: Men in Tights*. These humble, unaffected souls have Brooks' deepest admiration, but as filmmaker and satirist he's not for a second fooled by their unspoiled *Fiddler on the Roof* simplicity. Even Sholem Aleichem's Tevye belts out "If I Were a Rich Man" in private, and Brooks knows as well as we do all the anti-capitalist invective in the world can't turn Soviet Russia into Shangri-La. Money-love knows nothing of political overthrow or party decree, and whether a fellow labels himself Russian or Soviet, capitalist or socialist, his fundamental instincts remain unchanged. Even in Eden man wanted more, and if not even religion with all its "Thou Shalt Not"s and threats of Hell can

make people non-greedy, what chance does mere politics have?

In many ways, then, *The Twelve Chairs* shares much the same message as *The Producers*, in which even in his cardboard belt Max Bialystock still clings to his monogrammed smoking jacket and silk ascot from his theatrical glory days. Despite these now-ragged fashion trappings and a roomful of old play posters, we can only really take Bialystock's word for it that he was once "King of Broadway," but in a well-conceived flashback we actually see Ron Moody's once-stately Ippolit Vorobyaninov basking in extravagant pre-Revolution comfort, and we understand instantly why he misses it. As Brooks himself will insist as King Louis XVI in *History of the World—Part I*, and again as Rabbi Tuckman in *Robin Hood: Men in Tights*, "It's good to be the king," and clearly Vorobyaninov too has never recovered from having lost so much so quickly.

His only hope, it seems, lies in regaining possession of his dead mother-in-law's long-lost diamonds, but as Brooks' title song suggests, Vorobyaninov's quest is well-nigh doomed already. How difficult can it be to hunt down twelve government-seized dining chairs? Pretty difficult, since plans are already afoot to disperse them from the Soviet museum that's been housing them (seven end up in the hands of a Russian theater troupe; Vorobyaninov and Bender quickly rip the rest apart), and the one housing the gems will soon be found by others who, in one of Brooks' richest ironies, actually *do* spend the money for the common good.

"Hope for the Best, Expect the Worst" is *The Twelve Chairs*' theme song in every conceivable sense, entertaining us even as Brooks' lyrics clue us in on the film's decidedly Jewish philosophy in which optimism and anticipation meet with suffering and defeat at least as often as success and achievement. In the world of *The Twelve Chairs*—which is to say, of course, our world, the real world — we find not only that "some drink champagne" while "some die of thirst," but that the "deck is stacked" that way, at least long enough for many of the champagne drinkers themselves to get their pretty red carpets yanked away. "There's no guarantee," says Brooks, because not even the well-to-do can predict where and whom catastrophe will strike next, something millions of capitalist Americans learned with the Stock Market Crash of 1929, a mere two years after the incidents in *The Twelve Chairs*. In a world of such randomness and seemingly utter futility of effort, we've absolutely "no way of knowing which way it's going"—except that sooner or later it's probably going down.

Of course, as one of filmdom's all-time funniest men, Brooks isn't entirely pessimistic. As in *The Producers*, *Life Stinks*, and elsewhere, he still implies friendship bonds are ultimately more precious than stocks and bonds, that personal relationships, not personal belongings, are to be valued above financial gain. Still, the "Hope for the Best, Expect the Worst" philosophy makes no claim that even if we obtain the one we will ever rise above the other. As in *The Producers*, the unscrupulous anti-hero loses his fortune but wins the closest thing he has to a real friend, yet we're not at all convinced he's suddenly reformed his views on instant wealth. Vorobyaninov forms a seemingly permanent partnership with itinerant con man Bender, even fakes epilepsy to petition donations from sympathetic passersby, but we can't seriously believe he's happy about turning professional panhandler. He's "humbled," yes, but only because humility puts food in his mouth; he's accepted a "comrade," but only because anti-camaraderie means he's left defenseless. In *The Films of Mel Brooks* Neil Sinyard sums up the situation perfectly: "Although there are

moments of tenderness, *The Twelve Chairs* is a curiously loveless film, which is part of its point and poignancy. What the characters want, they cannot have; what they need, they do not want."

Film critic Leonard Maltin has argued that the "unsympathetic" nature of these characters accounts in large part for the film's lackluster box office, and he's probably right. Certainly the father-and-son warmth between *The Producers*' Max Bialystock and Leo Bloom never really develops for Vorobyaninov and Bender, and somehow even at the end, choosing to travel as a team rather than go it alone, they come across as more accommodating than affectionate. We've no doubt these two care more about each other than either lets on (their final scene team-up may well suggest, like the ending of *Casablanca*, "the beginning of a beautiful friendship"), but would either of these two selflessly sing the other's praises in court the way Leo sings Max's? Maybe, but likely only to save himself, especially con man Bender, who can talk his way out of anything.

Funnily enough, reducing the emotional remoteness of the two characters might not have required all that much extra work either. Perhaps if only once or twice Vorobyaninov had called his young partner "Ostap" instead of just "Bender," we'd better sense Vorobyaninov's gradual softening up, or maybe if Bender had just once called Vorobyaninov by his first name instead of "Old Man," we'd be less likely to find his threats and bullying so off-putting. Worse still, even given opening credits reading "RON MOODY as Vorobyaninov" and "FRANK LANGELLA as Ostap Bender," many fans may watch the movie from start to finish without ever getting a firm mental grasp on the main characters' names. Let's face it: with or without the informal "Ippolit" we once hear from Mrs. Ivanova on her deathbed, the name "Vorobyaninov" is quite a mouthful, and we really don't see or hear it often enough for either its spelling or pronunciation to really take hold. (At least Zero Mostel's character in *The Producers*, whose name we're given a good look at on his office door, barks out his own name for us each time he recalls how it once actually meant something, and Leo Bloom calls him both "Mr. Bialystock" and especially "Max" countless times.) Even if we don't find Vorobyaninov a hate-filled egotist, don't hold Bender's bullying against him, how well can we emotionally connect with characters so rarely called on by name?

Beautiful though it is, the film's setting perhaps makes *The Twelve Chairs* feel less than embraceable as well. *The Russians are Coming! The Russians are Coming!*, a big hit just two years earlier, involves Soviets too, but that film takes place in the U.S., with enough all–American types like Brooks' friend Carl Reiner, Eva Marie Saint, Brian Keith, Jonathan Winters, and Paul Ford running around to keep events nicely anchored in the comfy and familiar. Brooks' resolve to film overseas instead of on some semi-convincing Hollywood backlot really pays off art-wise and theme-wise, but the movie might have made more money updated to the '70s U.S., with Moody, DeLuise, and Langella playing greedy *American* fathers-in-law, priests, and street hustlers, not 1920s Russians. Money-stashing deathbed widows like Mrs. Ivanova live in America too, and perhaps wake from comas to find the family furniture auctioned off to pay hospital bills. No doubt Brooks could have made a very funny comedy with Moody, DeLuise, and Langella hungrily scouring 1970 California for the one lost chair with the secret loot. Why not — except, of course, that Russian lit fan Melvin Kaminsky had loved Ilf and Petrov's novel since he was fifteen and wanted to retain its flavor? Why not too, except that we've all seen

enough films and TV shows set in and about modern-day L.A. to last us ten lifetimes, thus making the snowbanks and sunsets of far-flung Yugoslavia seem as refreshingly unspoiled and exotic as the far side of the moon?

All of this is pointless speculation, however, and the sad truth is some movies are doomed to audience indifference even before the screenwriter first types the words "FADE IN." For all its beauty and brilliance *The Twelve Chairs* might have failed no matter what changes Brooks made. Then again, who knows? Released a year earlier, or maybe a year later, *The Twelve Chairs* might have gone right through the roof, broken records even. Who could have predicted a comedy as off-center as *The Princess Bride* would've ever found its niche, with all its medieval castles and highwaymen and damsels in distress? Or *Time Bandits*? Or *Monty Python and the Holy Grail*?

Still, *The Twelve Chairs* also isn't nearly as funny as most of those movies, and it depends a bit more than most Brooks films on our being transported to another world and time. Brooks could have shot the tale closer to home, today (goodness knows it would've been simpler), but we'd have lost something too. The greed-run-wild idea propels *Life Stinks* as well, recall (not that *Life Stinks* fared too well domestically either), but in '90s capitalist America, uncontrolled cupidity not only wasn't against the rules; it practically *was* the rule. If the two L.A. billionaires in *Life Stinks* set out to dislocate Midas-rich hotel owners or bankers instead of sickly homeless folks, who'd care *what* the winner built on the property he's after? Corporate dishonesty is so accepted, and expected, in modern America the idea of backstabbing economic competitors trying to turn millions into more millions seems less black-hearted avarice than good business. If IBM outsmarts Apple, or Apple outmaneuvers

IBM, few in the U.S. come down hard on the winner with a self-righteous "Shame on you." That's free enterprise, they figure; that's the American way.

Not so in *The Twelve Chairs*, though, whose anti-capitalist Soviet politics makes cash-madness like Bialystock and Bloom's in *The Producers* or Bolt and Crasswell's in *Life Stinks* feel less permissible — treasonous, even. The U.S.S.R.'s late–'20s political situation in *The Twelve Chairs* makes its protagonists' Daffy Duck devious "Mine, mine, all mine!" attitude come off as some mutinous, anti–Soviet crime against the State — enough so that a bluffing Bender is able to demand "in on" Vorobyaninov's scheme just by threatening to report him to the police. A decade or so earlier, back when the new Soviet Union was still good old entrepreneurial Russia, Vorobyaninov's greedy old mother-in-law could have stuffed a whole sofa with diamonds if she'd wanted to, but after the Revolution everything's changed. The outright every-man-for-himself selfishness of Ron Moody's Vorobyaninov, Frank Langella's Bender, and Dom DeLuise's Father Fyodor now amounts to anti–Soviet disloyalty, a political betrayal, a punishable offense.

Thus, in *The Twelve Chairs* avarice takes on far deeper meaning than in Brooks' previous film, and adding Father Fyodor as an even greedier profit hog gives the tale's underlying message still more impact. This isn't just some local bureaucrat or run-of-the-mill drifter who's dropped everything for a chance at lining his own pockets; this is the village priest, a man of God. Father Fyodor should be scolding such barefaced materialism, not relentlessly joining in, but in Brooks' work, mankind's craving for the forbidden has a way of squelching just about everything else, and of rendering true-blue loyalty to God, neighbor, and nation near-nonexistent, no matter who we are.

Father Fyodor's transformation even involves discarding his rabbinical-looking beard and priestly attire, as if he's denounced both soul-saving and socialism once Mrs. Ivanova tells him about the jewels. As a loyal Soviet, he is expected to reveal what he knows to the authorities so others may benefit too, not one man alone; Mrs. Ivanova has committed a crime hiding the gems to begin with — they're the State's now, not hers — but his plan to steal them is equally criminal. As a clergyman, he betrays his faith too; he tries stockpiling wealth that, distributed in the Biblical spirit of Christian charity, could feed the hungry, clothe the naked, or heal the sick, and, to make matters worse, capitalizes on a secret learned in a private deathbed confession. Mrs. Ivanova might expect a stranger like Ostap Bender to betray her trust, maybe even her own son-in-law — but her *priest*?

The old "what is" vs. "what was" conflict receives attention pretty much all through the film. Street signs have the names of toppled political greats X'ed out, and as Vorobyaninov's drunken onetime servant Tikon, Brooks himself bemoans the sudden equalization of everyone to "comrade" status, friend and foe alike. The contrast between Vorobyaninov's pre–Revolution and post–Revolution lives is particularly striking, with former "marshal of the nobility" Vorobyaninov dreaming (in flashback) of his days in uniform, recalling himself proudly seated, chin held high, atop a white steed. Remember in *The Producers*, when Max Bialystock shouts "Do you know who I used to be?" to a shaken Bloom? Nobleman-turned-nobody Voro-byaninov has "bottomed out" in much the same way, has become just another low-level Working Class Ippolit whose best days are behind him.

He's not at all happy about his new situation, either, so much so that only Bender's sheer forcefulness pulls the old man's secret about the gems out of him, and Vorobyaninov never even considers teaming with Father Fyodor even though working together is in all three men's best interest. United, each fortune-chaser could, albeit illegally, enjoy a third of the money; separately, at least one must do without entirely — two if Father Fyodor finds the gems first — making these three rivals in some sense represent just the sort of Russia the Revolution was meant to obliterate: the kind of out-for-self society in which a few grab up all for themselves, all others get nothing.

It's this very all-bets-are-off impropriety that gives *The Twelve Chairs* its biggest comic boost, and makes it accessible even to those who know next to nothing about the 1920s U.S.S.R. or the Russian Revolution. Allegiance to countrymen, religion, family — none of this means a thing when the prospect of instant wealth gets in the way. Without a shred of guilt, Bender blackmails Vorobyaninov into sharing his story about the lost jewels, misdirects poor Father Fyodor all the way to Siberia in search of a totally different, worthless set of chairs, and breaks into a recreation center with Vorobyaninov to steal the last of the real ones. Without thought to his own safety, Vorobyaninov single-mindedly walks a circus high-wire to steal a chair from a barely balanced tightrope walker; and without a thought to his soul, Father Fyodor lets his thirst for riches so consume him that at last he unwittingly corners himself all alone on a steep hilltop he's scared to climb down, trapped there with nothing but a ripped-apart chair and nary a diamond in sight.

We're pretty nicely amused by all this, too, off and on, and yet somehow none of these men's misadventures feel so outrageous as Bialystock and Bloom's efforts to stage *Springtime for Hitler* and strike it rich without going to jail. Brooks does his best to enliven *The Twelve Chairs'* sense of any-thing-can-happen insanity, and much of it works (fast-motion chases and scuffles, high-speed "Alvin and the Chipmunks" dialogue, etc.), but the film feels more self-consciously intellectual than *The Producers*, as if he's trying extra hard to impress us with cinematic beauty and grandeur and ambiance — what *The New Yorker's* Pauline Kael called "picturesque Grandma Moses atmosphere." If Brooks could've just made us laugh at least as often as he wows us with his craftsmanship, *The Twelve Chairs* would almost certainly be remembered as his finest film.

To some extent, though, Brooks' self-restraint tends to keep the whole picture playing pretty close to the vest, very much the same way *Life Stinks*, so long as homelessness remains a real-life social ill, can push the comic possibilities of a billionaire-turned-beggar just so far. At times even John Morris' music, so upbeat and playful nearly every second of Brooks' first film, sounds as poignant and powerful as something out of David Lean, and the *Dr. Zhivago*–esque costumes, settings, and locales carry with them such a European art house feel that anyone who's never seen *The Twelve Chairs* before might for a moment or two mistake it for a foreign film and expect subtitles any second. Does this explain why *The Twelve Chairs* made barely so much as a dent in the American box office on its initial release in 1970 — because U.S. audiences found the film's 1920s U.S.S.R. setting too off-putting, too alien? Probably so, a little, even though *Blazing Saddles, Young Frankenstein, History of the World — Part I, Robin Hood: Men in Tights*, and *Dracula: Dead and Loving It* are all set in distant pasts and foreign lands too, and each of these films has been seen by far more people than to this day even realize *The Twelve Chairs* exists.

Of course, Brooks' more famous other-time-other-place movies likely don't feel all that alien to Americans anyway, many of whom could never pinpoint Russia on a map or the Russian Revolution on a timeline but know Westerns, swashbucklers, and monster movies like the back of their hand. Having grown up on enough reruns of *Gunsmoke, Bonanza*, and *Rawhide* to choke a John Wayne horse, most Americans probably don't think of the Old West that Brooks laughs at with *Blazing Saddles* as the least bit exotic, and they've seen enough *Frankenstein* and *Dracula* films to feel pretty comfortable seeing Gene Wilder as Dr. Frankenstein and Leslie Nielsen as Dracula. Brooks' Sherwood Forest romp feels familiar too; Robin Hood remains such a round-the-world recognizable pop icon, like Zorro or Superman or The Lone Ranger, fans know pretty much what to expect going in. Most of the material in *History of the World — Part I* we've seen before too, really (even atheists know who Moses is), and the poster alone, with everybody running around in gladiator helmets and togas, brings back enough Sunday school memories of Samson and Delilah, David and Goliath, and all that to make most film fans feel they're treading on friendly terrain.

Some of *The Twelve Chairs'* characters have accents too, but surely this posed no real problem. Sid Caesar used make-believe accents all the time on *Your Show of Shows*, though admittedly he was aiming for laughs, not realism. Besides, of Brooks' three main stars, Ron Moody is English, New Yorker Dom DeLuise is about as American as they come, and Frank Langella, for all his princely, regal-rich diction, was born in New Jersey, and the largely Yugoslavian supporting cast, most of whom don't say much anyway, really don't jar the non–European ear any more than Peter Sellers' gloriously garbled French as Inspector Clouseau. If fans could fall in love with Don Adams' nasal duck quack as Agent 86 for five years on

Get Smart, voices like these should have been a snap.

Still, the movie does feel a little out of step with the rest of Brooks' work, and were it not for the broad comic presence of eventual Brooks semi-regular Dom DeLuise (and, though far less so, *The Producers'* Andreas Voutsinas in a small role), one might not believe Brooks the man behind *The Twelve Chairs* at all. The trademark Brooks kookiness is still here, but at times it seems oddly misplaced, as if it belongs in *Silent Movie* or *History of the World — Part I* but not here. We ought to fall down laughing when Vorobyaninov and Bender leap onto the back of a waiting horse and buckle the poor animal's knees — we're in stitches when Mongo knocks a similar horse flat with a punch to the head in *Blazing Saddles* — yet somehow here the sudden burst of slapstick feels out of place, as if Brooks has forgotten briefly he's set his film in a world Vincent Canby's *New York Times* review called "a Russia that is not too far removed from the world of Sholem Aleichem." Brooks has given the story so much texture up until now, put so much effort into capturing the innocence of Russian peasant life and the sentimental tragedy of onetime aristocrats reduced to face-in-the-crowd commoners, we've almost forgotten it's a comedy we're watching.

Indeed, of all Brooks' films *The Twelve Chairs* wavers the most between pie-in-the-face and poetic; in Disney terms, it's half Donald Duck cartoon and half *Bambi*, half Mickey Mouse short, half *Fantasia's* "Ave Maria," leaving us at times a little unsure quite what to make of it. Even the picture's casting feels a trifle off, even though practically every actor in it delivers a performance that is, taken strictly on its own terms, not only fitting but absolutely splendid.

The most obvious case in point here is, of course, Frank Langella, a then-rising young star whose late–'70s Broadway revival of the Hamilton Deane/John Balderston *Dracula* justly won him legions of fans who'd never heard of him before. Particularly suited to Byronic heroes and sinister villains, Langella ranks among the most gifted actors Brooks would work with, and his dark, faintly exotic features, roguish good looks, and riveting threat-whisper make him perfectly suited for the sly Russian ladies' man role Brooks has assigned him here. Regrettably, though, beyond a few early scenes in which Bender poses as a wounded war hero to petition charity and outsmarts his lover's husband by passing himself off as a doctor, Brooks doesn't push Langella very far comedy-wise, scripting Bender so sober-as-a-judge serious he might just as fittingly be played by a twenty-something Richard Chamberlain, Timothy Dalton, Daniel Day-Lewis, Kenneth Branagh, Liam Neeson, or Ralph Feinnes — virile, knavish-looking actors all, even pretty fair light comedians, but hardly likely to be named in the same breath with Dom DeLuise. One scene in particular, in which an enraged Bender bitterly shouts, "Parasite! Parasite!" at Vorobyaninov after the old man resists begging, plays almost exactly like Langela's incensed "Sacrilege! Sacrilege!" explosion in John Badham's 1979 *Dracula* adaptation. Powerful material, yes, and a marvelous acting opportunity for Langella — but who can laugh after a moment like this?

Thus Langella finds himself in the unenviable position of playing essentially a straight part in a comedy, his rakishly suave gravity at once precisely what the script calls for yet at the same time strangely at odds with the rest of Brooks' material. Were this a slightly more serious project, some poker-faced straight adaptation of Shakespeare or Henry James or one of the Brontë sisters, Langella would surely fit right in, but somehow when Langella bullies DeLuise or belts Moody in the stomach, it's not so much Abbott and Costello funny as just plain mean. Langella may be a fine comic, too, for all we know — for decades the closest we came to finding out was in light comedies like 1993's *Dave*, where he's cast as a bad guy and surrounded by low-key, understated costars — but even if Langella could have us rolling in the aisles, Brooks doesn't much try to find out. No matter how well Langella delivers his lines, and he delivers them superbly, the lines are rarely all that funny, and even if that's by design (keeping Bender a sane and sensible foil for the others, approaching his thievery with caution and refinement while Vorobyaninov and Father Fyodor foolishly leap without looking), opposite DeLuise and Moody he looks out of place.

English-accented Ron Moody, on the other hand, gets a luckier break in that Brooks gives him broader material to work with, lets him act much crazier, less in control of himself. Like Langella, Moody often veers dangerously close to serious drama, especially when he's playing patrician-turned-peasant Ippolit Vorobyaninov at his most utterly beaten and humiliated, but he's given plenty of chances to be funny too. While Moody's desperate-for-riches Vorobyaninov is several years older than traveling partner Bender, Brooks nevertheless makes him very much the over-hasty, out-of-control child of the pair; spoiled rotten by lost luxury, Vorobyaninov is the one whose rabid impatience and impulsiveness Bender has to constantly keep in check lest he snatch up a chair the moment he sets eyes on it and start ripping the seat cushions to shreds in full view.

A gifted comic performer, Moody knows just how to make all this frenzied over-eagerness sparkle too — so well it's hard to believe that beyond the occasional *Make Mine Mink*, *The Mouse on the Moon*, or *Unidentified Flying Oddball*, moviemakers

The Twelve Chairs (1970): Having traveled too far to give up his share of the valuable gems believed stashed inside one of a dozen scattered dining room chairs during the Revolution, smooth-talking Soviet drifter Ostap Bender (Frank Langella) prevents selfish cohort Ippolit Vorobyaninov (Ron Moody) from making off with the next-to-last chair.

rarely made use of his comedic talents on film. That's too bad; knees high, elbows bent, Moody even manages to give Vorobyaninov a funny run when he's chasing one of the chairs, and his comic mugging whenever his greed gets the better of him and his half-crazed ravings of "Hate! Hate!" as his loathing for Father Fyodor grows advance Brooks' themes even while they're making us laugh. The more of a "greedy pig" Vorobyaninov makes of himself, piling high his plate like Mt. Everest while invading a free buffet, requiring bodily restraint the second his eyes alight on one of the chairs, the more we "get" what Brooks is trying to say. In *The Twelve*

Chairs runaway greed turns grown men into children, and watching a "marshal of the nobility" behave like a spoiled, rapacious four-year-old is great fun. He even succeeds in giving this conceited, stuck-in-the-past fallen aristocrat the same semi-tragic, under-the-surface vulnerability of his child-corrupting Fagin character in the stage and screen versions of *Oliver!*, whose dishonesty we likewise find semi-forgivable because we pity his fear of being left fundless and friendless in his old age. Much as *Oliver!*'s Fagin squirrels away his boy thieves' best ill-gotten booty for his retirement, former nobleman Vorobyaninov's big concern when his mother-in-law dies is who will "take care of" him now, and here again Moody skillfully stirs up our compassion, condemnation, and amusement all at once — quite a tricky combination.

Still more colorful even than Moody's performance, though — way, way more colorful, in fact — is that of human pinball Dom DeLuise, who quickly became such fast friends with fellow Brooklynite Brooks and his family during the making of *The Twelve Chairs* that not only would Brooks direct the cherubic, high-energy actor four more times more over the years, but Brooks' wife Anne Bancroft wrote him his first-ever starring part in her 1980 directorial debut *Fatso*. It's easy to see why Brooks liked him. Besides being, like his costars, a marvelous (and vastly underrated) actor, DeLuise has the enviable advantage of both looking and sounding like a natural comedian; we expect him to make a movie funnier just by showing up, and whether he's being directed by Mel Brooks, Gene Wilder, or even animator Don Bluth, he never lets us down. With his Lou Costello excitability and Joe Besser prissiness, DeLuise's Father Fyodor gives *The Twelve Chairs* the kind of way-out, madcap wackiness not even Moody's daffiness can bring to it. Whenever DeLuise appears on screen, all hot-wired, stressed-out, and champing-at-the-bit, we forget all about epic Russian literature and remember, "Oh, yeah! This is a comedy! It's okay to laugh!"

Part of DeLuise's colossal comic appeal comes from his Brooklyn accent and very 1970s mannerisms, neither of which fit his 1927 Russian priest persona in the least but works great just the same. The last thing *The Twelve Chairs* needs is its one surefire laugh-getter squelching his comic instincts striving for Meryl Streep–type authenticity, but Brooks wisely gives DeLuise free rein. Would a real Russian utter such Americanisms as

"Come on, brain!" or "You dirty —!" when straining for a believable lie or, misdirected to Siberia, firing ill will at a chair-withholding Madame Bruns? Maybe not, but it sure is funny. Would a village priest really shove a grieving parishioner through a doorway like a sack of potatoes, or scramble over a front gate like some ill-bred schoolboy? Probably not, but why split hairs when we're dealing with DeLuise, the one actor to whom Brooks seems to have said, "Forget about art and drama and historical accuracy; just get out there and run wild"? As Father Fyodor, DeLuise enjoys Ron Moody's freedom to all but swallow the chairs whole the instant his character sees them, but, lacking Vorobyaninov's aristocratic dignity or Bender's threats to keep him in check, with Father Fyodor just about anything goes, especially during his dinner-demolishing, leg-hugging, finger-biting battle with the Brunses. Vorobyaninov thinks himself too proud to beg? Father Fyodor crawls like an animal at the Brunses' feet, and when DeLuise's voice, racing through Stan Freberg's entire "John and Marsha" novelty recording in just five seconds, shifts from urgently polite to *Exorcist*-level monstrous in mid-sentence ("My dear lady, don't you understand — I NEED THOSE CHAIRS?"), we know *The Twelve Chairs* couldn't possibly come up with a scene any funnier than this.

Regrettably, that turns out to be the case, too — *The Twelve Chairs* never does top Father Fyodor's madcap ruckus at the Brunses' — but that doesn't stop Brooks from giving us some really fine moments from his talented cast, himself included. Dressed like some burned-out, besotted refugee from the old Disney version of *Peter and the Wolf*, Brooks has his first self-directed on-screen role in this film (only his voice appears in *The Producers*), and though he doesn't have much screen time as Vororbyaninov's long-suffering but loyal ex-servant Tikon, he's given himself some nice material to play around with. His exaggerated drunken Russian shtick unsettles us a little when he first appears, especially in light of the movie's semiserious tone — it's as if radio comic Bert Gordon's Mad Russian were to suddenly turn up in *The Brothers Karamazov*— and it seems to take him awhile before he gets the timing and accent just right. But Brooks shares his pal DeLuise's enviable ability to perk up our enthusiasm the second we lay eyes on him, and after a slightly rocky start he really gets the hang of the character and does wonderful things with it.

Indeed, we're only just starting to embrace Brooks' slightly hammy approach before it's over with (*The New Yorker*'s Pauline Kael felt the film "never quite recovers from the loss of him"), and one wonders how much funnier, if thematically less potent, *The Twelve Chairs* might be had Brooks pitted Father Fyodor not against Vorobyaninov and Bender but Vorobyaninov and Tikon. The movie definitely would have lost something artistically — our feeling that Bender's life both before and after Russia's political upheaval has been one long, hard struggle, while men like Vorobyaninov have until recently been rich and idle, adds substance to the film's sociopolitical subtexts — but from a strictly financial standpoint more of Tikon's drunken incompetence might have meant funnier advertising, and funnier ads would almost certainly have meant bigger box office.

It couldn't have helped the promotional department either that, other than Brooks, *The Twelve Chairs* spends so little time spotlighting the rest of Moody, Langella, and DeLuise's supporting cast — or that so few of us would recognize them even if they did. They're fine actors too, every last one of them, but even the typical early-'70s Disney comedy — say, *The Boatniks* from that same year, whose under-five-minute roles include sitcom favorites Wally Cox, Vito Scotti, Florence Halop, Al Lewis, and Joe E. Ross, or the next year's *$1,000,000 Duck* with bit players Frank Cady, Hal Smith, Fran Ryan, and Bernard Fox — can get more marketing mileage out of its minor players than *The Twelve Chairs*' publicity people ever could have come up with here.

Elaine Garreau is both funny and touching in her brief but pivotal role as Vorobyaninov's conscience-stricken, dying mother-in-law Claudia Ivanova (she really does seem distressed about having hidden the gems, as much for having kept their fate from her son-in-law as for duping the State), and Branha Veselinovic, who as neighbor Natasha privately predicts Mrs. Ivanova's death a split-second after reassuring her all is well, is good too in a part that's even smaller. So are David Lander and Diana Coupland as unmercifully harassed Engineer and Madame Bruns, utterly dazzling in the Brunses' riotous indoor battle with Father Fyodor, then again giving up their chairs to this wacko later (Coupland's horrified scream of "No!" when the so-grateful-he's-giddy priest tries to say goodbye is just glorious!); *The Producers*' Andreas Voutsinas as prissy-pompous play producer Nikolai Sestrin, so insecure he moves to a higher step each time six-foot-plus Bender stands close enough to dwarf him; Vlada Petric as lily-livered theater prop thief Sevitsky, forever getting into tight spots for stealing; Robert Bernal in his half-minute bit as a persnickety museum curator; Will Stampe as the Moscow Railway Workers' Communal House of Recreation night watchman, who sentimentally reveals the "miracle" discovery of the gems, used to build the center where Vorobyaninov has filched a free meal — indeed, the whole cast is marvelous, no matter how large or small the role. How unfortunate, though, that ultimately most of these talented performers play walk-ons so don't-step-out-for-popcorn skimpy they make William Hickey's ditzy bar drunk and Estelle Winwood's "Touch Me Feel Me" lady in *The Producers* seem almost like that movie's main stars.

In *The Producers*, for instance, Brooks returnee Andreas Voutsinas plays a character so flamboyantly weird we can hardly believe our eyes, but here he's given barely thirty seconds to pull off the same miracle, and, funny as he is (and that's pretty funny), without benefit of Carmen Giya's offbeat costuming and more screen time he can't outclass himself no matter what he tries. That same shipboard theater segment even includes a bit part for an equally distinctive-looking Nicholas Smith playing First Actor — among its minor players, his is the one hey-I've-seen-that-guy face in the whole film — yet while TV's *Are You Being Served?* Britcom uses Smith's kindly uncle dorkiness, bald head, and Alfred E. Neuman ears to fine humorous effect, his task here seems pretty thankless — all that comic naturalness wasted on a part Smith could play in his sleep.

The Twelve Chairs includes several such missed opportunities. We all know how much Brooks loves song-and-dance sequences, for instance, yet despite the presence this time of Oscar-nominated *Oliver!* show-stopper Ron Moody, *The Twelve Chairs* would become the only Brooks comedy ever that didn't have one. He's written some spectacularly witty lyrics for the movie's Brahms-inspired opening credits theme, but perhaps Brooks felt pompous ex-aristocrat Vorobyaninov was too stuffy to launch into song, or he reasoned that a big, splashy extravaganza like *The Producers'* "Springtime for Hitler" or *Blazing Saddles'* "The French Mistake" would undermine the film's thematic integrity. Maybe so, but the scene in which Vorobyaninov is hit by stage fright posing as a theater troupe actor seems tailor-made for one of Brooks' big production numbers, and it's quite possible with just a little more rethinking he could have made it all work.

Given the thematic aptness of dropping erstwhile aristocrat Vorobyaninov into the middle of a production titled *The Rise and Fall of the Upper Classes*, Brooks couldn't replace the scene with just anything, but rather than some tune-free, all-talk stage play, why not instead shove a cash-desperate Vorobyaninov into some crazy Brooksian Russian operetta or ballet, show him dodging spins, leaps, and high-steps trying to run off with one of the chairs in mid-performance? Indeed, it's probably more in character for Vorobyaninov to try faking his way through songs and dance steps he doesn't know on stage than panic; after all, this is a man so blind to all but his own greed he ignores both crowds and heights to walk a circus highwire! Even if Vorobyaninov didn't sing and dance, though, just snatched up the chair and made a break for it, surely we'd have great fun watching him fleeing his pursuers crawling over the laps of audience members, knocking over sets, and ducking in and out among flabbergasted stage performers while clinging to an old chair.

Even without the hoped-for production number, though, *The Twelve Chairs* is still a nice little picture, albeit one with a comparatively somewhat limited audience appeal. Neil Sinyard quite rightly calls the film "a Mel Brooks movie for people who don't like Mel Brooks movies," but the unfortunate side effect of its more adult, sophisticated feel is that those who do like Brooks films won't feel entirely satisfied with this one. In one sense, the picture is a shorter (by nearly one-and-a-half hours), more intellectually ambitious version of Stanley Kramer's terrifically funny 1963 farce *It's a Mad Mad Mad Mad World*; it's Kramer's film scaled down but smartened up, given less action but more insight. Besides the greed-can-backfire, crime-doesn't-pay, cheaters-never-prosper message it shares with Brooks' film (and its closing argument that a good enough laugh can make almost anything bearable, even prison and broken bones), Kramer's movie hasn't a serious idea in its head, and that's precisely why we love it so much. Analyzing *It's a Mad Mad Mad Mad World* is like writing a master's thesis on why we love Bob Hope or *The Munsters* or *Hee Haw* or "Beetle Bailey." It's because they're funny, that's why, and sometimes that's more than enough.

The Twelve Chairs is funny too, if inconsistently, but where Kramer can cut easily from one group of crazies to another whenever it suits him (Sid Caesar and Edie Adams not colorful enough? How about Mickey Rooney and Buddy Hackett? Or Jonathan Winters and Phil Silvers? Or Milton Berle, Ethel Merman, Dorothy Provine, and Terry-Thomas?), Brooks has fewer options. Here fans can latch onto only one of two sets of competitors, either DeLuise's gooney-bird priest or Moody and Langella's mismatched pair, and if we don't like either set we're just out of luck. DeLuise, thankfully, makes a grand comic screwball, so whenever he's around we're having the time of our lives, even when his presence feels at cross purposes with the rest of the film, like Mickey Rooney's toothy Japanese in *Breakfast at Tiffany's* or Daniel Stern's slapsticky pitching coach in *Rookie of the Year*. With Moody and especially Langella, though, our reaction is more restrained. Moody's dog-on-a-leash impatience can be tremendous fun, and Langella's Russian roué charisma makes him a highly effective foil for Moody to play against, but even in mid-argument these two sometimes seem to be acting in completely different films, as if Moody has just been dragged in off the set of some '70s-era Disney comedy, Langella direct

from playing Heathcliff or Rochester in some new BBC adaptation of *Wuthering Heights* or *Jane Eyre*.

Strange as it seems having three such dissimilar talents "teamed up" for the same comedy, however, as disconcerting as we often find its uneasy union of painter's landscape magnificence, heartbreaking pathos, and rough-and-tumble farce, *The Twelve Chairs* nevertheless proves Mel Brooks capable of enormous artistry when art is what he's out for. Like some of his later works, *Life Stinks* and *Dracula: Dead and Loving It* in particular, *The Twelve Chairs* would have won greater acclaim had Brooks managed to double or even triple the number of laughs, but its heart is in the right place, with Brooks working hard to discover just the right balance between culture, character, and comedy. Two films later, teamed with Gene Wilder on *Young Frankenstein*, he'd accomplish just that, and *The Twelve Chairs* had a great deal to do with helping him get there.

CAST: Ron Moody (Ippolit Vorobyaninov); Frank Langella (Ostap Bender); Dom DeLuise (Father Fyodor); Andreas Voutsinas (Nikolai Sestrin); Vlada Petric (Sevitsky); David Lander (Engineer Bruns); Diana Coupland (Madam Bruns); Elaine Garreau (Claudia Ivanova); Will Stampe (Night Watchman); Mel Brooks (Tikon); Aca Stojkovic (Captain Scriabin); Robert Bernal (Curator); Nicholas Smith (First Actor); Branha Veselinovic (Natasha); Paul Wheeler, Jr. (Kolya); Mavid Popovic (Makko); Peter Banicevic (Sergeant); Bridget Price (Young Wife); Mladja Veselinovic; Rada Djurkin.

CREDITS: Director: Mel Brooks; Executive Producer: Sidney Glazier; Producer: Michael Hertzberg; Screenplay: Mel Brooks; based on the novel *The Twelve Chairs* by Ilf and Petrov (Ilya Faynzilberg and Yevgeny Katayev), as translated by Elizabeth Hill and Doris Mudie as *Diamonds to Sit On*; Editor: Alan Heim; Sound: Peter Sutton; Boom Operator: Ken Reynolds; Makeup: George Partleton; Unit Manager: Velia Janovelevic, Moma Pesic; Continuity: Ann Edwards; Sound Re-recording: Richard

Vorisek; Sound Editors: Thomas Halpin, Sanford Rackow; Property Master: Milan Cenio; Gaffer: Daagan Pavanovik; Key Grip: Ivan Pajdak; 2nd Assistant Directors: Peter Anderson, Vadivaje Vilotlavic, Tihajlo Cian; Assistant Editors: Richard S. Goldberg, Walter Rappaport; Opticals: Film Opticals; Production Supervisor: Fred Gallo; Production Manager: Ante Milic; 2nd Unit Photography: Eric Van Haaren Norman; Art Director: Mile Nikolic; Titles: Arthur Eckstein; Executive in Charge of Production: William Berns; Costume Designer: Ruth Meyers; Director of Photography: Djordje Nikolic; Assistant Director: Bato Cengic; Music Composer/Conductor: John Morris; "Hope for the Best (Expect the Worst)" Lyrics: Mel Brooks, from a melody by Johannes Brahms; Orchestration: John Morris, Jonathan Tunick; Color: Movielab; a UMC Pictures Crossbow Co. Production, 1970; 94 minutes.

3

★ ★ ★

"Have You Ever Seen Such Cruelty"

Blazing Saddles

★ ★ ★ ★ ★ ★

(1974)

Overseeing railroad work in the 1874 American West, nitwit white racists Lyle (Burton Gilliam) and boss Taggart (Slim Pickens) emperil black track-layers Bart (Cleavon Little) and Charlie (Charles Mc-Gregor) in quicksand, and Bart, enraged, hits Taggart with a shovel. At Taggart's request, greedy governor's assistant Hedley Lamarr (Harvey Korman) agrees to have ghoulish executioner Boris (Robert Ridgely) hang Bart, and plots to take over Rock Ridge, a tiny town worth millions once the quicksand-diverted railroad comes through, by having Taggart and a mob of thugs drive out the residents with a wave of destruction, assault, rape, and murder.

In Rock Ridge's church after the chaos, Rev. Johnson (Liam Dunn) declares plans to flee, but incoherent Gabby Johnson (Claude Ennis Starrett, Jr.) will stay, like Olson Johnson (David Huddleston), Dr. Samuel Johnson (Richard Collier), Howard Johnson (John Hillerman), and Van Johnson (George Furth). Their sheriff murdered,

they telegraph lewd, moronic Gov. William J. Lepetomane (Mel Brooks) for a new one, but Lamarr, convincing Gov. Lepetomane to appoint a black sheriff, sends Bart. As Lamarr has hoped, Sheriff Bart stuns and terrifies the lily-white bigots of Rock Ridge, but he easily escapes being shot to death when the townsfolk prove simple-minded beyond belief.

At an emergency meeting, schoolmarm Harriett Johnson (Carol Arthur) reads a nasty letter for the governor, while Bart befriends his one prisoner, Jim, The Waco Kid (Gene Wilder), an amazingly fast but alcoholic gunslinger. After Bart tells how a Jewish Indian Chief (Mel Brooks) let Bart's dark-skinned family pass West unharmed when he was a boy, Taggart sends brawny dullard Mongo (Alex Karras) to kill Bart. Mongo terrorizes the town until Bart defeats him with an exploding candygram, after which Bart is slightly better treated and even becomes Mongo's pal.

50

Lamarr hires saloon singer Lili Von Shtupp (Madeline Kahn) to entice and reject Bart, but Lili truly falls for him. Later, baffled by Lamarr's interest in Rock Ridge, Bart visits a track-laying Charlie for facts, and when Taggart and his mob ride up, Jim easily outguns all six. Lamarr next advertises for criminals to destroy Rock Ridge, and the residents grant Bart one day before they flee. After he and Jim spy on the villain sign-up, Bart forces a deal: his minority railway pals will help build a decoy Rock Ridge by morning for some free land. The citizens agree, and the fake town goes up, as does a toll booth to slow the enemy until decoy townsfolk are made. When the criminals ride up, Jim detonates dynamite with a bullet, and the citizens attack their foes en masse.

Events turn surreal as the chaos pushes through the film's frontier set and, acquiring more brawlers, into a musical by director Buddy Bizarre (Dom DeLuise), into the commissary for a big pie fight, and out the studio gates. Lamarr takes a taxi to a theater showing *Blazing Saddles*, but seeing Bart ride up on horseback on screen, exits, and fires on Bart, who nimbly shoots Lamarr dead. Jim arrives, and he and Bart watch the film, which ends with grateful Rock Ridge citizens, along with Lili and Gov. Lepetomane, saying tearful goodbyes to Bart. With Jim, Bart heads "nowhere special" by horse until the pair climb into a limousine and are driven into the sunset.

★　★　★

Excepting only *History of the World — Part I*, the uproarious 1974 comedy–Western smash *Blazing Saddles* qualifies as the most shamelessly offensive movie Mel Brooks ever made, and either despite this fact or because of it, it also happens to be one of his funniest. An R-rated laugh-riot running away in off-color directions his

clean-as-a-whistle TV world of *Your Show of Shows* and *Get Smart* never dared to, Brooks' third try as writer-director is sure to antagonize anyone who misses the days when comedy didn't have to shock to be funny, and sure to delight anyone able to overlook such excesses for the hundreds of non-shock gags in between.

Moviegoers who'd thought they'd seen and heard everything after 1968's *The Producers* soon realized they'd spoken too soon, and that all those Busby Berkeley Nazis and man-crazy little old ladies looked tame after *Blazing Saddles*, whose off-the-wall plotline — jive-talking black sheriff alienates, then rescues, dimwit racists in all-white Western town — slips in enough innuendo, racial epithets, and cattle-country vulgarisms to make *The Producers'* riskiest material up till then look downright innocuous. As a result, fans who prefer the relatively unobjectionable G and PG style of Mel Brooks behind films like *The Twelve Chairs* and *High Anxiety* may want to steer clear of it, but they'll miss out on some never-to-be-forgotten comedy if they do, because as frequent as they may seem to the feint of heart, the shock laughs still take a backseat to the sort of innocuous, funny-paper harmless entertainment that amused us in childhood. Either way, whether its gags are as unashamedly startling as something from Zucker-Abrams-Zucker or the Farelly Brothers or as Sunday school innocent as *Fibber McGee and Molly*'s open-closet Niagras or those beloved Ping Pong ball rainstorms on *Captain Kangaroo*, *Blazing Saddles* remains one funny, funny film.

It's funny enough, in fact, that fans who've seen only edited versions on TV may actually find many of the replacement jokes just as good as the ones cut. Some of the material initially left on the cutting-room floor (most of it involving either Sheriff Bart's Screwy Squirrel assaults on overgrown thug-lug Mongo or Brooks' dumb-as-dirt governor's visit to his constituents) is every bit as entertaining as the jokes the TV folks drop, and some of the minor scene-trims create new gags all their own. The TV censors snip a vulgar verbal response to a church house philosopher's Nietzsche quote, and, amazingly, we *still* laugh; now it seems the aghast minister seen next is floored by the profundity, not the swearing ("'Nietzsche,' he said! My word!"), the same way later on the entire town will be bowled over just hearing the name of film star Randolph Scott. No matter how it's sliced and diced, *Blazing Saddles* still gets laughs; it's positively tinker-proof.

That's assuming, of course, one finds oddball images like horses getting hanged and little old ladies taking fists to the gut like punching bags funny in the first place, and not everyone does, nor did they at the time. *Variety* found the film witty enough, certainly, declaring, "If comedies are measured solely by the number of yocks they generate … then Mel Brooks' *Blazing Saddles* must be counted a success," but not everyone was so charitable. The *New York Times*' Vincent Canby laughed some, but, unhappy with what he termed the film's "desperate, bone-crushing efforts" at comedy, felt himself "wanting it to be funnier," while *The New Yorker*'s Pauline Kael, whose earlier reviews had at least labeled *The Producers* "funny" and *The Twelve Chairs* "so-so," charged Brooks' latest with "a scarcity of comedy," claiming his "celebrated spontaneous wit isn't in evidence" and arguing his "desperate" older gags "never were very funny" to begin with.

Since what is and isn't giggle-worthy is so subjective, one can't very well fault these last two critics for finding *Blazing Saddles* less than the perfect comedy, and certainly it isn't as stylistically impressive as, say, *The Twelve Chairs* or *Young Frankenstein* in cinematography, sophisti-

cation of content, and all that. But unfunny? A Wild West comedy about a *Shaft*-flashy black sheriff taking on bad guys with plywood mannequins, Klan robes, and candygrams? No, Brooks might have made more artful comedies, but he rarely made one more mirth-provoking. *Entertainment Tonight* critic Leonard Maltin, clearly wishing later efforts might yet outclass it, put it this way: "None of Brooks' later films [ever] topped this one for sheer belly laughs."

All those "sheer belly laughs" came naturally to Brooks, whose third directorial effort actually furthers the sort of broad comedy he had already scripted so successfully in the '50s on *Your Show of Shows*, where Sid Caesar's gang had fans rolling with wild takeoffs on then-recent Westerns like *Shane* and *High Noon*. Here, though, the budget is much, much higher, allowing Brooks the "luxury" of shooting in genuine sand-and-sagebrush open-air, and the censors, instead of the old Broadcast Standards and Practices chopping axe, come armed with nothing but an MPAA poster rating. Consequently, the language may offend the rare moviegoer who rides into Brooks Country only by way of *The Producers* and *The Twelve Chairs* (less so those who've seen his post–'70s films), and the tale's race-related elements, satiric or not, will surely antagonize anyone who flinched at every *Hogan's Heroes* "Heil Hitler!" or protested the old Frito Bandito ads over at Frito-Lay. On the other hand, fans who can resist getting too bogged down in cultural sensitivity issues, who can take a joke even when they themselves bear some of the brunt of it, are likely to find *Blazing Saddles* one of the most rip-roaringly hilarious comedies ever made.

Hilarious, yes — but also controversial. Brooks noted later that, given the politically correct climate soon putting such a well-intentioned stranglehold on American entertainment, he might never have gotten away with many of *Blazing Saddles'* funniest bits had he not shot the film just when he did. The national mood has changed greatly since Brooks first wrote for TV in 1949, and many of Sid Caesar's characters — his make-believe Frenchmen, pretend Germans, phony Italians, sham Spaniards — might trigger protest launched in prime-time today. Perhaps now *Get Smart* couldn't slip its Oriental outlaw The Claw ("Not Craw — Craw!") past NBC so easily, or make a recurring villain of Bernie Kopell's Nazi-esque Siegfried. Indeed, could *The Andy Griffith Show* still find humor in a funny town drunk? *The Honeymooners* in "right in the kisser" threats of spousal violence? Maybe, given all those *Seinfeld* episodes raking in laughs with such touchy subjects as the physically handicapped and the mentally challenged — but then again, maybe not.

Certainly the timing seems to have been right from a satirical standpoint, considering such taboo-smashing shows as *All in the Family* (which clearly linked racism with ignorance just as Brooks does here) were scoring huge ratings on TV, and it surely helped too that by the mid–'70s fans of all races had already been rooting for slick, street-smart black heroes in films like *In the Heat of the Night* (1967), *Cotton Comes to Harlem* (1970, its cast including *Blazing Saddles* star Cleavon Little), and *Shaft* (1971). If ever the time had come for a cooler-than-cool hero like Sheriff Bart, the tricky young railroad worker spared from hanging by land-grabbers who hope his skin color alone will drive the bigoted, lawman-needy whites from tiny Rock Ridge, 1974 was it.

Alleviating some of this hypersensitivity too is the fact that Brooks' film is, to paraphrase one of its own gags, such an "equal opportunity offender," insulting just about everybody in equal measure. African-Americans in particular are surely well within their rights to bristle at the racial cruelty the movie's white oppressors fling about, but no way in the world could anyone watch the film seriously believing he alone has been singled out. Almost to a man *Blazing Saddles'* whites are depicted as ditzy, dishonest, or just plain mean, and if we just had a nickel for everything likely to offend *somebody*— women, politicians, clergymen, whites, blacks, Native Americans, Germans, Mexicans, Chinese, Arabs, Irishmen, Christians, Jews, homosexuals, Klansmen, bikers, recovering alcoholics, struggling drug addicts, the speech impaired, families of the mentally challenged — well, we'd have ourselves an awful lot of nickels, that's what. If none of this quite justifies all the ugly racial slurs the Rock Ridge bigots fling about so casually at their new sheriff's expense, at least the one big benefit of poking fun at so many different social groups is that sooner or later even the touchiest viewer cracks a guilty smile at something. "Aha!" Brooks can come back at us, finger waving. "You got all huffy about my black jokes, didn't you? But I notice you didn't mind one bit laughing at my white jokes and German jokes and gay jokes and Jew jokes, now did you?"

Perhaps the involvement of multiple writers made so many different bull's-eyes inevitable. As in his Sid Caesar TV days, Brooks didn't work mostly alone this time as he had in *The Producers* and *The Twelve Chairs*, but with others: director-to-be Andrew Bergman, whose initial *Tex X* script had impressed Brooks so much in the first place, and who soon proved he was no fluke with hits like *The In-Laws, Fletch, The Freshman, Soapdish,* and *Honeymoon in Vegas*; Norman Steinberg and Alan Uger, delivering what Brooks called their "Jewish comedy team" sensibilities (Steinberg later co-wrote Brooksfilms' *My Favorite Year*); and rising star Richard Pryor, who'd win an Emmy co-writing a Lily Tomlin TV special soon after the film's debut. In theory, with

Oblivious to his crooked assistant's scheme to drive out the all-white bigots of tiny Rock Ridge, dim-witted 1870s Gov. William J. Lepetomane (Mel Brooks) is literally floored by the thought of turning trailblazing hero, as sneaky subordinate Hedley Lamarr (Harvey Korman) convinces him to appoint the United States' first-ever African-American sheriff, in co-writer/director/lyricist Brooks' third movie and biggest hit, the uproarious *Blazing Saddles* (1974).

so many different writers, *Blazing Saddles* should be an aimless, haphazard mess, and while its "everything but the kitchen sink" style does at times make it feel that way (Cole Porter, *Bonanza*, and *Wide World of Sports* jokes — in one film?), it takes talent to make this much planning feel this random.

Like some screwball Tex Avery cartoon, *Blazing Saddles* revels in sheer un-

predictability, with its gags, as rubber ball pliable as a wad of Silly Putty, bouncing in at us from all angles and in all shapes. Except only a scene or two in *The Producers* (when Max expresses doubts about Leo's sanity to the audience) and *The Twelve Chairs* (with its "Bureau of Bureaus" joke), neither of his previous films step outside the bounds of believability the way Brooks does here. With *Blazing Saddles*, however, as with several later such comedies, stylistically pretty much anything goes.

Many of the laughs are anachronistic, springing from impossible-but-funny little timeline incongruities — nineteenth-century Klan robes with 1970s smiley-face emblems, for instance, or the Count Basie Orchestra in the desert in 1874. Others derive from cinematic in-jokes, references to films like *Cat Ballou* and Gabby Hayes and *High Noon*, or from making sport of the fact that what we're seeing is itself a movie, as when Harvey Korman's villainous Hedley Lamarr speaks to us straight-on or predicts his Academy Award chances come Oscar time. Still more come from corny puns, or "adult" shock effects, or old-time slapstick, or daffy song lyrics, or silly costumes, or goofy comic juxtapositions, as when Indian chiefs speak Yiddish and cattle populate saloons.

In short, where films like *The Producers*, *The Twelve Chairs*, *High Anxiety*, *Life Stinks*, and even *Dracula: Dead and Loving It* are somewhat limited as to the kinds of gags they can reasonably get away with, *Blazing Saddles* permits practically any sort of comedy imaginable. As in the classic Warner Bros. cartoons it references (by way of the Bugs Bunny–like ingenuity Sheriff Bart uses to defeat Mongo, his "Ain't I a stinker?"–type observations to Brooks' camera, even the use of the "Merrie Melodies" ditty "Merrily We Roll Along"), *Blazing Saddles* grants its creators the freedom to break just about any rule they like — including, following the long, slow death of the forty-year-old Hays Office Production Code, several rules of basic propriety as well.

Whether Brooks did the world any real favors helping obliterate such self-restraint remains questionable, but no one can deny *Blazing Saddles*' impact. For all the "I can't believe they just said that!" eyebrow-raising incited, the movie's break-with-tradition irreverence filled way too many theater seats in 1974 to pretend there was no market for it. Many might have cringed at the way it tested moralistic constraints perhaps still better left untested, or recoiled from it just as they had R-rated comedies like *The Graduate* and *M*A*S*H* a few years before, and maybe they were right to — yet in no time at all *Blazing Saddles* had become the year's second-biggest moneymaker (after *The Towering Inferno*), and all that soda and popcorn peddling spoke quite loudly indeed. Far from everyone who had helped make family-friendly comedies like *It's a Mad Mad Mad Mad World* and *That Darn Cat* and *The Love Bug* such hits just a few earlier before bought tickets, but all those thousands who did sent out a message to Hollywood that by now they'd pay to laugh at almost anything: the automatic pilot bit in *Airplane!*, the toilet bowl scene in *Dumb & Dumber*, the titlular sight gag in *American Pie*, any number of gross-out, ugly moments in *Scary Movie*.

With *Blazing Saddles*, we're sometimes struck, simultaneously, with both admiration and revulsion by what turns up on-screen. The notorious campfire incident, for example, in which Brooks, Bergman, Pryor, Steinberg, and Uger explore what logically should happen when movie cowboys gobble down all those beans, truly does give one pause for thought — at least when one ponders Brooks' explanation behind it in interviews later on. Why *is* it film fans can watch human beings beaten black-and-blue in saloon fights, strung up by lynch mobs, dragged through the dirt by horse rope, struck over the head with chairs, or gunned down in the street without batting an eye — yet a simple gag about flatulence, prior to 1974 anyway, raises cries of bad taste? Where were all these faultfinders when movie cowboys and Indians were getting shot off horses left and right? Why is it make-believe murder is just good clean fun, yet the perfectly natural, harmless after-effects of a good meal causes offense? Isn't this a little like looking the other way at rape and torture and cannibalism, yet protesting a belch or a burp or the mention of toilet paper?

Clearly, something is badly wrong here, and even if one finds Brooks' bean-eating bit disgusting, he at least deserves some measure of credit for reminding us what crazy, mixed-up hypocrites we are. What kind of cockeyed, upside-down place *is* Hollywood that filmmakers think stringing up, gun-blasting, and pistol-whipping Indian after Indian, scalping, tomahawking, and piercing with arrows cowboy after cowboy make great entertainment, but a simple case of the vapors is tasteless and extreme? And what kind of half-wit imbeciles are we ticket-buyers, too, that a little abdominal let-go can still shock us — but shootouts and slaughter seem as all–American and harmless as Mickey Mouse, Shirley Temple, and Rin Tin Tin? Are we out of our minds?

Of course, probably not too many spotted all this irony at the time, any more than anyone much questioned the logic behind a Western spoof whose pop culture nods aren't limited to just Westerns. A few of Brooks' references, to 1940's *The Grapes of Wrath* for instance, have about as much to do with cowboy flicks as *Robin Hood: Men in Tights'* Macaulay Culkin gag has to do with Robin Hood, but at least they aren't so hamfisted about calling attention to themselves — none of that "Well, I've got to go 'home alone' now" over-obviousness here. When *Blazing Saddles* slips in a joke that doesn't quite fit the genre, as when Mongo lopes up on an ox branded "YES" and "NO," Brooks doesn't even try helping us make the mental leap needed to get to the "LOVE" and "HATE" tattoos on Robert Mitchum's psycho-preacher in *The Night of the Hunter*,

and that's likely just as well. Charles Laughton's 1955 film has so little relation to *Blazing Saddles* (except by way of Henry Hathaway's 1968 Western *Five Card Stud*, in which Mitchum plays a similar murderous minister) that it's best just to sneak the joke in, say nothing, and casually zip right on.

Come to think of it, Brooks probably spends less time hovering over his humor here than in any of his other films. Several jokes, the "Dr. Gillespie" gag, for instance (alluding to the film and TV *Dr. Kildare* series inspired by the stories of Western novelist Max Brand), or the "laurel and a hearty handshake" salute to Stan Laurel and Oliver Hardy, come at us so unexpectedly and so fast we barely have time to absorb what we've just heard before something else steals our attention, and a few are so esoteric — the reference to bongo player Mongo Santamaria leaps to mind — that some may not realize a joke has been made at all. In the end it doesn't matter much, however, because for every gag that flies right over our heads, Brooks pelts another dozen or so at us that we grasp right off. Those of us who don't speak Yiddish won't have a clue why Madeline Kahn's suggestively monickered Lili Von Shtupp is so designated, for instance, and even fewer will "get" the reference to the human whoopee cushion Brooks' nitwit politico Gov. Lepetomane is named for, but that's okay; seconds after these two first appear we're too busy laughing at Lili's "siwwy song wywrics" and Lepetomane's running around cross-eyed with "GOV" on his coat to care.

Not *all* of *Blazing Saddles* hustles along at this same speed, of course. Material involving Gene Wilder's alcoholic ex-quick-draw artist Jim, a.k.a. The Waco Kid, can't help slowing things up a bit — for most of the picture, Jim is hung over, or passively playing chess with Cleavon Little's Sheriff Bart, or swapping stories with him, or quietly easing Bart's hurt feelings after a greeting to a little old lady has been paid back with a racist insult — and Alex Karras's simpleminded Mongo, with his drowsy, childlike delivery, can't keep the comic locomotive chugging along full-blast either. Still, quiet scenes like these, along with the final farewell between Rock Ridge rescuer Bart and the townspeople whose respect he has earned, give *Blazing Saddles* its most genuinely human moments, preventing this film, for all its verbal throwaways about Jesse Owens and Mr. Goodbar and Cecil B. DeMille, from turning into one of those funny but soulless comedies so popular after 1980's *Airplane!*— from the best of the bunch, like *The Naked Gun: From the Files of Police Squad!* (1988) and *Hot Shots!* (1991), to the rock-bottom worst — whose heroes' weighty, every-word-momentous delivery makes for plenty of Mad Hatter hilarity but no heart.

In *Blazing Saddles*, even surrounded by all that craziness, the emotional moments are played at least partially for real. The little old lady really does break Bart's spirit; Jim truly does care about cheering him up; Bart's railroad pal Charlie, reunited with the buddy he's thought dead, really is elated at seeing him; the townspeople, if not exactly converted, truly do have a change of heart; leaving town for "nowhere special," Bart and Jim, black man and white, truly are fast friends.

Indeed, as dizzily nonsensical as *Blazing Saddles'* dialogue often is (evildoers who believe Methodists as vile as rustlers and snipers, Supreme Court rulings that read like baseball scores), the film is far more sentimental than most of its successors. *Airplane!* is a bent, twisted joy, true enough, but when Robert Hayes, Lloyd Bridges, Robert Stack, and crew fire off their Gatling gun gibberish, they seldom shift gears; whether barking out orders, musing about failed romances, or brooding over some past disgrace, the rat-a-tat-tat deadpan remains. The same goes for most crazy-talk comedies, whose stars, from Charlie Sheen (*Hot Shots!*) to Emilio Estevez (*National Lampoon's Loaded Weapon I*) to Armand Assante (*Fatal Instinct*) to Billy Zane (*Silence of the Hams*) to Jay Mohr (*Jane Austen's Mafia!*), are asked to play the same one or two super-serious notes throughout. Ninety minutes later, we've laughed plenty, but have we felt anything? We like the actors, but do we really embrace the characters? *Blazing Saddles*, thankfully, tends to be a bit more emotionally satisfying, asking a tad more from its stars than just keeping a straight face.

The film is well-directed too. True, a few of the shots aren't all that attractive to look at, and, as occurs so often on TV, it's jarring whenever a glimpse through a doorway reveals not a "real" frontier street but a flat, painted backdrop, but elsewhere Brooks displays remarkably good technique. His slow, sweeping vistas, expertly supplemented by John Morris's splendid music (the opening and closing desert pans are particularly good) are really quite beautiful, and some of his visual tricks (point-of-view shots from a moving handcar; Jim's upside-down first glimpse of Bart; the horse-punch stunt; the line-of-dominos effect as quick-draw Jim shoots the guns out of hand after hand) provide some nice surprises. Then too, while it's true some might come a tad later than we'd like, Brooks' use of close-ups of both major and minor players helps immensely; these actors have gloriously expressive faces, and Brooks very nearly zeroes in on every last one.

When all is said and done, however, *Blazing Saddles'* most enduring element remains its once-in-a-million, absolutely inspired central idea: taking a streetwise, *Mod Squad*–snazzy black who knows what's what, dropping him smack-dab in the middle of a sleepy, backwards town full of all-white *Gunsmoke* types, stepping back, and watching the white folks' mask of "Do unto others" Bible-thumping wholesomeness get stripped away. Outrageous, status quo–smashing newcomer arrives and stirs things up — it's a classic comedy premise, seen again and again in any number of hit films (*M*A*S*H*, for instance, in which regulation-breakers Hawkeye and Trapper John take on lockstep, by-the-book military types) and TV shows (for example, *WKRP in Cincinnati*, wherein the new program director shakes up his catatonic, dead-last radio station by switching from "elevator music" drabness to kick-up-a-commotion rock 'n' roll). When Sheriff Bart rides into Rock Ridge, the culture shock blindsiding these milky-white ninnies, each expecting someone more akin to John Wayne or Roy Rogers, it feels like dropping a bomb; it's like seeing KISS booked at the Mayberry spring picnic, or Madonna as guest speaker for the Harper Valley P.T.A.

Ironically, though, the film's other plot, its "greedy criminals scheme to drive out property owners and steal their land" storyline, couldn't be more ordinary — we've seen this scenario played out in Westerns and near–Westerns for years, from *Shane* to *Once Upon a Time in the West* to *7 Faces of Dr. Lao* — but Andrew Bergman's idea to make the town's savior hip, urban, and black instead of square, folksy, and white is such pure gold it makes the movie's otherwise mundane townfolk vs. landgrabbers concept seem brand new. Like *The Producers'* Broadway Nazis and *Young Frankenstein's* capering Karloff, this one basic idea is so simple it's positively brilliant, like Jack Benny's radio writers coming up with Benny's first cheapskate gag, or "Peanuts" creator Charles Schulz's decision to put Snoopy atop his doghouse and start giving him his own thought balloons.

Mel Brooks himself, like Cleavon Little's Sheriff Bart, another "dazzling urban-ite" making a big impact treading unexpected terrain, comes across a pretty clever fellow as well. A longtime city dweller about as hay-bale-and-horse-trough rural as he is shy and retiring, the Brooklyn-born Brooks might seem like the last man in the world who ought to be directing a Western, no matter how many cowboy spoofs he once co-wrote for Sid Caesar, yet *Blazing Saddles'* "racism equals idiocy" theme, seen so often in his ongoing cinematic war on anti–Semitism, makes Brooks fit right in. During a brief flashback, in which an otherwise all-white wagon train rejects little Bart's family from its circle during a Sioux attack, the Yiddish-speaking Indian chief that Brooks plays makes all this clear when, finding their skin even darker than his own, sees these ill-treated outcasts as kindred spirits and affably lets them pass. Who knows what contributions this nice young family might make, if only the whites, like this sympathetic Jewish Indian, gives them a chance? Indians, blacks, Christians, Jews — history overflows with races and cultures targeted for persecution, and so it goes here as well. The citizens of Rock Ridge all but roll out the red carpet when they think their new lawman is white, then react in knee-jerk outrage upon meeting him firsthand, and they're as wrong about Bart as the Nazis were about the Jews, the pioneers about the Indians, and all the rest. Bart alone is quick-witted and capable enough to save these people, but bigots always resist what they don't understand, even when understanding is clearly in their own best interest.

Brooks underscores these bigots' idiocy repeatedly in the film. When the townspeople all turn their firearms on Bart early on, he easily outwits them with a preposterous but hysterically funny bit right out of Bugs Bunny in which, pointing his gun at his own head, he imitates first a ferocious killer, then the sort of frantic, 'fraidy-cat Negro stereotype so often associated (perhaps unfairly) with the '30s film roles of actor Stepin Fetchit. Much as *The Producers* equates Nazism with madness (primarily through Hitler-loving loony Franz Liebkind), Brooks here links racism with gullibility, narrow-mindedness, and naiveté. People like this practice racism because, as Bart tells us flat-out, they're just plain "dumb"—because, as Wilder's burnt-out gunslinger Jim puts it only half-jokingly, they're "morons." Perhaps one of his best running gags, in fact, giving nearly everyone in town a common last name (among its various Johnsons: Olson, Howard, Samuel, and Van), is Brooks' way of saying Rock Ridge is a community so inbred and so insular it wouldn't recognize broad-minded, tolerant, forward thinking if it rode into town on a horse—which is, of course, exactly what it does. Bart is the future, but the locals, still contentedly stuck back in the eighteenth century while Bart is already the living embodiment of the twentieth, just can't see it.

We see it, though, and the result is both funny and sad: the potential quicksand deaths of black railroad workers Bart and Charlie (Charles McGregor) being judged acceptable losses by their white employers; the whites' abandonment of pre-teen Bart's Indian-besieged parents, who, outcasts even in a crisis, are left to fend for themselves (the film's big group building project finale makes it clear that survival depends on putting racial issues aside and working as one); the little old lady's racist response to Bart's polite greeting. As in *The Producers*, in which Bialystock's desperate-for-cash womanizing and Bloom's blanket-toting hysterics make us snicker yet also feel sorry for both men, and in *The Twelve Chairs*, whose greedy Vorobyaninov and con artist Bender amuse even as they wander about homeless and poor, we chuckle, yes, but we're

thinking how pitiable poor Bart's predicament is too. We feel the same way when a worn-out Chinese laborer faints from heat exhaustion, for which he's callously docked a day's wages, and when the Rock Ridgers finally agree to accept black and Chinese residents in exchange for saving their town—but not, at first, the Irish. We laugh, but guiltily, like Mary Richards at Chuckles the Clown's funeral.

Brooks' comedic genius never soars higher than when he's being sly and sarcastic, taking jabs at us for our own defects, and *Blazing Saddles* is one of his best satires ever. His anti-racism slams are the most obvious, but bigotry isn't his only target, as we see in the weirdo state capital scenes with addlebrained Gov. Lepetomane, the largest of Brooks' five roles in the film. Akin to many a present-day politician, Lepetomane seems oblivious to much of the corruption in his own administration, giving up too much hands-on control to Harvey Korman's money-hungry attorney general Hedley Lamarr; works harder trying to secure a name for himself on building projects and first-ever legislation than curing social ills; betrays the public trust to further his own selfish ends; demands lapdog enthusiasm from underlings even when they disagree; and besmirches the integrity of his office by indulging his carnal appetites. Whether cheating Native Americans with toys instead of money, demanding sycophantic "harumph"s from his staff of yes-men, turning mental hospitals into self-named casinos, or chasing his buxom secretary, Lepetomane is a public disgrace—and yet, somehow, after all the Watergates and Iran-Contras and Monica Lewinskys, after all the ketchups-as-vegetables and price-hiked hammers and *Murphy Brown* unwed mothers, after all the ex-rock-and-rollers, ex-athletes, ex-astronauts, and ex-actors we've put in office, he's not the tiniest bit farfetched. In bits and pieces, we've elected men like Lepotomane into power by the hundreds over the years, in local, state, and national positions left and right.

For all its brilliance as satire, however, perhaps *Blazing Saddles* surprises one most for its achievement as parody, as lampoon. For all the too-casual tendency to label Brooks' films "spoof movies," the designation really does fit this time, right down to the picture's nonsense title and overblown theme lyrics. With *Blazing Saddles*, Brooks isn't just working within the genre but deflating it, exposing its square-dance-and-prayer-meeting small-town innocence for the hokey Hollywood whitewash it is. The Bible-toting preacher, the smiling shop clerk, the doting schoolmarm, the sweet little old grandmother type—in the *real* West, however saintly they may have seemed in their string ties, sunbonnets, and Sunday-go-to-meetin' clothes, it's doubtful many of these people showed nearly as much Christian spirit toward blacks as whites, and probably most had as little guilt about enjoying rights denied their black neighbors as laying claim to land already owned by the Native Americans they'd driven off. Brooks' affection for the genre he's lambasting is still here—he'd be thrilled to have a *Stagecoach* or *My Darling Clementine* on his resume—but for once he clearly steps outside of the celluloid universe he's honoring, sees it for what it is, and lets loose on it with both barrels. *Blazing Saddles* is the sort of Western in which a beloved old chestnut like "We'll head 'em off at the pass!" simply must go in—it's too eagerly awaited not to—but the character who utters it takes a bullet in the foot for his lack of originality.

When, furthermore, Brooks' bad guys, cleverly diverted by Bart to a hastily assembled duplicate of Rock Ridge, kick over a storefront's plywood facade and realize they've "been had," the act becomes a kind of metaphor for what Brooks himself is up to with the whole film: giving the whole Hollywood movie West a good swift kick and revealing it's all been a kind of cinematic magic show, a con, a fake, a trick. Brooks still treasures the original myth, still enjoys seeing it played out on film, but he has a fine time debunking it, too, just as we're able to still cherish every last half-hour of TV hits like *The Brady Bunch*, *Leave It to Beaver*, and *The Andy Griffith Show* even while making fun of their rosy depictions of resentment-free blended families, near-perfect parenting, and a small-town South with nary a rape, spouse-beating, or child neglect case in sight.

Brooks exposes the fakery behind Hollywood's make-believe West still better in the very next scene, as the Rock Ridge citizenry, emboldened by Bart's leadership, give Hedley Lamarr's hired guns the thrashing of their lives. The resulting free-for-all, a sight gag–loaded extravaganza made twice as much fun by John Morris's supercharged fight music, soon pushes right off Warner Bros.' *Blazing Saddles* lot and through to the next set, just as snippy director Buddy Bizarre (Dom DeLuise) and a cast of tuxedoed, top-hatted gay chorus boys try another run-through of a twinkle-toes dance number called "The French Mistake." If Brooks hasn't convinced us up till now that most of what we "know" about the Wild West is unalloyed Hollywood hokum, the resulting fist- and pie-fight among the Rock Ridgers, Lamarr's hoods, and Bizarre's dancing "Sissy Marys" makes it clear enough, bursting right through the WB commissary—whose diners include, as we've come to expect from the man behind *The Producers*, an actor dressed as Hitler.

This all comes through clearer still when Hedley Lamarr buys a ticket to *Blazing Saddles*' Mann's Chinese Theater premiere, and, the line between fantasy and reality by now impossibly blurred, discovers

Bart riding up on-screen for the big fight-to-the-finish, flees outside, nearly kills Bart, then gets gunned down himself atop the hand- and footprints of long-dead cinema stars. All that remains now is for pals Bart and Jim, back in the theater, to nestle in for the requisite "happy ending": Bart's delivery of a passionate, if Tinseltown artificial, noble hero speech to the tearful Rock Ridgers whose semi-respect he has finally won, then his rejoining Jim, seen even here with a cardboard popcorn tub, and riding with him on horseback just far enough to climb into a sleek studio limousine and get driven right off the picture and into the sunset. By turns madcap, sentimental, and even downright surreal, *Blazing Saddles'* final minutes, from the first thrown punch to the final Warner Bros. logo, delivers just one quirky surprise after another.

Brooks' casting choices, happily, prove every bit as satisfying. For years critics have argued that star Cleavon Little makes a less than ideal Sheriff Bart, speculated what might have become of *Blazing Saddles* had Brooks not gotten his hands on *Tex X* until a few years later, after co-writer Richard Pryor had won for himself just a little more Hollywood clout. Having fallen in love with his writing partner's raw, edgy take on the character during scripting, Brooks tried to convince studio execs Pryor should play Bart, but Brooks too lacked enough influence just then to pull the notion off. Given the huge success the then thirty-four-year-old comic would enjoy partnered with Gene Wilder starting with 1976's *Silver Streak*, the comic oater known early on as *Black Bart* surely would have pushed both Pryor and Wilder-Pryor to the top a few years early. As it was, Brooks might have won a more famous Bart (Godfrey Cambridge? Flip Wilson? Bill Cosby? Nipsey Russell?), but surely not one more gifted than studio-approved Cleavon Little, a multi-talented recent Tony winner for the Ossie Davis–linked 1970 Broadway

musical *Purlie* (and just emerging from the ever-revamped 1972–74 ABC hospital sitcom *Temperatures Rising*) who makes Gucci-snazzy ladies' man Bart smooth, smart, and savvy without miring the film so deeply in polyester-era trendiness it ends up looking like some mood ring/pet rock relic of the '70s.

Indeed, Cleavon Little exudes such winning, good-natured sweetness it's hard to envision Pryor's more acid-tongued, combative early '70s persona playing much better. Anyone who recalls Little's happy-to-help, delightfully peppy country preacher in Earl Hamner, Jr.'s 1971 telefilm *The Homecoming: A Christmas Story* (forerunner to Hamner's TV series *The Waltons*) knows how wrong Pryor would have been in the part, and as exciting as a pre–*Silver Streak* Pryor and Wilder team-up sounds, the '74 Pryor might have given Bart too much attitude; his "groovy"s and "baby"s might have rung truer than from nice guy Little (whose Bart, like Jim, disappoints us a bit when we see him smoking a marijuana joint; it lessens our opinion of him somehow — not to mention dates the film), but one can't see him delivering Bart's paternal, babysitter-like offer to entertain jail cell "guest" Jim with nearly this much warmth and magic. What a shame Brooks never called the actor back into service before Little's death in 1992; he was far too gifted with a light comic line to use just once.

Ironically, Brooks' *The Producers* pal Gene Wilder, called in as a last minute replacement to portray Bart's prisoner-turned-partner Jim, plays his role with even more laid-back lightness than Cleavon Little. Far funnier playing frenzied and frantic than listless and lazy, Wilder might not be the most obvious choice to play a battle-weary, worn-out drunk, and even billed second in the closing credits he doesn't have all that much to do, yet he works off Little just beautifully.

Their low-key styles, even if sometimes making Brooks' mostly villainous secondary players more colorful than his stars, complement each other nicely, a bit like the way TV's *Barney Miller* "cops" Hal Linden, Max Gail, Steve Landesburg, and gang tend to be less explosive personality-wise than many of their guest "felons" with their claustrophobic screaming fits, anti-government tirades, and hysterical were-wolf ravings. Besides, we've seen from *The Producers* and *Young Frankenstein* what Wilder unfettered can do, so we're just happy to have him aboard, whatever the occasion.

Harvey Korman, a bright spot in just about any project he appears in, gets put to far better use as devious political assistant Hedley Lamarr. At the time already seven years into his ten-year stay at TV's *The Carol Burnett Show*, where he'd played everything from Nazis to rubes with equal aplomb, Korman needs little more than a Snidely Whiplash mustache and Dick Dastardly sneer before he's off and running, piling on comedy and class in scene after scene. Oddly likable despite Lamarr's nastiness, Korman makes the perfect Brooks villain, somehow both menacing and cartoony at the same time, like Keenan Wynn or Cesar Romero over at Disney, or even the superb David Tomlinson, who made such a fine comic cad in that studio's *The Love Bug* in 1969. Indeed, Korman is so

Having tricked Hedley Lamarr's frontier roughnecks into attacking a hastily built replica instead of the real Rock Ridge, retired gunslinger Jim, a.k.a. the Waco Kid (Gene Wilder), and his quick-thinking buddy Sheriff Bart (Cleavon Little) lead the townsfolk in a Wild West street brawl, soon exposing the entire movie for the paint-and-plywood Hollywood mockup it really is in the Mel Brooks' *Blazing Saddles*, a three-time Oscar nominee and still one of the funniest movies ever made.

good we're not surprised Brooks kept going back to him (Brooks often joked that Korman was so tall he got more for his money), nor that, at least until *Dracula: Dead and Loving It*, the roles carried so many traces of Hedley Lamarr, especially the one in *High Anxiety*.

Giving Korman first-rate backup as Lamarr's onscreen assistant Taggart is co-star Slim Pickens, by then already a veteran of about fifty films, most of them Westerns, and gifted with one of the most memorable faces and voices in all of film. An actor who kept working right up to the very end of his life, Pickens still had another two dozen or so more films left in him even by the time of *Blazing Saddles* (a few even comic Westerns, like 1975's *The Apple Dumpling Gang* and 1976's *Hawmps!*), and the onetime rodeo favorite's delightful Deputy Dog exterior and *Lum 'n' Abner* drawl were already so indelibly linked with the Hollywood West one doubts even the most sheltered movie-goers in 1974 failed to recognize him right off—and smile, too. A genuine original, Pickens is just the sort of stand-out-from-the-crowd actor every Brooks comedy needs.

The same goes for opera trained actress-songstress Madeline Kahn, actually, whose role as Bart's antagonist turned admirer Lili Von Shtupp, she of the Marlene Dietrich song stylings, Mae West innuendo, and Elmer Fudd "wanguage pwobwems," provides some of the movie's most twisted humor. Her rather shocking song "I'm Tired," its "Falling in Love Again"-skewering lyrics and music both by Brooks himself, isn't very ladylike to say the least, but it certainly is funny (especially since Brooks uses it as yet another opportunity to poke fun at the Nazis, with Lili given a chorus line of armed and helmeted German soldiers as backup). Kahn, already an Academy Award nominee for 1973's *Paper Moon*, ended up with her second nomina-

tion for her dazzling work here, side-splittingly daffy material from an actress whose movie career (ending far too soon in 1999) was replete with such quirk-filled kooks, from her bossy, stressed-out fiancée in 1972's *What's Up Doc?* to her new-name-every-few-minutes femme fatale in 1978's *The Cheap Detective*. Search high, search low, the movies will never find another like Madeline Kahn.

Funny too, if markedly less famous, is actor Burton Gilliam, later re-teamed with *Blazing Saddles* co-writer Andrew Bergman in *Fletch* and *Honeymoon in Vegas* and, as Taggart's loyal but empty-headed sidekick Lyle, ideally suited to the kind of slapsticky, Saturday morning funnies–type comedy Brooks provides here. With his wide Cheshire Cat grin, Eb from *Green Acres* lankiness, and *Hee Haw* delivery, Gilliam takes a role easily little more than First Flunky or Roughneck Number One and gets laughs every time, just with an over-broad Jethro Bodine smile or funny French Stewart/Gilbert Gottfried squint. Rubber-jowled, wiry, and tirelessly expressive, Gilliam plays Lyle like some countrified Jim Carrey, like Jerry Lewis at the Grand Ol' Opry.

Another nice surprise comes from ex-football pro Alex Karras, still nearly a decade away from 1982's *Victor/Victoria* and his four-year *Webster* sitcom run, but already quite effective at comedy even this early in his career. As simpleminded strongman Mongo, a sort of frontier Big Moose from the old *Archie* comics, Karras gets the gag seen in just about every *Blazing Saddles* TV ad ever aired, in which Mongo, just as Brooks once saw a temper-gripped Sid Caesar do to an unruly animal that had thrown Caesar's wife, decks a horse in one hard punch. He also does a fine job gradually turning Mongo from Bluto to Pluto, from what at first seems some soulless, all-muscle killing machine like Gort the robot in 1951's *The Day the*

Earth Stood Still to a cuddly, Bart-devoted teddy bear akin to Karras's 1974 *M*A*S*H* soldier so over-grateful for Hawkeye's medical help he nearly drives the poor man crazy. One minute we're dreading the arrival of this monster, the next, thanks to Karras's endearing acting, we're half ready to adopt the big lug.

Even the film's small parts are pretty memorable, actually. The always welcome Dom DeLuise has less to do here than in *The Twelve Chairs*, but his out-of-nowhere appearance as Buddy Bizarre for the big finale is one of Brooks' best surprises — better than his *Robin Hood: Men in Tights* mini-role because it wastes less time and moves much faster. We're happy he's back, just as we are about his return in several other Brooks and Brooksfilms movies over the years.

DeLuise's wife Carol Arthur (*Silent Movie, Robin Hood: Men in Tights, Dracula: Dead and Loving It,* Brooksfilms' *Fatso*), who plays schoolmarm Harriett Johnson, is remarkably funny too, skillfully shifting from soft-spoken and shy to ribald and blasting in an instant. So too are the film's other Johnsons: familiar movie and TV actor David Huddleston as Olson Johnson (as in the comedy team Ole Olsen — with an *e* — and Chic Johnson); future *Magnum P.I.* TV regular John Hillerman, veteran of countless other film and TV projects (including, later, Brooks' *History of the World — Part I*), as town philosopher Howard Johnson, named for the famous hotel chain; George Furth (whose movies include *Oh, God!* and *The Man With Two Brains*, both directed by Brooks' friend Carl Reiner) as Van Johnson, after the boyish actor of the same name and whose squeaky-voiced style suggests a hybrid of Dick Van Patten, Dennis Day, and Ronnie Schell; Liam Dunn, also of Brooks' *Young Frankenstein* and several Disney films, as Rev. Johnson, who lets loose with bombastic prayers just

when absolute quiet is vital; vocally distinctive character actor Richard Collier, of comedies like *Rally 'Round the Flag, Boys!, Please Don't Eat the Daisies,* and *Mr. Hobbs Takes a Vacation,* as Dr. Samuel Johnson (like the dictionary creator); and Claude Ennis Starrett, Jr. as the Gabby Hayes–like Gabby Johnson, whose mush-mouthed jabber is used just often enough to become one of the picture's funniest running gags. The parts are small, yes, yet every last one of these actors brings to them something wonderfully eccentric and off-kilter.

The rest are good too: Charles McGregor as Bart's railroad buddy Charlie, whose obvious pleasure at finding his friend alive gives the film one of its warmest moments; Robyn Hilton as Miss Stein, Lepetomane's shapely secretary; frequent Western and horror actor Don Megowan as the over-cocky Gum Chewer shot by Lamarr; and Robert Ridgely, later of *High Anxiety, Life Stinks,* and (in essentially the same role) *Robin Hood: Men in Tights,* who is particularly memorable as Boris, a Quasimodo-by-way-of-Karloff hangman who nearly executes Bart. As for Mel Brooks himself, his aviator and voice-overs as a German dancer and cranky film-goer provide funny cameos but have little impact time, and his Yiddish-speaking Indian Chief, while making a bigger impression, isn't that large a part either. His bubble-brained Gov. Lepetomane, though, very much a precursor to *Spaceballs'* more consciously unscrupulous Pres. Skroob, squeezes endless terrific politician-as-dunderhead shtick into his few scenes. He's crude, lewd, and all that, yes, but he keeps the picture lively, too, letting fly with enough crazy-man energy to keep *Blazing Saddles'* potentially dull, static office material bouncing around like mad.

The music bounces as well. John Morris wrote the rousing title melody, Brooks the witty lyrics, and it's one of their perkiest tunes ever (and flexible; note the lazy, Otis Campbell stagger Morris creates for a drunken Gabby Johnson late in the film), especially in the closing credits, in which Morris, after wrapping a slower, richer version gripped by sentiment and grandeur, springs into it full force at the words "THE END" and takes off like lightning. *All* comedy credits should move this fast. Better yet, the song, like the movie's so-powerful-it's-ludicrous title, helps parody the genre: all those hyper-dramatic whip cracks, the wildly hyperbolic depictions of Bart's mild exploits, and the rabid ferocity with which singer Frankie Laine attacks the lyrics, seemingly unaware they are all just part of Brooks' big tease of the kind of overwrought title tune Laine had sung without a trace of irony in Westerns like *Gunfight at the O.K. Corral* and *3:10 to Yuma* for years.

"The Ballad of Rock Ridge" is a delight too, if a little naughty, brilliantly shifting from church-hymn piety to enemy-attack frenzy at the drop of a ten-gallon hat, as is the witty but bawdy "I'm Tired," Brooks' sly wink at the sort of Frederick Hollander-penned dance hall ditties sung by Marlene Dietrich in films like *The Blue Angel* (1930) and *Destry Rides Again* (1939). "The French Mistake," like *The Producers'* "Springtime for Hitler," seems both perfect for Broadway and a mockery of it at the same time. Brooks wrote the imaginative words and music for all those last three, but Morris's spectacular orchestrations of each is a marvel too.

Even discounting the hot-button issues it skewers and its R-rated sauciness, *Blazing Saddles* isn't perfect: it runs five minutes longer than *The Producers*, which itself starts losing fuel before it runs out of story; even some of its most colorful characters (notably Lili and Mongo) aren't all that crucial to the plot; sometimes one spots an obviously painted backdrop even where Brooks *isn't* commenting on Hollywood trickery; and so on. Still, the movie is incredibly, madly funny, so funny in fact *Films in Review*'s Michael Buckley said with it "the impossible has been achieved." *Blazing Saddles*, he argued, is "the first successful spoof of Westerns"—outclassing, presumably, even celebrated Oscar winners like 1948's *The Paleface* and 1965's *Cat Ballou*.

Voting *Blazing Saddles* sixth on their 1999 list of the past century's top U.S. comedies, the American Film Institute clearly agreed, ranking only *Duck Soup*, *Annie Hall*, *Dr. Strangelove*, *Tootsie*, and *Some Like It Hot* higher — no small feat for a man whose previous film, *The Twelve Chairs*, to this day most people have never even heard of. Like Sheriff Bart, rescued from death even with his neck in a noose, Mel Brooks had beaten unconquerable odds and followed up one of the '70s least seen movies with *the* big comedy of 1974. It was a truly fantastic achievement, a flat-out triumph — and *Young Frankenstein*, an even better film, lay only a few months ahead.

CAST: Cleavon Little (Sheriff Bart); Gene Wilder (Jim, The Waco Kid); Slim Pickens (Taggart); Harvey Korman (Hedley Lamarr); Madeline Kahn (Lili Von Shtupp); Mel Brooks (Gov. William J. Lepetomane/Indian Chief/ Aviator/Voice of German Dancer/Voice of Moviegoer); Burton Gilliam (Lyle); Alex Karras (Mongo); David Huddleston (Olson Johnson); Liam Dunn (Rev. Johnson); John Hillerman (Howard Johnson); George Furth (Van Johnson); Claude Ennis Starrett, Jr. (Gabby Johnson); Carol Arthur (Harriett Johnson); Richard Collier (Dr. Samuel Johnson); Charles McGregor (Charlie); Robyn Hilton (Miss Stein); Don Megowan (Gum Chewer); Dom DeLuise (Buddy Bizarre); Robert Ridgely (Boris the Hangman); Count Basie (Himself).

CREDITS: Director: Mel Brooks; Producer: Michael Hertzberg; Screenplay: Mel Brooks, Norman Steinberg, Andrew Bergman, Richard Pryor, Alan Uger; Story: Andrew Bergman; Director of Photography: Joseph Biroc, A.S.C.; Editors: John C. Howard, Danford Greene;

Production Designer: Peter Wooley; Choreography: Alan Johnson; Title Design: Anthony Goldschmidt; Sound: Gene S. Cantamessa; Rerecording: Arthur Piantadosi, Richard Tyler, Les Fresholtz; Set Decorator: Morey Hoffman; Property Master: Sam Gordon; Casting: Nessa Hyams; Unit Production Manager: William P. Owens; Special Costumes Designer: Nino Novarese; Wardrobe: Tom Dawson; Dialogue Coach; Herbert Winters; Makeup: Al Fama, Terry Miles; Hairdresser: Lola "Skip" McNally; Script Supervisor: Julie Pitranen; 1st Assistant Director: John C. Chulay; Special Effects: Douglas Pettibone; Music Editor: Gene Marks; Assistant Editors: C. Timothy O'Meara, Stephen Potter; 2nd Assistant Director: Leonard Smith, Jr.; Orchestrations: Jonathan Tunick, John Morris; Music Composer/Conductor: John Morris; "Blazing Saddles" Lyrics: Mel Brooks/ Music: John Morris/Singing: Frankie Laine; "The Ballad of Rock Ridge" Lyrics/ Music: Mel Brooks; "I'm Tired" Lyrics/Music: Mel Brooks; "The French Mistake" Lyrics/ Music: Mel Brooks; Filmed in Panavision; Color: Technicolor; A Crossbow Production; Warner Bros., 1974; 93 min.

4

★ ★ ★

"Put ... the Candle ... Back!"

Young Frankenstein

★ ★ ★ ★ ★ ★

(1974)

In early twentieth-century Transylvania, the will of Baron Beaufort Von Frankenstein is taken from the corpse's coffin and delivered by lawyer Herr Falkstein (Richard Haydn) to arrogant Dr. Frederick "Freddy" Frankenstein (Gene Wilder), the deceased's American great-grandson. Falkstein finds Freddy smugly arguing with an irksome student (Danny Goldman) and executing a cruel nerve impulse demonstration on elderly helper Mr. Hilltop (Liam Dunn)—and while Freddy calls himself "Fronk-en-steen" to reject lunatic grandfather Dr. Victor Frankenstein's dead-raising efforts, he soon leaves uptight fiancée Elizabeth (Madeline Kahn) behind to secure the Frankenstein castle.

Arriving, Freddy meets hunchbacked, bug-eyed servant Igor (Marty Feldman), pretty lab assistant Inga (Teri Garr), and horse-unnerving housekeeper Frau Blucher (Cloris Leachman), whom Freddy spies kissing a painting of his grandfather. That night, Freddy wakes after a bad dream about destiny, he and Inga trace haunting violin music to a secret

library where Freddy finds his grandfather's book, *How I Did It*. With Igor, an obsessed Freddy soon steals the seven-foot corpse of a freshly hanged murderer, then sends Igor to steal a suitable brain. Raiding the Brain Depository, however, a lightning-startled Igor drops the brain labeled "Hans Delbruck—Scientist and Saint" and replaces it with one marked "Do Not Use This Brain! ABNORMAL!"

Using storm-harnessed electricity, Freddy, Igor, and Inga revive the brain-implanted body, but the mute, zipper-necked Monster (Peter Boyle) attacks Freddy when Igor terrifies him lighting a match. The creature is sedated, and Freddy falsely reassures one-eyed, one-armed German Inspector Kemp (Kenneth Mars), sent by angry villagers, he has no monster-making plans. After Kemp leaves, however, Frau Blucher, who first lured Freddy to his grandfather's book, frees the brute, calming him with her violin until a blast of lab sparks sends him fleeing. After meeting a little girl (Anne Beesley) and a blind hermit (Gene Hackman), the

Monster is captured with the music, and Freddy brings him to tears, insisting he is loved. An unashamed Frankenstein now, Freddy unveils his creation before a crowd of scientists, but an exploding footlight distresses the Monster during a tux-and-top-hat dance with Freddy, and the audience jeers. Humiliated, the angry Monster shoves Freddy unconscious, assaults the crowd, and is captured by Kemp's men.

Anguished, Freddy begins an affair with Inga, then greets a visiting Elizabeth, whom the Monster kidnaps after assaulting a sadistic, match-wielding jailer (Oscar Beregi) and escaping. In the forest, Elizabeth falls for her captor's physical appeal, but the Monster follows violin music home, where, risking his own brain, Freddy cures his creation's cerebral-spinal fluid imbalance. When Kemp's rioters interfere in mid-transfer, the now articulate Monster stuns all by restoring order, so moving Kemp with his warm praise of Freddy's love and self-sacrifice that he is welcomed into the community. Days later, the newspaper-reading, pajama-clad Monster enjoys married life with seductive, hair-streaked bride Elizabeth, while Inga, singing the lullaby in her honeymoon suite, is delighted the brain transference has left a monstrously passionate Freddy a changed man.

★   ★   ★

Not everyone agrees the 1974 horror spoof *Young Frankenstein* is the very best comedy Mel Brooks ever directed, but those who like to think so will surely get no argument here. Oh, granted, his much-beloved debut effort *The Producers* has its legions of admirers too, all of them fond of pointing to Brooks' Best Screenplay Oscar win as proof his very first film was also his strongest, and his mock Western *Blazing Saddles* maintains such undying popularity many of its biggest backers refuse to

relinquish their preference for it — and that's just fine. Any filmmaker whose fans can't agree which of three "bests" is *the* best is definitely doing something right, and any comedy that shares the same spotlight with the likes of *The Producers* and *Blazing Saddles* must be a fine, fine movie indeed. If only every film comedy since *Young Frankenstein* merited such company, theater ushers would need angry-villager torches and pitchforks to chase us away.

At any rate, if *Young Frankenstein* isn't the finest movie Brooks ever filmed, it doesn't fall short by much, and for once the director's critics — if not downright hostile toward Brooks, usually at least fairly self-conscious about overpraising him — really seemed to sense a new maturity in his work and recognized he had the potential to be a truly magnificent filmmaker. The *New York Times*' Vincent Canby called the film Brooks' "most cohesive" project so far and found his madcap impulses "more disciplined" and "controlled" this time. *Newsweek*'s Paul D. Zimmerman, if missing the "true," "anarchic" Brooks, nevertheless labeled it "the most cinematically assured, coherent, and (relatively speaking) tasteful of Brooks' films," one showing sure signs of "aesthetic growth." Even *The New Yorker*'s Pauline Kael felt Brooks definitely "makes a leap up as a director" here, declaring *Young Frankenstein* "just about the only comedy of recent years that doesn't collapse." Indeed, it's rare to run across any big-time critic, then or now, whose appraisal doesn't applaud Brooks' heightened sense of self-assurance here — what the *Chicago Sun-Times*' Roger Ebert once called signs of "artistic growth," a "more sure-handed control" of some pretty far-out material.

For once, happily, the critics got it just right. Except perhaps the typical charges that Brooks includes a bit more off-color humor than absolutely necessary (less a problem here, given the film's PG rating, than in the R-rated *Blazing Saddles*, and far, *far* less so than in *History of the World — Part I*), about the only serious complaint one can level at this rousing little film is that, at 106 minutes, it might — *might* — run just a tad longer than it needs to. After all, the original 1931 *Frankenstein* itself runs thirty-six minutes shorter, and even its lengthiest sequel, 1939's *Son of Frankenstein*, still falls short by seven.

Since its fantastically funny Gene Wilder–Mel Brooks script plays so beautifully, though, who's counting? The extra time comes not from lazy dialogue delivery or too-slack editing but Brooks' careful, painstakingly meticulous re-creation of the look and feel of classic '30s Universal: those exquisitely old-fashioned screen wipes, those pin-drop quiet camera retreats and advances, all that marvelous Tom Swift monster-making razzle-dazzle. Like other light entertainments giving us perhaps just a wee bit too much of a good thing, *Young Frankenstein* more than makes up for the added time with added quality. Does anyone really mind that, at 140 minutes, *Mary Poppins* runs a bit long? That *Pollyanna*, at 138, edges awfully close to that? Hanging onto a few temptingly trimmable scenes hasn't exactly done Walt Disney's best movies any real harm, and with a script as fanciful, freespirited, and fun as Wilder and Brooks give us here, there's no reason at all Mel Brooks shouldn't be excused a few minutes extra too.

Of course, if *Young Frankenstein*'s 106 minutes felt like two hundred, we'd be singing a different tune, but it so obviously outclasses most other, speedier comedies of the early- to mid–'70s one can excuse it almost anything. Again, one doubts the appropriateness of the "genre parody" label fans are so quick to slap onto anything with Brooks' name (like 1975's *The Maltese Falcon* postscript *The Black Bird*, or 1987's *Dragnet*, it's as much comic sequel as concept spoof), but star Gene Wilder's inspired main idea — that Dr. Victor Frankenstein's pompous grandson inherits his forebear's cliff-top castle, finds his own obsession with raising the dead too great to resist, and fashions a monster of his own — yields such miraculous results it hardly matters. *Young Frankenstein*'s meticulous black-and-white re-creation of classic Old Hollywood charm is naturally just as striking as the blood red Hammer-style brightness of 1995's *Dracula: Dead and Loving It*, but Brooks' reverence-over-ridicule approach works better here because he finds so much else to laugh at; Brooks' vampire film runs sixteen minutes shorter, which should work to its advantage, but it also includes only about half as many good jokes — maybe not even that many.

If Wilder and Brooks avoid belittling the original *Frankenstein*, though, they certainly find laughs just about everywhere else. Besides several phenomenally funny multiple-minute scenes — the titular scientist's mid-bodysnatching encounter with an unsuspecting constable; the heroes' attempts to first befriend, then subdue their out-of-control Monster; the creature's visit with an accident-prone blind man; the "Puttin' on the Ritz" tap dance — scads of others are just quick little throwaways, dependent on perfect timing, artful set-ups, funny accents, clever casting. What's funny about a starched shirt collar? Nothing, unless it pops open a split-second after Gene Wilder's Freddy Frankenstein has declared how crucial it is he look "normal." "The Battle Hymn of the Republic?" Again, nothing, unless warbled by a kittenish Madeline Kahn as the Monster's new wife, all decked out like *The Bride of Frankenstein*'s Elsa Lanchester at bedtime, kicking off slippers like a Las Vegas showgirl. An unlit candelabra? Not a thing, unless Cloris Leachman's grim-faced housekeeper Frau Blucher warns Freddy to stay close to it for safety's sake. Neighing horses? Not funny at all, unless they whinny in horror every time they hear Frau Blucher's name.

Young Frankenstein wisely avoids trying to reproduce the self-aware, anachronism-loaded craziness that fueled *Blazing Saddles*, though a few of the musical references to "Chattanooga Choo Choo," "Just a Gigolo," and such may or may not fit the film's never-specified time frame, and once, during a scene with a little girl (Anne Beesley) who reminds one very much of the girl Boris Karloff's Monster accidentally drowns in the 1931 *Frankenstein*, Peter Boyle's Monster does come pretty close to looking right into the camera lens at the audience. It's also mercifully leery of the sort of terrible puns and wordplay that make Brooks movies like *Spaceballs* (Pizza the Hutt, Yogurt; etc.) and *Robin Hood: Men in Tights* (Achoo, the Sheriff of Rottingham, and such) often feel so juvenile even kids might groan. Otherwise, though,

the humor comes from all over. Many of the funniest lines — Marty Feldman's "Too late"; Wilder's "That goes without saying"; Leachman's "Yes!" — are amusing only because of what precedes them, or how they're said.

Part of the fun too, comes from nostalgia, the main source this time chiefly three Universal horror classics of the '30s: legendary director James Whale's 1931 *Frankenstein*, Whale's own still better 1935 sequel *The Bride of Frankenstein*, and its somewhat lesser Rowland V. Lee–directed 1939 follow-up *Son of Frankenstein*, whose title Wilder and Brooks' own calls to mind. Still, virtually Universal's entire seventeen-year series really gets spoof-saluted here, including Erle C. Kenton's *The Ghost of Frankenstein* (1942), Roy William Neill's *Frankenstein Meets the Wolf Man* (1943), Kenton's multiple-monster sideshows *House of Frankenstein* (1944) and *House of Dracula* (1945), and even Charles Barton's

Actors Teri Garr, Gene Wilder, Marty Feldman, and Peter Boyle enjoy director Mel Brooks' company in an off-camera moment from *Young Frankenstein* (1974), Brooks and co-writer Wilder's comic salute to the Universal horror films of the 1930s and '40s.

slaphappy Bud Abbott–Lou Costello comedy *Abbott and Costello Meet Frankenstein* (1948), filled to the beaker-brim with mad scientists, hunchbacks, grave-robbers, brain surgeons, cliffside castles, secret diaries, hidden passageways, lightning storms, electrical equipment, law officers, town elders, lynch mobs, and the like, all worked one way or another into Wilder and Brooks' ingeniously silly script. It's hard to say to which films actor Arthur Malet's Village Elder refers when he recalls all those chilling memories of what has befallen the town monster-wise "five times before" (not the America-set *Abbott and Costello Meet Frankenstein*, surely, but what of those "serious" ones relocating author Mary Shelley's Monster to neighboring Visceria?), especially since the Whale-Kenton-Neill entries include only two electrically charged monsters (Dr. Frankenstein's flat-topped original and its freaky, hair-streaked Bride) but at least seven different scientists who covertly try to revive or re-revive them. At any rate, we quickly grasp Wilder and Brooks' real point: in '30s and '40s horror films, as in Robin Hood flicks (remember the oft-burned little community in *Robin Hood: Men in Tights*?), life in a tiny European village is just one long trouble-plagued nightmare.

Much of *Young Frankenstein*'s extraordinary success with critics, in fact, derives from the fact that it feels so painstakingly well-researched, as if Wilder and Brooks had dissected every last atmosphere-laden frame of the Universal originals trying to pinpoint precisely what makes them tick. John Morris's gorgeous music, as deadly serious as that in any "real" horror film of the '30s and '40s, hasn't so much as one note that recalls the lighthearted whimsy of Morris compositions for comedies like 1979's *The In-Laws* or 1985's *Clue*, but it's so beautiful how can we object? Cinematographer Gerald

Hirschfeld too, already admired for his work on movies like *Fail-Safe* and *Goodbye, Columbus*, contributes perhaps his single finest accomplishment in film recreating the unique "feel" of James Whale's originals. *Young Frankenstein* looks so much like a 1930s-era horror film, in fact, anyone who's unfamiliar with its cast — that is, doesn't associate James Whale with the first half of twentieth-century cinema and Mel Brooks more with "part two" — might well imagine these productions were shot only a few years apart. Indeed, the effect is so persuasive we're not at all surprised seeing Hirschfeld reused on Gene Wilder's 1977 directorial effort *The World's Greatest Lover* and Brooksfilms' *To Be or Not to Be* (1983) and *My Favorite Year* (1982), all of whose lovingly textured visual styles help as much as the classic costumes and cars in convincing us we really have stepped back in time, respectively, to the 1920s, '40s, and '50s.

Young Frankenstein visually resembles Universal's classics in other ways too. Even with its nifty zip-up neck (replacing the two neck-bolt electrodes of the Whale-Kenton-Neill-Barton films) and effective use of actor Peter Boyle's naturally receding hairline, William Tuttle's makeup is closely modeled on Jack Pierce's timeless designs for Boris Karloff (duplicated later for Lon Chaney, Jr., Bela Lugosi, and Glenn Strange), and even Dorothy Jeakins' platform boots, blazer, and T-shirt look for Boyle's creature is patterned almost to the stitch after the outfit Karloff wears in the '31 original. The creation sequence's sputtering, spark-spewing electrical equipment has even more direct ties, much of it actually devised for Whale's initial production by gizmo wizard Kenneth Strickfaden, the rest added by Strickfaden himself at Brooks' request for the new film.

What's more, even many of *Young Frankenstein*'s specific scenes and performances are creative "lifts" from the old

Whale-Lee-Kenton-Neill-Barton films as well. Just like Colin Clive's fitful, feverish title researcher in Whale's '31 film, star Gene Wilder's stressed-out, single-minded Dr. Frederick "Freddy" Frankenstein often seems on the verge of madness, raving about success and raging against defeat with equal frenzy. Clive-like again, Freddy is headed for the altar too, with a pretty fiancée again named Elizabeth (played, inimitably, by the terrific-as-ever Madeline Kahn), who, as in *Frankenstein* and *Bride of Frankenstein*, respectively, is both confronted in her bedroom by her sweetheart's lumbering creation and then forcefully spirited away by it. Yet Wilder's quirkier, kinkier young scientist (and his arrival in his ancestor's homeland by train) is closely linked to *Son of Frankenstein*'s Baron Wolf von Frankenstein as well, since both are well-bred, upper-crust Frankenstein heirs who steadfastly deny all interest in monster-making even while gradually, secretly, getting drawn in. With his dashing mustache and dapper, high-class enunciation, Wilder even looks and sounds a bit like *Son of Frankenstein* star Basil Rathbone, and in the tension-thick dart game between Freddy and Kenneth Mars' prosthetic-armed, Nazi-like Inspector Kemp (a comic takeoff on Lionel Atwill's Inspector Krogh, whose weird windup-toy limb pivots are pretty funny even if one *hasn't* seen Mars' *Dr. Strangelove*–ian variation), the similarity between the two men's brisk, fast-clipped delivery is as uncanny as it is comical. Even Wilder's trademark frizzy hair calls up memories of *Son of Frankenstein*, though in this case the likeness (somewhat Wilder's natural state, admittedly) is more to kinky-locked child actor Donnie Dunagan's over-cute, sickly sweet moptop Peter von Frankenstein than to screen father Rathbone.

Son of Frankenstein also inspires Marty Feldman's hooded, hunchbacked sidekick Igor (here pronounced "Eyegore," Feldman tells us), or partly anyway, since both that film and *Ghost of Frankenstein* have horror star Bela Lugosi as a broken-necked, black-souled shepherd by that name, and this new Igor even plays a horn-like instrument like his sneakier, seedier prototype as well. Freddy's skinny, crazy-eyed helper still more closely resembles Dwight Frye's nasty, stooped-over Fritz in *Frankenstein*, though, with several of Fritz's actions as assistant to Dr. Henry Frankenstein paralleling Igor's almost exactly. Remember the sequence in which Igor helps Freddy make off with a corpse from the local cemetery? Fritz renders the same services in Whale's film, albeit with less whimsical results. The scene during which Igor, spooked by his own reflection in a lightning storm, accidentally drops a jar-housed "genius" brain he's stealing and replaces it with the brain of a killer? Fritz gets there first, minus a sight gag or two. The moment during which Igor casually lights a match and launches Freddy's monster into a fit of hysteria? Fritz again, though of course Frye's character, far more villainous than Feldman's good-hearted goof, torments Boris Karloff's monster with a torch not because Fritz doesn't know any better but because he's just plain mean.

Igor's role as hero, not heel, in Wilder and Brooks' film marks a major departure from the Universal originals, but when one considers how many scenes involving Wilder, Feldman, Boyle, Mars, Kahn, and others are at least semi-duplicates of material that worked so well for Universal, one realizes yet again how inadequate words like *spoof* and *parody* really are for the sort of films Brooks remains best known for. Wilder and Brooks, like their fans, dearly love all those great old monster movies and admire Mary Shelley's novel too, and while here and there *Young Frankenstein* does poke a little light fun at the genre's expense (the "five times before" line; Freddy's "There's always a device" observation seeking a trigger on a secret door; etc.), most of the time these two aren't even remotely trying to bring Universal's grand old *Frankenstein* saga to its knees.

The Universal series might have made a good target for this sort of debunking too, had Wilder and Brooks much interest in that sort of thing. For years Boris Karloff's Monster ran around terrorizing villagers in almost precisely the sort of sportcoat-and-T-shirt getup Hollywood swingers like Warren Beatty or John Travolta sported for *Tonight Show* appearances and movie premieres, but *Young Frankenstein* doesn't ridicule this at all really, even though the very idea of a walking corpse dressed flashily enough for a Rod Stewart album cover or a photo shoot at *GQ* seems too spoof-worthy to just let slip away. Comic Jerry Seinfeld once happily capitalized on this basic absurdity for one of his standup routines, yet Wilder and Brooks, beyond the terrified Freddy's desperate compliments about the monster's "handsome" looks, casually let it go, their only real laughs about the creature's attire coming from decking him out in tuxedos or pajamas.

Nor does *Young Frankenstein* take much advantage of another Universal horror tradition, either: the way presumably law-abiding shopkeepers and such always seem so eager to turn mob, though a disorder-wary Inspector Kemp's eventual riot stir-up near the end does at least get a few mild laughs out of it. Even TV's *The Simpsons*, whose Springfield lunkheads are forever running off half-cocked to demolish or set fire to something (their response to a near-miss with a comet: "Let's go burn down the observatory so this will never happen again!"), has more fun with the idea of small-town imbecility than Wilder and Brooks, whose rioters say and do lit-

tle all that much sillier than their '30s and '40s counterparts. The elegantly dressed scientific elite present for the monster's disastrous stage debut are, admittedly, rioters of a sort, and the idea to have them come prepared to hurl vegetables is a shrewd one (substitute film critics — or even ticket buyers — for the audience, and filmmakers Wilder and Brooks for their targets, and the satiric comment on the ever shaky audience-artist relationship becomes obvious), but then these upper echelon highbrows aren't exactly the local yokels of Whale, Lee, Kenton, Neill, and Barton, whose less sophisticated thinkers Wilder and Brooks mostly make fun of only by having one accidentally walk into a tree.

Still, since no law says parody absolutely *must* discredit the clichés and follies of the works it emulates, then of course Wilder, Brooks, and the critics can interpret the "spoof" concept as loosely as they like. If more or less repeating plot elements from *Frankenstein*, *Bride of Frankenstein*, and *Son of Frankenstein*, this time chasing more laughs than shivers, amounts to spoofing those films to some minds, who are we to argue? Even so, one wonders: Had writer Willis Cooper scripted *Son of Frankenstein* with as many jokes as *Young Frankenstein*, would that fact alone make it a spoof of the films that preceded it — or just another sequel that just happens to be funny?

Either way, several of the film's most memorable scenes — the shrewd, "What shall we throw in now?" in-joke nod to the drowning of the little girl Maria at the lake in the 1931 film; the Monster's brief sanctuary with the blind hermit in its 1935 sequel — are in fact comic restagings of classic Universal moments, but the material Wilder and Brooks come up with that isn't in Whale, Lee, Kenton, Neill, and Barton is often every bit as good: a medical school classroom lecture, shot with little real movement yet loaded with energy from a temperamental Freddy; a lovesick, Mrs. Danvers–from–*Rebecca* housekeeper who scares horses silly at just the mention of her name; a monster-and-mentor tap dance scene so exuberantly kooky one can hardly believe it was Wilder, not crazy-man Brooks, who kept insisting it go in the film; and a finale with a bespectacled, married monster reading the *Wall Street Journal* in pajamas while his creator honeymoons next door. The film's happy ending in particular, in which Freddy sacrifices a part of himself to stabilize the monster's "rotten" brain and is defended by his creation in a heartfelt speech recalling Leo Bloom's glowing tribute to his pal Max in *The Producers*, is a particularly happy surprise, probably the first movie version of Mary Shelley's novel ever in which neither scientist nor monster ends up dead.

Indeed, *Young Frankenstein* works so well even its seeming inconsistencies don't pose much of a problem. The peculiarly modern look of the medical school classroom scenes early on do disorient us a bit, since some of Freddy's blow-dried, very 1970s-ish students look more like extras from TV's *Welcome Back, Kotter* than early 1800s characters from Shelley, but then the Whale-Lee-Kenton-Neill-Barton saga never did worry about pinpointing either where it all takes place or even when, creating a sort of geographical-historical hodgepodge in which buckboards, trains, and autos exist side by side; where villagers use candles and torches even as scientists employ high-tech contraptions even Tom Edison might envy; where the accents vary from German to British to American; or where half the populace dress like nineteenth-century shepherds and milkmaids, the other half like a business-suited Don Ameche or a dressed-to-kill Claudette Colbert. Like James Barrie's Neverland in *Peter Pan*, whose Indians, pirates, mer-

maids, and such impossibly coexist, the Universal series is at once as '30s "modern" as some Humphrey Bogart gangster flick and as Old World European as *Heidi* or *Hans Brinker* or The Brothers Grimm.

Partly because of this tradition, partly because *Young Frankenstein* is simply too funny to nit-pick over, Wilder and Brooks get away with several such incongruities, including relocating the castle to Transylvania (the setting of the 1931 *Dracula*) instead of the unidentified village of Universal's first two films that, in *Son of Frankenstein*, bears the name of the family itself, or even nearby Visceria, locale of *Ghost of Frankenstein, Frankenstein Meets the Wolf Man, House of Frankenstein,* and *House of Dracula*. We're never fully sure, even, if the Frankenstein who wills Freddy his castle and the "famous cuckoo" who revived the dead are the same man — the distinction between great-grandfather Beaufort and his mad scientist son Victor got lost amid heavy editing — but then we aren't sure of such things in the originals, either. *Son of Frankenstein* suggests Dr. Henry Frankenstein (Victor both here and in Shelley) has but one heir, Wolf, but *Ghost of Frankenstein* introduces Sir Cedric Hardwicke as son Ludwig, so that by the time of *Frankenstein Meets the Wolf Man* we're unsure when "Frankenstein" means Henry or one of his sons.

What's more, by the time of *Ghost of Frankenstein*, Karloff's monster has an all new brain, Igor's, and is thus truly Igor for the rest of the series; has been stricken blind, not that one can tell from the way Bela Lugosi's *Frankenstein Meets the Wolf Man* performance has been so ruthlessly edited, nor as played by Glenn Strange later; no longer speaks, as in Whale and (with Lugosi's voice, Chaney, Jr.'s body) in *Ghost of Frankenstein*; and has been reduced from the scrappy, high-energy fugitive of the first two films to a shuffling, mannequin-stiff automaton — all mostly without explanation. Indeed, *Son of Frankenstein*, momentarily ignoring the Karloff monster's electrical origins, actually incapacitates the creature with a stray lightning bolt — only to perform a total flip-flop in *Ghost of Frankenstein* when yet another bolt hits and makes the brute stronger!

Given all this, we tend to give a "pass" to the occasional mild muddle here — when, for instance, Igor at first responds to Freddy's offer of medical help for his posture difficulties with a quiet, apparently deadly serious "What hump?" only to later completely contradict what we think we know about the character with a "Call it — a hunch!" joke in which he not only acknowledges his own infirmity but even points to it. For that matter, we're not even entirely sure Igor's name really is pronounced "Eye-gore." Since he seems so baffled when Freddy pronounces his own last name "Fronk-en-steen," maybe he's just making it up. If Freddy can get away with it, why not he? In any event, it's clear *Young Frankenstein* is the sort of film in which, because its source material has already set a precedent for it, even most of the inconsistencies don't much matter.

What does matter, though, is that Wilder and Brooks have created the most emotionally textured comedy of Brooks' career in film. Many of its most memorable scenes are also its most character-rich, Freddy's in particular: his bitter classroom indictment of his crazed ancestor's work, and his idiotic attempts to distance himself from his scandalous surname; his mid-nightmare chant about destiny, in which conflicting longings to both deny his heritage and embrace it duke it out in loopy singsong; his childish violence and sulky despondency after his attempt to bring life to the Monster seems to have failed; his quiet, paternal comforting of his persecuted "child" after his "nice boy" creation bursts into tears, and

his eventual forceful proclamation that his name is pronounced the traditional way after all; his worried-father heartache upon realizing the Monster is being hunted by angry mobs; and his selfless donation of part of his own vast intellect to help stabilize the Monster's defective brain. Even Wilder's classic "Puttin' on the Ritz" scene is loaded with character-revealing throwaways: the way Freddy gives his Monster treats as if he were a Pavlov dog or trained seal; presumptuously proclaims his work "genius" to the scientific community; and, like one of those "That's my boy!" fathers whose schoolboy son is doing him proud on Talent Night, mouths the words "I love him" while the creature out–Astaires Astaire. Even Freddy's merging of science and show biz to show off his Monster (complete with a tux-and-top hat dance number and one of Irving Berlin's classiest songs) reveals how much he relishes taking center stage, as do his protests when the Monster, terrified by an exploding stage light and enraged by flung vegetables, makes him look foolish before his experimenter colleagues.

The Monster's scenes likewise teem with emotion. Partly because Wilder and Brooks script it so splendidly, partly because Peter Boyle himself is such an intelligent actor, Boyle models his portrayal not on the robotic, blank-faced killing machines of Lon Chaney, Jr., Bela Lugosi, and Glenn Strange, but on the more expressive, lively depiction of Boris Karloff, whose creature elicits both scares and sympathy. Where the Monster of Kenton, Neill, and Barton (and Lee, to some extent) exhibit only marginally more humanity than the silent, stalking assassins of the *Halloween* and *Friday the 13th* films, Karloff's early performances are more soulful and searching; his creature kills, but as often as not because he's cornered or captured or confused, and he certainly doesn't clomp and stomp about like the groping, barely functional zombie of the series' final days, arms outstretched like some cartoon sleepwalker with splints up his sleeves.

While a few of Karloff's traits find their way into later performances (Chaney, Jr.'s *Ghost of Frankenstein* adaptation shares the original's fondness for music and children, for instance), compared to Karloff's, the Kenton, Neill, and Barton renderings each seem like a mere shadow of the Monster's former self, making us grateful Boyle opts for a more personality-heavy approach. One moment in particular, with Boyle's lullaby-enchanted man-child plucking imaginary daisies or stars or what-have-you from midair, directly alludes to a similar image from '31 in which Karloff's Monster is sedated by his creator and one of those quirky little strokes of acting genius not all the makeup and muscle pads in the world can provide. The scene in which Boyle's creature weeps like some lonely, bully-taunted schoolboy while "father" Freddy consoles him goes back to the '30s too, to *Bride of Frankenstein*, in which a blind hermit's gifts of food, music, and friendship reduces the poor Monster to tears. Again Wilder, Brooks, and Boyle win laughs without sacrificing characterization: as the well-meaning blind man accidentally turns a refreshing round of wine, soup, and cigars into a lap-scalding, thumb-scorching disaster, Boyle's Monster looks by turns baffled, patient, grateful, frustrated, and traumatized — and all without uttering a word.

When Boyle's creature finally does speak (Karloff's version speaks too, a little, in his second portrayal, as does Lon Chaney, Jr.'s, with Bela Lugosi's voice, in *Ghost of Frankenstein*), character-wise the results couldn't be more entertaining. His once erratic thinking corrected by a brain-boost from Freddy, the Monster delivers a speech in Freddy's defense so eloquent and

so heart-rending it rivals Leo Bloom's tender courtroom tribute to his friend Max Bialystock in *The Producers*; no burning windmills, exploding castles, or bursting dams this time — just a grateful "son" pouring out his soul expressing gratitude for a "father's" love. It's truly a wonderful scene.

Ironically, though ostensibly a tale about a monster, Brooks' fourth film remains one of his most human, and considering his claim that exploring characters' emotional neediness is so crucial to good storytelling, it's surprising so few of his later movies contained such moments. Just think how much richer *Spaceballs* might be letting us hear how Lone Starr, whose only family seems to be traveling buddy Barf, really feels about being an orphan with no real home, or how close the motherless Princess Vespa feels to safeguarding robot Dot Matrix. Just imagine how much more satisfying *Robin Hood: Men in Tights* might be if, instead of rebounding from the loss of parents and possessions in seconds, the once-wealthy Robin felt as humiliated by poverty as Max in *The Producers* or Vorobyaninov in *The Twelve Chairs*. Just picture how much better *Dracula: Dead and Loving It* might be if Dracula pursued Mina not just because she'd make an attractive vampire bride but because he truly loves her, or aches with such loneliness he can't bear it another day.

Much of the credit for all this emotion belongs, of course, to the creative collaboration between Mel Brooks and Gene Wilder, whose search for the big laughs is never so all-important that they forget Universal's *Frankenstein*, *Bride of Frankenstein*, and even *Son of Frankenstein* are less about graveyards and science labs than what Shelley's novel had been about in 1818: human yearning, desperation, longing. Shelley's scientist seeks the unknowable, pursues the unattainable, wants to create a brand new life "from scratch," like

God — or, like women, whom Brooks argued men envy their childbearing abilities; and her monster seeks only love, acceptance, friendship. Perhaps more than anything else, in fact, *Frankenstein* may be considered a tale about parental accountability. Like so many reckless modern fathers, Frankenstein brings into the world a new being, then takes no responsibility for it — creates a child, then abandons it to fend for itself.

By contrast, Freddy is a surprisingly good father, in his way, never forsaking his freakish offspring even when he knows full well he might be murdered by him. Where Shelley gives us a rash, incautious overreacher who rejects his own creation, Freddy is more Henry Higgins to the Monster's Eliza, over time thinking of him less as an experiment and more as a person he takes pride in and sees as a positive extension of himself. Amid his horror, Shelley's scientist can feel pity for his gruesome creation, but he can't bring himself to love him, yet Freddy does whatever he can for *his* Monster, tries his best to cure him, dry his tears, boost his self-esteem. At times we're still a little unsure where Freddy's paternal pride ends and his scientific self-satisfaction begins, but whatever his motivation it's clear that, like Higgins, by now too "grown accustomed to her face" to dump Eliza after her big "test" at the Embassy Ball, Freddy loves his Monster no matter how others react. To Freddy, his "son" will always be the best and brightest kid in class.

Young Frankenstein is filled with "bright kids." Acting as both writer and star (he and Brooks were Oscar-nominated for Best Adapted Screenplay), Gene Wilder takes the tale by storm right off, getting crazier and crazier still the more frantic events become. Ranting and raving with such delightful intensity he practically shakes the film from its sprockets, Freddy is Brooks' most dynamic character since Zero Mostel's Max in *The Producers*, and arguably the best movie role of Wilder's career. Invariably superb even in unruffled, quiet roles (as in the Cash Carter telefilms launched with 1999's *Murder in a Small Town* mystery for A&E), Wilder is his most engaging in parts tinged with madness — say, delusional, foul-tempered swordsman Philippe DeSisi in 1970's *Start the Revolution Without Me*, or pixilated confectioner Willy Wonka in 1971's *Willy Wonka and the Chocolate Factory* — and Freddy Frankenstein, a self-trumpeting know-it-all with a good heart but a short fuse, is just such a part. Whether singing, dancing, raging, or romancing, Wilder commands our attention no matter what Freddy is up to, and, demanding of himself twice as much energy as in *The Producers* and *Blazing Saddles* combined, is so Oscar-worthy wonderful one winces thinking how little chance to really shine this great talent had in most of his later films.

Still more discouraging is the fact that, after joining forces to such spectacular effect three times, Wilder and Brooks would part company so early on. With Wilder's increasing passion for directing and Brooks' rising love for acting, their careers by the mid–'70s were at cross-purposes. A Brooks film like *High Anxiety* might have made an equally terrific vehicle for Gene Wilder, and Wilder's 1975 *The Adventures of Sherlock Holmes' Smarter Brother* seems perfect for Brooks' gifts as director and co-writer, but by now both Brooks the movie star and Wilder the director were flying too high to make it happen. Even when Brooks shot *History of the World — Part I* in 1981, reuniting Brooks with returnees like Cloris Leachman, Harvey Korman, Dom DeLuise, Howard Morris, Ron Carey, and Madeline Kahn, Wilder was one of Brooks' few major "regular" actors not to appear. That's too bad too, because terrific as he is, Wilder was

Overcome by paternal affection for the misunderstood creation whose violent rampages have terrorized his village, fatherly scientist Dr. Frederick "Freddy" Frankenstein (Gene Wilder) consoles his lonely, heartsick "child," the Monster (Peter Boyle), in a warm moment from *Young Frankenstein*, director Mel Brooks' fourth film, for which Brooks' and Wilder's screenplay adaptation of the classic Mary Shelley novel received one of the film's two 1974 Oscar nominations.

films going back to 1968. Ironically, since only a few, like 1972's *The Candidate*, had been widely seen, and since only a handful were comedies, not many viewers in 1974 associated Boyle with laughs at all. Like co-star Madeline Kahn, Boyle had appeared in the CBS comedy-variety series *Comedy Tonight* in mid–1970, but it's doubtful many remembered, and even years later, when Boyle starred in ABC's 1986 sitcom *Joe Bash*, it's unlikely many recognized him from *Young Frankenstein*. Indeed, his matter-of-fact, serious-looking features seem so ideal for dramatic parts (the evil mine operator in 1981's *Outland*, for example), and so few of his post–*Young Frankenstein* comedies were big hits, it took until the late–'90s CBS sitcom *Everybody Loves Raymond* before TV viewers, most of whom before that series couldn't identify him by name, associated Boyle with comedy at all.

Happily, looks can be deceiving. Peter Boyle may look more like a university history professor than a comedian, but, like other outwardly businesslike Second City alumni (Edward Asner, Valerie Harper, Alan Alda, etc.), Boyle knows exactly how to go about making us chuckle when the material is well-written. Where Fred Gwynne could freely play *The Munsters'* Herman Munster as a sort of cowardly, tantrum-tossing toddler on TV, Boyle's role is more complicated. Until his final scenes, Boyle must convey all emotions through grunts and pantomime, and must make his Monster a more tragic figure we not only laugh at

more consistently effective directed by Brooks than by anyone else: himself, Sidney Poitier, Arthur Hiller — anybody. They never shared any scenes as actors, no, yet somehow when these two get together, it's magic.

Rivaling Wilder's awesome work is an equally fine performance from actor Peter Boyle, a Second City comedy veteran who had already held sizable roles in a dozen but feel for, and maybe even fear a little. In effect, he must play the Monster almost exactly as Boris Karloff might if asked to dance a buck-and-wing and emit puppy whines after a soup-scalding, and it's a task Boyle handles so nimbly it's real art. Academy Awards have gone out again and again to acting not half this good.

Marty Feldman, who would share screen credits with Peter Boyle again for *In God We Tru$t* (1980) and *Yellowbeard* (1983), Gene Wilder and Madeline Kahn in *The Adventures of Sherlock Holmes' Smarter Brother*, and Kahn in 1984's *Slapstick (of Another Kind)*, delivers his all-time most celebrated movie performance here too. His inimitable English accent sorely missed in *Silent Movie* two years later, Feldman is fully armed this time, and as stork-legged screwball Igor — whose hasty substitution of the brain of dead "scientist and saint" Hans Delbruck (funny how much that name sounds like "Mel Brooks") for that of a dangerous lunatic causes Freddy so much trouble — simply couldn't be better. Like Wilder, Feldman too would soon direct movies of his own (besides *In God We Tru$t*, he helmed 1977's *The Last Remake of Beau Geste*, a nice little comedy he and Brooks together might have done great things with), but *Young Frankenstein* tops all else in a career that, before his far, far too early death at forty-nine, included just ten films.

Before *Young Frankenstein*, most fans knew Feldman only from TV, where U.S. viewers had spotted him in variety series like NBC's *Dean Martin Presents the Golddiggers in London* in 1970 and ABC's *The Marty Feldman Comedy Machine* in 1972, the latter including Barbara Feldon from Brooks' *Get Smart* series and Spike Milligan of 1981's *History of the World — Part I*. Nevertheless, unforgettable to anyone who's ever stumbled across those cue ball eyes and pipe cleaner limbs, Feldman is the

sort of actor from whom we anticipate funny business just seeing his name. He can be tragic too, of course — the pitiable frailty that seeps into the line "What hump?" instantly recalls *The Hunchback of Notre Dame*'s Quasimodo or J. Carrol Naish's sad, misshapen Daniel in *House of Frankenstein* — but Brooks mostly just asks Feldman to be funny, and funny he is. Whether imitating Groucho Marx or Louis Prima, playing Charades with Inga or ferociously flirting with Elizabeth, Feldman makes an utterly glorious Igor, with lines only mildly funny from anyone else suddenly turning hilarious solely because of that musical, rapturous English lilt.

Famous for an equally musical, if decidedly American, lilt is *Blazing Saddles* returnee Madeline Kahn, who, along with the similarly excellent Cloris Leachman, was fast becoming the best all-around movie comedienne Brooks would ever have. Her operatic background and shrill, brassy intensity coming in handy for her thundering renditions of "Ah! Sweet Mystery of Life" and "The Battle Hymn of the Republic," Kahn is one of just a handful of early '70s talents whose voice alone, like Feldman's, is enough to trigger a big smile. Perhaps Kahn can't make quite the same impression playing Freddy's fashion-fussy, seemingly ultra-conservative fiancée Elizabeth as she could as *Blazing Saddles'* Lili Von Shtupp, crooning "I'm Tired" with a cartoon lisp and clad like some frontier Playboy Bunny, but Elizabeth's kooky, Monster-smitten transformation from demure, look-but-don't-touch china doll to flouncing, come-hither seductress is really something to see.

Already nominated for Best Supporting Actress Oscars for both *Paper Moon* in 1973 and *Blazing Saddles* in 1974, Kahn had become quite a success story in the mere two years since her sidesplittingly funny feature debut in *What's Up Doc* (1972, with *Blazing Saddles'* Liam Dunn and co-written by Brooks' *Get Smart* partner Buck Henry), and would keep on stealing scenes in comedy after comedy for years: 1975's *The Adventures of Sherlock Holmes' Smarter Brother* with Wilder, Feldman, and Dom DeLuise; 1978's *The Cheap Detective*, with DeLuise and past and future Brooks associate Sid Caesar, and written by Brooks' old TV ally Neil Simon; 1979's *The Muppet Movie*, with Brooks, DeLuise, Leachman, and *Blazing Saddles* co-scripter Richard Pryor; 1985's *Clue*, with Brooks players Lesley Ann Warren, Christopher Lloyd, and Howard Hesseman; and dozens more. Even when the movies weren't good, Kahn's chirpy, canary-bird perkiness was enough to partially redeem them, and *Young Frankenstein* carries so much comic sparkle it doesn't even need redeeming. Kahn, attacking her barely five-minute role with the same show-stopping gusto she'd give a full-blown starring part, just goes right ahead and lets fly at the role with everything she's got, adding still more great scenes to a comedy filled with great scenes.

Outstanding too in another small role is Cloris Leachman as horse-aggrieving housekeeper Frau Blucher. A Best Supporting Actress Oscar recipient for 1971's *The Last Picture Show*, the eventual four-time Emmy winner had already appeared in over a dozen films by the time of *Young Frankenstein*, and while only two were comedies (one, 1973's *Charley and the Angel*, would be the first of several at Disney), thanks to weekly TV Leachman likely had made more people laugh in the last half-decade than most of her co-stars put together. A near-constant TV presence in shows from *Kraft Television Theatre* to *Bob and Ray* to *Lassie* since the late '40s, over the past four years Leachman had won countless laughs, and two Emmys, as a sitcom semi-regular playing busybody landlady Phyllis Lindstrom on TV's *The Mary Tyler Moore Show*, a role she would con-

tinue on *Phyllis* (1975–77) soon after. Chalk-faced and corseted, her normally flowing blonde mane grayed and drawn back in a tight bun, she wins still more laughs here, in a role so unlike attractive, pant-suited feminist Phyllis that only Leachman's distinctive profile assures us it's the same actress.

She doesn't have many scenes, really, but when Leachman and Wilder get a real rhythm going (Frau Blucher's flirtatious "Ovaltine" overtures in Freddy's bedroom; the violin-punctuated "Yes!" exchange in Freddy's lab as Blucher reveals all) the verbal back-and-forth is so well timed those moments could play on radio and we'd still laugh. If *Young Frankenstein* is indeed a little too long, probably Leachman's role is the least essential (surely Freddy could have stumbled upon his grandfather's lab journal without help), but Leachman's German accent is so agreeable and her makeup so striking we'd hate to lose them. Her pained look of rejection when Freddy rebuffs her love-starved advances, like Feldman's "What hump?" line, suggests unexplored suffering behind all the laughs, but we love cigar-smoking, "boyfriend"-hungry Frau Blucher mostly just for giving the story an extra dash of comic weirdness, just as we love the normally radiant Leachman for her willingness to play down her natural good looks to provide it. Leachman's enthusiasm for playing dress-up (or, here, dress-down) made an impression on Brooks, too, who outfitted this talented lady in still stranger getups in *High Anxiety* and *History of the World — Part I*, and teamed her with another favorite, Harvey Korman, for not one but two roles on TV's *The Nutt House* in 1989.

Oddly, Brooks never did use actress Teri Garr again, despite the fact that both he and fans were delighted with Freddy's chipper young lab assistant Inga's effect on the film. A dancer in several Elvis Presley movies, Garr comes to the film with talents *Young Frankenstein* doesn't even tap, but she's certainly no stranger to comedy either. Garr had already spent the better part of the early '70s in TV comedy-variety shows like *The Ken Berry "Wow" Show*, *The Burns and Schreiber Comedy Hour*, and *The Sonny and Cher Comedy Hour*, and those experiences pay such huge dividends here it's staggering Brooks didn't use her bubbly, buoyant personality later on.

Thankfully, Garr found plenty of noteworthy roles elsewhere, in movie hits both dramatic (1977's *Close Encounters of the Third Kind*; '79's *The Black Stallion*) and comedic (1977's *Oh, God!*, directed by one Brooks ally, Carl Reiner, and written by another, Larry Gelbart; 1982's *Tootsie*, co-written by Gelbart, co-starring Brooks actor George Gaynes, and earning Garr a Best Supporting Actress Oscar nomination; 1983's *Mr. Mom*, with Brooks performers Jeffrey Tambor and Christopher Lloyd). It's *Young Frankenstein*'s Inga, though, for which she'll likely be most remembered, not because it's her best performance necessarily, but because it's so quirky and unconventional. Most of her other films set the action in the here and now and cast Garr as suburban housewives and mothers and businesswomen, but Brooks gives us a refreshing change of pace, a Teri Garr with tavern maid wardrobe and German accent, and as a result one of the few actresses in the world already so naturally adorable she rivals Goldie Hawn or Meg Ryan comes across still more adorable than usual. Though all grown up physically (as Freddy, conveniently forgetting fiancée Elizabeth, can attest even before their wedding night), Inga at times behaves like some sweet little schoolgirl half her age, oblivious to the effect her half-open robe might have on men and for whom "a roll in the hay" means exactly that. Both Garr and Inga are absolute delights.

Brooks returnee Kenneth Mars, playing his second nutty Mel Brooks German in six years, reveals yet again his tremendous vocal expertise, skills employed career-long in projects both live-action (*What's Up, Doc?*, with Madeline Kahn; *The Apple Dumpling Gang Rides Again*, 1979, with Brooks actor Tim Matheson; *Radio Days*, 1987, directed by Brooks' old TV co-writer Woody Allen; and so on) and animated (*The Little Mermaid*, 1989; *Thumbelina*, 1994; etc.). No doubt hoping to head off the inevitable comparisons between Mel Brooks Germans, Mars refuses to simply reproduce *The Producers*' sentimental peabrain Franz Liebkind, wisely creating instead a whole "new" character sounding, if anything, more like some militant, windy variation on his nose-in-the-air musicologist character from *What's Up, Doc?*, given a policeman's uniform, bushy mustache, "wooden" arm, eyepatch, and monocle — the last two items worn over the same eye!

The constabulary costume and prosthetic limb ideas originate, naturally, with Lionel Atwill's one-armed Inspector Krogh, whose mechanical-man mannerisms in the 1939 *Son of Frankenstein* Mars reworks for Inspector Kemp's weird wooden-limb spins and swivels. Ironically, Atwill's dead-serious shoulder, elbow, and wrist twists as Krogh were pretty funny even before Mars came along (the darts-in-the-arm bit appears first in *Son of Frankenstein*, for instance), but the near-impenetrable German accent is of course — or is it "off gourse?" — Mars' contribution. It's hardly a new idea, certainly, not even in Brooks (remember *Blazing Saddles*' Gabby Johnson?), and it would turn up again, sort of, in *Dracula: Dead and Loving It* later on, but it's a joke that works, especially since few actors anywhere can portray daffy Germans as superbly as Kenneth Mars. Only the fact that Kemp lacks as many close-ups as we might like prevents his making quite the impression he might have, and Mars delivers his verbal and visual shtick with so much aplomb, we're surprised his on-screen link with Brooks, not counting the Brooks-free 1989 TV movie *Get Smart Again!*, ended with this fine, funny film. We'd have loved seeing him again.

Surely the film's biggest casting surprise, however, comes from Gene Hackman, already a three-time Oscar nominee and a Best Actor winner for 1971's *The French Connection*, with other nominations and a Best Supporting Actor win for *Unforgiven* in 1992 still to come. While traces of wit had been sneaking into Hackman's work for years (1967's *Bonnie and Clyde*, for example), not until his well-intentioned Blind Man (or Blindman, as the credits spell it), clumsily putting his guest the Monster through such torture, had a movie really shown us just how funny he could be.

That would change somewhat after his work here, with his tongue-in-cheek Lex Luther in 1978's *Superman* (and two sequels) and the occasional odd comedy like *The Bird Cage* (1996) or *Heartbreakers* (2001), but even having seen those pictures we can hardly believe the same Gene Hackman famous for so many serious, pensive performances in films like 1970's *I Never Sang for My Father* and 1974's *The Conversation* could possibly be this funny. Funny he is, though, in a scene in which not one line, save maybe one quick espresso joke, would ever make us laugh until Hackman gives it his own special spin. Since Peter Boyle's character can't speak and Hackman's can't see, virtually all the humor must come from reactions: the Blind Man's attempts to decipher the Monster's grunts, or the Monster's alarm as his friend's enticing offers of soup, drink, and cigars one by one turn catastrophic. The resulting by-play, punctuated by some inspired slapstick, ranks

among the most slickly paced, funnybone-tickling material Brooks ever shot. Hackman, delivering lines as deceptively lackluster as "I didn't quite get that" and "An incredibly *big* mute" with quick-as-a-whistle timing even Abbott and Costello might envy, simply couldn't be better.

The smaller roles are well-handled too. In his final on-screen role, actor Richard Haydn, a thirty-film veteran most remember as good guy Max Detweiler in 1965's *The Sound of Music*, doesn't have much to do as attorney Herr Falkstein beyond notifying Freddy of his inheritance, but he's more than appropriately lawyerly and European. Even delivering laugh-free exposition, we embrace him more than we would most actors because, even if we can't place him, we sense we've seen and enjoyed Haydn in movies before. On the other hand, skinny, frail-looking Liam Dunn, back from *Blazing Saddles* and soon returning in *Silent Movie*, manages to be hilarious as elderly, pain-wracked test subject Mr. Hilltop without uttering a word, instantly explaining why directors like *Your Show of Shows* choreographer Gower Champion (*The Bank Shot*, 1974), Peter Bogdanovich (*What's Up Doc?*), and Robert Stevenson (*Herbie Rides Again*, 1974; *The Shaggy D.A.*, 1976) so often turned to him for small comic roles. As the snotty Medical Student who goads Freddy into an argument, meanwhile, Danny Goldman, one of Dunn's castmates in Disney's *The World's Greatest Athlete* a year earlier, is funny for the opposite reason: we're amused by the pompous, prissy voice he assumes, one recalling Steve Franken's as Chatsworth Osborne, Jr. on TV's *The Many Loves of Dobie Gillis* and Anthony Teague's as Bud Frump in 1967's *How to Succeed in Business Without Really Trying*. Oscar Beregi has a vivid accent too, albeit used for dramatic purposes, as the Sadistic Jailer who causes his own near-death cruelly taunting the Monster; Anne

Beesley is properly cute and likable as the Little Girl the Monster briefly plays with; and of course one is always delighted seeing familiar sitcom actor Arthur Malet, visible here as the Village Elder who recalls previous Frankenstein atrocities and whose delightfully eccentric voice has added an extra comic twinkle to movies as varied as 1964's *Mary Poppins* and 1966's *Munster, Go Home*, and was distinctive enough to stand on its own in animated projects like *The Secret of NIMH* in 1982 and Disney's *The Black Cauldron* in 1985.

As for Brooks' directing, perhaps one might question a choice or two here and there — say, his keeping the camera so far back during the Monster's first panic scene (Feldman's Igor triggers the creature's tantrum casually lighting a match for his cigarette, but we're so busy watching the Monster we barely notice what Igor is up to) — but overall this is fine, fine work. Besides all those slow, steady camera creeps, all that careful, conscientious attention to classic horror detail, we're struck even by the way Brooks introduces Wilder's Freddy; in *Robin Hood: Men in Tights*, not even Cary Elwes' debut moment as Robin gets much notice, but, putting Wilder front-and-center with a dramatic head shot right off, Brooks rivets our attention on character virtually right away.

Is *Young Frankenstein* Mel Brooks' greatest movie? *The Producers* and *Blazing Saddles* fanatics might not think so, but even if it isn't, it certainly proves the behind-camera Brooks had real talent — that, working with his creative batteries fully charged, he could be as fine a director as any Hollywood comedy could ask for. That he never quite duplicated its artistic or commercial success for the rest of the decade, or even the next several, proves nothing; with a cast and script this good, and Brooks on the creative roll of a lifetime, *Young Frankenstein* was tough to beat.

CAST: Gene Wilder (Dr. Frederick "Freddy" Frankenstein); Peter Boyle (The Monster); Marty Feldman (Igor); Madeline Kahn (Elizabeth); Cloris Leachman (Frau Blucher); Teri Garr (Inga); Kenneth Mars (Inspector Kemp); Richard Haydn (Herr Falkstein); Liam Dunn (Mr. Hilltop); Danny Goldman (Medical Student); Oscar Beregi (Sadistic Jailer); Arthur Malet (Village Elder); Richard Roth (Inspector Kemp's Aide); Gravediggers (Monte Landis, Rusty Blitz); Anne Beesley (Little Girl); Gene Hackman (Blindman); John Madison; John Dennis; Rick Norman; Rolfe Sedan; Terrence Pushman; Randolph Dobbs; Norbert Schiller; Patrick O'Hara; Michael Fox; Lidia Kristen.

CREDITS: Director: Mel Brooks; Producer: Michael Gruskoff; Screenplay/Story: Gene Wilder, Mel Brooks, based on characters from the novel *Frankenstein, or The Modern Prometheus* by Mary Wollstonecraft Shelley; Editor: John C. Howard; Director of Photography: Gerald Hirschfeld, A.S.C.; Unit Production Manager: Frank Baur; Assistant Director: Marvin Miller; 2nd Assistant Director: Barry Stern; Music Composer/Conductor: John Morris; Orchestrations: Jonathan Tunick, John Morris; Production Designer: Dale Hennesy; Set Decorator: Bob deVestel; Title/Graphic Designer: Anthony Goldschmidt; Casting: Mike Fenton, Jane Feinberg; Makeup Creator: William Tuttle; Men's Wardrobe: Dick James, Ed Wynigear; Women's Wardrobe: Phyllis Garr, Carolyn Ewart; Makeup Artist: Ed Butterworth; Costumes: Dorothy Jeakins; Hairdresser: Mary Keats; Gaffer: James Plannette; Property Master: Jack Marino; Assistant Property Master: Charles Sertin; Special Effects: Henry Millar, Jr., Hal Millar; Construction Coordinator: Hank Wynards; Camera Operator: Tim Vanik; Script Supervisor: Ray Quiroz; Production Mixer: Gene Cantamessa; Production Rerecording: Richard Portman; Sound Editor: Don Hall; Assistant Editors: Stanford C. Allen, William D. Gordean; *Frankenstein* Laboratory Equipment Provided by Kenneth Strickfaden; Film Equipment: Panavision; Prints: Deluxe; Produced by Gruskoff/Venture Films, Crossbow Productions, Inc., and Jouer Limited; 1974, Twentieth Century–Fox; 106 minutes.

5

* * *

"DON'T YOU KNOW THAT SLAPSTICK IS *DEAD*?!"

Silent Movie

* * * * * *

(1976)

After dropping off a pregnant woman (Carol Arthur) at a Hollywood maternity hospital, convertible-cruising Mel Funn (Mel Brooks) and pals Marty Eggs (Marty Feldman) and Dom Bell (Dom DeLuise) pass the gate guard (Chuck McCann) at Big Picture Studios, where recovering alcoholic Funn hopes to restart his directing career. Learning from the Studio Chief (Sid Caesar) Big Picture needs a hit movie soon, before heartless conglomerate Engulf & Devour takes over, Funn pitches his idea: a modern-day silent movie! The Studio Chief finds the idea absurd until Funn promises to get big-name stars for the film, and suddenly the project is an immediate "go."

Passing a tailor shop patron (Harry Ritz) and acupuncture patient (Arnold Soboloff), the three men stop at Burt Reynolds' estate, and, denied entry, invade the star's shower. Tossed out, they try in disguise, badgering him until he signs up, as newspapers tossed at an elderly vendor

(Liam Dunn) attest, just as they will through most of Funn's star-signings. They next sign James Caan in his wobbly star trailer, and in New York City Engulf (Harold Gould) fumes over Funn's scheme. Back in Hollywood, after incidents involving a blind man (Charlie Callas), his dog, spicy food, and a motorcycle officer, Funn, Eggs, Bell, and the Studio Chief learn Engulf & Devour is on its way, and Funn promises the Studio Chief he will secure even more big stars.

Donning clumsy suits of armor, they sneak into a studio commissary where, recognized by an eager Liza Minnelli, Funn signs her up, and at Engulf & Devour's West Coast office Devour (Ron Carey) alerts Engulf to Funn's plan to sign Anne Bancroft next. Soon Funn, Eggs, and Bell appear as exotic showmen The New Flamencos at the Rio Bomba Club to meet Bancroft, over whom the Maitre d' (Fritz Feld) makes a huge fuss. Recognizing them, Bancroft has great fun dancing with the trio and agrees to be in their movie, enraging Engulf, who arrives too late.

After the ailing Studio Chief is rushed to a hospital, Funn, Eggs, and Bell run into aged dancers, elevator troubles, and a negligent nurse while visiting him. After they accidentally play havoc with his health, the Studio Chief urges Funn to sign French mime Marcel Marceau by phone. Marceau's one-word answer: "NO!" Spying a race-injured Paul Newman in an electric wheelchair, however, Funn, Eggs, and Bell chase him in wheelchairs until, recognizing them, he asks to be in their film.

Engulf next hires showgirl Vilma Kaplan (Bernadette Peters), and at the Rio Bomba she seduces the lovestruck Funn away from his pals. Days later, Eggs and Bell prove she is a spy, and Funn, heartsick, starts drinking again. Vilma really loves Funn, however, quits Engulf & Devour, and helps find him and sober him up so he can direct his film, which he completes in record time.

At the premiere, the movie turns up stolen, and sexy Vilma stalls the audience while Funn retrieves his film from Engulf & Devour's fireplace. Engulf & Devour pursues Funn, Eggs, and Bell in a wild car chase involving student drivers and bug exterminators, until the villains are trounced by Coca-Cola "grenades," lovebirds Funn and Vilma make wedding plans, and the film, unwound but now unspooling from Eggs' body, wins raves. Funn's silent movie is a spectacular smash hit.

★   ★   ★

Probably not too many fans of *Silent Movie* (1976) count it as their favorite Mel Brooks comedy, and despite the fact that Brooks' fifth directorial outing wasn't a bad little money-maker when it first debuted, the picture runs so rarely on commercial TV it's quite possible all but his most rabid fans have even forgotten all about it. Perhaps because so many Brooks projects shot both before it and after it seem so much — well — noisier by comparison, *Silent Movie* tends to get overlooked, like some quiet, efficient housecat who's caught hundreds of mice over the years entirely unobserved while the family watchdog, all bay and bark and bluster, calls attention to itself nightly yapping at imaginary prowlers and snapping like mad at its own shadow on the floor.

Those who sing *Silent Movie*'s praises, though, do sing them fairly loudly, and surely any comedy that Pulitzer-winning *Chicago Sun-Times* critic Roger Ebert once rated four-stars-out-of-four merits a closer look. *Silent Movie* is, after all, one of the most ambitious comedies of its century, not because the Buster Keatons and Harold Lloyds hadn't already mastered material like this long before, but because the whole idea of shooting a silent film in the mid-'70s must have sounded as out-of-step crazy as if Ford Motors had suddenly brought back running boards, hand-cranks, and rumble seats. Besides, where in 1976 could one still find old-style Hollywood slapstick anymore? In a Disney picture like *Gus*, maybe, and in *The Pink Panther Strikes Again* with Peter Sellers' Inspector Clouseau, but that was pretty much it outside of TV, where the new *Happy Days* spin-off *Laverne & Shirley* was doing all it could to take over where *Here's Lucy* had left off.

True, the plot, involving efforts by alcoholic movie director Mel Funn (Mel Brooks, in his first starring role) to save career and studio by signing big-name stars for an all-new silent film, feels fairly lightweight, and as far as drama goes even Fred MacMurray, Dean Jones, and Kurt Russell faced crises this grave in many a Disney farce of the '60s and '70s. Somehow, though, the film ends up such an agreeable, old-fashioned charmer we can't much care, and given such ace backup from Brooks' fine cast and, when he really cuts loose anyway, John Morris's buoyant score, we just can't help liking it. Seeing Brooks' Mel Funn and pals Marty Eggs (Marty Feldman) and Dom Bell (Dom DeLuise) pratfall their way through *Silent Movie* is like watching a whole slew of Three Stooges shorts back to back, minus the "sointainly"s and "Wise guy, eh?"s but in full color, and provided one enjoys watching three forty-something oddballs in goofy outfits falling out of cars, tumbling down hillsides, and bouncing off elevators, *Silent Movie* can be considerable fun.

Of course, if, on the other hand, one never much cared for Larry, Moe, and Curly to begin with (or Joe, or Curly Joe), Brooks' fifth directorial effort might make for some slow going. *Silent Movie* is consistently pleasant and diverting, but film fans either like silent comedy or they don't, and those who don't will find its enticements only modestly satisfying no matter how many celebrities Brooks might cart in. Silents don't often rent too well on video, and outside of cable and pay TV movie channels, most of us will never stumble upon Charlie Chaplin's *The Circus* or Harold Lloyd's *For Heaven's Sake* on regular TV in a lifetime — and even if we did, we probably wouldn't watch, however fond we may be of *Mr. Bean* reruns, whose semi-articulate title oddball himself gurgles a little dialogue at times, his background happily tittering with audience laughter.

Silent Movie serves up some Rowan Atkinson–level laughs too, occasionally, though few on the actual soundtrack, of course, so when a joke isn't working we're more conscious of it than in, say, *The Producers*, where the comic back-and-forth discharges with such rapidity the material doesn't have time to die. Brooks' laughs

here don't fly quite that fast, though — how can they, with our stopping everything to read off cards all the time? — so when the jokes die here, they take their sweet time doing it. Even at just eighty-six minutes *Silent Movie* feels a half-hour too long, and while it's true even many of Charlie Chaplin's best silents exceeded this length, Brooks' picture, albeit a much lighter, fluffier affair, plays better seen in bits and pieces than in one stretch.

Trimming a few of its longer scenes might have helped (sixty seconds or so of Funn, Eggs, and Bell sliding off commissary chairs and tables in suits of armor is one thing — but nearly two full minutes?), or dropping some gags about Paris fashions, spicy foods, acupuncture, blueberry pies, and seeing-eye dogs that, while funny, sidetrack the plot more than enhance it. A bit more music would have been nice too, since the zippier Morris's melodies are the more we like the film — anything to perk up our interest enough so we don't mind not hearing anything when the actors' lips are moving. As it is, with too many scenes stretched too thin, too many dull moments left soundless beyond the odd drum roll or cymbal crash, *Silent Movie* sometimes gets thwarted by its own gimmick. The initial idea of a slaphappy silent for the '70s naturally grabs our attention, yet once we realize just how silent that silence really is, we start missing the human voice pretty quickly.

Brooks' opening joke, for instance, the one in which chums Funn, Eggs, and Bell interrupt a drive through Hollywood to give an expectant mother a lift, plays so quietly and so still we're already starting to squirm a little. No doubt 1920s filmgoers, still a half-century away from the non-stop barrage of noises and visuals of *Star Wars* and *Raiders of the Lost Ark*, would have loved *Silent Movie* just as it is, but by the time John Morris's rousing title tune finally charges up at us and the opening credits roll, we've never been so glad to hear music in our lives. Certainly we *shouldn't* grow that impatient — something's definitely wrong when we get all fidgety every time our MTV-diminished attention spans get taxed even the least little bit — but then even all those aforementioned *Mr. Bean* sketches come at us only a delightful quarter-hour or so at a time.

Still, even if Brooks credits us with greater powers of concentration than most of us care to put to work anymore, one greatly admires *Silent Movie* just for daring the attempt. For that matter, when one considers the fiscal risks shooting nontalkies in the mid–'70s in the first place, the fact that *Silent Movie* exists to squabble over at all commands our respect right there. Not surprisingly, *Variety* credited Brooks with "a lot of chutzpah" just for having attempted such a film, noting too that *Silent Movie* works "surprising well" considering "verbal comedy," not visual, "has always been [Brooks'] forte as a writer-director-performer." One can imagine the dumbstruck stares Brooks must have gotten before everyone finally realized his plans for a silent comedy truly were for real — especially since not even fellow writer-director-star Charlie Chaplin (still alive in 1976, by the way) had shot a motion picture without sound for the last forty years.

Indeed, Chaplin's *Modern Times* (1936) had come and gone long before most of *Silent Movie*'s potential audience was even born, yet shooting the film when he did was one of the shrewdest moves of Brooks' entire career. After the powerful double whammy of *Blazing Saddles* and *Young Frankenstein*, Brooks was perhaps the only director in the world just then who could have lured fans into theaters for a film called *Silent Movie*, and he was very, very smart to attempt it before the window of opportunity closed. In 1976 Mel Brooks' directorial star had never shone

brighter, and if anyone was going to meld the age of John Travolta and Barbra Streisand and Benji with the era of Francis X. Bushman and Mary Pickford and Rin Tin Tin, the time was now.

Silent Movie is far more than just a creative publicity stunt, however; it's a labor of love, too, Brooks' way of tackling another so-called "spoof movie" in the tradition of *Blazing Saddles* and *Young Frankenstein* while revisiting the celluloid snickers of his boyhood at the same time. Though the silent comedy of Harold Lloyd and Buster Keaton and the Keystone Kops was well on its way out by the time Brooklyn newborn Melvin Kaminsky came along in 1926 (cinema's breakthrough talkie *The Jazz Singer* arrived the next year), the young Mel Brooks had caught just enough of the art form's waning days to make him a fan, and it shows. Brooks' colossal affection for the material he's toying with is unmistakable, and much of what he does here really does feel like a throwback to an earlier era — if not to the early '20s, at least back to his own '50s TV hit *Your Show of Shows*, whose star Sid Caesar plays the desperate-for-a-hit studio chief whom Mel Funn talks into financing his movie to start with. Shot both in color and, at times, off-color for a "with it," up-to-the-minute 1970s PG, *Silent Movie* nevertheless plays like the sort of family-friendly lunacy in which Carl Reiner, Howard Morris, and Imogene Coca could easily feel right at home.

Even with all the updating, of course, *Silent Movie* remains, like so many parodies, less censure than homage, with silents like *The Freshman*, *The Gold Rush*, and *The Kid Brother* losing nothing in the ribbing. What's more, the films Brooks takes comic cues from this time are funny already, unlike the Western and horror films toyed with in his two then most recent works. It's not the works of D.W. Griffith and Fritz Lang he's spoof-saluting, but the rib-tickling likes

Filmmaking buddies Dom Bell (Dom DeLuise), Marty Eggs (Marty Feldman), and Mel Funn (Mel Brooks), whose plans for recovered alcoholic Funn's big directorial comeback hinge upon signing up big-name Hollywood stars for a modern-day silent film, cruise the streets of Tinseltown, in *Silent Movie*, the 1976 comedy directed and co-written by longtime silent film fan Mel Brooks.

of Mack Sennett and Hal Roach — men who *want* us to laugh. Maybe the fact that it's a movie about making movies, with Funn's project-pitching so like Brooks' own, makes it true lampoon, but, as in Robert Altman's *The Player*, that's really more a swipe at Hollywood deal-making than silents themselves. It's easy to punch holes in Charlton Heston or Kirk Douglas or John Wayne, but how does one ridicule the clown-car craziness of a Jerry Lewis, Pee-wee Herman, or Jim Carrey?

Such intellectual issues notwithstanding, the film's very muteness makes it one of the most genuinely inventive comedies of the 1970s. Like his black-and-white classic *Young Frankenstein* and his multipart *History of the World — Part I*, *Silent Movie* is an event picture, one whose very contents provide its own best advertising. To audiences in 1936, silent pictures were already passé, but to filmgoers in 1976, a good many of whom didn't know Fatty Arbuckle from Fred Astaire, *Silent Movie* looked like quite literally something they'd never seen before.

Co-writers Ron Clark, Rudy DeLuca, and Barry Levinson were latecomers too, not just to silent film but Brooks. Though one of his least discussed films, artistically *Silent Movie* may be among Brooks' most pivotal, employing three new writers fated to shape his work for the rest of the decade. Much as *Young Frankenstein* had been Gene Wilder's idea before Brooks helped rethink it, *Silent Movie* was the brainchild of 1970's *Tim Conway Comedy Hour* producer Ron Clark, who recruited Rudy DeLuca and Barry Levinson from *The Carol Burnett Show*, where Conway had been its most popular guest in the Lyle Waggoner days and finally a full-time cast member its last four years. Since all three writers (four, with Brooks) had TV sketch comedy ties, small wonder both *Silent Movie* and, later, *High Anxiety* so often feel like films which Burnett, Conway, Wag-

goner, Vicki Lawrence, and *High Anxiety*'s Harvey Korman might fit right into.

Small wonder too, considering how nicely so many of *Silent Movie*'s individual bits turned out, Brooks would so happily invite Clark, DeLuca, and Levinson back in various capacities in later films. *High Anxiety* would showcase the same writing team the next year, DeLuca and Clark would provide story ideas to *Life Stinks* (which DeLuca co-wrote), and DeLuca and Levinson, who appear in *Silent Movie* as actors — they turn up in the gang of corporate "yes" men who report in to the profit-inquiring higher-up plotting to ruin Funn's studio chief boss — were joined by Clark on-camera for *High Anxiety* and *History of the World — Part I*, with DeLuca going it alone in *Spaceballs*, *Life Stinks*, *Robin Hood: Men in Tights*, and *Dracula: Dead and Loving It*.

They make a fine quartet, Brooks and these three, and influential, too; for better or worse, their softer, fairly content-tame scripts for *Silent Movie* and *High Anxiety* lend Brooks' work a boy-wins-girl, all's-well-that-ends-well amiability still making an impact right up through his final films, though *Young Frankenstein*'s marital bliss finale points the way as well. For some, the Brooks-Clark-DeLuca-Levinson teaming ends for good the sly, cynical Brooks who'd once been such an expectation-smashing original, the one whose "good guys" in *The Producers* and *The Twelve Chairs* were as scheming and devious as the villains in some films. To them, Brooks' work from '76 on lacks the same comic edge; it feels so "family hour" inoffensive that, edited only slightly, a movie like *Dracula: Dead and Loving It* might easily air on The Disney Channel right alongside low-risk fare like *Rent-a-Kid* and *Safety Patrol* and *The Paper Brigade*. Others, mindful of upcoming attacks on political corruption, medical incompetence, and corporate greed in later

Brooks films, and glad to avoid a *History of the World—Part I* "R" rating, don't much mind at all.

Indeed, many fans genuinely admire *Silent Movie* for its relative self-restraint (though they may be less than thrilled with its admittedly funny boardroom table gag), and certainly it contains enough sharp-edged social satire to more than make up for a light touch. In *Silent Movie* Brooks gives us a film company named Big Picture Studios, its front gate sign boasting not of its movies' quality but their sheer multi-million-dollar scope; film projects "green-lit" solely on the basis of star power, not the intelligence of the scripts; quality-blind executives who can't tell good footage from bad, and who, behind doors labeled "Current Studio Chief," occupy offices from which they're sure to be ousted after the next big flop; hostile swallow-up threats from cold, soulless conglomerates (here Engulf & Devour, a '70s in-joke to Paramount's takeover company Gulf & Western); business-suited, interchangeable corporate underlings who move in lockstep, thinking only what the boss thinks and following his lead entirely; and movie stars themselves who can't stop admiring their own good looks and flaunting their wealth with their limousines, mansions, and high-class clothes. As in *The Producers* and *Young Frankenstein*, the public is fickle too, responding to Funn's silent film (of which, tellingly, we see not a single frame, save an MGM-type logo with Sid Caesar's Studio Chief depicted as a braying donkey) with flag-waving, balloon releases, and an arm-in-arm parade that, as it does for vegetable-assaulted tap-dancers Freddy Frankenstein and his Monster, just as easily might have gone the other way. The satire may not be as pointed as in earlier Brooks films—denouncing Nazism and racism hits a lot harder than poking fun at Hollywood moviemaking—but that's okay, isn't it? Can't comedy sometimes just be fun?

Silent Movie makes it pretty clear Brooks believes so. We're not tossed much food for thought here, nothing akin to the "put aside your prejudices" messages that lent so much depth and texture to *Blazing Saddles* and especially *Young Frankenstein*, but *Silent Movie* still includes more than its share of good laughs. None of it's particularly highbrow, no (how can one achieve sophisticated, witty dialogue when practically nobody talks?), but anyone who wouldn't smile just a little seeing Mel Brooks, dancing with wife Anne Bancroft, slamming his tango partner's head into a tabletop in mid-dip, then, with Feldman and DeLuise, battering-ramming the poor woman's head into a wall just doesn't know how to laugh. George Bernard Shaw won't get much serious competition here, admittedly, and neither will Noel Coward, or James M. Barrie, or even Neil Simon for that matter, but a number of *Silent Movie*'s slapstick ideas are so classic-comedy funny they're like full-color, celluloid adaptations of "Golden Age" bits from old radio and TV, bits like Fibber's spill-out closet from *Fibber McGee and Molly* or that great old conveyor belt gag from *I Love Lucy*. A self-obsessed movie star casually soaps himself down in the shower and finds six extra hands assisting with the scrubbing; a steamroller driver, unaware he's seeing two men, not one, protruding from opposite ends of a giant overcoat, faints dead away believing he's squashed a man flat; sleeping marrieds, their motel Murphy bed suddenly given a big yank from a drunk in an adjoining room, crash backwards and right through the wall; Coca-Cola cans, pop-top "pins" pulled, get tossed like grenades and leapt upon by "soldiers" from big business—not exactly intellectual humor, any of it, but we've got *Private Lives* and *Pygmalion* and *The Admirable Crichton* and even *The Sunshine Boys* for that, and for what it is, it sure is funny, funny stuff.

Silent Movie is far more artfully assembled than one might imagine, too. Its opening "HELLO" and closing "GOOD-BYE" messages provide Brooks with a pretty nifty bookend for all that oddball material in between, and for all its popularity among fans of off-color humor, Brooks' *History of the World — Part I* feels like a lost, aimless muddle compared to what we see here. Maybe we can't figure out why Orson Welles' narration keeps coming and going, or why some segments chew up dozens of screen minutes while "The Old Testament" lasts only a handful, but with its single-plot, A-B-C linear storyline, *Silent Movie* doesn't face these problems.

The picture does have problems enough of its own, though, as that aforementioned Liza Minnelli segment makes clear. Overlength doesn't matter much when a scene like this works, but not all the rat-a-tat-tat tympani John Morris can rustle up to accompany Brooks, Feldman, and DeLuise's slipping and sliding stunts can keep us from losing interest eventually. "All right, already," we're muttering to ourselves. "It's hard to sit down in a suit of armor. We get it; we get it!" Besides that, *Silent Movie* doesn't make particularly good use of Liza Minnelli, whose only real contribution besides a few quick falls is to sit at a commissary table, dressed a little like Glenda the Good Witch from mother Judy Garland's *The Wizard of Oz*, waiting patiently while Funn, Eggs, and Bell clatter and crash about like three half-wit Tin Men gone blind. Remarkable: Brooks goes to all that trouble hiring Liza Minnelli, one of the all-time greatest singer-dancers in the history of stage and screen entertainment, and what does he do? He puts her in the one movie of his career in which we couldn't hear her sing even if he asked her to, and not only that, gives others all the dancing scenes, leaving her material any well-known Hollywood actress of the '70s could play just as well,

from Jill Clayburgh to Cicely Tyson to Glenda Jackson to Karen Black.

The film does at least make good use of Mel Brooks himself, though, and in showcasing so prominently the way-out talent once recognized only as an unfamiliar writing credit wrapping each week's *Your Show of Shows*, *Silent Movie* actually marks something of a comic milestone. By now fans had grown used to seeing this once strictly behind-the-scenes funnyman taking small on-camera roles, but in *Silent Movie* writer-director-producer Brooks takes top billing as an actor for the first time. The lobby posters had advertised his first and third films as "Mel Brooks' *The Producers*" and "Mel Brooks' *Blazing Saddles*," and *The Twelve Chairs* and *Young Frankenstein* had heralded the tag line "A Mel Brooks Film," but the promotional materials this time sounded the difference loud and clear: "Mel Brooks in *Silent Movie*." No more off-screen voice-overs as in *The Producers* and *Young Frankenstein*, no more supporting parts as in *The Twelve Chairs* and *Blazing Saddles*; this time Mel Brooks himself was his own undisputed name-above-the-title star.

Of course, Brooks' recuperating alcoholic character Mel Funn is accompanied just about everywhere by his two goofy sidekicks Eggs and Bell, and the posters boast prominent photos of Feldman and DeLuise, so it's not as if Brooks carries the film all by himself. Funn functions more like The Three Stooges' Moe or The Marx Brothers' Groucho than some stand-alone comic like W. C. Fields or Red Skelton or Danny Kaye. Still, *Silent Movie* is clearly more Funn's story than anyone else's — it's Funn whose big idea it is to jump-start his career making a silent film — and considering how little actual screen time Brooks had in *The Twelve Chairs* and *Blazing Saddles*, skeptics could be forgiven for fearing he might be overreaching a bit suddenly taking center stage.

They needn't have worried. With his vividly expressive face and wild-man gesticulations, Brooks was born to play parts like this, and in his silly Thurston Howell III yachting outfit and overstuffed yellow Studebaker, Brooks looks so off-the-beaten-path ridiculous that just seeing him is good for a big laugh. In movies without sound, we crave visual exaggeration, want our heroes overstated and off-kilter and sensationalized. Then again, magnificently visual as Brooks is all decked out like Phil Silvers in *The Boatniks* or Tony Curtis in *Some Like It Hot*, hearing this madman run wild is half the fun, and a silent, semi-restrained Brooks somehow seems like only half a performance. He's got the looks and mannerisms of a classic comic, but somehow that wonderfully raspy Brooklyn voice, part Jack Klugman, part Bud Abbott, part Andy Devine, practically *begs* us to hear it, and while we all know Mel Brooks' inimitable voice so well by heart we actually do seem to hear it in our heads, how much nicer to enjoy the real thing.

Brooks' buddies Marty Feldman and Dom DeLuise both have that classic comic look too — bug-eyed, beanpole-thin Feldman in his form-fitting jumpsuit and pilot's skullcap, DeLuise with his marvelously lovable Spanky McFarland chubbiness and Howdy Doody grin — so much so one suspects, had they been around during the heyday of Abbott and Costello, the Marx Brothers, and Laurel and Hardy, Brooks, Feldman, and DeLuise might have made a hit comedy team in their own right. Like latter-day screen partners Peter Cook and Dudley Moore or Tim Conway and Don Knotts, these three crazies simply came along at the wrong time, a few decades too late.

That's not to say the team-up entirely lives up to its promise, however. Marty Feldman's ear-tickling British and Dom DeLuise's bubbly Brooklynese, so appealing in the actors' earlier Brooks films, possess yet two more great accents we desperately miss the sound of, and while Feldman's fantastic taffy-pull limberness, barely hinted at amid Igor's slinking about in *Young Frankenstein*, this time fires up full-blast, for some reason DeLuise's extraordinary gifts for slapstick aren't particularly well served. Eventually, Brooks fans will grow used to this — by 1989, in *Spaceballs*, DeLuise won't even be visible on-screen, and by *Robin Hood: Men in Tights* he'll be delivering every line of dialogue sitting in a chair — but the funniest of DeLuise's '70s work has him running around half-crazy, spinning wildly and irretrievably out of control. We do enjoy passing glimpses of DeLuise's genius here, of course, just as we do in his brief *Blazing Saddles* bit, but most of the really funny slapstick ends up in Feldman's corner (quite a good place for it, too, as Feldman's whole body seems built from licorice whips and pipe-cleaners), while DeLuise, so fabulously "wired" in *The Twelve Chairs*, mostly just plays Dom Bell all lovable and needy and sweet — Baby Huey in fedora and trenchcoat instead of bonnet and diaper. We really like Dom Bell too, obviously (DeLuise's is the sort of face that boosts any film a notch just being there), but anyone who's seen the actor's combination psychopath-pussycat in Burt Reynolds' *The End* (1978) knows DeLuise is perfectly capable of playing bashful and bombastic at the same time.

Bombast, obviously, is something *Silent Movie* could use a good deal more of — film critic Leonard Maltin was right to call Brooks' efforts "only mild instead of the knockout they should have been" — but the gags would play a lot milder without Mel Brooks, Marty Feldman, and Dom DeLuise. We *expect* laughter from these fellows; they've amused us so often before and since we take one look at them now and somehow the jokes seem grander, the script itself funnier than perhaps it genuinely is. What's more, as costumed by Patricia Norris, and driving that crackerbox yellow car, the *Silent Movie* Brooks, Feldman, and DeLuise are as broadly drawn as some trio of rubbery, visually exaggerated characters mixed-and-matched from the Sunday funnies: Dagwood Bumstead, Jughead Jones, and J. Wellington Wimpy, maybe, or Smokey Stover, Andy Capp, and Sgt. Orville Snorkel. They're living, breathing cartoons, these three, men we anticipate comedy from right off— exactly what a movie like this needs when forcing us to lip-read half the time and stalling its own progress with title cards the other half. Cast this same film with, say, John Agar, Kenneth Tobey, and Clint Walker, the serviceable if lackluster comics equivalents of Maj. Steve Trevor, Bruce Wayne, and Rex Morgan, M.D., and the whole effect falls flat.

That's why the casting for Brooks' subplot about Funn, Eggs, and Bell's search for "some really big stars" for Funn's picture is so important too, and while few of the names signed on give us much hope we'll be rolling in the aisles, we're still pretty well wowed by the high-class crowd Brooks runs with these days. Impressed by Oscar winner Gene Hackman's surprise pop-up as the Blind Man in *Young Frankenstein*? *Silent Movie* gives us not just one Academy Award recipient but two— Liza Minnelli, a two-time nominee and 1972 winner for *Cabaret*, and Brooks' ultimately five-times nominated wife Anne Bancroft, winner for 1962's *The Miracle Worker*— along with nominee James Caan, just four years after 1972's *The Godfather*; future winner Paul Newman, eventually an eight-ceremony nominee and three-time recipient then still riding high after 1973's *The Sting*, and after nearly a quarter-century of hits a full-fledged movie star if ever there was one; universally renowned mime Marcel Marceau, famous if not exactly

beloved in America (whose citizens have long been more inclined to beat mimes senseless than make stars of them); and eventual Emmy winner Burt Reynolds, already well on his way to becoming the '70s' hottest moviehouse draw and barely a year shy of his box-office blockbuster *Smokey and the Bandit*.

Marcel Marceau ends up with one of the *Silent Movie*'s cleverest jokes (rejecting a movie offer from Funn, Eggs, and Bell, it's the world's most famous mime who utters the one word of audible dialogue in the film), and we're not too surprised to find ourselves smiling at least a little at his brief bit of walk-against-the-wind nonsense. The man is a professional comic, after all, which only adds to the movie-within-a-movie irony of it all; Funn snares every big star he goes after *except* the one who's most qualified to do it. We are surprised by how much we're amused by some of Brooks' more "serious" guest stars, though, all of whom do good work even with the odds against them. Liza Minnelli probably finds the least success, though not through any fault of her own, since *Silent Movie* never pushes her all that far; she does end up flat on her back once, felled in a commissary by blundering armored "knights," but it's really stars Brooks, Feldman, and DeLuise who carry most of the comic load. Minnelli has a great smile, just the right bubbly spirit, and in her fairy princess outfit looks as cute as the proverbial button, but she's asked mostly to react, not take charge. James Caan fares slightly better, at least getting to deliver a few clumsy punches to bystanders' heads trying to point and pivot in boxing gloves, but most of the real laughs come from our heroes' attempts to steady their balance in Caan's studio trailer, a broken spring turning even sprinkling too much pepper or eating too many melon balls into a mild earthquake. Like Minnelli, Caan accomplishes what's asked of him just fine, is just as slick and smooth and professional as anyone could ask — it's just nobody's asking much, that's all.

A twinkly-eyed Burt Reynolds, whose winning Johnny Carson era *Tonight Show* guest persona he exaggerates to great effect here, has better luck, tweaking his own "Mr. Smooth" image as rich, narcissistic ladies' man and seemingly having real fun doing it. Gazing adoringly at himself in mirrors, living in a mansion bedecked with signs and photos bearing his name and face, Reynolds proves what a great sport he is right off, sending up himself, and Hollywood, with so much self-mocking glee we're convinced he's having the time of his life. There's wit to both the acting and scripting here, with an instant classic sight gag with Brooks, Feldman, and DeLuise turning up in the actor's shower that's as hilarious for Reynolds' priceless comic reactions as anything else. Similarly sporting, Paul Newman tries a little comic self-deprecation too, showing up hospitalized, still dressed for the track and lounging outdoors by a wrecked race car, but most of Newman's laughs come from Brooks' crazy *Ben-Hur* takeoff, with Newman zipping all over the hospital grounds in his motorized wheelchair, a similarly transported Funn, Eggs, and Bell in hot pursuit. The material lacks the satiric edge evident in Reynolds' bit, but it does inject some renewed energy, certainly a big plus in a movie whose characters can only mouth their words. Still another is Anne Bancroft's segment (definitely overlong, but fun), in part because of her engaging, entirely unexpected cross-eyed Marty Feldman imitation, in part because Brooks gives Bancroft some pretty nifty comic dance material to play around with, and just when the movie's really starting to need it, too. Her role in *The Turning Point* notwithstanding, who'd have guessed Bancroft was this fine a dancer — or, before *To Be or Not to Be*, such a good light comedienne?

Reynolds, Caan, Minnelli, Bancroft, Newman — probably both Funn and Brooks would be better off stacking the deck chasing after big-time comedy stars instead of so many super-serious dramatic types, but honestly, how many actual high-profile jokers were there in 1976 that he could have tossed into the deck? Excepting maybe *The Sunshine Boys'* recent Oscar-winner George Burns, few of the truly great names (Bob Hope, Phil Silvers, Red Skelton, Jerry Lewis, Lucille Ball, Danny Kaye) were still selling tickets, and most of the young up-and-coming (Steve Martin, Robin Williams, John Candy, Richard Pryor, Chevy Chase) were still just up-and-coming.

Then again, since Brooks' comedies so often perform better in TV reruns and home video than in theaters, perhaps what's finally important is how recognizable its stars are today, not then. It's debatable how many seats to its initial unveiling they actually filled (probably not many), but quite a number of *Silent Movie*'s supporting players are actually far better known now than they were in 1976, with singer-dancer-actress Bernadette Peters being perhaps the prime example.

Looking back, Bernadette Peters' involvement in a project as ballyhooed as *Silent Movie* in 1976 seems almost as unexpected as Brooks' hiring of a relatively unknown Gene Wilder for *The Producers*, or Frank Langella for *The Twelve Chairs*. Peters had shot only two films before *Silent Movie*, with only the second, Robert Aldrich's 1974 film *The Longest Yard* (starring Burt Reynolds, who of course works for Brooks here) a full-blown hit, and while she'd made quite a splash both on and Off Broadway, her first Tony win, for 1985's *Song and Dance*, was still nearly a decade off, and wouldn't have made her easy to identify for much of anyone except

New York theatergoers anyway. Even her short-lived but high-profile sitcom *All's Fair* was still a year off, and while Peters was already guesting fairly often on prime-time TV (one attention-getting turn on *The Carol Burnett Show* even helped win its writers, *Silent Movie* scribes Rudy DeLuca and Barry Levinson among them, a 1974 Emmy), she still wasn't yet really a household name.

Peters is astonishingly well-suited to working with Mel Brooks, however, and with her pouty, Shirley Temple–like little-girlishness, Peters seems very nearly as much a cartoonish figure as Brooks, Feldman, and DeLuise. Perhaps because her Vilma Kaplan character is a sultry, sexy nightclub singer, Peters reminds us a great deal of some sort of cross between Jessica Rabbit and Betty Boop (mostly Betty Boop — if, that is, we could hear that unforgettably striking singing voice), with traces of Olive Oyl and a grown-up Nancy or Little Lulu thrown in. Luckily for the film's post-release chances, Carl Reiner's *The Jerk* (1979) and John Huston's *Annie* (1982) would soon boost her stock several notches, all of which means time has proven Brooks either extremely smart or remarkably lucky hiring Peters on her way up. Too bad he doesn't let us hear her sing.

And that's not all, since Brooks found similar success, at least briefly, with some smaller parts as well. Onetime *Get Smart*

Shapely nightclub star Vilma Kaplan (Bernadette Peters), movie director Mel Funn (Mel Brooks), Funn's Studio Chief boss (Sid Caesar), and Funn's pal Dom Bell (Dom DeLuise) nervously await audience reaction to Funn's risky silent film venture in *Silent Movie*, director Brooks' fifth movie and the first reuniting him with real-life former employer Sid Caesar, for whom Brooks had helped write hundreds of comedy sketches in the live–TV days of *Your Show of Shows* and *Caesar's Hour*.

guest Harold Gould (he'd costar in the TV movie *Get Smart Again!* in 1988) had been seen in films since 1965, and he'd given stars Paula Prentiss, Richard Benjamin, and Brooks actor Kenneth Mars great backup in the 1967–68 sitcom *He & She*, but the '70s were clearly the years that made Gould's face and voice, if less so his name, well-known. By 1976 he'd spun his *Mary Tyler Moore Show* guest part as Rhoda Morgenstern's dad Martin into a multi-season gig on *Rhoda* (slews of other regular series roles soon followed), and the '70s' first half-dozen years alone showcased the actor in several commercial and cult favorites: *The Sting* (1973), *The Front Page* (1974), *Love and Death* (1975), *The Strongest Man in the World* (1975), *The Big Bus* (1976), and *Gus* (1976). Gould always makes us feel happier about a movie he's in, no matter whether he's playing a decent man or a crook. He's so good, if a tad underutilized, as Brooks' raging, fuming comic villain Mr. Engulf (particularly in the bit in which, like Lon Chaney, Jr. or Old Yeller post-wolf bite, he's spewing foam and literally going for an employee's jugular) one regrets Brooks didn't reuse him in later films, where his distinctive, high-class speaking voice would have played beautifully. Like Peters', Gould's presence in itself didn't drag in all that many couch potatoes (this is really Brooks, Feldman, and DeLuise's picture), but a familiar face can bring with it plenty of good will, especially when the familiar faces never actually say anything.

Jack Riley, by this time well into his 1972–78 role on TV's *The Bob Newhart Show*, even in his small role here as one of Engulf & Devour's employees, tugs a few instinctual smiles from us as well. He doesn't do much, no, but better someone we find funny elsewhere than someone we've never thought funny at all, and if only for his work opposite Newhart alone it's no surprise to see him turn up again,

both in a serious Brooksfilms effort like *Frances*, and for comic effect in *High Anxiety, History of the World — Part I, To Be or Not to Be*, and *Spaceballs*. He's handed better material in all of these films, which is good to see. Riley's a funny man, and he deserves it.

We smile too at the work of impressionist Charlie Callas, fresh from a huge likability boost from his semi-comic role alongside Robert Wagner and Eddie Albert on TV's *Switch* (1975–78). The voice of the title character in Disney's *Pete's Dragon* the next year, Callas was riding high in 1976, but even saying nothing he's funny in his not exactly P.C. role as a goofy-looking blind man whose dog an unthinking Eggs accidentally switches with an unruly lookalike. Brooks would use Callas again too, unforgettably in *High Anxiety* (ironically, as a mental patient who *thinks* he's a dog), a good deal less well in *Dracula: Dead and Loving It* (as another asylum resident we barely even notice).

Slightly less recognizable at the time, though inches away from their big breaks, were two other actors who, like Gould, Riley, and Callas, would find their greatest successes on TV. The first, Ron Carey, whose six-year stint as Officer Carl Levitt on *Barney Miller* had barely begun in 1976, is billed surprisingly high in *Silent Movie's* opening credits, and while nobody will ever remember his toadying Mr. Devour as vividly as *High Anxiety's* lovable chauffeur Brophy, we can certainly see plenty of talent in his scenes opposite Harold Gould's Mr. Engulf. With his short stature and (sadly, unheard here) highly distinctive big-city accent, Carey reminds one of a 1970s, New Yorker version of *New Faces'* similarly named Robert Clary, and *Silent Movie* puts him to work far more creatively than one might expect when one considers Carey's biggest box office hit before this was in Neil Simon's *The Out-of-Towners* (1970), where he only turns up for about one minute. Brooks definitely knows talent, though, using Carey again not only for *High Anxiety* and *History of the World — Part I* but also as Dom DeLuise's big-screen brother in Brooksfilms' 1980 release *Fatso*, Anne Bancroft's one and only attempt at directing on film.

The second future TV favorite is Howard Hesseman, who even after parts in *Shampoo* (1975), *The Sunshine Boys* (1975), and, with Gould, *The Big Bus* (1976) was still two years from playing disco-hating deejay Dr. Johnny Fever on *WKRP in Cincinnati* and still farther from his short stopovers on *One Day at a Time* and *Head of the Class*. Sadly, except for the paycheck, and the priceless opportunity to watch Brooks at work on a movie set, Hesseman might as well not be in *Silent Movie* at all; like Rudy DeLuca and Barry Levinson, Hesseman is filmed too far back for his now familiar face to really register, and his Engulf & Devour executive is a role so tiny he's little more than an extra. Still, here again we have a name that meant practically nothing to moviegoers in 1976 that now represents a face definitely worth searching for. Too bad Brooks never put Hesseman to work once both he and we really understood what this zany could do.

So things go too with comic Chuck McCann, whose touching 1968 role in *The Heart is a Lonely Hunter* was only the beginning for an actor whose years of movie, variety show, sitcom, kiddy show, and commercial appearances were already making him well-liked if not always easy to attach a name to. Here he's seen only as a movie studio gate guard, an awfully small part for a comic two years away from second billing opposite Tim Conway in the admittedly lesser *They Went That-A-Way and That-A-Way*, but McCann doesn't seem to mind; in 1993 he'd play a still smaller part as a villager in *Robin Hood: Men in Tights*, and he'd win a really solid Brooks role in 1995's *Dracula: Dead and*

Loving It, complete with silly accent and mustache. Good for him; he's a funny man, and anybody who remembers him as Bob Denver's caterer-turned-astronaut pal on Saturday morning TV's *The Far-Out Space Nuts* is sure to be delighted just seeing him.

At best, perhaps, not one of these people was more than moderately celebrated in 1976, but the more cable and pay TV setups pipe these faces into our living rooms in repeats, the more embraceable and marketable *Silent Movie* becomes. The film has plenty of additional such talents on hand besides: *Blazing Saddles'* Carol Arthur, Mrs. Dom DeLuise, as the Pregnant Lady whom Funn, Eggs, and Bell give a lift and who is later seen in *Fatso, Robin Hood: Men in Tights* and *Dracula: Dead and Loving It*; *Blazing Saddles* and *Young Frankenstein* returnee Liam Dunn as the elderly news vendor who keeps getting beaten senseless by newspaper bundles flung from a truck; longtime Barry Levinson script collaborator (and later, for a time, his wife) Valerie Curtin as an Intensive Care Nurse; legendary "Take my wife, please!" comedian Henny Youngman, here doing the old "Waiter, there's a fly in my soup" gag and soon back for *History of the World — Part I*; and, as Man in Tailor Shop, another comedy legend, Harry Ritz, the youngest of the great Ritz Brothers comedy team (the other brothers were Al and Jim), whom fellow Brooklynite Brooks had admired as both kid and comedian, delighting in their work even more than Charlie Chaplin's.

Of course, *Silent Movie*'s muteness hurts these actors' bankability a little too. Ron Carey and Chuck McCann in particular have highly distinctive voices — Carey's bantie-rooster New York feistiness on *Barney Miller*, Chuck McCann's "Hi, guy!" oafishness in the old Right-Guard commercials. The way these actors sound is every bit as valuable a comic asset as their colorful smiles, scowls, and smirks, yet in *Silent Movie* they must win laughs from looks and shtick alone.

This problem strikes hardest with Brooks' old TV boss Sid Caesar, whose greatest talent Brooks once claimed was his gift for silly dialects. Here's a man whose screaming Germans and gibberish-spewing Italians had fans in stitches week after week, yet all his laughs as chief of Big Picture Studios are visual. Even his gruff, Yonkers-bred "normal" voice ranked among the most distinctive on TV, yet his chuckle-grabbing here must come only from sight gags (at which Caesar is, thankfully, brilliant as ever) and title card laugh lines Caesar-fied for us only because, having heard his articulations elsewhere, we can imagine how this great vocal genius might say them.

For that matter, even longtime comedy bit player Fritz Feld, whose trademark champagne cork imitation here depends on an onomatopoeic printout version, and our own recollection from past Feld appearances, is likewise deprived of his distinctively haughty pronunciations. Thank goodness that voice, and that wonderful, wonderful "POP!" has been preserved for us elsewhere.

Silent Movie's momentum is a tad off too, now and then, though the slack comes about only rarely from Brooks' directing, which is less artful than his James Whale–styled helming in *Young Franken-stein* but certainly splashy and cheerful throughout — a sort of creative midpoint between *The Producers* and *High Anxiety* and definitely work Brooks could be proud of. No, when *Silent Movie* isn't working the fault is rarely Brooks' either as performer or director, but rather because eighty-six minutes of silent comedy these days is awfully difficult to sit still for. Even John Morris's excellent score, said to be minute-for-minute one of the most music-packed in comic cinema, still falls uneasily quiet

for far too long. So long as the scenes are fast-paced or really super-silly, *Silent Movie* holds up just dandy, partly because great comedy always does, and partly because Morris's upbeat backup is so finger-snapping entertaining even without any action. His melodies for the motoring scenes, the blind man bit, the Burt Reynolds intro, the wheelchair chase — absolutely perfect, every last one, great listening even with the visuals turned off. When the comedy starts dragging, though, or just isn't visually involving, we really need something else to fill up the emptiness, and the occasional light *thud* or *boink* or *tinkle* just won't do it. In such cases we want John Morris hitting us full blast, with music so good it's memorable all on its own.

Both benefited and bedeviled by its own premise, *Silent Movie* wasn't the best-reviewed American comedy of 1976 — that honor went to Martin Ritt's *The Front*, a film well-served by Brooks allies Woody Allen and Zero Mostel — nor was it the biggest moneymaker, Brooks alumni Gene Wilder and Richard Pryor pulling in the topmost tallies for Arthur Hiller's *Silver Streak*. It ranked right up there, though, on both scales, just as any film should that wins so many laughs on such a gamble. In years to come Mel Brooks would make funnier films than *Silent Movie*, but not many, and never again would he take a directorial risk this chancy that would turn out this well.

CAST: Mel Brooks (Mel Funn); Marty Feldman (Marty Eggs); Dom DeLuise (Dom Bell); Bernadette Peters (Vilma Kaplan); Sid Caesar (Studio Chief); Harold Gould (Engulf); Ron Carey (Devour); Carol Arthur (Pregnant Lady); Liam Dunn (Newsvendor); Fritz Feld (Maitre d'); Chuck McCann (Studio Gate Guard); Valerie Curtin (Intensive Care Nurse); Yvonne Wilder (Studio Chief's Secretary); Arnold Soboloff (Acupuncture Man); Patrick Campbell (Motel Bellhop); Harry Ritz (Man in Tailor Shop); Charlie Callas (Blindman);

Henny Youngman (Fly-in-soup Man); Eddie Ryder (British Officer); Al Hopson (Executive); Rudy DeLuca (Executive); Howard Hesseman (Executive); Lee Delano (Executive); Jack Riley (Executive); Inga Neilsen (Beautiful Blond # 1); Erica Hagen (Beautiful Blond # 2); Robert Lussier (Projectionist); Burt Reynolds, James Caan, Liza Minnelli, Marcel Marceau, Anne Bancroft, Paul Newman (Themselves).

Credits: Director: Mel Brooks; Producer: Michael Hertzberg; Screenplay: Mel Brooks, Ron Clark, Rudy DeLuca, Barry Levinson; Story: Ron Clark; Production Designer: Al Brenner; Editors: John C. Howard, Stanford C. Allen; Director of Photography: Paul Lohmann; Costume Designer: Patricia Norris; Choreography: Rob Iscove; Music: John Morris; Orchestrations: Bill Byers, John Morris; Conductor: Lionel Newman; Casting: Mary Goldberg; Production Consultant: Ron Clark; 2nd Unit Director: Max Kleven; Production Manager: Frank Baur; Assistant Director: Ed Teets; 2nd Assistant Director: Richard Wells; Makeup Artist: William Tuttle; Makeup Man: Charles Schram; Camera Operator: Ed Koons; Assistant Art Director: Steve Berger; Men's Wardrobe: Wally Harton, Jay Caplan; Ladies' Wardrobe: Nancy Martinelli; Hairdresser: Mary Keats; Gaffer: Michael Marlett; Property Master: Tommi Fairbanks; Assistant Property Master: Richard Evans; Key Grip: Tom Prophet, Jr.; Set Decorator: Rick Simpson; Construction Coordinator: Hank Wynands; Script Supervisor: Ray Quiroz; Assistant Editor: David Blangsted; Sound Editor: Don Hall; Rerecording Mixers: Richard Portman, Don MacDougall; Music Recording: Kevin Cleary; Special Effects: Ira Anderson, Jr.; Titles: Anthony Goldschmidt/Pacific Title; Filmed in Panavision; Color: Deluxe; Crossbow Productions, Inc.; Released by 20th Century–Fox, 1976; 87 minutes.

6

* ★ ★

"WHAT A DRAMATIC AIRPORT!"

High Anxiety

★ ★ ★ ★ ★ ★

(1977)

Badly shaken by his flight, noted psychiatrist Dr. Richard H. Thorndyke (Mel Brooks) disembarks in Los Angeles, where he is to take over as head of the Psycho-Neurotic Institute for the Very, *Very* Nervous, a respected cliffside asylum for the mentally ill. After a series of deeply unsettling airport experiences, Thorndyke soon meets his new "driver and sidekick" Brophy (Ron Carey), a photo-snapping chauffeur delighted by Thorndyke's arrival yet strangely suspicious of the sudden death of Thorndyke's predecessor, Dr. Ashley, a respected therapist planning big changes at the Institute — and whose abrupt demise Brophy gravely attributes to "foul play."

At the Institute, Thorndyke is welcomed with great enthusiasm by Dr. Philip Wentworth (Dick Van Patten), likewise distressed by "strange" goings-on at the asylum — and noticeably afraid of interim chief Dr. Charles Montague (Harvey Korman), a sly psychiatrist deeply resentful of his demotion, and Nurse Charlotte Diesel (Cloris Leachman), Montague's rigid, rather mannish lover.

Unpacking, Thorndyke is greeted by beloved mentor Prof. Lilloman (Howard Morris), an elderly consultant overjoyed to see his star pupil and insistent he try out the view from his office balcony. Uneasy, Thorndyke reluctantly agrees, but one look at the surf below plunges him into a wild panic, proving Thorndyke still suffers from High Anxiety, a debilitating fear of heights Prof. Lilloman insists must be cured lest its devastating effects someday cost Thorndyke his life.

In league with Nurse Diesel, Montague thwarts Thorndyke's look into the asylum's low recovery rate by newly unhinging one cured patient, Mr. Cartwright (Ron Clark), and replacing another, wealthy Arthur Brisbane (Albert J. Whitlock), with a lunatic who thinks he's a dog. Worse still, the lovers hire deranged killer Braces (Rudy DeLuca), Dr. Ashley's murderer, to kill panicky Dr. Wentworth by causing a cerebral hemorrhage by way of loud music in a locked car.

Baffled by this second death, Thorndyke leaves with Brophy for a psychiatric convention in San Francisco, where Diesel and Montague, exploiting Thorndyke's phobia, shrewdly book him on the hotel's topmost floor. Here Thorndyke meets Victoria Brisbane (Madeline Kahn), frantic daughter of the *real* Arthur Brisbane, who convinces Thorndyke to help her set her father free.

Disguised as Thorndyke, Braces shoots a hotel guest, and Thorndyke, framed for murder, flees. After Brophy enlarges a photo proving his boss's innocence, however, Thorndyke is nearly strangled to death in a phone booth before impaling Braces on broken glass in mid-struggle. Determined to clear his name, Thorndyke re-teams with Vicki and sneaks back to the Institute, where Prof. Lilloman reveals Brophy, a "mental breakdown" victim, has been locked away.

Freeing Brophy, the trio set out with him to rescue Vicki's father before Diesel and Montague's crony Norton (Lee Delano) can fling him from a madhouse tower. Only after Prof. Lilloman reveals that Thorndyke's High Anxiety began after a fall from a high chair during a parental quarrel can Thorndyke find the courage to ascend the tower, stop Norton, and narrowly sidestep a maniacal Nurse Diesel, who falls to the rocks below. His lover dead, a cowardly Montague quickly gives himself up, and Thorndyke and Vicki, their worries over, enjoy a happy honeymoon.

★　★　★

Of all Mel Brooks' comedies after *Young Frankenstein*, his 1977 Alfred Hitchcock spoof *High Anxiety*, that way-out, neurosis-nutty takeoff on everything from *Rebecca* to *Psycho* to *North by Northwest* to *The Birds*, is still the one whose original critical assessment remains the most baffling. Overall the best directed, edited, scripted, and acted comedy Brooks would helm for the rest of his career, *High Anxiety* showcases some of his finest work ever as director, writer, actor, even as songwriter and singer, yet its unaccountably ho-hum reviews keep this deliriously demented comic tale of murder, madness, and medical malpractice even now his most inexplicably under-appreciated laugh-getter since 1970's *The Twelve Chairs*— this despite the fact that never again after *High Anxiety*'s release are Brooks' characters this deliciously eccentric, his storylines this richly intricate, or his scene-for-scene gag-to-laugh ratio this gloriously, intoxicatingly high.

Critical response to *High Anxiety* wasn't bad, really — just subdued. *Films in Reviews*' Rob Edelman, at least, called it "ninety-two minutes of hilarity," with Brooks' humor "present in all its outrageous glory," and the *New York Times*' Vincent Canby thought it "witty and disciplined" despite a "built-in problem" of having "nothing to send up" since Hitchcock's work is so waggish to begin with. *Variety*'s reviewer, though, while mostly pleased, noted an "uneven" quality, lots of "highs and lows," "valleys and peaks" instead of constant brilliance; the *Chicago Sun-Times*' Roger Ebert felt Hitchcock's "spoof-proof" wit causes Brooks to "bury his own comic talent" trying to mimic him; and Leonard Maltin would later label the picture "uneven" and only "so-so."

Most of the complaints are legitimate, too, yet looking back at it today one can't imagine so few saw how special *High Anxiety* really is — not because Brooks, Ron Clark, Rudy DeLuca, and Barry Levinson's *Silent Movie* follow-up is perfect by any means, but because it pulls off the difficult trick of somehow resembling both real-life and cartoon at the same time. Brooks violates the cinematic "fourth wall," just as Hitchcock does with Barbara Harris's closing wink in *Family Plot*, or with his own in-joke cameo turns, but we're still "sold" quite fully on the man-on-the-run intrigue too. His murder plot feels real enough to make an exciting crime yarn even without the laughs, yet even the craziest actions centered around it play just right too. Like Gene Wilder's scholar-turned–grave robber in *Young Frankenstein* or Peter MacNicol's lawyer-gone-buggy in *Dracula: Dead and Loving It*, *High Anxiety* belies its surface look of sanity and stability and, in true Hitchcock style, just keeps lobbing something more and more outlandish at us at every turn.

Esteemed psychiatrist Dr. Richard Thorndyke, played to such matchless comic perfection by longtime therapy fan Brooks himself, is the director's first protagonist since his two-for-one antiheroes from *The Producers* who seems like someone we'd meet in real life, in depots and bus stops and subways, in line for restaurant tables and car rentals and theater tickets. Yet for all his Fred MacMurray average-ness, for all his '50s-businessman hats, topcoats, and three-piece suits, even he isn't entirely run-of-the-mill. On the outside he's as reliable and rational and real as they come, yet shove this same solid, sensible professional inside an airplane or too close to a balcony railing and poor Thorndyke crumbles, is reduced to a hysterical Leo Bloom–type wreck in nothing flat. Educated yet infantile, practiced yet pitiable, Thorndyke is Brooks' comic juxtaposition theory personified, sagely sniffing out madhouse mismanagement one minute, wailing for "Mama" the next. And in *High Anxiety*'s cuckoo-crazy universe such oddball behavior isn't all that unusual. "Dr. Montague," Thorndyke observes at one point, "I'm a little disturbed," and it's surely by design Brooks has his foible-laden therapist hero express his bafflement about his new workplace's patient recovery rate just that way. In *High Anxiety*, who *isn't* "a little disturbed"?

Not its doctors and nurses, assuredly.

Indeed, nearly everyone on staff at Brooks' cliffside Psycho-Neurotic Institute for the Very, *Very* Nervous (love that name!) harbors some oddball eccentricity, insecurity, or even full-blown dementia behind his seemingly "normal" outward calm: Dr. Charles Montague (Harvey Korman), whose dapper, David Niven eloquence and pin-striped, classy distinction disguise the masochistic, simpering child-man underneath; his starched-stiff lover Nurse Charlotte Diesel (Cloris Leachman), her already creepy mannishness only hinting at the sadistic, homicidal fiend behind so much evil; stone-cold ward guard Norton (Lee Delano), his rage barely more contained than the patient's who ripped half his mustache off his face; panicky, guilt-wracked Dr. Philip Wentworth (Dick Van Patten), snapping to attention like an abused lapdog when Montague and Diesel yank his leash; Prof. Lilloman (Howard Morris), as spookily corpselike in open-eyed slumber as he is lovably paternal awake; hyperactive driver Brophy (Ron Carey), yammering over-insistent self-assurances one minute, about-face jittery disbelief the next; Thorndyke's unseen secretary, her nasal outer-office squawk caused more by self-pinched nostrils than bad intercoms. Thorndyke's "new home," as Brophy so unsettlingly puts it, may purport to cure the patients under its care, but its healers and helpers too are all just a teensy bit "off."

Like Tippi Hedren's Melanie Daniels in Hitchcock's *The Birds*, who seems to invite chaos to tiny Bodega Bay just by setting foot there, so Thorndyke attracts lunacy wherever he goes, as if a magnet attuned solely to maniacs and madmen. We recognize Brooks' parks and wharves and lounges as coming from a world like our own, yet — as in Hitchcock, where showers become crime scenes and phone booths targets for mad birds — the erratic and offbeat turns up amid even these standard-issue locales. An airport here is no normal airport, but a spot where wild-eyed strangers leap at us like psychopaths, where take-charge security types are just twisted, brain-sick weirdoes. Here car radios emit death rays and phone cords turn strangle wires, and in hotels seething-mad bellhops snap at a hat's drop, horror hostish staffers operate maintenance carts like bulldozers, the fellow sipping drinks at the piano bar itches to kill us, and the chap by the elevators frames us for murder. Compared to the otherworldly spaceships-and-castles locales of *Spaceballs* or *Young Frankenstein*, perhaps, Brooks' far subtler milieu of therapist's offices, dining rooms, and lecture halls looks as commonplace as anything in Frank Capra or Preston Sturges or Howard Hawks, yet *High Anxiety* plays more like Capra's *Arsenic and Old Lace* or *You Can't Take It With You* than *It Happened One Night* or *Mr. Deeds Goes to Town*, and if dead bodies suddenly turned up in window seats or half-crazed relatives turned up in togas and tutus we wouldn't be at all surprised.

Indeed, the fact that *High Anxiety* plays as much like Charles Addams as Mel Brooks fits the film just beautifully, at once giving Brooks' plot a darker, more menacing edge that pushes his already fantastic cast of zanies into whole new realms of wild hilarity. Who *wouldn't* laugh at Mel Brooks and Madeline Kahn, disguised as a scrappy old Jewish couple, carping and kvetching their way past airport security

Eager to chauffeur his new employer from the airport to the "head shrink" position awaiting him at the nearby Psycho-Neurotic Institute for the Very, *Very* Nervous, photography-loving "driver and sidekick" Brophy (Ron Carey) tries hard but finds he just "ain't got it" as he helps psychiatrist Dr. Richard H. Thorndyke (Mel Brooks) with a heavy steamer trunk, in *High Anxiety* (1977), writer-director-lyricist Brooks' comic homage to Alfred Hitchcock, the cinematic Master of Suspense.

behind bagged groceries and baggy clothes? Cloris Leachman as a death-masked, steel-brassiered nurse–Nazi stomping about after hours in police uniform and hot pants? Harvey Korman in plastic werewolf fangs, crawling around firing paper clips at hysterical mental patients? From start to finish, *High Anxiety* keeps piling on one outrageous bit of insanity after another, leaving us a movie so quirkily engaging one can only guess at least some of its early detractors, already a little irked over Brooks' taking top billing in *Silent Movie* and now resentful of his unexpected new turn as Cary Grant-ish, James Stewart–esque leading man, simply couldn't see past such personal jealousies to what a charming, endearing little black comic gem it really is.

One of its big victories is that, until 1991's *Life Stinks*, *High Anxiety* is the last Brooks film in which the humor is almost solely story- and character-driven, and arises as a natural outgrowth of plot and personality instead of just because, independent of any other clear purpose, Brooks simply hopes it might pull in a laugh. Beyond the occasional Frank Sinatra or Jack Benny gag, virtually nothing turns up without reason, and the film's three or four blatantly cinematic bits (in which characters react self-consciously to set-shattering camera dollies and ear-piercing music cues) work just fine given its "Hitchcock spoof" design. It's as if Brooks, recalling how strictly Hitchcock planned, plotted, and storyboarded every scene, fights hard to keep *High Anxiety* as pure and on-focus as possible, wanting not even one second left slack, uncalled-for, or uncontrolled.

All this added effort tightens Brooks' narrative magnificently, too. Oh, yes, he still can't resist a few out-of-nowhere gags — for all the movie's direct-from-Hitchcock origins and thematic hints at normality-gone-berserk, its daffy parody of *The Birds* doesn't advance character or plot one iota — but even these little extras don't sidetrack the film in the least. When Madeline Kahn's perky, pretty Victoria Brisbane pulls up for a secret rendezvous with framed-for-murder Thorndyke in a bold checkered-spotty auto perfectly matching her bold checkered-spotty pantsuit, the joke may simply reveal an unexpected character quirk (Vicki as compulsive fashion fanatic), or it may be a subtle nod to costume legend Edith Head's down-to-the-last-detail perfectionism outfitting Hitchcock's leading ladies — but even if it's nothing more than a Brooks-loony sight gag dropped in just for the sheer goofy fun of it, it still doesn't damage the film any because, coming unobtrusively as it does, without dialogue, Brooks doesn't permit it to seriously stall the action.

Instead, excepting the inevitable sendups of specific Hitchcock scenes, images, and camera angles, the humor in *High Anxiety* reflects moment-to-moment developments in story, character, and concept almost nonstop. In any other post–*Young Frankenstein* Brooks film, perhaps, putting the then-fiftyish Brooks in baby bonnet and highchair might invite charges of over-the-top artistic recklessness, proof positive of a Mel Brooks so Jerry Lewis shameless he'll do just about anything for a laugh (strikingly, the much-maligned Lewis, a pretty fair actor-writer-director too when he wants to be, dons baby togs for a similar scene in 1964's *The Nutty Professor* — featuring Howard Morris!), yet here even an image this idiotic feels not only allowable but downright essential. Hitchcock's *Spellbound* and *Marnie*, remember, also elucidate adult psychosis with a childhood trauma flashback, and if Brooks is self-restrained enough to hold his squabbling parents/ squalling toddler bit to the mere handful of seconds seen here — well, fine and dandy. What's more, where later Brooks films might let Baby Thorndyke fall from the highchair just for a cheap laugh, here the scene does exactly what it's meant to: explains why a perfectly rational, level-headed therapist like Richard Thorndyke falls apart every time he looks down too fast or leans over a rail too far.

Likewise, the riotously funny bit about poor Zachary Cartwright (co-writer Ron Clark), the patient recovering from sharp pains and werewolf dreams, and the wild scene about the lunatic who thinks he's a cocker spaniel (Charlie Callas), might be just a pair of meaningless sight gags in later Brooks films, yet here they serve a multitude of legitimate purposes. Through them, we learn that Thorndyke feels genuinely troubled (even if financially well-rewarded) by therapy's failure to cure his needy charges; that vile, money-hungry Dr. Montague and Nurse Diesel will go to any lengths to prevent patient recovery, including inflicting cruel new torments on Cartwright and passing off a "dog" patient for the *real*, cured Arthur Brisbane (Albert J. Whitlock); and that madness and mental upset, themes introduced the instant we meet heights-traumatized Thorndyke in mid–plane flight, will remain among *High Anxiety*'s primary subtexts right up to the very end.

When, moreover, Thorndyke encounters the crazy-eyed woman and half-naked pervert at the airport early on, such gags appear not for mere whimsy's sake, but to further Brooks' ongoing madness-anxiety motif. *High Anxiety* depicts an entire universe of mental instability, one lending clear thematic purpose to what at first seem simple comic throwaways: Thorndyke's dizzy spells and panic attacks; Nurse Diesel's mad dinner table tirade; Thorndyke's compulsive teeth-brushing to a methodical child's rhyme; the rock-affixed "WELCOME" note from inmates of the Violent Ward; Diesel and Mon-

tague's kinky whips-and-chains escapades; Brophy's habit of talking to and repeating himself; the lunatic sporting a violence-procured half-mustache; the patient who thinks he's a dog; Cartwright's pains and monster dreams; agitated Dr. Wentworth's brain hemorrhage, caused by mind-blasting hard rock; Vicki's edge-of-sanity paranoia and hormone-frazzled nerves; Thorndyke and other therapists' hangups about using body part terminology before two little girls; Vicki's substitution of "Little Girl's Room" for "bathroom"; the sadistic, heavy-breathing bloodlust of metal-toothed hit man Braces (Rudy DeLuca); Vicki's rapture thinking Thorndyke's strangle-gasps and Braces' death throes an obscene phone call; elderly Prof. Lilloman's eyes-open cat naps; an emotionally stunted Thorndyke's discovery he really fears not heights but parents; and Nurse Diesel's deranged death-laugh while falling from a madhouse tower. In this regard, *High Anxiety* represents Brooks at his most artistically self-disciplined; like Hitchcock, who could so ingeniously sustain, say, bird imagery all through *Psycho* or food imagery all through *Frenzy*, Brooks knows how to weave elaborate variations on a single idea through virtually every scene.

Consider, for instance, Brooks' persistent use of disguise imagery, the way his characters are forever masquerading as or mistaken for someone else. The *Dragnet*-serious policeman who lures Thorndyke into an airport restroom isn't "real" at all but a half-nude deviate chasing a cheap thrill; Nurse Diesel plays nightstick-and-handcuff traffic cop for her sick role-playing games with bondage fetishist Dr. Montague; Montague dons fake monster fangs to scare poor Mr. Cartwright quite literally out of his wits; the doglike Arthur Brisbane Thorndyke meets isn't Vicki's cured, rich father but some crazed impostor; Montague poses as a "Mr. MacGuffin" by phone to reassign Thorndyke to a hotel's top floor (a MacGuffin, recall, was Hitch-cock's term for quest items his characters seek out — the wine-bottled uranium in *Notorious*, the government secrets in *North by Northwest*, the stolen money in *Psycho* — but in which Hitchcock had little interest); the Thorndyke who guns down a colleague is really toothy hitman Braces in a rubber mask; and to evade capture Thorndyke and Vicki must pose as a scrappy Jewish couple.

In *High Anxiety*, as in Hitchcock, artifice and imposture hoax and hoodwink us at every turn. The ostensibly homicidal woman at the airport isn't out to kill Thorndyke but to greet a much-missed relative; former madhouse chief Dr. Ash-ley is dead not of a heart attack but "foul play"; the Institute wears the outward trappings of a true hospital, yet seldom ac-tually cures anyone; even basically honest, medical-minded sorts like Thorndyke re-veal they too love psychiatry largely be-cause that's where "the real money is," be-cause it makes them "a nice living"; the supposed death threat hurled through Thorndyke's window is really a friendly welcome note; Nurse Diesel pretends to free timid, guilt-ridden Dr. Wentworth from her criminal stranglehold, but se-cretly plans to have him murdered; Prof. Lilloman isn't really dead, just asleep, both eyes open; Thorndyke isn't afraid of heights but parents; and on and on. This is funny, funny stuff, yet artful too; it's subtle; it's smart.

The window–lattice web gag involv-ing scared, spider-snared Dr. Wentworth, for example, with Dick Van Patten replac-ing *Suspicion*'s Joan Fontaine, doesn't show up just once and vanish, any more than the dizzying spiral effect bombarding Thorndyke's anxiety attacks. Those same shadows appear behind Nurse Diesel re-peatedly, accentuating her evil (later the hoop-latticed windows creating them be-come heart-shaped ones at Thorndyke's

honeymoon motel), while Thorndyke's dizzying anxiety vortex pattern fills in the main credits lettering and the words THE END. A similar whirlpool pattern ap-pears — by coincidence, but no less in-triguing for it — when the ink from Thorn-dyke's newspaper spins down his tub drain like *Psycho*'s chocolate syrup "blood," and at times the net-like webs and whirlpool-ish spirals form a single design, as in the vortex-mesh floor tile pattern at Thorn-dyke's feet at the hotel elevators. That one's coincidence too, surely, as may be the use of the color red — Thorndyke wears a bright red necktie only when pitched wildly out of control, either during his symbolic vortex tailspins or when he's framed for murder by his double and turns wanted-for-murder renegade — but the significance of the color in *Marnie* (and the gunshot flash in *Spellbound*, which also emphasizes stark, snowy whites) makes one wonder.

Even the music takes a thematic ap-proach, with the superb Mel Brooks/John Morris title song appearing not only at be-ginning (wildly up-tempo, building in-credible suspense) and end (waltz-like, played atop freeze-frames recalling Bro-phy's photos), and Morris' five-note mu-sical cue echoing its title, but in full-lyrics form when Thorndyke sings and in casual, all-whistle prelude as he tries sidling away from attack-ready birds. What's more, the way its title functions both as synonym for the hero's heights aversion and metaphor for the perils of romance gives both song and film still more textural richness. As in Hitchcock, whose titles often hold double meanings (Does *Psycho* mean "madman," or is it short for psychology/psychoanaly-sis? Does *Spellbound* imply the protago-nist's guilt-amnesia, or his pretty psychi-atrist's lovesick attraction to him? Does the "plot" in *Family Plot* allude to cagey household intrigue, or the corpseless fam-ily gravesite?), *High Anxiety* implies both falling and falling in love — risky ventures, both — and since this sort of motif-focused scripting and scoring isn't easy, writers Brooks, Ron Clark, Rudy DeLuca, and Barry Levinson and composer Morris all deserve real credit for handling it with so much finesse.

Indeed, had every post–'70s Brooks comedy been scripted and executed with as much screen-savvy as *High Anxiety*, it's practically guaranteed Brooks' career as writer-director would have been far, far more successful. Brooks' revue picture *History of the World — Part I*, for all its structural daring, screams for a narrative drive this solid; *Spaceballs* for a hero and heroine with this much attention-riveting nuttiness; *Life Stinks* for a cast of second bananas with this much sublime goofiness; *Robin Hood: Men in Tights* for this kind of split-second timing; *Dracula: Dead and Loving It* for so many quality jokes packed into so little space. Asking Brooks to come up with another *The Producers* or *Blazing Saddles* or *Young Frankenstein* every few years might have been unrealistic — even Orson Welles never topped *Citizen Kane*— but two or three films as well-done as *High Anxiety* for each decade of Brooks' career? Heaven — sheer comic Heaven.

Yet for some strange reason, as outstandingly effective as *High Anxiety*'s comic and visual style so obviously is, critics seem largely to have passed Brooks' sixth film by with relatively little fanfare. The question is, why? How can so many gifted reviewers have possibly been so blind?

The most common complaints leveled against *High Anxiety* at the time of its initial release are simply these: first, the notion that somehow Westerns (*Blazing Saddles*), horror films (*Young Frankenstein*), and even Chaplin-style silents (*Silent Movie*) are fit material for parody but the films of Alfred Hitchcock are not; and, second, the idea that spoofing Hitch-

cock's best moments and simply restaging them for a laugh (as Brooks does the *Psycho* shower scene, the playground attack from *The Birds*, etc.) are not really the same. One can't easily refute either charge, and yet *High Anxiety* is simply too never-let-up entertaining to dismiss so quickly no matter how good a point its naysayers might have. Even if they're right, the dialogue still sparkles, the comedy still crackles, and the whole wacky, wonderful project just keeps on being relentlessly funny anyway.

In any event, the first criticism — that Hitchcock pictures simply don't make good source material for a Brooks lampoon — springs mostly from fans who feel Hitchcock's movies, like his sly, sponsor-skewering introductions for TV's *Alfred Hitchcock Presents*, make such wickedly witty self-parodies already (think *The Trouble with Harry*, or *To Catch a Thief*, or *North by Northwest*, or *Family Plot*) making fun of them further proves downright redundant. One might easily ridicule some stuffy, self-important *War and Peace* or *Wuthering Heights*, they argue, but what of something more tongue-in-cheek, a *Gulliver's Travels* or a *Catch-22*? Brooks' and Buck Henry's *Get Smart*, after all, lampooned Ian Fleming–style spy capers black and blue week after week for five years yet came no nearer derailing Eon Productions' James Bond movie juggernaut than the likes of *Agent 8¾* and *Carry on Spying*. The Bond films, like the best of Hitchcock, started spoofing *themselves* from Day One, so what possible impact could mere parody have?

What's more, these "you-can't-kid-a-kidder" types insist, lampoons work best when Brooks spoofs entire genres, not entire careers, and the work of just one filmmaker, especially one as distinctive as Hitchcock, simply makes too precise and tricky a target. Nearly everybody recognizes the conventions of old-style horror

films, after all, even those who've never actually seen one — baying wolves, mad scientists, cobwebs, castles, and all that — but
Hitchcock's favorite story elements are less
universal, far more film specific. How is
the non–Hitchcock fan to know *High Anxiety*'s Richard H. Thorndyke is a take-off
on Cary Grant's Roger O. Thornhill in
North by Northwest? That camera-toting
chauffeur Brophy is Hitchcock's twinkle-
eyed salute to James Stewart's photographer hero in *Rear Window*? The answer,
naturally, is that of course he can't.

What makes *High Anxiety* unique,
however, is that its script is crafted with
such skillful thematic and narrative over-
lap such minor knowledge gaps carry practically no negative impact whatsoever. Even
those who *don't* "get" Thorndyke's name
still embrace him as a human being in ways
they never would the deadpan-serious heroes of spoofs like *Hot Shots!*, *Fatal Instinct*,
or *Mafia!*, whose purported "character"
moments always feel cocky and cynical, as
if the very idea of genuine feeling is just a
joke. We care about Thorndyke, so missing
the Hitchcock connection hardly matters;
we're far too engaged in rooting for him,
fearing for him, to believe for a second we're
getting shortchanged on anything. Besides,
so what if we don't recall Grant's character
name in *North by Northwest*, with that loss-
of-identity-themed "nothing" middle initial *O*? That doesn't make Thorndyke's
middle name *Harpo* any less loopy, does it?
And as for the link between Brophy's pic-
ture-taking and Stewart's in *Rear Window*,
again, what of it? Brooks gets several agreeably silly non–Hitchcock yuks from Brophy's shutterbugging anyway (Thorndyke's
airport action-posing, the wall-sized picture blow-up, etc.), and the fact that one
snapshot clears his boss of murder lends
Brophy's photo-fixation a new import that
works just fine on its own.

The second criticism, on the other
hand — the charge that restaging Hitch-

cock's best scenes with a slight comedic
twist falls short of true parody — proves a
bit more problematic. It was in her review
of *High Anxiety* that *The New Yorker*'s
Pauline Kael argued that "all Brooks does
is let us know he has seen some of the same
movies we have," that he holds only "a
child's idea of satire" comprised mostly of
mere "imitations," and it's a valid charge:
the idea that making fun *of* a film and just
having fun *with* it aren't identical, that
comic ridicule and comic re-enactment
aren't the same. Brooks himself surely
grasps this distinction, but at times his signals feel mixed; we know from interviews
he aims not to "trash" the Robin Hood legend with *Robin Hood: Men in Tights* so
much as play around in it, yet the studio's
"The Legend Had It Coming" ads imply
plans to discredit the saga once and for all.
It doesn't much matter either way — who
said a spoof can't revere as well as revile? —
but for a man so vocal about critics' re-
fusal to fully endorse his films or cut-no-
slack condemn them, it's ironic he too
"plays it both ways," upends Hitchcock
without debunking him. If Brooks feels
Hitchcock needs deflating, fine, but since
he clearly doesn't (he even dedicates the
film to him), small wonder such taunt-free
tweaking left some critics cold.

Happily, however, such larger issues
for once prove inconsequential in the final
analysis, since *High Anxiety* succeeds quite
admirably where many a Brooks film since
has come up short: it entertains almost
round-the-clock, and maintains a gag momentum more zesty and zippy than anything Brooks would ever achieve again. If
helmeted loony Franz Liebkind's pro–Nazi
stage play in *The Producers* is "a love letter
to Hitler," *High Anxiety* is a love letter to
Hitchcock, a glowing tribute to the Master and his movies, yet somehow the fact
that Brooks here again reduces spoof cinema to little more than wholesale hero-
worship doesn't matter because the picture

is just so doggone much fun. What if its tone *is* all salute and no censure? *High Anxiety* still musters more first-rate side-splitters its first half-hour than *Dracula: Dead and Loving It* can its full ninety, and with an entertainment index that high we can forgive almost anything. Where most *Young Frankenstein* follow-ups suffer from too much awkward silence, a few too many punchlines left hovering in space after their comic impact has long died away, *High Anxiety* just keeps cheerfully bubbling along at a truly phenomenal comic pace, and second after second one just can't help smiling at *something*— a quirky camera angle, a loony line reading, a zany plot twist — till the very last scene.

We've already said *High Anxiety* "goofs" on Hitchcock wonderfully well without being at all Hitchcock-dependent, and that's absolutely true; the ads call the film "a Psycho-Comedy," but one needn't know *Psycho* inside and out to have a great time. Still, just as horror buffs get "more bang for the buck" from *Young Frankenstein* than someone who's never seen a Boris Karloff movie in his life, so does anyone who's a real nut on Hitchcock come better prepared than anyone else to fully appreciate what *High Anxiety* is all about. Fortunately, even the most casual viewer usually picks up on Brooks' big *Psycho* and *The Birds* nods (we see these two parodied on TV all the time — on *The Simpsons*, or *Just Shoot Me*, or *The Golden Girls*), and they're funny enough we don't even mind that, story-wise, neither one really adds up to much. Drenching Thorndyke in bird dung from dive-bombing pigeons is funny but fairly pointless (unless one thinks of them as *mad* birds — which is pretty logical, actually), and the bellboy's shower attack on Thorndyke with a rolled-up newspaper advances the insanity theme nicely but not really the plot. Comedy-wise, though, Brooks' hat-tipping hits all the Hitchcockian high spots just right; we rec-

ognize right off what he's driving at (Thorndyke as bird-beset Tippi Hedren, Thorndyke as nude-helpless Janet Leigh), laugh exactly for the reasons we're meant to, and eagerly look forward to the next scene.

Hitchcock's most obvious influence, of course, springs from the main storylines of three of his best films, *Spellbound* (1945), *Vertigo* (1958), and *North by Northwest* (1959), the first two ranking among his most psychology-focused, the third among his most wittily suspenseful. In fact, one of *High Anxiety*'s real achievements is its masterly incorporation of all three plots into a smooth, unbroken whole without relying too rigidly on any one, with Brooks essentially playing the trouble-besieged heroes of all three films simultaneously — and playing them very nicely indeed.

Brooks' madhouse setting is essentially a '70s version of *Spellbound*'s Green Manors, where Ingrid Bergman's therapist heroine learns the new administrator played by Gregory Peck is in fact an amnesiac present at the real director's murder, committed, as here, by another top-level employee — with Brooks more or less playing both the Bergman and Peck roles. (Mel Brooks as Ingrid Bergman — now *that's* comic juxtaposition!) Like Bergman, Thorndyke gradually unearths dark secrets posing as normalcy at his new workplace, but like Peck, whose disguise stems from a long-buried childhood shock revived upon witnessing the true chief's murder, Thorndyke is more sickly infant than mature grown-up, a wounded child-man still haunted by boyhood trauma. His rival, Korman's envy-filled Dr. Montague, thus becomes a younger, spryer adaptation of Leo G. Carroll's character in *Spellbound*— who, like Montague and Nurse Diesel with Dr. Ashley, has killed his would-be replacement to save his own job. *Spellbound* also gives Brooks something else to play around with: Michael Chekhov's kindly old mentor figure, expertly played here by Brooks' *Your Show of Shows* playmate Howard Morris, director of Brooks' "Mr. Big" pilot for *Get Smart* twelve years earlier. As gray-bearded, bespectacled, German-accented Prof. Lilloman, whose hypnosis sessions help his favorite pupil confront the buried source of his psychosis just as the Chekhov character helps Peck, Morris nimbly reworks Chekhov's role as Bergman's aged instructor and Sigmund Freud at the same time. What's more, Brooks tricks us into thinking Dr. Lilloman has been slaughtered in his chair almost exactly as Hitchcock fools us about Chekov; Nurse Diesel's fork-to-the-table lunge hints vaguely at Peck's uneasiness at fork marks on tablecloth white; Thorndyke's all-white bathroom recalls (by accident?) Peck's "freak-out" as so much unsullied whiteness plunges him into a sort of snow-blind trance; and the half-a-mustache incident suggests the female patient in *Spellbound* who bit off a man's mustache with her teeth!

Thorndyke's fear of heights, meanwhile, springs chiefly from *Vertigo*, and while Brooks resembles James Stewart about as much as he does Ingrid Bergman, anyone who's seen the 1958 original knows exactly what Brooks is up to. Like its own poster art, *High Anxiety* depicts the hero's mental distress by envisioning Brooks screaming like a banshee, limbs flailing, plummeting into a spinning black-and-white cartoon abyss, a sort of Spirograph vortex with Thorndyke falling like dead weight into its center. It's easily the film's strongest image, its emotional and aesthetic center, and the connection between it and Stewart's *Vertigo* nightmares before his guilt-induced nervous breakdown (Stewart's head encircled by dizzy-sick descent-into-madness animation, his limp silhouette plunging from a great height) needs little explanation. We needn't dwell

either on how closely Brooks' madhouse architecture resembles the Spanish mission murder site in *Vertigo*, or how clearly the big Thorndyke-climbing-the-tower scene that ends the film draws inspiration from *Vertigo*, in which Stewart loses his girlfriend not once but twice — once when, counting on Stewart's heights phobia to prevent his chasing her to the top, a duplicitous Kim Novak pretends to leap to her death when in fact another corpse is hurled over the edge, then again when, fears defeated, he forces Novak up the tower again only to see her fall for real. Overlooked more often is the fact that, like much of *High Anxiety*, *Vertigo* takes place in and about San Francisco, a city renowned for its steep hills, its constant sense of moving less side-to-side as up and down. Where better for a tale of a man terrified by sudden dips and drops, either in *Vertigo* or right here?

As for *North by Northwest*, it's amazing Brooks reworks so much of that 1959 thriller without spoofing its two most famous scenes — Cary Grant chased by machine-gunning cropduster, then across Mount Rushmore — but it's still *North by Northwest* that provides the framework for the film's final third. Actually, Brooks, Clark, DeLuca, and Levinson considered trying some sort of cockeyed tribute to Hitchcock's cropduster business, but what *High Anxiety* really needs from its source it has in spades: the fugitive factor, a sudden, deck-stacking upsurge of man-on-the-run jeopardy. A sort of late-'50s version of *The Thirty-Nine Steps* and *Saboteur*, *North by Northwest* cuts off Grant's Roger Thornhill from help on all sides, sends him fleeing both spies chasing him because he knows too much and misled police because they know too little, and *High Anxiety*'s last half-hour works much the same way. The scene in which Thornhill, framed for homicide, wanders into a hotel lobby murder gun in hand superbly re-stages the scene in which Grant ends up holding the death-blade the spies' knife-throwing expert has just hurled into a United Nations diplomat. Even Thorndyke's clothes bring to mind those worn by Grant (like Thornhill, he sports the same outfit for much of the film), whose insecticide-choked business suit needs cleaning after his cropduster escape just as Brooks' does after the attack by all those birds. Notable too (and quite common in Hitchcock) is the way Thorndyke uses psychology to slip past security by acting so loud and obnoxious the officers let him pass just to get rid of him. What Grant does to escape gun-toting spies in *North by Northwest* isn't exactly the same — Thornhill *wants* to get arrested, deciding he's safer in jail than with known killers — but his noisy art auction ruckus yields the same response: he tricks the police into doing precisely what he wants them to. Even Brooks' ending is pure *North by Northwest*: just as Hitchcock has cliff-clinging Grant reaching out to Eva Marie Saint, has his film go hazy, then reveals Grant pulling Saint up onto a honeymoon train berth for a romantic finale, Brooks has Thorndyke and Vicki spin about in dancer ecstasy, then dissolves to a similar newlywed finale depositing the two love-birds onto the bed of their honeymoon suite.

Yet while *Spellbound*, *Vertigo*, and *North by Northwest* give Brooks his primary support, *High Anxiety*'s Hitchcock links run far deeper than just this. We've named several already, but we haven't noted how Ron Carey's bowtie-and-cap outfit resembles Bruce Dern's cabby attire in *Family Plot*; how Cloris Leachman's corpse-white Nurse Diesel calls to mind Judith Anderson's sour-faced housekeeper Mrs. Danvers from *Rebecca*; the way the red screen-burst as hired killer Braces plots Thorndyke's murder from a lounge barstool suggests the flashes of scarlet trig-gering Tippi Hedren's childhood flash-backs in *Marnie*; how the rain-slashing windshield wipers on Dr. Wentworth's sabotaged car echoes Janet Leigh's ill-fated car trip in *Psycho*, the brake tampering assault on Bruce Dern and Barbara Harris in *Family Plot*, and Cary Grant's near car crash after being force-fed vodka in *North by Northwest*; the way Nurse Diesel's crazed leap at Thorndyke in the tower, like the airport lady incident, recalls Mrs. Bates' knife thrust at Martin Balsam's detective in *Psycho*; how Braces' bayside phone booth attack on Thorndyke echoes the assault on a "caged" Tippi Hedren in *The Birds* (whose Bodega Bay locale even lies near San Francisco), the trapped-and-helpless shower murder in *Psycho*, and even James Stewart's bay-leap to rescue a suicide-faking Kim Novak in *Vertigo*; how Madeline Kahn's Vicki, charging in with her floppy hat and flowing blonde tresses, resembles Karen Black's disguised kid-napper in *Family Plot*, and how her classy coolness recalls provocative "Hitchcock blondes" like Grace Kelly, Kim Novak, Eva Marie Saint, and Tippi Hedren; the way Harvey Korman's charismatic Dr. Montague exudes the dapper-but-deadly menace of Hitchcock villains from *Vertigo*'s Tom Helmore to *North by Northwest*'s James Mason to *Family Plot*'s William Devane; the way Braces' gasping, near-erotic sadism and "kill him" repetitions suggest Barry Foster's feverish mantra ("Lovely. Lovely.") as he rapes and strangles in *Frenzy*; the way Thorn-dyke's anatomical euphemisms and Vicki's use of the phrase "Little Girl's Room" echo Norman Bates' inability to say the word "bathroom" in *Psycho*; how Brooks' shooting-through-the-glass-table bit (in which Brooks' camera can't "see" around all that re-situated dinnerware) recalls shots through upturned drinking glasses (*Spellbound*), see-through ceilings (*The Lodger*), and the like; the way Brooks' mid-film crooning of the title song calls to mind Doris Day's warbling of "Que Sera, Sera" in the 1956 *The Man Who Knew Too Much* remake; how the broad daylight park bench scene reflects a similar fugitive-and-lover meeting in *Frenzy*; the use of violin-heavy Bernard Herrmann–type background melodies, and weirdo musical cues recalling Miklos Rozsa's work in *Spellbound*; the way Brooks employs slow-moving tracking shots to gradually close in on his targets; and so on, and so on, and so on.

High Anxiety profits from non–Hitchcock allusions too. Brooks' *Wizard of Oz* gag, with cackling, black-cloaked Nurse Diesel sailing to her death more or less astride a broomstick, may *seem* out of nowhere, but is it really? With Diesel's Hitchcock prototype, *Rebecca*'s stone-cold Mrs. Danvers, herself so Wicked Witch–like, and Thorndyke so Dorothy-esque (and Cowardly Lion-ish) with all his tornado-style panic imagery, Brophy his Toto-like sidekick, and the way the power to solve his crisis has lain inside himself all along? (Brooks references *The Wizard of Oz* again in *Spaceballs*, whose *Star Wars* story source revisits the same themes.) Nurse Diesel also suggests Louise Fletcher's cold, cruel Nurse Ratched in the 1975 movie of Ken Kesey's *One Flew Over the Cuckoo's Nest*, a more disturbing mental hospital film, and on a more cryptic note, Neil Sinyard notes in *The Films of Mel Brooks* that Diesel's claim that the late Dr. Ashley's biggest plan for the Institute was hanging new drapes (in the Psychotic Game Room — another great name!) lies rooted in Vincente Minnelli's 1951 version of William Gibson's psychiatric novel *The Cobweb*. (*Spellbound*'s Salvador Dalí–designed dream sequence involves drapes too — symbolic ones cut in two by huge scissors — but maybe that's best not gotten into.) Not too many recall *The Cobweb* these days, but that Brooks does speaks volumes; this man really knows his

movies. Far more fun, if unrelated to psychiatry or Hitchcock, are Brooks' wacky takeoff on singer Frank Sinatra, whose jazz-hipster style and snappy lyric-mangling Thorndyke approximates in his impromptu piano bar act just brilliantly (Sinatra, by the way, presented Brooks his Best Screenplay Oscar for *The Producers* in 1968) and his oddball pre–*To Be or Not Be* salute to that other "Old Blue Eyes," Jack Benny, whose memorable "Oh, Dennis!" radio entreaties to kiddish crooner Dennis Day Jack Riley's desk clerk emulates to perfection. Incredibly, though, all but the barest handful of *High Anxiety*'s pop culture in-jokes stem directly from Hitchcock, thus making Brooks' sixth film his most tightly focused, thematically unified work ever — and clearly one of his very best.

As for *High Anxiety*'s very best, one hardly knows where to begin, since Brooks really hits the ground running this time and just keeps topping himself. Should we mention the movie's manically frenzied first five minutes, editor John C. Howard's feverishly Hitchcockian montage of airport bag-handling, rail-clutching, and escalator-exiting so powder-keg pressurized the hero is left dumbstruck with exhausted disbelief? That exquisitely daffy moment in which, upon mere mention of the words "foul play," Thorndyke and Brophy find Bernard Herrmann–esque suspense music blasting from out of nowhere — then spy a full-scale orchestra passing their limo in a bus from behind? That gloriously goofy bit in which Prof. Lilloman and a hypnotized Thorndyke duke it out like boxers in a ring — and striped-shirted, bowtied Dr. Montague joins in as referee?

High Anxiety includes literally hundreds of nice moments, large and small, and while the movie may not be exactly error-free (a boom mike wobbles into frame in an otherwise fine mirror shot,

and Thorndyke is asked *if* he'll be attend-
ing a convention at which he's "principal
speaker" later on), its best scenes are so
well-directed even Hitchcock might have
been pleased. Remember that early camera pan, with its window-by-window survey of a landing airliner's beaming, carefree occupants — and, finally, Thorndyke's
terrified face gazing with horror at the
runway below? Had Hitchcock helmed
that scene, he'd have won raves for his
planning, and Brooks should too for cap-
ping it off with such a great final joke, just
as he does again when, as the passengers
disembark one by one, we at last see
Thorndyke drop off his airsick bag with
the flight attendant as he steps off. This
isn't just good directing, but good comedy, based as much on character as a good
gag. Particularly admirable is Brooks' expert handling of jumpy-jittery Dr. Wentworth's final scenes, with first a spectacular long shot of Nurse Diesel at her office
files, seen through a glass fish tank in
which tiny sharks (nicely suggestive of
both Diesel herself and glitter-gummed
Braces) swim about menacingly; then the
stylized *Suspicion* shot of Wentworth
snared in the window shadow web; a mas-
terfully executed zoom-in on Diesel's
reflection in the limo Brophy polishes outside; a blood-chilling zoom-in on Diesel's
piercing, murderous eyes, eerily dissolving
into a magnificently matched shot of the
headlights on Wentworth's night-driving
car; some splendid over-the-roof, over-
the-shoulder, through-the-back-glass,
through-the-windshield tension-builders
as Wentworth flees the Institute in the
rain; several excellent shots of a wildly agitated Wentworth through steering wheel
and driver's window as he tries desperately
to shut off his caterwauling, eardrum-
blasting radio (some extraordinarily cutting satire on modern music at work here,
by the way, proof yet again Brooks is
working from an exceptionally strong

script), and kick his way out of his locked
car; and a final close-up of the dead,
eardrum-damaged Wentworth amid the
lonely sounds of pouring rain. The whole
ordeal is filmed magnificently, as if, as in
Young Frankenstein, emulating Hollywood's finest gives Brooks' own directing
a real shot in the arm, re-energizes it,
makes him try little filmmaker's tricks he
might never even have tried on his own.
Where in most of his post–'70s efforts
Brooks tends to keep his camera too still
for too long, or too centered, or too far
back, or sometimes just plain doesn't
shoot from enough angles, *High Anxiety*'s
whole "Hitchcock spoof" premise forces
him out of his usual "comfort zone" in
wonderful new ways.

What fans love most about *High Anxiety*, though, besides its unbelievably high
number of really solid, big-time laughs, is
its cast, one exuding so much fantastic
comic chemistry it's hard to imagine
Brooks would rehire most of them only to
keep them sometimes whole centuries
apart for *History of the World — Part I*.
Harvey Korman, Cloris Leachman, Madeline Kahn, Howard Morris, Ron Carey, *and*
Mel Brooks, all in one film — and every last
one of them given a chance to really shine?
Seemingly impossible, and yet in *High
Anxiety* that's exactly what Brooks delivers.

No doubt Harvey Korman's snide,
sneaky-sinister Dr. Montague looks and
sounds a bit too much like his iniquitous
Hedley Lamarr from *Blazing Saddles* for
some tastes (a little unfair, really, since lily-
livered, spineless Montague is too hen-
pecked even to boss around Nurse Diesel),
but why nit-pick when Korman's so
terrific? His decade-long *Carol Burnett
Show* TV stint paying off in every scene (he
must have had great fun reteaming with
Burnett writers DeLuca and Levinson),
Korman makes this infantile deviate
delightful to watch, whether cowardly

begging for mercy after the jig is up or just sprinting down staircases like some late-for-dinner schoolboy, and some of his scenes — the werewolf and referee bits in particular — are among the best in the film.

Every bit as fantastic, though, is Cloris Leachman, who, having so gleefully tossed every trace of vanity aside playing grim-visaged Frau Blucher in *Young Frankenstein*, pushes herself still further here as Korman's nasty sidekick, macho malefactress Nurse Diesel. How many other Best Supporting Actress Oscar winners (*The Last Picture Show*, 1971) would

bury their natural good looks under this much bad costuming, hair, and makeup again and again just for the sake of making a movie for Mel Brooks? Not many, but, like Korman, with whom Brooks reteamed her twice in years to come (in *History of the World — Part I* on film, NBC's *The Nutt House* on TV), Leachman is clearly one of Brooks' biggest fans, and some of the scenes she tackles here — the fork-through-the-tabletop bit, the traffic cop dominatrix gag, the *Wizard of Oz* death scene — make this Medusa-monstrous, cast-iron Lady Macbeth one of the funniest comic villainesses in years.

Emulating the lyric-twisting stylishness of Frank Sinatra and the upbeat vitality of Doris Day's "Qué Será, Será" from Alfred Hitchcock's 1956 *The Man Who Knew Too Much*, heights-wary therapist Dr. Richard H. Thorndyke (Mel Brooks) wows hotel lounge patrons with an exhilarating rendition of the movie's Brooks-penned title song, in writer-director-producer Mel Brooks' *High Anxiety*, in which even composer John Morris's clever background melodies suggest those in classic Hitchcock films.

Brooks' pal Howard Morris, whose post-debut addition to *Your Show of Shows* Brooks himself had been hoping for in 1951, scores a real hit too, and despite the fact that he's no slouch as a director himself (*Who's Minding the Mint?*; *With Six You Get Eggroll*; *Don't Drink the Water*; TV hits from *The Dick Van Dyke Show* to *The Andy Griffith Show* to *Hogan's Heroes*), he works with Brooks just beautifully. Prof. Lilloman may not have many big scenes, but we're won over by this huggable old gent all over again each time we see him (for the split-second we think he's been murdered, we feel unforgivably betrayed), and we like Thorndyke still more because Lilloman seems so weepy-eyed fond of him. What's more, since the real-life Morris has so much boundless bantamweight energy, the scene in which this "frail," "aged" elder therapist dances and dodges about punching Thorndyke silly takes us by welcome surprise. Even in "little old man" getup, Morris's enthusiastic, love-of-the-gag exuberance remains flat-out irrepressible.

Equally good, and even more bounce-off-the-walls lively, is *Barney Miller*'s Ron Carey as Thorndyke's "driver and sidekick" Brophy. A sort of two-legged, cabby-capped Chihuahua utterly devoted to Thorndyke — and utterly devastated, like the little "Say it ain't so, Joe" boy after the Black Sox Scandal, when it seems his beloved "Doc" has turned killer — Brophy talks nearly as fast as he snaps pictures, and spouts high-speed street slang like some adult Dead End Kid hopped up on pep pills. Given one of Brooks' few real running gags ("I got it! I got it!" — then, "I ain't got it!" when tackling some challenge he's just not up to), Carey has better scenes here than in later Brooks films, and, with Carey playing them for all they're worth, the result is great, great fun.

And Madeline Kahn? To nobody's surprise, she's as arresting as ever, not merely as the ultra-paranoid, end-of-her-tether Vicki who charges into Thorndyke's hotel room demanding he close the drapes and crawl around on the carpet like a bug, but even more so the shrill, squabbling "housewife" Vicki who helps him avoid capture in baggy-garbed, cat-spectacled disguise. In this latter scene in particular Kahn delivers a caricature-type performance so robust and farcical it not only stands up quite nicely alongside Brooks' efforts as her celery-toting "husband" but even the broad, both-barrels comedy of a Lucille Ball or Carol Burnett — and that's high, high praise indeed.

As for Mel Brooks himself, *High Anxiety* proves he's not just a great comic but a fine, fine actor too. Like Kahn's Vicki, Thorndyke isn't as sketch comedy showy as one might expect after Brooks' early efforts, but Brooks' comic instincts are so perfect we don't mind one bit. Even his age here, fifty-one, seems just right given Brooks in essence plays a Cary Grant–James Stewart composite (both men were in their fifties for their final Hitchcock films), and his mock Sinatra and crabby old man routine are so tailor-made for his one-of-a-kind show-biz talents that one can't help smiling just thinking about them. Even when Brooks briefly plays Braces, his face magically takes on such dull, empty blandness we're half-convinced we're seeing not Thorndyke at all but Braces in a rubber mask. Put simply, as both actor and funnyman, Mel Brooks has never been better.

The rest of the cast is uniformly strong as well. In his first teaming with Brooks, TV vet Dick Van Patten, then topping his *Mama* teen stardom with *Eight is Enough*, has too few scenes to leave much lasting impact — we instantly like and feel sorry for Dr. Wentworth, but the instant he's gone we're already forgetting him — yet Van Patten's acting couldn't be better, and his pantomime-panic hard-rock

Mel Brooks directs his own performance in *High Anxiety*.

demise matches Brooks' deft directing of it shot for shot. *Silent Movie* alumni Charlie Callas, Jack Riley, and Arnold Soboloff have still fewer scenes, but Callas's dog bit is a low-comedy scream, one of those rare laugh-about-it-going-home bits every screen comic hopes for; Riley's hotel clerk is sure to please all of us who'd give almost anything to have the real Jack Benny back again; and Soboloff's Dr. Colburn — the paintywaist-pompous Q & A participant whose over-sanitized sex lecture inquiries drop a hundred I.Q. points once two little girls walk in — adds immeasurably to our hilarity seeing adult professionals squirm like a roomful of embarrassed four-year-olds. *Blazing Saddles'* Robert Ridgely does a fine job too in his brief turn as the airport flasher (intimidating one second, swishy-prissy the next), as do several others given even tinier, more "serious" parts, among them Lee Delano as the half-mus-

tached Norton and — in one of Brooks' most interesting tributes — Hitchcock's visuals wizard Albert J. Whitlock, who not only provides *High Anxiety*'s fine special effects but plays Vicki's captive dad Arthur Brisbane.

Most surprising of all, though, are the unexpectedly engaging performances from Brooks' co-writers Ron Clark, Rudy DeLuca, and Barry Levinson, the last two on-screen again after a few small parts in *Silent Movie*. As werewolf-wary Zachary Cartwright, Clark superbly seesaws between sad-sack sobriety one minute, freaked-out frenzy the next; DeLuca lends killer-for-hire Braces just the right measure of sicko-psycho savagery; and Levinson's peevish bellboy Dennis, with his womanish, Bernard Herrmann–type screech, proves just as vital to Brooks' *Psycho* gag as his mindful re-creation of Hitchcock's original. Their long-lasting fame may rest on their talents writing behind the scenes, but their double-duty here works out great; these three men can act.

Truth be told, not very much about this funny, funny picture *doesn't* work, and were *The Producers*, *Blazing Saddles*, and *Young Frankenstein* not so unbelievably, uncommonly good all else gets lost in the shuffle, *High Anxiety* would almost certainly be cited as one of Brooks' best works. Those critics ranking it a notch or two lower than these films are quite right to do so, too, but others, those who don't rank it among Brooks' five or six best movies — well, those critics, bless them, are just plain wrong. Like over-confident load-lifter Brophy, they *think* they've got a firm handle on things, but for all their certainty and expertise they "ain't got it" either — and one of these days they'll see it. It may take a few years, but if scared-silly Richard Thorndyke can finally climb that madhouse tower, surely an overlooked Mel Brooks treasure like this one can scale its way to the top as well. Even Brooks' theme song has it all figured: "*High Anxiety*, you win.*"

CAST: Mel Brooks (Dr. Richard H. Thorndyke); Madeline Kahn (Victoria Brisbane); Cloris Leachman (Nurse Charlotte Diesel); Harvey Korman (Dr. Charles Montague); Ron Carey (Brophy); Howard Morris (Professor Lilloman); Dick Van Patten (Dr. Philip Wentworth); Jack Riley (Desk Clerk); Charlie Callas (Cocker Spaniel); Ron Clark (Zachary Cartwright); Rudy DeLuca (Braces, the Killer); Barry Levinson (Bellboy); Lee Delano (Norton); Richard Stahl (Dr. Baxter); Darrell Zwerling (Dr. Eckhardt); Murphy Dunne (Piano Player); Al Hopson (Man Who Is Shot); Robert "Bob" Ridgely (Flasher); Albert J. Whitlock (Arthur Brisbane); Pearl Shear (Screaming Woman at Gate); Arnold Soboloff (Dr. Colburn); Eddie Ryder (Doctor at Convention); Sandy Helberg (Airport Attendant); Fredric Franklyn (Man); Deborah Dawes (Stewardess); Bernie Kuby (Dr. Wilson); Billy Sands (Customer); Ira Miller (Psychiatrist with Children); Jimmy Martinez (Waiter); Beatrice Colen (Maid); Robert Manuel (Policeman at Airport); Hunter Von Leer (Policeman at Airport); John Dennis (Orderly); Robin Menken (Cocktail Waitress); Frank Campanella (Bartender); Henry Kaiser (New Groom); Bullets Durgom (Man in Phone Booth); Joe Bellan (Male Attendant); Mitchell Bock (Bar Patron); Jay Burton (P atient); Bryan Englund (Orderly #2); Anne Macey (Screaming Woman); Alan U. Schwartz (Psychiatrist).

CREDITS: Director: Mel Brooks; Producer: Mel Brooks; Screenplay: Mel Brooks, Ron Clark, Rudy DeLuca, Barry Levinson; Editor: John C. Howard; Costume Designer: Patricia Norris; Special Visual Effects: Albert J. Whitlock; Music Composer and Conductor: John Morris; "High Anxiety" Lyrics/Music: Mel Brooks, Sung by Mel Brooks; Production Designer: Peter Wooley; Director of Photography: Paul Lohmann; Production Manager: Ernest Wehmeyer; Assistant Director: Jonathan Sanger; Assistant to Producer: Stuart Cornfeld; 2nd Assistant Directors: Mark Johnson, David Sosna; Production Consultant: Ron Clark; Casting: Melnick/Holstra; Continuity Sequences: Harold Michelson; Set Decorators: Richard Kent, Anne MacCauley; Costumers: Jered Green, Nancy Martinelli, Wally Harton; Makeup: Tom Tuttle, Terry Miles; Hairdressers: Sugar Blymyer, Linda Trainoff; Still Photographer: Elliott Marks; Production Mixer: Gene Canamessa; Camera Operator: Ed Koons; Assistant Art Director: Edward Richardson; Assistant Editor: Mary Scott; Apprentice Editor: Thomas G. Jingles; Special Effects: Jack Monroe; Gaffer: Michael J. Marlett; Key Grip: Guy Polzel; Property Master: Bill MacSems; Script Supervisor: Marie Kenney; Assistant to Mr. Brooks: Roslyn Chaitoff; Construction Coordinator: Hendrik Wynands; Orchestrations: John Morris, Jack Hayes, Ralph Burns, Nathan Scott; Rerecording Mixer: Richard Portman; Sound Effects: William Hartman, U.P.S.E., Richard Sperber; Scoring Mixer: Danny Wallin; Music Editor: John R. Harris; Production Accountant: Abe Glazer; Transportation: Transcord; Film Equipment: Panavision; Color: Deluxe; Titles and Opticals: Pacific Title; Released by 20th Century–Fox; A Production of Crossbow Productions, Inc.; 20th Century–Fox Film Corporation, 1977; 94 minutes.

7

★ ★ ★

"It's Good to Be the King!"

History of the World—Part I

★ ★ ★ ★ ★ ★

(1981)

Narrator Orson Welles' look at history begins with carnal, ape-like "Prehistoric Man," then a "Stone Age" segment in which a slow-witted caveman (Sid Caesar) struggles with fire; faces an early art critique; instates primitive marriage; tests the first spear; employs ancient funeral rites; and develops comedy and music based on pain. Next, in an "Old Testament" segment, God gives Moses (Mel Brooks) three stone tablets bearing fifteen Commandments — until, dropping one tablet, Moses quickly improvises and shares with his followers only the remaining ten.

A longer sequence, "The Roman Empire," reveals a busy, decadent Rome where jobless "standup philosopher" Comicus (Mel Brooks) learns from agent pal Swiftus Lazarus (Ron Carey) he is set to perform at Caesar's palace. En route they are dazzled by slave auction reject Josephus (Gregory Hines), who jokes and dances to avoid execution, and pretty palace vestal virgin Miriam (Mary-Margaret Humes), who risks injury protesting a driver's at-

tack on an ailing chariot horse called Miracle. Comicus punches her attacker, pulls a stone from one of Miracle's horseshoes, and is himself rescued from injury by Josephus, who strikes the angry driver — and insults a police officer. Josephus seems sure to die until litter-bearers arrive with lustful Empress Nympho (Madeline Kahn), whom Miriam persuades to grant Josephus a palace job as wine steward.

Performing before gluttonous Emperor Nero (Dom DeLuise), warrior Marcus Vindictus (Shecky Greene), a prissy Court Spokesman (Howard Morris), and others, Comicus risks death when his jokes insult Nero's weight and dishonesty — as does Josephus after he spills wine on the angry ruler. Comicus's admirer Miriam begs help from Empress Nympho, who suggests Nero let them fight each other to the death. Nero agrees, but Comicus and Josephus are too squeamish for murder, battle Nero's men, and flee, escaping by chariot to Judea with Swiftus and Miriam thanks to Miracle, a marijuana smoke screen, and a water-parting assist from a time-displaced Moses. In Judea, Comicus soon works as a waiter for Jesus (John Hurt) and his apostles at The Last Supper, where Renaissance artist Leonardo Da Vinci (Art Metrano) captures the historic event on canvas.

After a song-and-dance from Torquemada (Mel Brooks), the sadistic Grand Inquisitor of "The Spanish Inquisition," the tale shifts to "The French Revolution," where sly Count de Monet (Harvey Korman) and swishy aide Bearnaise (Andreas Voutsinas), fearing revolt, dress palace menial Jacques (Mel Brooks) as look-alike deviate King Louis XVI (Mel Brooks), whose plan to ravish chaste Mademoiselle Rimbaud (Pamela Stephenson) before releasing her jailed father (Spike Milligan) fails when Jacques frees the old man. Soon, however, rabble-rouser Madame Defarge (Cloris Leachman) and a peasant mob take presumed king Jacques and the Rimbauds away for beheading. All seems lost until Miracle, the chariot horse from the "Roman Empire" sketch, defies time and space by galloping up with old pal Josephus, who saves the three prisoners and rides off with them toward a "big ending" followed by coming attractions for a make-believe *History of the World — Part II*: "Hitler on Ice," "A Viking Funeral," and "Jews in Space."

★   ★   ★

Somewhere buried deep inside Mel Brooks' raucous, rollicking 1981 big-screen comedy revue *History of the World — Part I* lies an absolutely brilliant film, a classic, a masterpiece, and every half-dozen minutes or so, just when we've almost given up on it completely, Brooks unearths such an unexpected flash of comic genius he very nearly convinces us the picture we're seeing isn't unspooling half as badly as we've thought and is every bit as good a comedy as he or anyone else ever made. At the top of its game, *History of the World — Part I* rivals the very best moments of *The Producers*, *Blazing Saddles*, and *Young Frankenstein*, and had Brooks somehow managed to sustain this same level of excellence all the way through, and curb whatever ill-heeded impulse led him to seek out an "R" rating instead of his usual 1970s "PG," this freewheeling grab bag of costumes, capering, and cartoon kookiness might well have turned out his best project yet.

Unfortunately, though, while Brooks' and Buck Henry's Secret Agent 86 from TV's *Get Smart* series may have "missed it by that much," *History of the World — Part I* misses its mark a bit wider. As hit-or-miss erratic as it is occasionally inspired (and let's state here again that several moments here rank among the best of his career), Brooks' seventh film seems dead-set on making us squirm, either with restless impatience over its drag-its-heels inertia or just plain red-faced embarrassment over its endless sex, drug, and potty jokes. The satiric intent is clear — strip away mankind's outward nobility and expose us for the unconscionable, self-serving animals we often are — and the image of history as one long catalog of incautious hedonism is doubtless as wickedly accurate as it is unflattering, but, through guilt by association, Brooks comes off as shameless as the hopped-up sex fiends he's vilifying. It may be Old Roman decadents, not Brooks, debauching and doping onscreen, but it's Brooks' film, so he comes out looking as depraved as they do. Like Blake Edwards, who went from merely implying nudity in *A Shot in the Dark* to baring Dudley Moore waist-down in *10* and Julie Andrews waist-up in *S.O.B.* around this same time, Brooks isn't really any more artful just because he's freed up. If anything, it's the other way around.

Making matters worse, Brooks' enthusiastic "tribute to [the] majesty" of epic-makers Cecil B. DeMille and D. W. Griffith suffers the same make-it-or-break-it weakness of 1976's *Silent Movie* as well: a central gimmick that, for all its admirable novelty and aesthetic daring, proves both the film's best friend and worst enemy. In the case of *Silent Movie*, at times that picture's very muteness pushes gags through that would kill most films, yet that same silence also keeps its nutty main trio at arm's length, and robs us of stars Mel Brooks, Marty Feldman, and Dom DeLuise's singular verbal charm. Similarly, because of *History of the World — Part I*'s vaudeville sketch show style, we no sooner start to care about its best characters (Ancient Romans Comicus, Josephus, Miriam, and Swiftus in particular) than Brooks drops them, sometimes for the rest of the film. Where *Silent Movie* asks us to connect with people who don't talk, *History of the World — Part I* connects us with people who do talk, just about win us over, then pretty much vanish into thin air.

This peculiar distancing effect might be irrelevant were the film's individual segments both fast-paced and funny enough to make up for it, like, say, Monty Python's "best of" movie *And Now for Something Completely Different*, resting only a quick couple of minutes on each section before racing right on, but *History of the World — Part I* lopes along in fits and starts, touching just long enough on what does work but lingering way, way too long on what doesn't. No sooner does Brooks hit real pay dirt with something truly special (a tablet-dropping Moses' impromptu reduction of fifteen commandments to ten; his 2,000-Year-Old-Man-ish robbery at bow-point; the doubling of the Las Vegas Caesar's Palace for Nero's; the "Inquisition" song; Leonardo Da Vinci showing up in person to paint the Last Supper) than along comes something so snail's-pace lazy we can hardly believe the near-nonstop comic energy of *The Producers* and the

spin-its-wheels listlessness of this funny but much less spirited film were written and directed by the same man.

Take Brooks' "Roman Empire" section, the segment with the most noticeable extremes of cinematic-comedic highs and lows. Brooks wins us over early with his expertly staged camera pans of wacky Old Roman street markets (funny stuff, when it's not wallowing in crudeness, if nowhere near as upbeat and animated as its counterpart in *The Twelve Chairs*), and he follows these strengths with others, too, from Johnny Carson–era show-biz in-jokes to the welcome return of Madeline Kahn, Howard Morris, and Dom DeLuise. "The Roman Empire" rarely achieves the hurricane hilarity material like this demands, though, especially the "Caesar's Palace" bit, yet no one on-camera or off- seems bothered by how much time gets eaten away per laugh. It's as if Fritz Freleng's 1955 Bugs Bunny short "Roman Legion Hare," with all its Nero, chariot, and soldier gags, were being reshot at TV movie length but just a fraction of the speed, with Bugs kept still way too long while Freleng shows off his fancy-schmancy cartoon costumes and sets. The scene shifts and shot cuts *should* fly fast and furious, the zingers bouncing like pinballs, but that's just not happening; a truly great cast has been costumed and coiffured just fine, then left all dressed up with no place to go.

Indeed, Warner Bros.' great old Bugs Bunny cartoons make a fair point of reference for a film like this. How many history-mangling one-reelers did the Warners gang cook up for old Bugs, and all of them zipping along at a pace the post–'70s Brooks might have done well to take pointers from? Remember Bugs' medieval mockeries "Knights Must Fall," "Knightmare Hare," "Knighty Knight Bugs," and "Shishkabugs"? His pirate flicks "Buccaneer Bunny" and "Captain Hareblower"? His American Revolution gala "Bunker

Hill Bunny"? The Columbus caper "Hare We Go"? The Viking romp "Prince Violent"? In cartoon after cartoon Bugs ran roughshod over cowpokes, camel-drivers, and cavemen, always at a much, much faster clip, and 1953's "Yankee Doodle Bugs," in which he narrates a cockeyed U.S. history lesson on everything from King George III to Betsy Ross to George Washington, might have taught *History of the World — Part I* a thing or two about keeping the craziness moving. In films like these, he who hesitates is lost.

Well — semi-lost, anyway. Brooks' movie keeps spinning back on itself too ingeniously to lose its way entirely. His big "French Revolution" finale, for instance, provides one of his all-time cleverest endings, brilliantly blasting all logic and, as in

Blazing Saddles, celebrating film's unique capacity for anything-can-happen unpredictability. With his own guillotine-slated Jacques spirited off by Gregory Hines' "Roman Empire" rescuer (driving a horse named Miracle, no less), almost as if Jacques and his Old Rome counterpart Comicus were the same man, Brooks' wild wrap-up makes little sense, really, but what better way to wind up a movie this structurally unbalanced and jagged? It's all nonsense, and thus pure Mel Brooks: preposterous, inventive, totally off-the-wall.

For all its "Looney Tunes"–speedy potential, however, the Ancient Rome section trudges along more like some toga-clad elephant than a WB Tasmanian Devil, spotlighting one by one tap great Gregory Hines as slave-for-sale Josephus, Dom

Fleeing soldiers dispatched by a furious Emperor Nero, comedy agent Swiftus Lazarus (Ron Carey), vestal virgin Miriam (Mary-Margaret Humes), palace wine steward Josephus (Gregory Hines), and "stand-up philosopher" Comicus (Mel Brooks) narrowly avoid capture, in the "Roman Empire" segment of Brooks' *Caesar's Hour*–type revue *History of the World—Part I* (1981), Brooks' seventh film, and the first since *The Producers* crediting him as the sole screenwriter.

DeLuise as spoiled-rotten Nero, Brooks as joke-slinger Comicus, Madeline Kahn as sex-crazed Empress Nympho — yet never asking any of these stars to employ much energy. Hines does some mild sandal-shuffling yet moves just a few feet, music-free, so we barely sense his huge talent from what little we see here; once-irrepressible DeLuise, whose post–*Silent Movie* weight gain suits his new pampered potentate persona just dandy, needn't exert himself much beyond his *Spaceballs* voice-overs later on; Brooks' purposely unfunny stand-up needs camera action we just don't get; and Kahn's insatiate empress chiefly just loafs or reviews her stud-troops, with all the visual ado of a schoolgirl choosing sides in gym. As in *Robin Hood: Men in Tights*, whose characters often act as if the *Wild Kingdom* folks have just shot them all with tranquilizer guns, the "Roman Empire" gang lacks nearly enough get-up-and-go.

Occasionally Brooks and editor John C. Howard do pace a major out-of-the-blue "Roman Empire" gag just fast enough, of course — say, when Brooks' time-defying Moses, arms aloft, parts the waters in mid-holdup, for one (though this gag may offend some), or Da Vinci's gung-ho prep work for an apostle "group portrait," even if it does follow some religiously disquieting by-play between Christ and Comicus — but little else Ancient Rome–ish builds up much steam. Every time we're ready to leave behind Brooks' marijuana-stoned pursuers to rejoin our heroes' far more exciting chariot escape, the film cuts back to them and drags it all out longer, and while in *Blazing Saddles* such flip-flopping works great (recall that great fever-pitch fight scene, whose cuts back to Buddy Bizarre's hissy-fit gays heighten the finale's comic momentum, not stalls it), *History of the World — Part I* doesn't know when to quit. More furiously edited, and with enough slam-bang *Blaz-*

ing Saddles–type frenzy behind it, this might be unforgettable; as is, we're re-assembling it all in our heads, making tighter cuts, adding more music, trying to give the scene more "oomph."

Musically, in fact, even Brooks' long-time tunesmith John Morris seems only semi-inspired this time around (one of Morris's best *The Twelve Chairs* melodies even turns up, recycled for the "Viking Funeral" preview), composing his overall least engaging Brooks score until *Life Stinks*. His tunes here are far better than most of *us* could come up with, certainly, but his work in *The Producers* lays his output here in the dust, and the instrumentals for Brooks' own compositions actually give the film more buoyancy than Morris's disconcertingly muffled, lyric-free title song, which does at least suggest the epic scope of Griffith and DeMille just as Brooks surely intended. The song works, but it's not nearly as much fun as his theme for 1977's *High Anxiety*— a movie which, even with a near-identical cast, stays well-paced whether Morris writes music for it or not.

Brooks' and Ronny Graham's waggish "The Inquisition" song (an instant classic, thanks to the nutty lyrics they've given their own tune) helps a good deal, as does Brooks' own phony sequel sneak-peek song "Jews in Space" (an embryonic version of his 1993 *Robin Hood: Men in Tights* theme), but even these and the best of Morris's work can only really counteract the film's nailed-to-the-floor inaction just so far. The music feels fairly skimpy this time too, creating the uneasy feeling (as does the directing and editing) that Brooks' actors, instead of getting plenty of back-up help in post-production, have been abandoned. Even when Comicus and Josephus flee Roman guards, Morris spices things up only fitfully (at least compared to, say, John Addison's ongoing fight-and-chase music in 1970's *Start the Revolution*

Without Me), and we yearn for all that madness-run-amuck exuberance so much that when chariot-mates Brooks, Hines, Ron Carey, and Mary-Margaret Humes belt out a riff on Johnny Burke and Jimmy Van Heusen's great old title number from 1942's *Road to Morocco*, we're suddenly having such a fine time we're disappointed they stop so soon. Unlike in *High Anxiety*, which benefits from a single plot and lickety-split pacing, in *History of the World— Part I* the material is too often left to sink or swim on its own, and what little action we're given is just slack enough that, when Morris falls silent, we really miss him. The whole "Caesar's Palace" visit badly needs a *Blazing Saddles*–type pick-me-up (like *Spaceballs'* spaceship set, Nero's hall needs lots of razzle-dazzle to remedy all that pin-drop-in-a-morgue emptiness), and the "death battle" between Comicus and Josephus cries out for a little high-octane action music to jazz up the stock-still camerawork. Not to belabor the WB idea, but Milt Franklyn or Carl Stalling surely wouldn't cast poor Bugs adrift this long.

Far more than Brooks' earlier movies, in fact, this one often looks and feels as much like a filmed stage show as film, with attention-grabbing costumes and sets but little action, and given its "revue movie" premise maybe that's intended. In honest-to-goodness floorboards-and-footlights revues, the only movement comes when a theatergoer physically stands up to try another seat, the only editing when the actors forget their lines, or the curtain drops too early, or somebody gets yanked off-set with a stage hook. None of this alters the fact that the film feels mobility-starved, though, and don't think the critics didn't notice. Roger Ebert's *Chicago Sun-Times* review, for one, decries the "expensive sets sitting around waiting for Brooks to do something funny in front of them," while Pauline Kael's *New Yorker* write-up notes that even when Brooks and his pals "are

racing about, the movie feels static" anyway. Indeed, it's almost as if Brooks imagines — not that we really believe it, given his wondrous visual expertise in *The Twelve Chairs* and *Young Frankenstein*— that with stars and sets like these, details like cuts and camera angles don't matter.

A little more characterization and plot focus would have helped some of this too. In *The Films of Mel Brooks* Neil Sinyard cites several likely influences on Brooks' seventh film: Richard Lester's 1966 take on *A Funny Thing Happened on the Way to the Forum*, the madcap Roman Empire musical with former Brooks loony Zero Mostel and based on the Broadway hit co-written by Brooks' *Your Show of Shows* buddy Larry Gelbart; Lester's witty 1973 satiric swashbuckler *The Three Musketeers*, whose featured player Spike Milligan Brooks uses again here; the Monty Python gang's 1979 Crucifixion-era comedy *Life of Brian*, again with Spike Milligan in a bit role; Charlie Chaplin's 1940 rise-of-Hitler satire *The Great Dictator*, whose peasant-poses-as-tyrant plot Brooks' "French Revolution" section vaguely calls to mind; and several others. All of these films tap the same basic material Brooks has fun with here, but with one key difference: where *History of the World— Part I* rarely follows the same heroes and villains for more than half-hour at a stretch, each of these other movies sticks with a single comedy-adventure all the way through.

Perhaps the one genre spoof Sinyard doesn't hint at as an inspiration to Brooks (though likely it should have, as it plays better as sheer film) is TV mainstay Bud Yorkin's already alluded-to farce *Start the Revolution Without Me*, starring Brooks' own Gene Wilder and Donald Sutherland as *two* sets of mismatched twins, one privileged, one pauper, who botch last-minute efforts to avert the French Revolution. The parallels to Brooks' 1789 saga are obvious — the rich vs. poor theme, the mistaken identities, the Louis XVI palace setting, the presence of Orson Welles as inside-scoop narrator — yet Yorkin's film hits the mark so much more often one almost — almost — wishes Brooks had been a little less artistically ambitious and made a full-length story of one of his best segments.

Running slightly shorter than Brooks' film, its crazy scrambling about given several times the hustle-bustle and backed up by composer John Addison with several times the music, Yorkin's movie has nearly ninety-one minutes to tell just one story, and create full-blown characters of finer idiosyncratic depth. Hugh Griffith's King Louis XVI, a sort of reverse-gender version of Marion Lorne's lovably dotty Aunt Clara on *Bewitched*, is such a frail, pitiable old cuckold he quickly steals our hearts, but with Brooks' broader, raunchier Louis, one-dimensionalized to play up the vileness-of-humanity angle, what we see is what we get. He's more attention-grabbing because he's more shocking, yes, but it's Brooks' outrageousness we respond to, not psychological depth; Louis stands out, but only in the way Brooks' cartoony Nazi mad scientist does in *The Muppet Movie* — as caricature, not character. And what of the evil Gene Wilder twin, with the "pet" stuffed falcon, the hissy-fit insistence on being named first, the kinky bedroom games, the paranoid outrage over imagined insults? For all Brooks' laudable structural risk-taking, character-wise *History of the World — Part I* has few such involved creations — not unexpectedly, no, but disappointing even so.

Many critics were disappointed too, and not just about characterizations. Leonard Maltin has called the movie "scattershot," with "gags that range from hilarious to hideous," a film whose material finally "all just lies there" with "no more momentum"; *Variety* bewailed the "inconsistent level of inventiveness" and "fee-

ble" French Revolution segment that "comes up lame"; and Roger Ebert called it "a rambling, undisciplined, sometimes embarrassing failure." "Failure" may be a tad harsh, but Ebert's right thinking this is no *The Producers*, and, critics ourselves, we too can't help mentally re-writing, re-directing, and re-editing a little when the momentum starts lagging.

During the summer of its first release, Ebert hit upon the movie's chief frailty when noting Brooks "never seems to have a clear idea of the rationale" behind what's onscreen. Having made six single-plot films in a row, evidently Brooks simply wants to make an old-fashioned revue, like *New Faces* or his 1950s TV work — a fine idea, too, granting rich opportunity to, say, write Sid Caesar that great caveman skit *Your Show of Shows* never got around to, or Howard Morris that big, splashy Roman Empire skit NBC never could have afforded on new-show-a-week live TV.

Unhappily, though, despite its all-too accurate observation that the human race has been made up of pretty much nothing but greedy, appetite-driven deviates from Day One (terrific gag material, proof yet again Brooks is never savvier than when he's satirizing human failings), the film reveals no particular logic behind, say, spending only about ten minutes total in the Stone Age and Old Testament but over an hour in Ancient Rome and 1789 France. For much of the sprawling length of "The Roman Empire," after Brooks' five-minutes-per-era pacing goes right out the cinematic window, we're still trying to get our bearings. Up until now we've thought we'd seen what he's is up to, but all of a sudden we're not so sure, and when his stand-alone "Spanish Inquisition" section briefly revives the pattern he's already rejected once, we're stumped all over again. For all its strengths, and it has many, *History of the World — Part I* needs some pretty significant re-conceptualizing to truly work; it needs to be rethought, reformulated, re-visualized to really make it to the top rung. Small wonder *Variety* found the film "disappointingly uneven."

Consider: Brooks wants to survey human folly and depravity through the ages, and that's a fantastic plan, as well as the film's single most effective unifying theme. Yet with Earth's entire multi-millennial history to select from Brooks picks so few events to make fun of (cinematically overused ones at that, mostly) we can't help feeling cheated. The Spanish Inquisition is fairly fresh terrain, excepting the old "Nobody expects the Spanish Inquisition!" *Monty Python's Flying Circus* skit and a few other pop culture nods, but films like *Roman Scandals* (1933), *Androcles and the Lion* (1952), and *A Funny Thing Happened on the Way to the Forum* (1966) had already giggled their way through Old Rome long ago, and *Start the Revolution Without Me* had played Louis XVI, Marie Antoinette, and crew for laughs over a decade before. The Stone Age segment would get upstaged by *Caveman* the very year of its release too, and two sitcoms, *The Flintstones* (1960–66) and *It's About Time* (1966–67) had mined rock-and-cave gags on TV every single week for years. Even the Old Testament section had been beaten to the punch at least twice not much earlier, by *Monty Python's Life of Brian* (1979) and *Wholly Moses* (1980), leaving Brooks precious little to laugh at that, in one way or another, hadn't already been laughed at before.

Brooks thinks the picture needs a narrator, too, and even recruits no lesser talent than fellow writer-director-actor Orson Welles as conductor — again, stellar thinking, provided Welles doesn't become intrusive — yet after the first five minutes he drops Welles for so long at a stretch we've nearly forgotten he's even in the film. One can't imagine many more authoritative tour guides than Welles, who'd

already narrated not only Yorkin's film but the 1961 Bible epic *King of Kings* (James Earl Jones maybe? William Conrad? John Huston, director-narrator of *The Bible*?), but still, the question remains: Why hire Welles at all if after the first few minutes Brooks plans to have him do little more than read off placards? Even admitting the whole thing's starting to wear thin by the time Brooks has Welles calling his cavemen by name (history records the actual names of these guys? Come on!), why bring Welles aboard at all if he's so halfhearted about using him?

Brooks believes his historical stopovers need distinct title card-signaled section divisions as well, and we're behind him one hundred percent, yet we're mystified why some of the actual sections themselves ("The Stone Age," "The Old Testament," etc.) last only slightly longer than his mock "Coming Attractions" trailer for an imaginary *History of the World— Part II* while others ("The Roman Empire," "The French Revolution") take up roughly a third of the film. The *basics* of design exist here, yet beyond mere chronological order and its insightful history-as-depravity subtext, the movie seems aimless. Why hover so long over some eras but not others, and why call the film *History of the World — Part I* and cover so little real history? Moses is here, sure, and Nero, and King Louis XVI, but even if the *Part I* section of the title means the film is intended (albeit jokingly) to carry Brooks' cruise through time only so far (that is, the French Revolution), why cover just six incidents along the way? Where are Atilla the Hun and Galileo and Joan of Arc and Columbus and Shakespeare? Why no Genghis Khan or Confucius or Socrates or Cleopatra?

Ironically, perhaps the very best solution to Brooks' organizational difficulties lay under his nose all along: namely, his old TV-and-recording partner Carl

Reiner and their delightfully aged yet age-less creation, Brooks' seen-it-all, done-it-all 2,000 Year Old Man. Mel Brooks and Carl Reiner penning *History of the World — Part I* together — now that's a revue movie we'd like to see, yet Brooks tackles the writing this time entirely on his own, to far lesser effect than in *The Producers*, sorry to say, and Reiner's involvement as no-nonsense straight man to Brooks' daffy old coot is precisely what this film needs. Without Reiner on hand to ask questions ("Did you know King Arthur?"; "Robin Hood — did he exist?"), all those now-classic "2,000 Year Old Man" routines might be little more than one man's aimless, incoherent ramblings — hilarious ones, yes, but ramblings all the same. Even granting most of the recordings' big laughs come from Brooks (he's clearly Costello to Reiner's Abbott, Lewis to Reiner's Martin), Reiner's extraordinary gift for making even Brooks' most off-the-cuff randomness feel as well polished as a Reiner-scripted *Dick Van Dyke Show* episode is in large part what made the whole concept work. Mel Brooks' nutty spontaneity as the Old Man gave the duo's superb exchanges their unbridled silliness, but it was Carl Reiner's question-formulating reporter who most gave them structure — or at least made us *think* they had structure, which in the long run may be every bit as important as the real thing.

Indeed, Brooks' first film of the '80s feels like such a natural outgrowth of "The 2,000 Year Old-Man" one marvels he didn't just bring Reiner in and make its Old-Man-and-Interviewer pattern the basis for the whole film. If *History of the World — Part I* needs one big change to make it all work, it's some sort of sensible central framework for its disparate elements to hang on, and his and Reiner's classic "Old Man" shtick might have provided the perfect skeleton. What would have been so wrong (other than that

Brooks had a yen to script by himself again, something he'd netted an Oscar for on *The Producers*) if the story had been told in interview form, with Brooks' irascible old immortal relating firsthand his recollections of the great events of human history? Why not have the Old Man tell Reiner (and show us in flashback) how he attended the first cave man funeral, saw Moses bring the Ten Commandments down Mt. Sinai, served Christ's apostles at the Last Supper? Brooks might have had to alter his phony "Coming Attractions" finale a little (the "Jews in Space" gag, while funny, breaks from the film's titular "world history" proposition anyway), but even if this section were lost completely, it's a small price to pay for a film with a stronger spine to support it, not to mention a singularly lovable lead character to boot.

Regrettably, however, the *History of the World — Part I* Brooks finally settles on is a curiously shapeless affair, all lopsided and off balance, like unwatched clay on a potter's wheel. At times it even seems to lose sight of its own premise (as funny as "Jews in Space" is, it's not history), and occasionally even Brooks' behind-the-scenes expenditures feel a bit off. Should a revue picture look like a real movie, or should its visual style somehow testify to its stage show roots? Evidently even Brooks can't decide, shooting his big "French Revolution" climax with *You Are There*-ish semirealism, and his "Stone Age" and "Old Testament" bits with papier-mâché boulders and painted-backdrop deserts that always look a touch lighter or hang a tad flatter than the real thing. His "Spanish Inquisition" set alone, a sprawling epic with its Olympic-size moat, enormous one-armed bandit, and giant underwater menorah, takes up so much space and looks so great the James Bond people could have used it for a grand finale — but why devote so many of one's resources to just one scene? Why not spend a few of those man-hours and dollars shooting Sid Caesar's caveman outdoors, or having Brooks' Moses tromp down a *real* mountain? Outdoor filming doesn't come cheap, but surely the "Spanish Inquisition" set needn't be *that* big.

What's finally most irksome about *History of the World — Part I*, though, is how boorish and, to some, even downright dirty it seems after Brooks' earlier films. We can see what's ahead from the very first scene, when Brooks' Stanley Kubrick–inspired "Dawn of Man" segment veers from "G"-rated *2001: A Space Odyssey* tribute to gutter-humored locker room sleaze. As satire, admittedly, what Brooks delivers hits dead-on (as soon as the words "Our Forefathers" turn up on-screen, reducing mankind to a race of salacious, sex-obsessed apes, we can see humanity isn't coming out of this unscathed), but surely he needn't have resorted to gags this near-pornographic to let us know we're all brute beasts. Animals *kill* too, after all, and having our now "civilized" forebears slowly rise to full height and suddenly turn on one another like savages might have cut us down to size equally well, man-to-man violence being at least as vile as anything ape-to-ape. (One idea: Show Brooks' primates fighting early on, gradually rise up illuminated with the spark of humanity — and then go right on fighting exactly as before.) As it is, Brooks' opening makes both the best and worst possible first impressions — best because we can see Brooks' satiric talents are fired up full-blast, worst because we're watching guiltily, like a child with a stack of *Hustlers*.

One would like to report that this first joke is just a fluke, just a momentary lapse of good taste, but the sad truth is the film only gets worse in this regard, not better. Except maybe its brief "Old Testament" bit and end-of-film mock promos, not one segment can be seen straight through in polite company — "polite" here meaning anyone who prefers his comedy clean and classy to crude and lewd. The *Animal House* beer-and-toga types will love this movie, and one can easily picture housefuls of Friday night high-schoolers snickering like crazy at every last expletive and excretion, at least till the folks get home (assuming they'd even care, having left a pack of hormone-charged teenagers unsupervised to start with). For just about everyone else, though — well, just forget right now about inviting the Bible class over, or the girlfriend's parents, or anyone from the school board, and by the time we're a millimeter away from Paris gang rape jokes, we've never missed the '60s TV innocence of *Get Smart* so much in our lives. Urine, flatulence, orgies, incest — the fixation on body parts and body functions never wears down, but it wears out its welcome early, and the way the scenes slog along so only makes things worse. Bad enough Brooks thrusts such repugnant sights as urinating cavemen our way (which does, at least, carry some witty satiric implications about the artist-critic relationship; we'll grant it that) — must he drag it all out so long?

Some of the costumes offend, too. Roman orgy candidates, buttocks bared, line up, rear ends dead-ahead; Gregory Hines' Josephus dons what amounts to an ostrich feather loincloth for one of Brooks' raciest sight gags ever; and Pamela Stephenson's Mademoiselle Rimbaud sports a dress cut just enough inch-fractions low VCR freeze-frame buttons are bound to be clicking away. Add to this all the sexual innuendo and downright vulgarities (which, in the Roman Senate scene, does at least function satirically, and in the *Oedipus Rex* joke somehow appears highbrow and lowbrow at the same time), and the reasoning behind the "R" rating becomes all too clear. One hates to sound

Mel Brooks in Roman regalia for *History of the World—Part I.*

so prudish, since nobody expects '80s Brooks to play like '60s Disney anyway, and no one's denying his constitutional right to make movies like this, but it's a huge relief to see him tone things down a little in *Spaceballs* later on. Envelope-pushing is one thing, but a Brooks film shouldn't make us feel smutty for laughing, or socially irresponsible giving it our support, as if buying a ticket to it or renting it gives Hollywood the go-ahead to befoul us more. Granted, Brooks' gross-out body-process jokes look tame alongside those in *There's Something About Mary* and *Scary Movie*, but we're grateful beyond measure he got most of this out of his system.

Even cleaned up a little and rated "PG," however, *History of the World — Part I* would still suffer a bit. Steve Gordon's 1981 hit *Arthur* includes off-color elements too, but mellow and light as it is, it's also a stronger film, not just because it picks one story and sticks to it, but because it uses its time to create rich, three-dimensional characterizations that emotionally really do connect. One does question the wisdom behind lovable drunkard jokes (though it's surely no more reckless than the marijuana jokes here), but Dudley Moore's lovelorn, spoiled little rich boy Arthur Bach will outlive Brooks' Moses, Comicus, Torquemada, Jacques, and King Louis XVI in the popular imagination even if *History of the World — Part I* airings outnumber *Arthur* TV reruns ten to one.

Granted, the friendship between Brooks as "standup philosopher" Comicus and Gregory Hines as slave pal Josephus has promise (we feel for Josephus when he's mistreated, and admire Comicus for not "cutting him loose" to save himself), as does the way urine-disposer Jacques uses his King Louis masquerade not to deflower Mademoiselle Rimbaud but help her free her captive father. Since these two relationships are better developed than,

say, those in his "Stone Age" bit, we see Brooks really can do better character work given more time, and again we wonder if he shouldn't have made two films here, not one. The notion of Comicus and Josephus, free man and slave, joining forces to flee Nero is a fine idea for a whole film — a sort of lunatic, character-driven hybrid of *Spartacus, Some Like It Hot, The Defiant Ones*, and *The Three Stooges Meet Hercules*. The same goes for the Jacques/Mademoiselle Rimbaud story; one can imagine how Brooks might have taken the "court flunky poses as king to save girl's father" idea and really run with it. Sadly, though, since both stories only run about sitcom length, the characters can develop just so far, and since neither is even half as clever as Brooks' and Buck Henry's *Get Smart* pilot, the added human interplay can only make up for so much. Put simply, Brooks has in effect divided his usual hour-and-a-half movie into two thirty-plus-minute sitcom pilots, with fifteen minutes' worth or so of hit-and-miss ape man, caveman, song and dance, and mock trailer material slipped in.

Hats off to Brooks for trying something so artistically risky, though, and a few critics who normally might have stomped him black-and-blue for hit-or-miss disorganization seem not to mind this time. Who complains about third act troubles in a film with no plot? Not *The New Yorker*'s Pauline Kael, who'd charged Brooks with filmic "ineptitude" and "amateurish" camera placement in her semi-positive *The Producers* review, yet has a fine time here even if his *Young Frankenstein* expertise has fallen off. She does suggest he "isn't a great director," but she's so in love with him as "a great personality," an "uncontrollable original" she barely minds the no-rules slackness. It loosens him up, she says, and lets his "maniacal, exuberant compulsion to flaunt show-biz Jewishness" burst through. For Kael, the film is about "show business through the ages," is an uproarious "parody of the Broadway-Hollywood approach" to subjects from prejudice to religion to poverty. She's right, too, but it's still amazing she prefers this movie to, say, *High Anxiety*, even though that film is so much better scripted, edited, acted, and directed it puts this later picture to shame.

Disproportionate and sluggish as it is, though, Brooks' first film of the '80s still looks like a minor classic compared to most comedies released that year. *Arthur* got better reviews, as did writer-director Alan Alda's *The Four Seasons*, and a few others like *Stripes* and *Time Bandits*, but in many respects Brooks' movie came out smelling like a rose. *Chu Chu and the Philly Flash* didn't do stars Alan Arkin and Carol Burnett any favors, and *Charlie Chan and the Curse of the Dragon Queen*, starring two-time Oscar winner Peter Ustinov, sounds like a winner but didn't win over most audiences. Sitcom star Tony Danza worked from stronger scripts nearly every week on *Taxi* than the one he signed up for with *Going Ape!*, and his TV costar Andy Kaufman fared little better with the robot love story *Heartbeeps*. Actor-director Jerry Lewis had a surprise hit with *Hardly Working*, his first big release in years, but nobody imagined he'd outclassed 1963's *The Nutty Professor*; the Chevy Chase vehicles *Modern Problems* and *Under the Rainbow* left fans longing for the days of *Foul Play* and *Seems Like Old Times*; and *The Cannonball Run*, a huge hit, brought '70s superstar Burt Reynolds some of the worst reviews of his career. Let's just come right out and say it: a few bright spots aside, comedy-wise 1981 was one lousy year.

Nothing's lousy about this film's casting, though. A handful of favorite faces are missing, sure — Gene Wilder is noticeably absent, as are Kenneth Mars, Dick Shawn, Marty Feldman, and several others we wouldn't mind seeing again — but otherwise *History of the World — Part I* is the ultimate Mel Brooks family reunion. Where else could one find Sid Caesar, Madeline Kahn, Dom DeLuise, Ron Carey, Howard Morris, Cloris Leachman, and Harvey Korman all in one place?

The only problem is that most of these actors actually *don't* appear all in one place, their characters often being kept apart, if not by separate subplots, by entirely different story lines set whole centuries apart. The effect is a little like watching Irwin Allen's 1957 film *The Story of Mankind*, whose title and episodic structure *History of the World — Part I* somewhat resembles, thrilled by the prospect of seeing the Marx Brothers reunited on film for the first time in eleven years — only to discover good old Groucho, Chico, and Harpo aren't even reassembled as a team!

Keeping them together or apart, however, *History of the World — Part I* spotlights some great, great actors, its own writer-director himself headlining the whole affair in high style. Given his career-long love affair with Jewish-themed humor, and especially after his phenomenal success as the 2,000 Year Old Man, Mel Brooks couldn't possibly have found a better Moses than Mel Brooks (funnyman Brooks is rarely more endearing than when he plays old men, as his marvelous Uncle Phil characterizations from TV's *Mad About You* so well proved), and his singing, dancing Torquemada during his bigot-bashing "Spanish Inquisition" bit is so spectacular that after the Grand Inquisitor hits his last high note the movie just can't top it. What a delightful performance!

Brooks makes a sensationally insidious King Louis XVI too, gunning down commoners like clay pigeons, scoping out hoop skirts like some triple-X porn addict, and quickly turning "It's good to be the king" into one of his most quoted lines.

Louis is such a depraved, dirty-minded little deviate we couldn't stand too much of him (the whole unsavory "French Revolution" section leaves us feeling tainted a little), but Brooks does a superb job creating a second villain so unlike his first one; his singing, swinging Torquemada is a black-hearted scoundrel too, but he looks like Mother Teresa beside Louis, who seems utterly beyond redemption. Brooks' clown-for-hire good guy Comicus is a far more lovable creation, enough so we wouldn't mind seeing more of him once "The Roman Empire" wraps — which, in effect, we do since Brooks' urine-hauling lackey Jacques from "The French Revolution" is essentially the same character, as we realize upon the Frenchman's unexpected "reunion" with Comicus's slave buddy Josephus at the end of the film.

As for Josephus himself, dancer Gregory Hines does just fine in a part initially slated for *Blazing Saddles* co-writer Richard Pryor — who, thanks to either studio insistence or unforeseen health crises never was able to join Brooks onscreen. It might have been nice had Pryor been replaced again with Cleavon Little, then still very much alive and well and whose twinkle-eyed sparkle always lends a little extra pizzazz, but Hines had quite a career ahead (*The Cotton Club*, *White Nights*, *Tap*), and Brooks was smart to grab him on the ground floor. It's too bad he's given so many gross-out jokes (the ostrich plume eunuch gag; a really disgusting bit involving a plastic tongue), but even with a rather sober-looking outward appearance Hines holds his end of the funny business amazingly well. He's perhaps not the ideal Brooks choice (the name "Gregory Hines" doesn't exactly shout hilarity like "Marty Feldman" or "Dom DeLuise"), but considering how many career comedians surround him, what Hines so ably pulls off here is a minor miracle.

Like Hines, *Blazing Saddles* and *Silent Movie* graduate Dom DeLuise undertakes some pretty undistinguished comedy too (sorry to say, the flatulence gags aren't the half of it), but his depiction of one of Old Rome's sorriest overlords as a man of slothful, gluttonous decadence matches exactly the popular conception, sprung mostly from Hollywood performances by the likes of Peter Ustinov and Charles Laughton, of Nero as a lazy, food-gobbling hothead. At the time probably only Ustinov himself (remember his rum-besotted *Blackbeard's Ghost* pirate and coin-clutching *Robin Hood* lion-prince for Disney?), or possibly James Coco (still fresh from his cuisine-craving Hercule Poirot takeoff in *Murder by Death*), could have made a comparable Nero, and while we miss the roller-coaster energy DeLuise brought to live-wire Father Fyodor in *The Twelve Chairs*, not to mention the cherubic sweetness of *Silent Movie*'s Dom Bell, we can't deny that his slower, more laid-back surliness this time fits Nero's cinema-fed image to a tee. Even given physically straitjacketing material like this, the one-of-a-kind DeLuise still shines like a beacon.

Playing the sex-obsessed Empress Nympho, the ever-extraordinary Madeline Kahn does nice work too but has less going for her here than in her first three Brooks films, chiefly because the character's sketch show confines limit our getting to know her. Of course, Kahn's a natural scene-stealer no matter what project she's in, from her 1972 *What's Up Doc?* debut right up to her career-closing years on TV's *Cosby*, and we can't take our eyes off her again here, even when she's playing a part so unabashedly matter-of-fact about her own promiscuity she makes even *Blazing Saddles*' Lili Von Shtupp look schoolmarm-ish. Oddly, even when Nympho acts noble and generous, as when twice rescuing an execution-fated Comicus and Josephus as a favor to Mary-Margaret Humes' vestal virgin Miriam, she seems more sketchily drawn than genuinely multi-dimensional. At least when *Blazing Saddles'* Lili aids Sheriff Bart it's because she's fallen head-over-heels in love with him, but Nympho lacks any particular motivation save helping out Miriam. Why she likes Miriam, though, we're never told, and since Kahn and Dom DeLuise have almost zero screen contact, we're none too clear on how Nympho feels about her husband either. Kahn's just as leap-off-the-screen watchable as ever, but Brooks' praiseworthy attempt to make *History of the World — Part I* something offbeat and special undercuts the character's appeal a bit.

The same holds for Harvey Korman, playing a character almost as disagreeably nasty as Brooks' King Louis XVI. We're amused by Korman's leering, sneering Count de Monet, but we can't follow his exploits even half so spiritedly as his *Blazing Saddles* and *High Anxiety* villains, nor his one incontestable Brooks good guy, *Dracula: Dead and Loving It*'s flabbergasted, blustery old Dr. Seward. Korman himself we like just fine (Korman we *always* like just fine), but the part itself is pretty one-note compared to what we know this former *Carol Burnett Show* loony is capable of. We're delighted seeing him again, even taking pratfalls that probably sound a lot funnier on paper than they are onscreen — but couldn't Brooks put him to better use than this?

We're glad to see Korman's *High Anxiety* crony Cloris Leachman too, but the same problem holds: maximum talent, minimal screen time. Her *A Tale of Two Cities*–inspired crone Madame Defarge arrives too late in the story to linger with us long after the closing credits, yet Leachman launches herself into the part just as rabidly as if she's been hired to play it all the way through. Thanks to some expert makeup, Leachman has never looked worse, either, not even in *Young Frankenstein* or *High Anxiety*, but with Brooks this

actually quite fetching actress always seems to have a field day cosmetics- and costume-wise, like some fun-loving grade schooler playing dress-up at Halloween. Brooks lets her really run wild this time, too, quite literally warts and all, and while thick-accented rabble-rouser Defarge repels as much as she attracts, Leachman scores high on guts alone — especially in a part without benefit of real single-plot drama behind it.

As Comicus's agent-pal Swiftus Lazarus (remember famous show-biz rep Swifty Lazar?), third-time Brooks cast member Ron Carey has a little more emotional impact, but we lose him right after he, Comicus, Josephus, and Mirium escape to Judea — unfortunately, just as he's starting to become a team player. As he does so many characters, Brooks scripts Swiftus's language a little more crudely than absolutely necessary, but the *Barney Miller* regular's boyish enthusiasm makes up for a lot, even when the camera is so busy focusing on Comicus's Nero-galling standup routine it virtually ignores Swiftus, reduced by then to shouting warnings from half a set away. Carey's a natural comedian, and more than one of Brooks' later pictures could have used him.

One such picture, at least, 1991's *Life Stinks*, did use Howard Morris, too, whose role as Nero's emasculate Court Spokesman doesn't really ask much of him, especially since this is the same human pogo stick who gave even the already excellent *Your Show of Shows* a definite shot in the arm and after just five appearances made rock-tossing nitwit Ernest T. Bass one of *The Andy Griffith Show*'s most popular characters. Morris isn't bad here at all, just squandered a bit, the handful of lines he has here being not nearly enough to develop a real character. His delivery is as good as ever, and we like the "cretins at Sparta" wordplay, but the part itself is so scanty we'd never even notice he's meant to be gay if Nero and Comicus didn't point it out. While it's doubtful we'd want the character lingering on the film's full length, fans who loved sentimental, grandfatherly Prof. Lilloman from *High Anxiety* are bound to feel sorry about the lost screen time.

As vestal virgin Miriam, pretty newcomer Mary-Margaret Humes makes a surprisingly endearing Brooksian love interest, supplying a sort of Doris Day–like, Meg Ryan–ish guilelessness we find pretty refreshing in a film so loaded to the gills with sleazos, sickos, and scuzzos. Having Miriam make the Comicus/Josephus/Swiftus team a foursome is a smart idea, implying silliness in Miriam even when we've seen little evidence of it, the way Dorothy Lamour seems funnier with Hope and Crosby than no-nonsense Jon Hall, Robert Preston, and Ray Milland—even in a similar sarong. Still, best known as the mother in TV's *Eerie, Indiana* (1991–92), Humes didn't procure much celebrity from her work here, chiefly because, like so many later Brooks actresses, she looks too sensible to provide much comic jolt—besides which, she really isn't given much funny to do.

As "The French Revolution" segments Mademoiselle Rimbaud, Pamela Stephenson has the same problem—even more so—despite later appearing in several comedies and even a 1984–85 TV stint on *Saturday Night Live*. Unlike, say, *SNL* comediennes like Gilda Radner, Julia Sweeney, and Victoria Jackson, Stephenson simply doesn't seem off-center enough, as if she's been cast strictly on acting talent and beauty—the perfect combination for drama, but all wrong for comedy unless the dialogue is sharp enough. Since Stephenson's isn't, she ends up, through no real fault of her own, barely remembered for anything beyond some good line readings and a fabulous face and figure. To this day most Brooks fans can't mentally separate Stephenson from Humes without checking the cast list, something one could never say about Cloris Leachman and Madeline Kahn.

Shecky Greene faces much the same difficulty playing Roman war hero Marcus Vindictus. Despite a striking likeness to musical comedy star Anthony Newley, and despite being a standup great himself, Greene just plain looks too actor-ish for a film like this, as if he's wandered in from some serious Old Rome flick like *Spartacus* or *Quo Vadis?* or *Ben-Hur*. He gives his lines a nice light touch, but he's so sturdy and stalwart one imagines, in their day, anyone from Richard Burton to Richard Harris playing the role just as well. Sure, they could do it, but who'd want them to? Why not cast against type, not to it, hire someone more like a young Woody Allen or Wally Cox?

Say what one will, though, *History of the World—Part I* boasts enough famous names for any ten films. Only here could Brooks' *Your Show of Shows* mentor Sid Caesar play a Chief Caveman, followed up just minutes later, uncredited, by *Caesar's Hour*'s Beatrice Arthur as a sarcastic unemployment clerk, right alongside *High Anxiety* co-writers and costars Rudy DeLuca (Speared Caveman; Captain Mucas), Barry Levinson (Column Salesman), and Ron Clark (Stoned Soldier # 1), and even Charlie Callas (Soothsayer) and Jack Riley (Stoned Soldier # 2) from the same film. Brooks' *New Faces* (and future) buddy Ronny Graham shows up too, in his first Brooks-helmed roles (as Oedipus and Jew #2), as do future returnees Art Metrano (Leonardo Da Vinci), Pat McCormick (Plumbing Salesman), Ira Miller (Roman Citizen), Johnny Silver (Small Liar), and John Hurt (Jesus), then fresh from Brooksfilms' 1980 drama *The Elephant Man*. In his third Brooks role, meanwhile, we're given a powdered-up Andreas Voutsinas, of *The Producers* and *The Twelve Chairs*, as foppish Frenchman Bearnaise, while *Blazing Saddles*' John Hillerman shows up as a Rich Man, and *Silent Movie*'s Henny Youngman as a Chemist and Fritz Feld as the Last Supper Maitre d'. Let's not forget either, besides Spike Milligan as Monsieur Rimbaud, actor-director Paul Mazursky (Roman Officer), *Playboy* founder Hugh Hefner (Entrepreneur), Jackie Mason (Jew # 1), Phil Leeds (Chief Monk), onetime Sid Caesar TV lead-in Jack Carter (Rat Vender), Jan Murray (Nothing Vendor), and actor-ambassador John Gavin (Marche). It's an amazing variety of big-name talent, both comedic and otherwise. Small wonder fans of the film like it so much; it's a celluloid toy-and-gumball machine, with celebrities as the toys and gumballs.

In the end, in fact, even if all the comic cameos in the world can't replace smoothness of execution, three-dimensional characters, and just plain good taste, *History of the World — Part I* still strikes our comic fancy if for one reason alone: it comes to us from Mel Brooks, a man who never gives up trying for a laugh. No matter how badly some of his material might stumble, he keeps on slugging away, and sooner or later his determination always pays off. Don't care for toilet humor? Maybe the "V and X Cent Store" gag will make up for it. Semi-blasphemy jokes make one cringe? Maybe seeing Louis XVI skeet-shooting catapulted peasants will do the trick.

Uneven, poorly paced, superficial, vulgar — yes, *History of the World — Part I* is all of these, yet its flashes of satiric genius, its tablet-fumbling lawgivers, time-displaced painters, and bathing beauty nuns make it also so much more than that we're willing to overlook plenty. Paraphrasing Brooksfilms' *My Favorite Year*, "with Brooks you forgive a lot," and thanks to its many high spots, from tap-dancing sadists to spaceship-piloting Jews, *History of the World — Part I* redeems itself countless times and becomes a "magical history tour" whose failings often get lost in the shuffle along with everything else. Like Torquemada and King Louis, Mel Brooks transcends even the harshness of history, outlasts all criticism, fair and unfair. A man this funny is one for the ages.

CAST: Mel Brooks (Moses/Comicus/Torquemada/Jacques/King Louis XVI); Dom DeLuise (Emperor Nero); Madeline Kahn (Empress Nympho); Harvey Korman (Count de Monet); Cloris Leachman (Madame Defarge); Ron Carey (Swiftus); Gregory Hines (Josephus); Pamela Stephenson (Mademoiselle Rimbaud); Shecky Greene (Marcus Vindictus); Sid Caesar (Chief Caveman); Mary-Margaret Humes (Miriam); Orson Welles (Narrator); Howard Morris (Court Spokesman); Rudy DeLuca (Captain Mucas/Speared Caveman); Charlie Callas (Soothsayer); Dena Dietrich (Competence); Paul Mazursky (Roman Officer); Ron Clark (Stoned Soldier # 1); Jack Riley (Stoned Soldier # 2); Art Metrano (Leonardo Da Vinci); Diane Day (Caladonia); Henny Youngman (Chemist); Hunter Von Leer (Lt. Bob); Fritz Feld (Maitre d'); Hugh Hefner (Entrepreneur); Pat McCormick (Plumbing Salesman); Barry Levinson (Column Salesman); Sid Gould (Barber/Bloodletter); Ronny Graham (Oedipus, Jew # 2); Jim Steck (Gladiator); John Myhers (Leader of Senate); Lee Delano (Wagon Driver); Robert D. Goldberg (Senator # 1); Alan U. Schwartz (Senator # 2); Jay Burton (Senator # 3); Robert Zappy (Roman Citizen); Ira Miller (Roman Citizen); Milt Freedman (Roman Citizen); Johnny Silver (Small Liar); Charles Thomas Murphy (Auctioneer); Rod Haase (Roman Officer); Eileen Saki (Slave); John Hurt (Jesus); Jackie Mason (Jew # 1); Phil Leeds (Chief Monk); Jack Carter (Rat Vendor); Jan Murray (Nothing Vender); Andreas Voutsinas (Bearnaise); Spike Milligan (Monsieur Rimbaud); John Hillerman (Rich Man); Sidney Lassick (Applecore Vendor); Jonathan Cecil (Poppinjay); Andrew Sachs (Gerard); Fiona Richmond (Queen); Nigel Hawthorne (Citizen Official); Bella Emberg (Baguette); George Lane Cooper (Executioner); Stephanie Marrian (Lady Marie); Royce Mills (Duke D'Honnefleur); Mike Cottrell (Tartuffe); Gerald Stadden (Le Fevre); John Gavin (Marche); Rusty Goff (Le Muff); Earl Finn (Caveman/Disciple); Leigh French, Richard Karron, Susette Carroll, Sammy Shore, J. J. Barry, Earl Finn, Suzanne Kent, Michael Champion (Other Cave People);

Henry Kaiser, Zale Kessler, Anthony Messina, Howard Mann, Sandy Helberg, Mitchell Bock, Earl Finn, Gilbert Lee (Other Disciples); Molly Basler, Deborah Dawes, Christine Dickinson (Game Show Girls); Lisa Sohm, Michele Drake, Jeana Tomasino, Lisa Welch, Janis Schmitt, Heidi Sorenson, Karen Morton, Kathy Collins, Lori Sutton, Lou Mulford (Vestal Virgins); Scott Henderson, Michael Miller, Royce D. Applegate ("Coming Attractions" Performers); Beatrice Arthur (Dole Office Clerk, uncredited).

Credits: Director: Mel Brooks; Producer: Mel Brooks; Screenplay: Mel Brooks; Editor: John C. Howard; Director of Photography: Woody Omens; Production Designer: Harold Michelson; Special Visual Effects: Albert J. Whitlock; Associate Producers: Stuart Cornfeld, Alan Johnson; Editor: Danford B. Greene; Assistant Editors: Carol Anne DiGiuseppe, George A. Martin, Stephen Lovejoy; Assistant Choreographer: Charlene Painter; Costume Designer: Patricia Norris; Choreographer: Alan Johnson; Music: John Morris; "The Inquisition" Lyrics/Music: Mel Brooks, Ronny Graham; "Jews in Space" Lyrics/Music: Mel Brooks; "Funkytown" Lyrics/Music: Steve Greenberg, performed by Lipps, Inc.; Music Editor: John R. Harris; Orchestrations: Jack Hayes; "The Spanish Inquisition" Orchestration: Ralph Burns; Production Designer: Stuart Craig; Director of Photography: Paul Wilson; Production Manager: Ralph Singleton; Assistant Director: Jerry Ziesmer; 2nd Assistant Director: Mitchell Bock; Casting: Mike Fenton, Jane Feinberg; Art Director: Norman Newberry; Production Sound Mixer: Gene S. Cantamessa, C.A.S.; Supervising Sound Editor: Robert R. Rutledge; Sound Editor: Scott A. Hecker; Rerecording Mixers: Arthur Piantadosi, C.A.S., Les Fresholtz, C.A.S., Tex Rudloff, C.A.S.; Camera Operator: Chuy Elizondo; Special Photographic Effects: The Magic Lantern; Set Decorator: Antony Mondello; Property Master: Jack Marino; Set Construction: Christina Productions; Publicity: Irene Walzer; Titles/Graphics: Intralink Film Graphic Design; Special Effects: Phil Cory; Still Photographer: Elliott Marks; Stunt Coordinator: Gary Combs; Script Supervisor: Betsy Norton; Production Coordinator: Judi Rosner; Assistants to the Producer: Leah Zappy, Randy Auerbach; Accountants: Jim Turner, Lenna Katich; Research: Lillian Michelson; Women's Wardrobe: Nancy Martinelli; Men's Wardrobe: Jered Edd Green; Makeup: Robert Norin; Hair Stylist: Vivian McAteer; Gaffer: Gibby Germaine; Key Grip: Gerald King; Transportation: Transcord; "THE FRENCH REVOLUTION": Production Manager: Alexander De Grunwald; Assistant Directors: Brian Cooke, Michael Stevenson; Production Auditor: John Trehy; Location Manager: Terry Needham; Casting: Maggie Cartier; Art Director: Bob Cartwright; Set Decorator: Harry Cordwell; Property Master: Bert Hearn; Camera Operators: John Morgan, Ginger Gemmell; Gaffer: Maurice Gillett; Sound Mixer: Mike Sale; Continuity: Penny Daniels; Stunt Coordinator: Bill Hobbs; Wardrobe Supervisor: David Murphy; Chief Hairdresser: Paula Gillespie; Chief Makeup Artist: Jill Carpenter; Makeup Artist: Eric Allwright; Construction Manager: Reg Richards; Production Coordinator: Loretta Ordewer; Locations: Beinheim Palace, Oxford, England; Shepperton Studio Centre, England; Color: DeLuxe; Opticals: Pacific Title; Filmed in Panavision; A Brooksfilms Production, Released by 20th Century–Fox, 1981; 92 minutes.

8

★ ★ ★

"SONDHEIM! SEND IN THE CLOWNS!"

To Be or Not to Be

★ ★ ★ ★ ★ ★

(1983)

In 1939 Warsaw, Poland, married actors Frederick and Anna Bronski (Mel Brooks, Anne Bancroft) wow Theatre Bronski patrons with song and dance, the loudest applause coming from young aviator Lt. Andre Sobinski (Tim Matheson), who has a secret crush on Anna and sends her roses each night. As Frederick plays a comic Hitler, the Führer-bashing ditty he, Ravitch (George Gaynes) and Ratkowski (George Wyner) perform is halted by reprisal-wary Dr. Boyarski (Earl Boen) from the Foreign Office. To avoid closure, Frederick drops the Nazi skit and pompously replaces it with his own portrayal of Hamlet. During his "To be or not to be" soliloquy, however, he is outraged when Andre walks out to meet with Anna. When Sobinski repeats this insult the next night, a livid Frederick has little time to protest. The Nazis have just invaded, sending Andre racing back to his squadron and the troupe hiding in the basement as Nazi bombs drop overhead.

Weeks later, their estate now Gestapo Headquarters, Frederick and Anna must live with homosexual dresser Sasha (James Haake), while in London Andre's RAF comrades foolishly give Warsaw-bound "countryman" Prof. Siletski (Jose Ferrer) names of loved ones, including spies for the underground. Andre sends Anna the message "To be or not to be," which Siletski thinks is in code, but, suspicious when Warsaw "native" Siletski does not recognize Anna's name, Andre alerts his superiors and is parachuted into Warsaw to kill Siletski before the Gestapo gets the list.

In Warsaw, Andre briefs Anna at Sasha's apartment, where he sleeps as Gestapo take her to a Nazi-seized hotel. Here she finds early-comer Siletski, who accepts her "love code" story, takes a call from Gestapo chief Erhardt about tomorrow's talk, and asks her to dine later. Anna goes home to change as an irate Frederick finds Andre in bed, then, back at the hotel, is held there as actors Ratkowski and Dobish (Jack Riley), as Gestapo, escort Siletski to a Gestapo office set, where Siletski gives the list to Frederick, who poses as Erhardt. Detecting the ruse, an armed

136

Siletski is killed by Andre in mid-escape, and Frederick plays Siletski to help Anna and burn a duplicate list. Told by Capt. Schultz (Christopher Lloyd) of schedule changes, Frederick visits the real Col. Erhardt (Charles Durning), submits names of two just-executed spies, and goes home.

The next day the Gestapo, rounding up gays, capture Sasha and close the theater. Later, Andre, unaware Erhardt only wants to arrange a show for Hitler, sees Anna "captured," and soon Frederick arrives as Siletsky just after Anna exits — and after Siletski's corpse, lost in transit, is reported found. Left alone with the body, Frederick shaves Siletski's beard, affixes a spare, uses Erhardt's humiliation to free Sasha, and escapes with "Gestapo" men Ravitch, Andre, and others.

At the show, "intruder" Jewish actor Lupinski (Lewis J. Stadlin), Frederick as "Hitler," and other fake Nazis divert attention so the others can escape in clown disguises, including Gruba (Estelle Reiner) and nearly a dozen Jewish relatives in hiding. After "Hitler" saves Anna from an over-ardent Erhardt, all narrowly escape in Hitler's plane to England, where the "Führer" puts a scare into pub patrons and Frederick gets to play Hamlet in London — the perfect happy ending until a young British naval officer (Paul Ratliff) heads backstage at the line "To be or not to be."

★　★　★

Died-in-the-wool Mel Brooks fanatics may find the very idea unthinkable, but the 1983 Alan Johnson–helmed remake of director Ernst Lubitsch's 1942 Jack Benny classic *To Be or Not to Be* very nearly didn't secure its own chapter in this book, was almost left, so to speak, "on the cutting room floor" except for some short-lived mention alongside the star's acting turns on TV's *The Tracey Ullman Show* or *The Simpsons*. Since Brooks neither wrote nor directed this film, and since so many scenes and lines spring directly from Lubitsch's original, giving *To Be or Not to Be* a spot all to itself in a book titled *The Big Screen Comedies of Mel Brooks* seemed out of step with the rest of the material, like devoting an entire chapter to, say, Brooks' acting in James Frawley's *The Muppet Movie* or Penelope Spheeris's *The Little Rascals* or Ezio Greggio's *Silence of the Hams*. Granted, Brooks is funny in all these films, just as Woody Allen brightens Paul Mazursky's *Scenes from a Mall* (1991) and Carl Reiner amuses in Norman Jewison's *The Russians are Coming! The Russians are Coming!* (1966), but since Brooks didn't direct, they're really all somebody else's projects, and warrant coverage in some other *The Big Screen Comedies of …* book. Indeed, not even 1954's *New Faces*, 1971's *shinbone alley*, or 1973's *Ten From Your Show of Shows* have been awarded their own chapters here, even though an off-screen Brooks either directly or indirectly contributed scripted material for all three films. When one is talking about the movie comedy of Mel Brooks, somehow "merely" producing, writing, or acting alone just doesn't feel like enough.

For better or worse, however, in the end *To Be or Not to Be* finally won out, primarily because Brooks both produces and stars in the film, using Lubitsch's characters and concepts to lambaste Adolf Hitler and his Nazis both behind the scenes and on the screen. A handful of other reasons contributed to its inclusion too, though: because, to begin with, in any number of interviews Brooks himself so often spoke of *To Be or Not to Be* with such proprietary affection, far, far more so than for any of his other non-starring Brooksfilms releases; because he contributes song lyrics to the movie much as he has for several of his "written and directed by" films; because the character he plays (along with that of his wife, Anne Bancroft) dominates the story; because the film's conspicuous anti–Nazi "Jewish-ness" represents the most overt embodiment of themes so many of Brooks' own movies have addressed less directly; and even because in a telling scene from 1987's *Spaceballs* he proudly displays video copies of *To Be or Not to Be* right alongside such no-doubt-about-it Brooks efforts as *The Producers*, *Blazing Saddles*, and *Young Frankenstein*. It's still a little "iffy" whether spotlighting in these pages a film Brooks neither wrote nor directed is a good idea—1999's *Screw Loose*, an Ezio Greggio–helmed comedy in which Brooks receives top billing, almost appeared here as well, and was eventually rejected—but since the Mel Brooks who helmed *Spaceballs* seems to think of *To Be or Not to Be* as one of the at-that-time nine "big screen comedies of Mel Brooks," we'll take the same risk here and say so too. What can it hurt?

One thing the film *hasn't* hurt is Ernst Lubitsch's original, one of the most controversial comedies of its era but also one of its most daring and distinctive. That classic film, a marvelously satiric assault on World War II Naziism—in which a team of Polish actors led by Jack Benny and Carole Lombard's husband-and-wife team Joseph and Maria Tura must resort to deception to help Maria's young aviator admirer (Robert Stack) save members of the Warsaw underground from the Gestapo—ranks high on most lists of great comedies, its stature increasing daily. Indeed, how can it not, with Benny's beloved genius in radio, movies, and TV treasured more and more the farther distant that Golden Age becomes, and Lombard's 1942 plane crash death seeming more tragic than ever as admiration for her screwball comedy hits like *My Man Godfrey* (1936) and *Nothing Sacred* (1937) remains on the rise? Thanks to Brooks, Lubitsch's film is better known now than ever. Like Lubitsch's 1940 *The Shop Around the Corner*,

which most people had never even heard of until Nora Ephron's 1998 update *You've Got Mail*, Brooks' film has actually given Lubitsch's a much-needed profile hike. If it has done the 1942 version any injustice at all, really, it's only that some videophiles favor Johnson's adaptation just because it's in color and not black-and-white.

To Be or Not to Be is more steadfastly funny than Lubitsch's film, yet never so slapsticky and over-broad as to make a mockery of tiny, war-torn Poland's WWII persecution. Brooks and director Alan Johnson haven't outdone Lubitsch, but this is as ridicule-rich a stick-it-to-the-Nazis comedy as anything since *The Producers*, whose "Springtime for Hitler" number helped ready choreographer Johnson for directing here. Except for a brief hat-tip to Steven Sondheim's *A Little Night Music* song "Send In the Clowns" and a self-referential closing credits gag, only in one swift voice-over vowing to drop Polish for English does the movie step outside its own cosmos, and even toning down his usual craziness the story seems so perfect for Brooks' bold, assertive style it's hard to believe soft-spoken Jack Benny had played this same part. Who'd ever guess a role once performed by a man so even-tempered and serene even his wildest tirades rarely rose above an exasperated "Well!" or "Now cut that out!" would end up revisited by someone as famously over-excitable as Mel Brooks? Yet even with the added emphasis on comedy, *To Be or Not to Be* never disgraces itself, even trying out several all-new ideas that play so well one could splice them right into the 1942 Edwin Justus Mayer script (and Melchior Lengyel story) with little disruption.

Indeed, one of the greatest testaments to writers Thomas Meehan and Ronny Graham's accomplishment here is to observe how, after one has seen both films, the mind tends to become a little cloudy as to exactly which elements belong to which.

In Nazi-occupied Warsaw, Polish stage star Anna Bronski (Anne Bancroft) barely gives actor-singer husband Frederick (Mel Brooks) time to recover from finding Anna's RAF aviator suitor Lt. Andre Sobinski (Tim Matheson) asleep in his bed before the flirtatious pair involve him in a desperate plan to rescue unsuspecting Poles from the Gestapo, in director Alan Johnson's 1983 remake of *To Be or Not to Be*— a project Brooks both produced and starred in but chose neither to write nor direct.

"Oh, I love that scene!" we exclaim confidently, or "What a terrific line! That's so clever it *must* be from Lubitsch, right?"—and when at last we realize no, it's *not* in Lubitsch at all but plays so smoothly and effectively it just as easily might be, we grasp even more clearly what an amazing feat Meehan and Graham have pulled off.

Some of this confusion, and this is a real tribute to the intelligence of Mayer's 1942 script, comes built-in, since Lubitsch's movie boasts one of the most difficult to summarize plotlines in comic cinema. Though matters invariably become clear if we'll just wait around a bit, we aren't always instantly sure what's going on, so somehow even when the film is humming along nicely, the story, like the Shakespearean tragedy from which it takes its title, defies easy encapsulation. As with *Hamlet*, another tale of actors, traitors, and tyrants, explaining *To Be or Not to Be* to one who hasn't seen it just can't do it justice. To say it's a comedy about Polish actors who dupe and sham their way out of Nazi Germany is accurate, but it ignores countless tricky surprises, and, *Hamlet*-like again, its labyrinthine twists and turns get tangled in memory just after we've seen it.

Our mild disorientation results partly because Lubitsch gives us so many characters, often in near-identical Nazi uniforms (or costumes, in the case of its Polish actors only posing as Nazis), and because so many exotic names get bandied about: Tura, Ravitch, Bronski, Dobish — and even two, Robert Stack's Lt. *Sobinski*, a hero, and Stanley Ridges' Prof. *Siletsky*, a villain, that sound so alike we'd be surprised if the actors themselves didn't get confused. We're thrown off a little too, if enthusiastically, by the way the plot keeps ingeniously crisscrossing itself, with characters visiting and revisiting hard-to-identify locales for reasons which, clear as they seem to Lubitsch's stars, we're sometimes a little less sure of. To heighten suspense, the 1942 film even, and quite skillfully, withholds information briefly, cleverly "conning" the audience itself for short periods much as its villains are fooled by the heroes: people we think are Nazis turn out to be just actors rehearsing; rooms we think are military offices reveal themselves as mere stage sets; characters whose seemingly self-motivated actions suggest they are cold, efficient spies for the underground prove only common citizens running errands for soldiers unable to take the risk themselves.

Though sacrificing some of Lubitsch's edgy, Gestapo-around-every-corner desperation in the process (an unfortunate loss, sometimes resulting from shooting in color as much as anything else), the Johnson/Brooks *To Be or Not to Be* clarifies some of Lubitsch's more will-o'-the-wisp cryptic elements to create a slightly less complicated, if slightly less artful, alternative. We still have quite a number of difficult-to-distinguish surnames (oddly, while the Turas here become the Bronskis in the original Bronski's absence, the Sobinski/Siletski business remains intact), and even a few more, since Meehan and Graham add on several all-new parts Lubitsch never thought of. Otherwise, though, Johnson's remake is a tad easier to follow; now when we're seeing actors *play-*

ing Nazis and not "real" Nazis, we're usually clear about it, just as we usually know when the sets are just sets. Neither do we make the minor mistake, as one might in Lubitsch, of believing the Carole Lombard/Anne Bancroft character an official agent for the Polish underground when, aiding Sobinski, she slips top secret information to her freedom-fighter countrymen at a Warsaw bookstore; this time the bookstore idea is dropped, costing the film a bit of absorbing secret agent intrigue but keeping us from briefly wondering, needlessly, if Maria/Anna has been a spy all along.

Furthermore, this time we see Frederick and Anna Bronski lose their ritzy mansion to the Nazis (it becomes Gestapo headquarters, even) rather than simply hear about it as in Lubitsch, where the first Tura residence we see is a tiny apartment one might think has been theirs all along. We aren't thrown as many curves by Bancroft's Anna as Lombard's Maria either; we don't expend as much effort trying to figure out how honest or dishonest she is. Lombard's character definitely takes her romance with Andre a step farther than Bancroft's, for instance, flying with the lovesick soldier in his plane even, so what in Brooks seems a semi-"innocent" flirtation in Lubitsch feels more serious, as dishonest as Prof. Siletski's faked affection for Warsaw before his Polish patriot facade gets stripped away. Perhaps neither woman intends to push her playful come-ons to their logical conclusion, but of the two, Lombard's Maria is clearly more brazen, so we're unsure how far to trust her moral compass, uncertain how far she'll go to get what she wants or do what she must. Will she really cheat on her husband? Murder Siletski? What *is* off-limits with this lady?

That we feel we can predict Anna's behavior a bit more than Maria's creates its own set of problems, of course. The shift to a more vulnerable, less take-charge Maria/Anna, much like the decision to jettison the scene from Lubitsch in which Sobinski scrambles around through a snowy Polish countryside narrowly escaping Nazis who've seen him parachute in, perhaps diminishes our admiration for the characters a little, makes them seem less heroic and brave. Somehow we miss all that watch-your-back, risk-taking Mata Hari gravity with which Carole Lombard bestows Maria Tura (Lombard's character tends to *take* action, while Bancroft's more often gets acted *upon*), but in a plot that's confusing enough as is, not having to figure out why Maria/Anna is sneaking handwriting samples and typing up phony suicide notes is actually something of a relief.

Occasionally, though, Meehan and Graham devise an idea so perfect one marvels Edwin Justus Mayer didn't use it for the original film. In Lubitsch the Turas' actor friend Bronski (Tom Dugan) disguises himself as Hitler for the finale, but somehow it's more fitting "great, great Polish actor" Joseph Tura, who has already portrayed Gestapo officer Col. Erhardt (Sig Rumann) and Prof. Siletski, should play Hitler too and thus pull off the ultimate con. Besides, who better to impersonate Hitler than a self-serving show-off whose delusions of grandeur mirror Hitler's on a smaller scale? What better writer's joke on both actors *and* autocrats than to have one massive ego outwit another? Meehan and Graham correct this oversight, mindful of the delicious irony of seeing irrepressibly Jewish Brooks, Nazi-obliterating author of *The Producers* and *Springtime for Hitler*, finally play the Führer himself, make a self–"Heil"-ing mockery of this black-hearted monster once and for all. To remake *To Be or Not to Be* with Mel Brooks involved and *not* let Brooks himself smash this anti–Semitic madman to smithereens would have been inconceivable.

The film succeeds elsewhere too. Some will object to the reinvention of Maria/Anna's elderly female dresser as male homosexual Sasha (James Haake), either on religious grounds or simply because they feel the writers strain too hard here for some trendy, '80s–Hollywood touch, yet Sasha's near-execution keeps us mindful that the real-life Gestapo were killers, not funnymen. Meehan and Graham achieve similar results adding a family of Jewish relations the Bronskis help friend Gruba (Estelle Reiner) hide from the Nazis, and while one wishes their personalities were better differentiated, the presence of all these tucked-away mothers, fathers, daughters, and sons creates just enough *Diary of Ann Frank* earnestness to keep the fun and games from going too far. Two scenes in particular, both with Eda Reiss Merin as a trembly old Jewish woman so shaken by a theater-ful of Nazis she very nearly bolts in a blind panic, even bring to mind *The Sound of Music*, in which, for all its upbeat whimsy, we're still half-afraid the Nazi-surrounded Von Trapps are "whiskers on kittens" away from getting machine-gunned or loaded on boxcars or worse. Nobody's likely to confuse the movie with *Schindler's List*, no, but it's easy to see from its Polish-persecution additions it might have worked even as a dark-and-deadly dramatic thriller.

And why not, too? Like most great war and espionage tales, *To Be or Not to Be* is about trickery, disguises and deception, and the 1942 Edwin Justus Mayer/Melchior Lengyel storyline even one-ups this by adding two more forms of deceit: show business, which of course relies heavily on makeup, costumes, and vocal trickery; and extramarital sex, which similarly depends on excuses, lies, and sneaking around. The film's very title suggests how tightly the worlds of espionage, theater, and cheating are bound together: it starts out as merely the classic *Hamlet* line Frederick utters on-stage; next becomes a sort of lover's "all's clear" for wife Anna and her airman beau letting them know Frederick will be occupied while they romance backstage; then is mistaken for a wartime spy code by which intelligence agents are somehow exchanging top secret information.

To Be or Not to Be's themes of impersonation and betrayal pervade every scene. Anna plays the role of faithful wife around husband Frederick, yet privately invites advances from other, younger men, Tim Matheson's Lt. Andre Sobinski in particular. Jose Ferrer's Warsaw "native" Prof. Siletski is in fact a Nazi spy duping Andre's comrades out of names and addresses of loved ones in the Polish underground. A married Anna must feign attraction to Prof. Siletski to save her husband, and a disguised Frederick, to convince the Gestapo that Siletski, not he, is the impostor, must affix a fake beard to the dead man's shaved shin. The Bronskis' friends Ravitch (George Gaynes), Ratkowski (George Wyner), Dobish (Jack Riley), Lupinksi (Lewis J. Stadlen), and others, besides playing Nazis on stage, must employ German accents and costumes to get out of Poland alive. Another friend, James Haake's Sasha, dresses as a woman to flee the Gestapo's roundup of gays, while still others, like Estelle Reiner's Gruba, her daughter Rifka (Marley Sims), son-in-law (Larry Rosenberg), and grandson (Brooks and Bancroft's son Max), must don clown costumes to escape a soldier-filled theater. Playhouse back rooms are camouflaged as Gestapo offices, black limos double as Nazi command cars, steamer trunks hiding dead spies pose as innocent-looking costume trunks — in *To Be or Not to Be*, disguises and deception abound.

To Be or Not to Be includes some quality in-jokes, too, occasionally. It's unlikely many besides the rare Jack Benny biographer or two will spot Benny's birth name, Kubelsky (here spelled *Kubelski*) on the Bronskis' Nazi-appropriated mansion, but it's a nice touch, albeit a still nicer one had someone thought to reference Benny's professed age for over a quarter-century by making the house number a more fitting "39" instead of "52." The movie's Stephen Sondheim gag inspires more immediate recognition, at least for anyone who remembers his song "Send In the Clowns" from the Broadway musical *A Little Night Music*, and while it's not exactly an inside joke, really, anyone who's seen the 1980 Bancroft-directed Dom DeLuise film *Fatso* might enjoy noting this makes the second time in the '80s a Brooks comedy has featured the old Ben Bernie, Maceo Pinkard, and Ken Casey tune "Sweet Georgia Brown," sung here in Polish by Brooks and Bancroft in what *The New Yorker*'s Pauline Kael labeled the "high spot" of the whole film.

The movie has dozens of high spots, many of them shrewdly character-derived. This is the sort of comedy in which a simple line like "This is bad too," only semi-amusing from anyone else, becomes funny just because it comes from Brooks' vain, self-involved Frederick Bronski, unsure which is the greater tragedy: Poland's invasion, or the fact that, twice in a row, the young pilot in Row Two has walked out mere seconds into his big *Hamlet* soliloquy. The remark is a Meehan and Graham original, yet so perfectly attuned to Tura/Bronski's basic arrogance it could easily have been given to Jack Benny (whose carefully developed radio persona depended on just such pretend pomposity already) without changing a thing. Brand-new or borrowed, though, the dialogue in *To Be or Not to Be* is almost always smartly written, even among 1982 hits like Barry Levinson's *Diner*, Larry Gelbart's *Tootsie*, *Victor/Victoria* (all Oscar writing nominees), Woody Allen's *A Midsummer Night's Sex Comedy*, *Night Shift*, and Brooksfilms' *My Favorite Year*.

Reviews for *To Be or Not to Be* weren't exactly four-star, but critics were kind enough to Johnson's revisions to suggest Brooks might have been wise to try shooting a few remakes of his own. *Newsweek*'s David Ansen labeled it "entertaining in its own right," proof "delight can strike twice in the same spot," *Variety* called it "very funny stuff indeed," Roger Ebert claimed it "works as well as a story as any Brooks film since *Young Frankenstein*" in the *Chicago Sun-Times*—well, anyway, one gets the general idea. Not everyone agreed, naturally—*The New Yorker*'s Pauline Kael found it "benign but not really very funny," for instance, and *The New Republic*'s Stanley Kauffmann called it one of those "bad before they are made" projects, one doomed in this case by forty-one years having elapsed between 1942 and 1983—but no matter how unimpressed, few suggested Johnson, Brooks, Bancroft, or anyone else had disgraced themselves or Lubitsch in the attempt. Too bad so few films Brooks actually directed in the post-'70s were received this well.

Too bad Brooks didn't do more acting work during this era too. As splendid as the great Jack Benny was, Brooks not only proves a worthy stand-in but an excellent one, and the idea of turning Tura/Bronski into a vaudeville-type song-and-dance man who only aspires to Shakespeare instead of specializes in it gives him plenty of room to make the role his own. Where Benny's Joseph Tura only acts on stage, Frederick Bronski isn't so much specialist as all-around showman, providing extrovert Brooks not only occasion to sing (in Polish) and dance to "Sweet Georgia Brown" but to "A Little Peace" and "Ladies," both co-written with his old *New Faces* ally Ronny Graham. Better still, the film gives Brooks, like Bronski, the greatest acting challenge of his life: portraying not only flawed but lovable Bronski, complete with all his petty jealousies, vanity,

and take-his-wife-for-granted cluelessness, but also Bronski as Hamlet, Bronski as Gestapo officer Col. Erhardt, Bronski as enemy spy Prof. Siletski, and even Bronksi as Hitler—*two* Hitlers, in fact, both the butt-of-his-jokes version sneered at on stage, and the nasty, hate-filled genuine article at the end of the film. With all that singing, dancing, and running around in disguise, *To Be or Not to Be* is just the sort of movie that, thirty years earlier, would have been perfect for Bob Hope.

To no one's surprise, Brooks handles each and every one of these tasks marvelously, and it's nice seeing a more mature, vulnerable Brooks on display for a change too. Sure, Bronski childishly competes with Anna, but he loves her too, and we respect him for eventually forgiving Anna and her starstruck young admirer for their impropriety. "It's easy" to fall in love with Anna, he tells Andre quietly, and we're pleased he's befriended his rival by the end of the film. We're touched too by the scene in which Bronski, having rescued Anna from the Gestapo disguised as the traitorous Prof. Siletski, muses over having finally produced true art without any applause.

These are fine, fine scenes, and if it's true all that affection for Lubitsch keeps Brooks' wild man instincts a little too reeled in to suit fans hoping for another scenery-chewing screwball like *Blazing Saddles*' Gov. Lepetomane or *History of the World— Part I*'s King Louis XVI, maybe that's not such a bad thing. Some of the remake's Nazis do, admittedly, have a touch of *Hogan's Heroes* incompetence about them, but events never turn quite so farcical squads of Gestapo can't still unsettle a little, and Brooks' slightly more controlled performance helps considerably. Like *High Anxiety*, *To Be or Not to Be* proves Brooks can play characters as well as caricatures, and if reverence for Lubitsch, Benny, and friends had anything at all to do with helping *To Be or Not to Be* steer clear of *History of the World — Part I*–style urine, flatulence, and pot jokes and returning Brooks' comedy to a less gratuitously vulgar PG, fantastic. Sure, a less disciplined Brooks would have been funnier, and probably would have made the film a bigger hit — but nobody wants to see Ernst Lubitsch reshot like the Farrelly Brothers, especially in a story in which it's the power-mad Nazi aggressors, not the victimized, overmatched Poles, who are supposed to look like fools.

Playing Bronski's partner-spouse Anna, Brooks' own show-biz wife Anne Bancroft makes a tantalizing co-star. As beautiful and elegant as she is talented, Bancroft brings with her more a sense of natural polish and poise than pratfall-and-spit take hilarity. She doesn't come to the part with some built-in comedic assist — say, the schoolgirl squeal of a Peggy Cass or the stork-like lankiness of a Mary Wickes — and so must pull laughs solely from razor-sharp timing, artful reactions, and a way with a good line. More than up to the task, Bancroft also makes expert use of the remake's new emphasis on song and dance, two skills already exhibited for Alan Johnson when he was choreographing her Emmy-winning TV special *Annie, The Women in the Life of a Man* in 1970, a project teaming her with Brooks and Thomas Meehan as well. Her blissful team-up with Brooks for "Sweet Georgia Brown" gets the movie off to a fine start, and even when she isn't dazzling us with her musical expertise, she makes an amazingly fine screen comedienne, especially considering her film career before '83 had given her so little practice. Besides *Silent Movie*, recall, the eventual Tony-, Oscar-, and Emmy-winner's then three decades in film included only four true comedies, all of which (*The Kid From Left Field*, 1953; *The Graduate*, 1967; *The Prisoner of Second Avenue*, 1975; the Bancroft-directed

Brooksfilms effort *Fatso*, 1980) are at least as heavy on drama as laughter. Even *To Be or Not to Be* takes itself fairly seriously for a Brooks movie, but Bancroft brings out its comic best, making lines like Anna's exasperated "Ten minutes ago it was *my* chair" and "We're living in a rat hole!" some of the most laugh-worthy in the entire film.

In a somewhat less engaging role, actor Tim Matheson, who as a teenager achieved pop culture immortality voicing boy heroes on still-popular '60s TV cartoons like *Jonny Quest* and *Space Ghost*, does fine work too, if inevitably overshadowed by the two main stars. Like Robert Stack from the 1942 film (and a Matheson co-star in another WWII comedy, *1941*), Matheson is just low-key enough that he can come off a little colorless if the role isn't pretty exceptional, and since Lt. Andre Sobinski is fairly standard "eager young hero" stuff, he can't bring much more to it than what's written: boyish enthusiasm, lovestruck loyalty, and selfless patriotism, all of which, of course, he handles like the pro he is. Matheson's disarming boy-next-door sincerity may even be just what's needed to tiptoe the fine line between comedy and drama; like Jonny Quest himself, Matheson always seems boyish and grown-up at once, and, amid farces like *National Lampoon's Animal House* (1978) and *A Very Brady Sequel* (1996), showing a knack for comedy-drama both before and since in films like *Yours, Mine and Ours* (1968), *A Little Sex* (1982), *Fletch* (1985), and *The Story of Us* (1999), Matheson supplies a crisis-era realism some kookier, crazier personality might have tossed off-balance. He's funny but never too funny, serious but never too serious.

Another fine actor, Charles Durning (who in 1979 had already shared scenes with Brooks in *The Muppet Movie*), enjoys slightly more comic elbow room. Where

Matheson's Andre must come across heroic, rugged, and dashing enough for Anna to fall for, Durning can make Gestapo chief Col. Erhardt nearly as ridiculous and blundering as he likes. After all, he isn't the picture's real villain — that role goes to Jose Ferrer's disloyal Prof. Siletski, and other bullet-flingers — and is more of a sputtering nincompoop akin to Werner Klemperer's Col. Klink from *Hogan's Heroes* (who, by the way, like Erhardt, blames his mistakes on an aide named Schultz). Consequently, the corpulent, endlessly exuberant Durning plays Erhardt as broadly smug and silly as he can get away with. Given his ballroom dancer past, and his Oscar-nominated song-and-dance turn in the movie version of *The Best Little Whorehouse in Texas* the year before, it's surprising Durning has no musical number, but, again, that wouldn't really fit *To Be or Not to Be*'s semi-serious style. Besides, who cares? Bouncing and bounding his way to a second straight Best Supporting Actor nomination, Durning is so wonderfully animated he's practically singing and dancing anyway.

Gangly, grasshopper-limbed Christopher Lloyd's overzealous Capt. Schultz gives the film a nice humor-hike too, just as we'd expect from a multiple Emmy-winner then in his last days as bewildered '60s burnout Reverend Jim on TV's *Taxi*. Like other Brooks actors who only seem wackier now thanks to later comic associations, so does the marvelously eccentric-looking Lloyd brighten his material after-the-fact because of all the spaced-out weirdoes he's given us since: wiggy inventor Doc Emmett Brown in the *Back to the Future* movies, for instance, or hairless, dorky Uncle Fester in his *Addams Family* films. As with Brooks, we've seen Lloyd much, much loonier than Schultz is written here, but his expressive face and raspy voice make him joyous to watch even in straight dramatic roles, and he certainly attacks his

small part with more oafish, gung-ho gusto than most actors ever could have mustered. He's like a lanky, Nazi Barney Fife.

The great Jose Ferrer, a three-time Oscar nominee and a winner for *Cyrano de Bergerac* (1950), provides one of the closest casting matches to the 1942 original, reminding one very much of Stanley Ridges but bringing with him a vastly more famous name. Ferrer may seem an odd choice for comedy, but he had already played a villain in the 1976 spoof *The Big Bus*, and two of Brooks' '50s TV peers had used him in comedies already: Carl Reiner in 1967's *Enter Laughing* and Woody Allen in 1982's *A Midsummer Night's Sex Comedy*. Besides, Nazi-in-Allied-clothing Prof. Siletski is perfectly suited to Ferrer's cultured, stately style and ultra-elegant diction, and while Ferrer likely would have "clowned it up" if asked, it's probably best he doesn't. Like Tim Matheson, Ferrer can't risk being too funny lest he tip the comedy scale too far; just as Anna would never fall in love with an RAF Stan Laurel or Harpo Marx, Frederick isn't likely to fear a Nazi-fied Jerry Lewis either, so Ferrer does the next best thing: makes Siletski smooth, suave, and sinister while leaving the major "funny fascist" shtick to Charles Durning and Christopher Lloyd.

The remaining parts are all much smaller, but they too are uniformly well cast. One of its more recognizable faces is George Gaynes, who had already worked for two of Brooks' old TV co-writers the previous year, Carl Reiner in *Dead Men Don't Wear Plaid* and Larry Gelbart in the Gelbart-scripted *Tootsie*, and who here plays Ravitch, one of Frederick's actor friends. Gaynes wasn't especially well-known to movie fans at the time of *To Be or Not to Be*, but was on the threshold of becoming so with his 1984–86 sitcom *Punky Brewster*, a slew of critically reviled but money-making *Police Academy* farces, and the debut year of the 1992–95 series *Hearts Afire*, which in its second season dropped not only Gaynes' daffy senator character but most of its political satire shrewdness as well. Gaynes doesn't have all that much to do here, but he shines whenever Ravitch must be all mock Gestapo boom and bluster, and *Police Academy* enthusiasts, seeing him in his policeman-like Nazi uniform, are today sure to enjoy the accidental connection.

As Ravitch's acting sidekick Ratkowski, rising Brooks favorite George Wyner from *My Favorite Year* and later *Spaceballs* appears in most of these same scenes. Like Gaynes, Wyner's "Where've I seen that guy?" face and delivery remain better known than his name, even though he's logged enough film and TV screen time to make some of the world's biggest stars look like beginners. Ratkowski isn't all that well-defined as a character, and Wyner could switch dialogue with Gaynes halfway through without many of us even noticing, but we're happy seeing him, and he even gets one line ("You even *drive* like an understudy") that's among the very best in the film.

Given slightly more opportunity to shine is TV and stage veteran Lewis J. Stadlen, barely recognizable behind beard and accent as Lupinski, who in one of the film's most tense moments gets to deliver an impassioned anti-racism diatribe, inspired by Shylock's famous speech from *The Merchant of Venice*, to Frederick's pretend Hitler amid a lobby-ful of armed, Jew-hating Nazis. Perhaps best known up till then for playing snippy governor's aide Taylor the first season of TV's *Benson*, Stadlen would appear years later with Brooks players Nathan Lane and Mark Linn-Baker in the 1996 revival of Brooks' friend Larry Gelbart's *A Funny Thing Happened on the Way to the Forum*, but marketing-wise his name and face probably didn't ring much of a bell. Even so, when Lupinsky tells off the Nazis for their brutality, he fulfills the dreams of countless millions whose lives Hitler either snuffed out or otherwise turned completely upside down. It's a superb scene, loaded with empathy and richness and heart, and Stadlen brings it to touching life just splendidly.

A more instantly recognizable TV personality, actor Jack Riley not only gets to play his share of bogus Nazis but has a funny running gag in which his character, Dobish, gets a little too helpful for his own safety trying to feed lines to Frederick as Hamlet — a joke marred only slightly when a foot-stomp from Frederick is aimed just a little bit too far to one side to possibly connect with Dobish's fingers from below. It's a small part, sure, but we're so fond of Riley from his six years on *The Bob Newhart Show*, not to mention bit roles in past and future Brooks productions like *High Anxiety*, *History of the World — Part I*, *Spaceballs*, and *Frances* (as well as Brooks ally Gene Wilder's *The World's Greatest Lover*), he actually stands out in memory more than most.

The same holds for Ronny Graham as Sondheim, whose unconscious, top-of-his-lungs backstage shouting and theatrical last name aren't exactly highbrow comedy material but turn out pretty funny just the same. Something of a cross between *The Producers*' William Hickey and screeching standup Gilbert Gottfried, Graham, a key contributor to Larry Gelbart's *M*A*S*H* series in mid-run and another Gene Wilder *The World's Greatest Lover* actor, had been affiliated with Brooks since *New Faces of 1952* (for which he won a Tony) and its 1954 movie adaptation, and by the time of his death would take on *Spaceballs* and *Life Stinks* as well. As usual, teaming with Brooks works to mutual advantage. Their scenes together are short ones, but work they do.

Another standout, in a much bigger part, is James Haake as Anna's homosexual backstage helper Sasha, whose explanations about being forced to wear a pink triangle by the Nazis and his later arrest give both Haake and Bancroft a terrific acting opportunity. In fact, Bancroft's Anna reveals more depth of feeling reacting to Sasha's humiliation and capture than almost anywhere else, and while a near-unknown to viewers, Haake not only provides many of the film's most emotional moments but many of its funniest. It's the sort of role sure to offend almost anyone — those who object to homosexuality on moral grounds, others because Sasha comes across so stereotypically womanish — but it's certainly hard not to laugh at Haake's over-the-top yelping and mincing about.

The rest of the cast proves equally reliable. Estelle Reiner, wife of Brooks' longtime pal and "2,000 Year Old Man" partner Carl Reiner (and an actress that year in Reiner's *The Man with Two Brains*), has a nice part as Gruba, whose Jewish relatives the Bronskis help hide. Fans of the Reiners' actor-director son Rob Reiner will recall her "I'll have what she's having" bit from 1989's *When Harry Met Sally*, but she's given more than just one scene here and fares quite well. Earl Boen, also of *The Man With Two Brains*, is good too as Foreign Office caller Dr. Boyarski, seen briefly warning the troupe against baiting Hitler, and Eda Reiss Merin, whose films would one day include 1953's *Lili*, '84's *Ghostbusters*, '85's *The Black Cauldron*, and '91's *Don't Tell Mom the Babysitter's Dead*, has two near-wordless scenes as the Frightened Jewish Woman that are both deeply moving and just plain fabulous. Fine too are, as Bieler, Zale Kessler, a would-be Hitler in *The Producers* also seen in the Neil Simon–penned *The Cheap Detective* in 1978; as Gen. Hobbs, Ivor Barry, whose roles included many a witty butler and chauffeur on TV (*Bridget Loves Bernie*, for one) and in movies ('74's *Herbie Rides Again*, for example); as Major Cunningham, William Glover, later of Disney's animated *Oliver & Company* (1988) and one of Ivor Barry's co-stars in '69's *The King's Pirate* and '74's *Lost in the Stars*; as a Nazi Officer, Henry Brandon, whose films include both "serious" hits (*The War of the Worlds*, 1953; *The Ten Commandments*, 1956; *The Searchers*, 1956), and comedies (*The Paleface*, 1948; *Scared Stiff*, 1953; *Casanova's Big Night*, 1954; *Auntie Mame*, 1958); as Officer in Command Car, Frank Lester, seen earlier in 1975's *The Rocky Horror Picture Show*; as Hitler, Roy Goldman, a *M*A*S*H* enlisted man its final two seasons; as the Elite Guard Officer, John McKinney, used by Brooks' pal Gene Wilder in 1984's *The Woman in Red*; as an English Pub Waitress, Paddi Edwards, who in '89 would voice characters in Disney's *The Little Mermaid*; as the Narrator, actor Scott Beach, visible in several film classics (*American Graffiti*, *The Right Stuff*, *Stand by Me*, *Tucker: The Man and His Dream*, *Mrs. Doubtfire*); and as the Startled British Officer, Terence Marsh, production designer on quite a number of well-known films (*Dr. Zhivago*, *A Man for All Seasons*, *Oliver!*, *Scrooge*, *The Hunt for Red October*, *Clear and Present Danger*, *The Shawshank Redemption*, Gene Wilder's *The World's Greatest Lover*), including Brooks' own *Spaceballs* and even *To Be or Not to Be*.

Thanks to Marsh's work, along with the care taken by costume designer Albert Wolski, director of photography Gerald Hirschfield (of *Young Frankenstein* and *My Favorite Year*), and others, *To Be or Not to Be* looks and feels authentically 1930s to practically the last detail. If its overall look has one flaw, in fact, it's that the film seems enveloped by such a glossy, reverential shimmer it often appears shot through some sunlit white fog, like some aging movie queen whose face is kept unfocused by lens-dabbed Vaseline. Instead of the crisp, clear look of *My Favorite Year*, another retro-comedy, *To Be or Not to Be* keeps us squinting through museum case glare.

Still, such problems arise only because its creators handle *To Be or Not to Be* with so much respect. John Morris's musical score is one of his classiest, Mel Brooks and his co-stars treat the invasion of Poland like the outrage it was, and director Alan Johnson depicts the Polish, Jewish, and Allied struggle with the appropriate respect without letting its comic possibilities entirely slip away. *To Be or Not to Be* isn't Mel Brooks' funniest comedy, but it's surely one of his best as actor instead of director. Like the Ernst Lubitsch version, this is a film that deserves to be seen.

CAST: Mel Brooks (Frederick Bronski); Anne Bancroft (Anna Bronski); Tim Matheson (Lt. Andre Sobinksi); Charles Durning (Col. Erhardt); Jose Ferrer (Prof. Siletski); George Gaynes (Ravitch); Christopher Lloyd (Capt. Schultz); Earl Boen (Dr. Boyarski); George Wyner (Ratkowski); Lewis J. Stadlen (Lupinski); Jack Riley (Dobish); James Haake (Sasha Kinski); Ronny Graham (Sondheim); Estelle Reiner (Gruba); Zale Kessler (Bieler); Ivor Barry (Gen. Hobbs); William Glover (Major Cunningham); John Francis (Brtish Intelligence Aide); Raymond Skip (RAF Flight Sergeant); Marley Sims (Rifka); Larry Rosenberg (Rifka's Husband); Max Brooks (Rifka's Son); Henry Kaiser (Gestapo Officer); Milt Jamin (Gestapo Soldier); George Caldwell (Gestapo Guard); Wolf Muser (Desk Sergeant); Henry Brandon (Nazi Officer); Lee E. Stevens (2nd Nazi Officer); Frank Lester (Officer in Command Car); Roy Goldman (Hitler); Robert Goldberg (Hitler Adjutant); John McKinney (Elite Guard Officer); Eda Reiss Merin (Frightened Jewish Woman); Manny Kleinmuntz (Frightened Jewish Woman's Husband); Phil Adams (Airport Sentry); Curt Lowens (Airport Officer); Robin Haynes, Ron Kuhlman, John Otrin, Blane Savage, Joey Sheck (Polish Fliers); Ron Diamond (Pub Bartender); Gillian Eaton (Pub Barmaid); Paddi Edwards (Pub Waitress); Terence Marsh (Startled British Officer); Winnie McCarthy (Picadilly Usherette); Paul Ratliff (Naval Officer); Scott Beach (Narrator); Sandra Gray, Laine Manning, Antonette Yuskis, Clare Culhane, Leeyan Granger, Stephanie Wingate (Ladies); Ian Bruce, John Frayer, Edward J. Heim, Spencer Henderson, George Jayne, Bill K. Richards, Neil J. Schwartz, Tucker Smith, Ted Sprague (Klotski's Klowns); Scamp (Mutki the Dog).

CREDITS: Director: Alan Johnson; Producer: Mel Brooks; Screenplay: Thomas Meehan and Ronny Graham, based on the 1942 film *To Be or Not to Be*, directed by Ernst Lubitsch, from the screenplay by Edwin Justus Mayer and the story by Melchoir Lengyel; Associate Producer: Irene Walzer; Executive Producer: Howard Jeffrey; Editor: Alan Balsam; Music: John Morris; "Ladies" and "A Little Peace" Music/Lyrics: Mel Brooks, Ronny Graham; Orchestrations: Jack Hayes; "Sweet Georgia Brown" and "Ladies" Orchestration: Ralph Burns; Production Designer: Terence Marsh; Director of Photography: Gerald Hirschfeld, A.S.C.; Costume Designer: Albert Wolksi; Production Supervisor: Jack Frost Sanders; Casting: Terry Liebling; Production Manager: Jack Frost Sanders; Assistant Director: Ross G. Brown; 2nd Assistant Director: Pamela Eilerson; Art Director: J. Dennis Washington; Set Decorator: John Franco, Jr. ; Set Designers: Craig Edgar, Joseph E. Hubbard; Property Master: Dennis J. Parrish; Production Sound Mixer: Gene S. Cantamessa, C.A.S.; Camera Operator: Michael A. Benson, S.O.C.; Assistant Cameraman; Marc D. Hirschfield; Gaffer: Ronald W. McLeish; Key Grip: Robert West, Sr.; Construction Coordinator: S. Bruce Wineinger; Construction Foreman: Guy Allan MacLaury; Assistant Editor: Nancy Forner; Script Supervisor: Cynnie Troup; Assistant Choreographer to Mr. Johnson: Charlene Painter; Women's Costume Supervisor: Ann Somers Major; Men's Costume Supervisor: Bruce Ericksen; Make-up Artist: John M. Elliot, Jr.; Hair Stylist: Cheri Ruff; Still Photographer: Stephen Vaughan; Unit Publicist: Bruce Bahrenburg; Re-recording Mixers: Bill Varney, C.A.S., Gregg Landaker, C.A.S., Steve Maslow, C.A.S.; Supervising Sound Editor: Louis L. Edemann; Sound Editor: Rick Franklin; Music Editor: Eugene Marks; Music Scoring Mixer: Danny Wallin; Production Coordinator: Anna Zappia; Production Controller: K. Lenna Woodward; Leadman: William Maxwell III; Swing Gang: John Scott III; Dolly Grip: Bill Beaird; Boom Operator: Raul A. Bruce: Best Boys: Michael Blymyer, Al Budniak, Joe Collins, Chuck Sereci; Assistant Property Masters: Hope Parrish, Mary Mathews; DGA Trainee: Dennis P. Maguire; Assistants to Mr. Brooks: Leah S. Zappy, Michele Markus; Assistant to

Mr. Johnson: Tom Gillman; Assistant to Mr. Jeffrey: Pattie Pica; Production Assistants: Princess McLean, Stanley Gibbs; Video Playback Operator: Lindsay P. Hill; Negative Cutting: Jack Hooper; Transportation Coordinator: Michael Connolly; Craft Service: Penny Brocato; Stunt Pilots: Art Scholl, Bernie Godlove; Stunt Coordinator: Dick Ziker; Stuntmen: Buddy Joe Hooker, Harvey Parry; Apprentice Editor: Patrick W. Magee; Polish Dialogue Coach: Iwonia Izoebska; Polish Translation of "Sweet Georgia Brown": Tad Danielewski; Mutki's Trainer: Weatherwax Trained Dogs; Opticals: Pacific Title; Title Design: Wayne Fitzgerald, Modern Film Effects; Title Illustrations: Bart Doe; Production Suggested by: William Allyn, David Lunney; Lenses/Panaflex Cameras: Panavision; Color: Deluxe; Soundtrack available on Island Record and Cassettes; Recorded in Dolby Stereo; Lightflex System on: Lightflex America, Inc.; A Brooksfilms Production; 1983, Distributed by 20th Century–Fox Film Associates; 108 minutes.

9

★ ★ ★

"MAY THE SCHWARTZ BE WITH YOU!"

Spaceballs

★ ★ ★ ★ ★ ★

(1987)

Nearing planet Druidia in *Spaceball I*, a giant spaceship from air-stealing planet Spaceball, helmeted villain Dark Helmet (Rick Moranis) and ship head Col. Sandurz (George Wyner), under orders from Pres. Skroob (Mel Brooks), prepare to kidnap rich, spoiled Princess Vespa (Daphne Zuniga) to force from her father King Roland (Dick Van Patten) Druidia's air shield combination. Vespa, meanwhile, rejecting dozy fiancé Prince Valium (JM J. Bullock), flees her wedding with robot Dot Matrix (Joan Rivers/Lorene Yarnell) in her sportscar-like spaceship — and is fired upon.

Frantic, King Roland calls space drifter Lone Starr (Bill Pullman) and vows a huge reward for Vespa's safe return. Eager to pay off cheese-dripping mobster Pizza the Hutt (Dom DeLuise), Lone Starr and dog-like pal Barf (John Candy) make a quick rescue in their flying Winnebago *Eagle 5*, escaping as their pursuers, attempting Ludicrous Speed, badly overshoot the mark.

At first resenting Vespa's bratty arrogance, Lone Starr softens after a rough landing on a desert moon when his ship runs out of fuel. While Barf and Dot sleep, he reveals he was found on a monastery doorstep in infancy, and shows Vespa an ancient medallion that may hold clues to his identity. Vespa reveals she must marry a prince, but soon the two are inches away from a kiss before Dot, programmed to protect Vespa's pre-wedding virtue, urgently intervenes.

Overcome by desert heat, Lone Starr, Barf, Vespa, and Dot are aided by six happy dwarfs, who escort them to a mysterious underground temple. Inside, they meet tiny philosopher Yogurt (Mel Brooks), benevolent wielder of The Schwartz, a wondrous magic also used by Dark Helmet. Though a Schwartz ring-wearing Yogurt can decipher the language on Lone Starr's medallion, he insists Lone Starr will learn its meaning later and teaches him how to use the Schwartz's magic.

Finding Yogurt's lair, Dark Helmet disguises himself as Vespa's father and abducts her and Dot in *Spaceball I*. Given fuel, a fortune cookie, and the Schwartz ring by Yogurt, Lone Starr follows with Barf while Vespa faces surgical restoration of her old nose unless her father gives up the combination. Horrified, Prince Roland relents, but a prison guard-attired Lone Starr and Barf free Vespa and Dot from a cell and head for Druidia as *Spaceball I* transforms itself into *Mega-Maid*, an enormous housekeeper with a vacuum that is sucking Druidia's air.

Using the Schwartz, Lone Starr restores the air, flies inside *Mega-Maid*, and sneaks about alone to destroy the ship. Engaging Dark Helmet in a battle of Schwartzes, Lone Starr outsmarts his foe, activates the Self-Destruct sequence, and flees with his pals just before *Mega-Maid* blows up, hurling Pres. Skroob, Dark Helmet, and Col. Sandurz onto a planet of stuffy talking apes.

Even Pizza the Hutt's death can't cheer up Lone Starr after he returns Vespa to Druidia, but when Barf opens the fortune cookie, Yogurt appears, identifying Lone Starr's medallion as a birth certificate proving him a prince. Fueling the *Eagle 5* with Yogurt's Liquid Schwartz, Lone Starr — whom Vespa loves even more since he has taken no reward for saving her — races back to Druidia and, in prince attire, stops the wedding, and happily marries an admiring Vespa himself.

★   ★   ★

Of all the big-screen comedies directed by Mel Brooks in the two decades following the 1970s, his nonsensical 1987 sci-fi parody *Spaceballs* stands out like an interstellar beacon as his most irrepressibly goofy, his most nonstop full of life. A somewhat belated takeoff on producer George Lucas's original *Star Wars* trilogy (*A New Hope*, 1977; *The Empire Strikes Back*, 1980; *Return of the Jedi*, 1983) with a few faint traces of other well-known sci-

ence fiction movie and TV adventures lightly peppered in, *Spaceballs* is easily Brooks' silliest post–'70s film, the one most reminiscent in overall style and spirit to the rambunctious, bend-all-rules lunacy of his instant classic mock Western megahit *Blazing Saddles* some thirteen years before. Like that 1974 comic smash, *Spaceballs* unabashedly calls attention to the fact that its characters exist only within the confines of a Hollywood movie (no, its heroes don't ride off the set in some rocket-loaded studio limousine, but given the picture's blatant preoccupation with its own "cinema-ness," they easily could), relentlessly pokes fun at political corruption and incompetence, and involves an easygoing, weak-willed citizenry menaced by predatory outside forces. Indeed, so conceptually similar are the two films that both at one point even end up alluding to classic Warner Bros. cartoons.

Excepting Brooks' several behind-the-scenes roles as actor and producer, *Spaceballs* makes the first clear-cut Mel Brooks movie in a half-dozen years, and while nothing here quite reaches the inspired madness of his big *History of the World — Part I* "Inquisition" number, the film's overall effect ultimately proves slightly more satisfying. Where his 1981 revue often feels undermined by its own shaggy-dog shapelessness, *Spaceballs* floats just a little higher because its story — a sweet, sentimental "Cinderella" or "Snow White" type fairy tale not unlike *Robin Hood: Men in Tights* six years later — taps into very nearly the same old-fashioned, "Jack the Giant Killer," "Brave Little Tailor" essence of the George Lucas original. Like *Star Wars*, whose gray-bearded mystics and jabbering elf-gnomes feel as much at home among spaceships and ray-guns as castles and magic wands, *Spaceballs* somehow manages to feel both futuristic-advanced and fable-ancient at the same time, and it's certainly no accident both Lucas's instant-classic *Star Wars* preamble ("A long time ago, in a galaxy far, far away...") and Brooks' ("Once upon a time warp...") sound so very much like space-age variations on Hans Christian Andersen or the Brothers Grimm.

It's easy enough to find fault with *Spaceballs*, of course (goodness knows it's not Brooks' best film), but on its own dopey terms it succeeds so often one feels downright callous speaking ill of it. Do its strictly linear plotline and classic boy-wins-girl scenario make it less structurally ambitious than *History of the World — Part I*? Absolutely, yet it's more tasteful too, only rarely too embarrassing to view in polite company, and even then for only for a split-second's word-slip at a time. Does it lack the good-citizenship respectability of *Life Stinks*, with its virtuous vagrants and hobos with hearts of gold? Definitely, but it's also more eye-candy extravagant, and outclasses its side-street, pavement-and-pothole shabbiness a million to one. Are its hero and heroine roles, for all their fairy-tale good looks and romantic charm, cast to lesser effect than those in *Robin Hood: Men in Tights*? Unquestionably, but its colorful supporting cast largely makes up for it, with one or two new additions nearly in the same league as Gene Wilder, Cloris Leachman, Harvey Korman, or Madeline Kahn. Is the film just a tad too funny-book juvenile in light of the subtler, softer Victorian sophistication of *Dracula: Dead and Loving It*? Surely, but it also includes so many more jokes the blatant immaturity of some of its worst ones are fairly easily brushed aside.

Truth be told, *Spaceballs* works so well as sheer dumb fun it's tempting to overlook its shortcomings entirely — quite a tall statement considering how many such shortcomings the picture actually has. To begin with, its two leads, then-rising stars Bill Pullman and Daphne Zuniga, seem all wrong for Mel Brooks — too sta-

ble-looking somehow, too rational, as if both would feel more at home in some non-comedy Brooksfilms effort like *Frances* or *84 Charing Cross Road*. Yet not even this seemingly fatal weakness sinks the film, in part because both Pullman and Zuniga are too gifted to let it (they're no Burns and Allen, but they do emit a certain low-key charm), in part because *Spaceballs* just keeps on trying whether everything's hanging together or not. The film's overall comic rhythm, for example, doesn't work all that well — somehow its sprawling, cavernous spaceship interiors only underscore those uneasy moments when the jokes fall flat, as if the movie itself is a comic "dying" onstage in a near-empty theater — but its best bits are so unpredictably quirky it very nearly doesn't matter. Private-owner spaceships designed like Mercedes sportscars and camping-trip Winnebagos? Diabolical madmen with Dilton Doiley eyeglasses and a passion for play dolls? Chambermaid-shaped space tankers that suck entire atmospheres into oversized vacuum cleaner bags? Who except Brooks and his crew could even dream up such ditsy stuff?

That crew includes co-scripters Thomas Meehan and Ronny Graham, two writers well suited to working with Brooks here. Meehan had won an Emmy co-writing *Annie, The Women in the Life of a Man*, a 1970 TV special starring Brooks' wife Anne Bancroft; had helped adapt Harold Gray's "Little Orphan Annie" comic for Broadway's *Annie*, 1977's Best Musical Tony hit; with Graham, already linked with Brooks on '54's *New Faces*, had given Brooks and Bancroft the "new" *To Be or Not to Be*; and, with Brooks, would win a Tony turning *The Producers* into the 2001 Broadway smash. Not everything this offbeat trio tries works, but that even one filmgoer anywhere guessed right off that the air-thieving spaceship *Spaceball I* would unfold itself into a mammoth

Mega-Maid contraption is inconceivable, and making the mental leap from spaceship to vacuum monster to *Planet of the Apes* homage even more so. Besides the usual boy-girl, good guys–bad guys predictability typical of most films, *Spaceballs* is rarely what we expect, and that's one of the best things about it. Talking pizzas? Robot gangsters? Outer space truckstops? Raspberry jam catapults? Breathable oxygen in pop-top cans? Could *you* fit so much lunacy into just one film?

The *Spaceballs* universe is the sort of place where fairy tale castles coexist with rockets and spaceports, where kings and princes still wear tights and crowns and flowing locks, spacemen coveralls and cowboy hats, and governors and gangsters tuxedos and pin-striped suits. Like *Star Wars*, whose spaced-up versions of *Wizard of Oz* characters (C-3PO a super-articulate Tin Man; Chewbacca a heroic Cowardly Lion; R2-D2 a chirping, mechanized Toto; Darth Vader a he-man Wicked Witch; etc.) and scenes (saving a kidnapped heroine; waylaying guards for their uniforms; and so on) forever mix with ideas from *The Searchers* and *The Hidden Fortress* and *Triumph of the Will*, *Spaceballs* takes way-out inspiration wherever it can find it. The *Wizard of Oz* allusions are even bolder here than in Lucas: fair maidens still get liberated, and uniforms stolen, and the Wizard-like Yogurt, who repeats Prof. Marvel's

Having crash-landed on a desert moon after their flying Winnebago runs short of fuel, spoiled, sullen Princess Vespa (Daphne Zuniga) relaxes her "Druish princess" arrogance long enough to accept physical and emotional warmth from devil-may-care space drifter Lone Starr (Bill Pullman), in *Spaceballs* (1987), director Mel Brooks' funny if somewhat belated *Star Wars* takeoff in which Brooks also produces, co-scripts, co-authors the film's theme song, and takes on two key acting roles.

phony-baloney entrance in his first scene, replays the *Oz* hag's wild death-babble in his last. Whatever else *Spaceballs* may be — corny, ill-paced, clumsily edited, visually inconsistent, even poorly cast — it rarely lacks for sheer off-the-wall whimsy. We know going in Brooks will fire off references to rocket-and-ray gun flicks, but not, in a purported sci-fi spoof, to Mr. Coffee and Doublemint and Kentucky Fried Chicken, to *The Bridge on the River Kwai* and *Lawrence of Arabia* and *Indiana Jones and the Temple of Doom*.

Of course, unpredictability cuts both ways in movies like this, and heaven knows many a film spoof has been crippled by too many hat-tips to irrelevant sources. *Spy Hard* scores a good hit on '60s spy flicks with its *Thunderball*–skewering title sequence and theme, but what do its takeoffs on *Speed* and *Sister Act* have to do with anything even remotely James Bond? *Mafia!* feels dead-on yukking it up in *Godfather* and *Casino* territory, but what's the thinking behind all those *Forrest Gump* and *Twister* jokes? *Scream* and *I Know What You Did Last Summer*, sure, but what's *Scary Movie* up to bothering with the likes of *The Matrix* and *Titanic* and *Amistad*?

Brooks' pictures at times lose focus the same way (how *does* that *Robin Hood: Men in Tights* Macaulay Culkin bit help spoof Robin Hood again?), but in *Spaceballs* the real riddle isn't so much what's included as what's left out. *Spaceballs* is the sort of sendup that makes room for jokes about *Rambo*, "Prince Valiant," *The Untouchables*, Milkbone dog biscuits, Pepto-Bismol, and Ace pocket combs, yet beyond *Star Wars*, *Star Trek*, *Alien*, and *Planet of the Apes*, doesn't seem all that earnest about "goofing" on science fiction at all. Where's Brooks' jab at *2001: A Space Odyssey*, for instance? Not that we're that eager to see Stanley Kubrick's classic defiled all over again (not after Brooks'

funny but tasteless tackling of it in *History of the World — Part I*), but surely some sly allusion to HAL the computer or looming black monoliths or embryonic starchildren belongs more here than in a film about the Roman Empire and French Revolution.

Why no takeoffs on *Forbidden Planet*, either, or *Silent Running*, or *Close Encounters of the Third Kind*, or *E.T.: The Extra-Terrestrial*? What of *This Island Earth*, *War of the Worlds*, or *The Day the Earth Stood Still*? True, most of these films had been razzed to death already, and simply stuffing *Spaceballs* full of pointless allusions to *Earth vs. The Flying Saucers*, *The Space Children*, and *It Came From Outer Space* isn't truly spoofing them anyway. Like most American parodists, Brooks rarely pushes lampoon beyond simple comic cross-referencing (again one recalls Pauline Kael's *High Anxiety* protest that "all Brooks does is let us know he has seen some of the same movies we have"), so none of that's fixable adding more name-dropping. Still, given Brooks leaves even Lucas only kidded and not clobbered, why so much *Star Wars* and so little else? *Invaders From Mars*, *Invasion of the Body Snatchers*, *The Thing from Another World*— not one of these prime targets makes Brooks' cut, yet he finds room for not one but two films by David Lean, who never lensed any significant science fiction in his life. What gives?

What gives, obviously, is thematic continuity. If bedeviling the first three *Star Wars* films was Brooks' chief aim, maybe he should have dropped the non–Lucas gags entirely. Or maybe he should have widened his scope, not narrowed it, leaving the *Star Wars* material pretty much as is but dropping in comic nods toward anything and everything "outer-spacy," from the old *Flash Gordon* serials to Fritz Lang's *Metropolis* to Georges Méliès' *A Trip to the Moon*. It's hard to say just how Brooks should have given *Spaceballs* a tighter grip, but as a whole the existing film feels off balance — way too heavy on *Star Wars*, way, way too skimpy on just about everything else — and quite frankly, without much real conviction no matter what target Brooks is aiming at.

Roger Ebert notes this absence of point-of-view in the *Chicago Sun-Times*, calling the film a "no-brainer satire" and asking what Brooks "really think[s] about *Star Wars*, or anything else." Its sights set more on mimicry than true take-'em-down-a-peg derision, *Spaceballs* parodies *Star Wars* mostly by just reproducing it topsy-turvy. Cocky loner Han Solo and wizard-in-training Luke Skywalker merge into magic-endowed flyboy Lone Starr; Solo's shaggy pal Chewbacca is half-canine Barf; spunky Princess Leia is spoiled heiress Princess Vespa; ebony-visored tyrant Darth Vader is black-masked weakling Dark Helmet; hobgoblin space prophet Yoda is pygmy philosopher Yogurt; and so on. It's funny, but don't kids do this sort of thing all the time at summer camp, sitting at fireside making up loopy new lyrics to "Jingle Bells," "On Top of Old Smokey," and the TV theme from *Branded*? Do we need an Oscar-winning screenwriter for *this*?

Probably not, no, and Ebert is right about Brooks' "aiming low" here. Less satirizing *Star Wars* as sillying it up with bad puns and juvenile character names, *Spaceballs* tackles its subjects a bit like the way TV's *The Flintstones* does with all its "Ann-Margrock" and "Rock Vegas" gags, or the way ad execs give cereal and corn chip mascots funny labels like Count Chocula and W. C. Fritos. After all the comedic stretching and squeezing, is space cinema itself left any the worse for wear? No, because Lucas fan Brooks is only pillow fighting here, firing off pain-free Nerf pellets and Silly String, as his targets' continued success (*Star Wars'* later "prequel" series; endless *Star Trek* spin-offs; still more *Alien* movies; a big-budget relaunch of *Planet of the Apes*) makes clear.

Doubtless we're again defining "parody" too strictly here — it's the parodist's right, not ours, to decide how harsh-edged he wants to be — and one can almost hear Brooks saying as much in response: "For crying out loud, this is comedy, not brain surgery! You laughed, didn't you? What more do you *want*?" Still, *Spaceballs* seems like the perfect place to let space-age filmdom have it right between the eyes, yet except for one or two mild throwaways (robot Dot Matrix's dread of the inevitable sci-fi laser shootout, or Dark Helmet's ire over those pointless "prepare to" commands), *Spaceballs* spends less time sending up its genre than its medium. Moviemaking itself takes some hits, directing our attention to key personnel (boom operators, stunt doubles) and techniques (zoom-ins, dissolves), but Brooks' ideal forum for shooting a film *about* shooting a film is *Silent Movie*, not here. Where, say, '97's *Austin Powers: International Man of Mystery* mocks its source even as it celebrates it (Austin's otherwise useless set-up-the-story spy boss is named Basil Exposition; the villain devises an over-intricate, barely supervised execution instead of just killing the hero right off; etc.), and '95's *The Brady Bunch Movie* comes down hard on the '70s sitcom's mind-blowing absurdity (toilet-less bathrooms, quarrel-free parents, children too good to be true, homily-for-every-crisis dads), *Spaceballs* largely lets sci-fi cinema off scot-free.

Spaceballs' top-heavy emphasis on the Lucas films, furthermore, has, like the Schwartz, a downside to its upside too. Everyone from *Mad* magazine to *Saturday Night Live* to *Donny and Marie* had targeted *Star Wars* already, a fact Roger Ebert recognized when observing that, "in bits and pieces, one way or another, this movie ha[d] already been made over the last ten years by countless other satirists" — that "the strangest thing about *Spaceballs* is that it should have been made several years ago, before our appetite for *Star Wars* satires had been completely exhausted." Considerably less charitable, *Films in Review*'s Michael Buckley, calling it "light years unfunny" agreed: *Spaceballs*, he declared, came "nine years too late" to feel as fresh and novel as it should.

That's the bad news, though. The good news is that, for all its over-familiarity, the movie is still Brooks' most winningly funny comedy since *High Anxiety*. As with that film, whose most inspired bits often have little to do with spoofing Hitchcock, many of *Spaceballs*' best laughs arise when it ignores sci-fi and just lets Brooks be Brooks. True, some of its worst puns are real clinkers (that three such talented writers — *three!* — could still think that terrible "strawberries" line Brooks-worthy right to the last boggles the mind), but a few of its wittiest (the "Metamorphosis" nod, for one) take us by such surprise we laugh right off, and certain fast-as-lightning exchanges charge along so swiftly they tap the razor-sharp timing of an Abbott and Costello, whose classic "Who's on First?" bit Dark Helmet's videocassette confusion calls to mind. The crackerjack give-and-take as Barf parrots Lone Starr's "activate this/switch on that" instructions works well too, like the perfectly set-up by-play over Pres. Skroob's luggage, and Brooks' wild climax comes closer to the anything-goes ending in *Blazing Saddles* than anything he would ever shoot again.

Even when *Spaceballs* does reference pop-culture sci-fi, however, the success rate remains pretty high. *Planet of the Apes* has seen itself — well — aped in pop culture from the minute we first left Charlton Heston pounding his fists in the sand, but we've never, ever seen its famous ending reworked so cleverly as Brooks, Meehan, and Graham do here. The film's *Alien* linkup, meanwhile, doesn't add much storywise, but it pays off too, even if only Ridley Scott nuts notice the familiar-looking uniforms, equally familiar casting, or the clever "return" of actor John Hurt. Even children, though, will recall Chuck Jones' 1955 "One Froggy Evening" cartoon, Michigan J. Frog, and the Milt Franklyn version of "Hello, My Ragtime Gal," and find it great, great fun.

Unfortunately, while Brooks' timing here is flawless right up to Pullman and Candy's final punchline, the effects work and even Brooks' directing veer perilously close to ruining the whole bit. That Brooks' puppet alien looks pretty phony up-close is bad enough, but the second he tries making him dance, the scene nearly collapses on itself. Such obvious fakery plays just fine on, say, TV's *Sesame Street*, but for a big-budget film, Brooks' first directorial effort since 1981, six years seems like plenty of time to figure out where to put the camera so a trick-revealing tail rod wouldn't show. We're only half-serious, of course; Brooksfilms had been turning out nearly a film a year since 1981, so it's hardly as if Brooks had been planning all this a whole half-decade (just getting *Spaceballs* launched at all must have been tough), and anybody who can't even take a vacation photo without getting the horizon crooked can imagine the problems on a movie set. Still, we are a little surprised the director of visual triumphs like *The Twelve Chairs* and *Young Frankenstein* couldn't have set up at least a slightly better shot, whatever the practical difficulties.

Beyond that, though, most of the special effects are really quite striking. Our first-scene glimpse of Pres. Skroob's *Spaceball I*, a Brooksian exaggeration of Lucas's opening shot in *Star Wars*, not only makes for a nice sight gag (and one of the few bits that tease Lucas's directorial technique rather than just replaying *Star Wars* with kooky names), but as Brooks' camera slowly pans the ship inch by inch, we really do feel we're out there in space. The

Monty Python and the Holy Grail folks might point out to us that, like that film's Camelot, "it's only a model," but the scene plays so smoothly we're perfectly happy to just mentally file that little bit of actuality away and get swept up by the whole vacuum-of-space grandeur of it. *Spaceball I*'s gradual conversion into Mega-Maid later creates much the same effect, tickling us while filling us with a real sense of gee-whiz-will-you-look-at-that wonder — again, this ship looks *huge*— and its eventual self-destruct countdown and detonation play well too, complete with escape pod blast-offs and flying debris.

The model shots of Lone Starr's Winnebago spaceship *Eagle 5* look surprisingly realistic too, especially during its emergency landing on desert terrain, and the shots of Druidian monarch King Roland's Disney-esque castle and planet Druidia's transparent air shield almost make up for the video-game crudeness of some of the pictures on spaceship view screens. Admittedly, even at their best *Spaceballs*' visuals are rarely as sophisticated as those in *Star Wars* (the budget's big, but it's not that big), yet since this isn't "serious" action-adventure, they don't have to be. The film's logic is hardly flawless either — we all know a helmetless Barf and Princess Vespa couldn't survive in the airless cold of space, realize with or without rockets a Winnebago makes a poor projectile, understand perfectly any vehicle the size of *Spaceball I* could never set down outside Yogurt's temple unheard — but because this is only a takeoff on *Star Wars* and not the real thing we don't care. What was it the theme song from TV's *Mystery Science Theater 3000* said? "Just repeat to yourself, 'It's just a show; I should really just relax'"? That's Brooks' spirit exactly.

As in *History of the World — Part I*, then, we're a tad surprised where Brooks chooses to concentrate some of his energies (surely his *Alien* puppet bit could stand some of the funds and focus put into that needless five-second shot of Princess Vespa's Mercedes spaceship launchpad), but who are we to complain? It's not *our* money, and it's not as if we don't keep smiling. Lorene Yarnell's Dot Matrix outfit isn't as intricately designed as the one Anthony Daniels wears as Lucas's C-3P0, either (Joan Rivers' voice-overs don't play nearly as well, even if Daniels too performs behind a face-plate with no movable mouth), but who cares when we're in such fine company? Even when we're left a bit disappointed over the bargain basement shabbiness of the occasional zip-up bear suit, dollar store underwear, or painted-on dog spots, we're won over all over again by something so tiny and so simple it shouldn't even matter — the way Barf's ears perk up when something grabs his attention, maybe, or the way Dot Matrix's heretofore lifeless eyes suddenly grow red with horror in the dark as her beloved Princess Vespa is cruelly spirited away.

John Morris triggers much the same effect with his music, pleasing us most of the time as long as he keeps the melodies coming, creating a big black hole of emptiness whenever he leaves us for dead. His main theme for the film seems near-perfect for Brooks' concept, recalling not only John Williams' fantastic *Star Wars* theme but even the "happily ever after" triumph of Lucas's "Throne Room" conclusion, in which Princess Leia rewards Luke and Han for a job well done. Even when Brooks replays scenes over it spotlighting his main cast, the tune meshes just fine, and Morris's "Love Theme," a dandy mix of fairytale fantasy and boy-loves-girl romance, and his high energy rhythms for *Eagle 5*'s exciting crash landing on Yogurt's Tatooine-like home world and *Mega-Maid*'s ultra-majestic unveiling (great use of the kettle drum, too — off-screen and on) are absolutely first-rate, underscoring not only the film's increased closing-half intensity but also reminding us, unfortunately, of how sparse Morris's music seems the movie's first half.

Indeed, the original *Spaceballs* music album (labeled *Spaceballs: The Soundtrack*, a witty extension of one of the movie's best jokes) contains barely more than seven minutes of Morris's instrumentals, the rest going to popular 1980s rock performers The Spinners, The Pointer Sisters, Berlin, Kim Carnes, Jeffrey Osborne, and Van Halen. That's about the size of it, too, since for all the effectiveness of Morris's best music, here again, as in *History of the World — Part I*, he doesn't include nearly enough of it. His infrequent *Jaws*-like strumming during that long, long, long scene introducing *Spaceball I*, for instance, milks viewer anticipation just fine (and prepares us for *Mega-Maid*'s sharkish "mouth" later on), but fans who don't see the wit behind Brooks' lava-slow camera pan may grow impatient — and wonder if filling the film's first minute-and-a-half with nothing but dull engine drones barely punctuated by strings may have been a bad move, especially since Brooks cuts from this straight to an on-ship scene with even less movement.

We value Morris's music most, in fact, when it suddenly up and disappears on us, as in *Spaceballs* it too often does, usually just when the movie could really use a good pick-me-up. The worst lags seem to turn up whenever scenes linger too long aboard *Spaceball I*, whose wildly oversized bridge set so dwarfs even Brooks' funniest stars it tends to leave all but their very best zingers dying in midair. Widescreen works just great for showing off super-big sets, but it can mean the kiss of death unless things keep hustling along lickety-split, and Brooks' *Spaceball I* scenes, comprised mostly of actors just standing about planning and plotting, play so softly and so still we'd almost swear we can hear the camera whir. What we really hear, if anything, is faint "engine noise," but, as with Brooks' *Spaceball I* exteriors, the end result sometimes feels awfully static, like wax figures in a tomb. Running longer than any other Brooks-directed movie except *Young Frankenstein*, *Spaceballs* could stand to lose a few minutes — and add more instrumentals.

As in *Robin Hood: Men in Tights*, many of those minutes could have been trimmed from too many split-second hesitations between lines, since the characters in *Spaceballs* often seem to talk about half as fast as those in *The Producers* — and in dialogue only about half as hyper-witty and sharp-edged. Maybe it's because, despite the PG rating, Brooks is deliberately aiming more at children this time than adults, but *Spaceballs* just isn't as smartly written as movies like *High Anxiety*, and Bill Pullman and Daphne Zuniga's exchanges in particular, while acted well enough, rarely rival the high-voltage crackle of the Howard Hawks–type routines they vaguely resemble.

Indeed, most of the film's conversations feel way too casual, as if the actors all imagine they've been handed such surefire comic gold they needn't rush, but the truth is *Spaceballs* just doesn't need ninety-six minutes to tell this story no matter how much the lines might get sped up. The plot just isn't that complicated, and the characters, especially Brooks' imitation Han Solo and Princess Leia, are essentially the same as in *Star Wars*, Frank Capra's *It Happened One Night*, and just about every Disney-animated fairy tale ever made. However much we might hate to lose any of its best free-floating "extras," *Spaceballs* would play just as well cut down to the length of the average *Get Smart* two-parter. (At about twenty-three minutes per show, even a three-parter would've run nearly a half-hour shorter!) Would *Spaceballs*' story suffer any had Brooks cut the transporter beam joke? The Doublemint twins gag? The voice-created sound effects bit? Not really, no, and Brooks could have dropped the whole subplot about Lone Starr and Barf's "need" for some quick cash to pay off gooey, oozy Pizza the Hutt without crippling matters much at all, as we soon see once Brooks kills off Pizza near the end and thus negates that whole storyline anyway.

Spaceballs also loses momentum from too much go-nowhere dialogue that, as in Brooks' Sherwood Forest comedy again, spin the picture's wheels in place just a little too long without good reason. The second Leslie Bevis's Commanderette Zircon character makes her very first "beaming" reference, for instance, only somebody who's stayed hidden under a dilithium crystal all his life won't know she's talking about *Star Trek*, yet even after giving us an equally obvious clue involving *Spaceball I*'s Scottish transporter chief, before long Brooks still insists on having his own Pres. Skroob character allude to Gene Roddenberry's TV classic by name. Does he really think we're not following his line of thought here? Does he really believe, when Pizza the Hutt gets Barf's name, we need him to repeat the insult for us even after Barf corrects him? Wouldn't Brooks be smarter to just cut Pizza's follow-up and keep his plot moving ahead full-speed?

Speaking of moving ahead, *Spaceballs* certainly does so casting-wise, anyway. In 1987 some fans felt alienated seeing so many new faces on-screen, wondered if maybe Brooks (or the casting department, or the studio, or *somebody*) hadn't tried a little too hard to seem late-'80s "with it" hiring so many then-rising stars, especially ones young and fetching enough to maybe lure in teenagers who perhaps wouldn't be much interested in a fairy tale romance between, say, a fiftyish Gene Wilder and a forty-something Madeline Kahn. Well, maybe — but who knows? It is true, any-

way, that the number of returning Brooks players is pretty small. Besides Wilder and Kahn, *Spaceballs* offers nary a Cloris Leachman, Harvey Korman, Ron Carey, or Howard Morris in sight, though longtime Brooks cronies Dom DeLuise, Dick Van Patten, and a few scattered others like Ronny Graham and Rudy DeLuca do appear in bit roles. Not since *The Twelve Chairs*, whose only on-screen returnee from *The Producers* was the relatively unknown Andreas Voutsinas, had a Brooks film come along with so few repeat performers in the lead roles.

The peculiar truth is, though, that however much it may seem *Spaceballs* sets out to win over a more hip crowd (certainly all that trendy hard rock blasting away all over would make it seem so), of its major stars only thirty-three-year-old Bill Pullman and twenty-four-year-old Daphne Zuniga, as star-crossed flirts Lone Starr and Princess Vespa, play characters whose fresh-faced, adolescent get-up-and-go gets much emphasis. Ironically, while young-ish *SCTV* favorites John Candy and Rick Moranis have only a few years on Pullman, and both seem sort of college-kiddish what with Candy's doglike Barf's literal puppy-dog playfulness and Moranis's nerdy whiner role, Candy's Zero Mostel–like girth and Moranis's autocratic bossiness as the pain-inflicting Dark Helmet elsewhere make even these thirty-something teen-pleasers seem nearly as seasoned as a Marty Feldman or a Howard Morris. Excepting the occasional Michael Winslow, Sal Viscuso, or JM J. Bullock, the rest of the main cast — Golden Age TV veteran Dick Van Patten as Princess Vespa's father King Roland, George Wyner as *Spaceball I* chief Col. Sandurz, Joan Rivers as the voice of Princess Vespa's android helper Dot Matrix, Rudy DeLuca as Vinnie the robot gangster, white-haired Ronny Graham as the minister who weds Lone Starr and Princess Vespa, Mel Brooks himself as both Yogurt and air-thieving Pres. Skroob — skew fairly middle-aged to say the least, and seem no younger overall than the casts of any other Brooks film of the past twenty years.

So much, then, for all those complaints about *Spaceballs'* supposed all-consuming quest for kid-appeal. That said, though, how does the cast fare acting-wise? Do Brooks' new actors prove funny enough to work alongside Mel Brooks? Do the veteran stars still manage to shine?

In many ways Brooks hit it lucky with Bill Pullman, an expert actor who, having turned up only in the 1986 comedy *Ruthless People* before an eagle-eyed Brooks snatched him up, was just starting out in film when *Spaceballs* arrived but had roles in all manner of high-profile projects coming up just ahead. Significant parts in *The Accidental Tourist, Rocket Gibraltar, The Serpent and the Rainbow, A League of Their Own, Newsies, Malice, Sleepless in Seattle, Sommersby, Wyatt Earp, Casper, While You Were Sleeping*, and *Independence Day*, among others, all in just that very first decade after working for Brooks? An impressive accomplishment, to say the least.

Lone Starr is a big part for an actor with just one film behind him too, and Pullman is just personable enough to make it all work fairly well. Unfortunately, despite his obvious way with a line, Pullman's natural straight-faced everyman aura comes across a trifle bland alongside Candy, Moranis, and Brooks, and *Spaceballs'* costume and set planners, playing to the role's rough-hewn earthiness, engulf the sandy-haired, fairly nondescript actor with so many ho-hum golds, beiges, and browns even a high-flying maverick like Lone Starr can't help fading into the background a little. Talented as Pullman is, Lone Starr still comes off only slightly more attention-grabbing than the likable-but-colorless types Pullman would play so well in films like *Sleepless in Seattle*, and it

doesn't help that, since he's so rarely shot in-tight and alone, he never gets much chance to really stand out. Odder still, while *Get Smart* lampooned James Bond by securing Don Adams, an actor whose way-out voice, looks, and mannerisms contrasted wildly with those of spy movie star Sean Connery, *Spaceballs* for some reason seems to be casting *to* type here, not against it. How can Pullman "send up" Harrison Ford's Han Solo when he looks and acts so much like the real thing?

Pullman's young costar Daphne Zuniga (who just two years earlier had played another reluctant traveling companion-turned-sweetheart in Rob Reiner's *The Sure Thing*) isn't exactly a hundred-and-eighty-degree contrast to Carrie Fisher, either, as a sight gag about Fisher's *A New Hope* hairdo reveals, but she is more pompous and pouty than Princess Leia, which at least helps differentiate the two a tad. Some of Zuniga's spoiled rich girl gags are fairly funny, too, briefly (the hairdryer bit, the hairdo joke — the latter a nice riff on *Star Wars*, whose outraged Luke turns one-man army seeing kindly old mentor Obi-Wan Kenobi struck down), but in a sense that's all they are, too: routines, the sort of over-broad uppiteness we've seen again and again on *Newhart* and *Designing Women* on TV. In the final analysis Princess Vespa is only slightly less shallow when *Spaceballs* ends than when it starts, and a little "Druish princess" surliness goes a long way. Though she does make more lasting impact than most post-'70s Brooks actresses (Quick: Who played Miriam in *History of the World — Part I*: Pamela Stephenson or Mary-Margaret Humes?), in the end Zuniga appeals more for her youth and beauty than because she's the next Cloris Leachman or Madeline Kahn. Like Pullman, who looks too leading-man solid ever to match the natural-born nuttiness of a Candy, Moranis, or Brooks, Zuniga handles her dialogue just fine — by no stretch at all is she a bad actress — but were she teamed with the *real* Joan Rivers and not just a blank-face gold robot with Rivers' voice, it's a fair bet Rivers would blow her right off the screen.

Having over the years blown many a good comic off the screen — "blowed 'em up good, blowed 'em up real good" his *SCTV* "Farm Film Report" character might say — John Candy by contrast couldn't be better suited for the world of Mel Brooks, and it's a real shame these two crazies never teamed up again before Candy's far, far too early death in 1994 at forty-four. An out-and-out master at creating breakout characters for both the Second City comedy troupe and *SCTV* (3-D horror star Dr. Tongue, polka king Yosh Schmenge, chain-smoking lothario Johnny LaRue), the rotund, endlessly inventive Candy reminds one very much of Brooks favorite Dom DeLuise,

with, at times, even a bit of Zero Mostel, James Coco, Jackie Gleason, Oliver Hardy, and Lou Costello thrown in. While we won't pretend his sweet-tempered man-dog Barf pushes Candy's colossal talents nearly as far as his now-classic fruitcakes on *SCTV* (minus all the dog business, Barf remains fairly standard sidekick-buddy material), the actor's ever-buoyant affability and winning delivery often makes his dialogue play funnier than it really is, and his very presence in the movie — just seeing his name on the poster or video art, even — gives us incredibly high hopes for it. Not too many actors could have held their own in films opposite comic scene-stealers like Steve Martin, Bill Murray, and Chevy Chase, but Candy stays funny opposite anybody, and, cast among lesser loonies Pullman and Zuniga, he outshines his costars without even breaking a sweat.

Their vessel's escape pods already piloted to safety by circus acrobats, zoo animals, and assorted other shipboard eccentrics, sycophantic Col. Sandurz (George Wyner), self-important space bully Dark Helmet (Rick Moranis), and administrative screw-up Pres. Skroob (Mel Brooks) brace for the worst as their computer counts down the seconds until their air-stealing spaceship self-destructs, in director Mel Brooks' *Spaceballs* (1987).

Though they actually have no scenes together, Candy gets great backup from *SCTV* pal Rick Moranis, another of those rare Brooks actors whose name alone promises a laugh-a-minute, rollicking good time. Proof positive one needn't be physically larger-than-life to somehow still *be* larger-than-life, Moranis brings just as much talent as his friend (Remember *SCTV*'s parka-clad, beer-loving Bob McKenzie? Those uncannily accurate impressions of Dick Cavett, Woody Allen, and Merv Griffin?), and his tyrannical yet nerdy scene-stealer Dark Helmet, stomping around in tights and boxers like Steve Urkel convinced he's King Kong, is one of *Spaceballs'* best assets. Probably only Woody Allen himself would've made a nicer surprise behind that huge mask, and he and Candy help so much just being there we're only sorry more *SCTV* alumni (Joe Flaherty, Eugene Levy, Dave Thomas, Andrea Martin, Catherine O'Hara, Martin Short, etc.) couldn't have joined up too. If Brooks must seek new faces, *SCTV* is clearly a good place to find them.

A much bigger surprise is actor George Wyner, returning from *My Favorite Year* and *To Be or Not to Be* and, as Dark Helmet's gutless yes-man Col. Sandurz, an unexpectedly solid foil for both Moranis and Brooks here. Perhaps because Wyner looks so much like the fellow who cashed our last paycheck or filed our taxes we tend to forget the seemingly zillions of sitcoms he's appeared in, or his role as the butt of Chevy Chase's wisecracks in his 1980s *Fletch* movies. *Spaceballs* might have been far funnier casting some more overtly comic weirdo (imagine Dom DeLuise crawling out of Lady Liberty's nose!), but Wyner's anguish-by-proxy look of empathy as Dark Helmet castigates (castrates?) one of his male minions and his speech-impeding pucker bracing against the deadly pressures of "ludicrous speed" make him well worth reusing.

Fans are always happy stumbling on TV favorite Dick Van Patten again as well, his Archie Andrews speaking voice and Andy Hardy grin as well-suited to his second of three Brooks films as to his half-dozen or so Disney pictures of the 1970s. What a great sport, too; Brooks wants him duded up like some aging Buster Brown in Goldilocks curls, and Van Patten goes right along with it as if he's just happy to be asked. King Roland's low-key anxiety won't steal many scenes (his best bit is some minor babbling about his car-dealer cousin, carried off in endearing MacLean Stevenson style), but *Eight Is Enough*'s Van Patten plays worried fathers better than anyone, even dressed more like somebody's dotty old aunt than her dear old dad. As with Wyner, might some more hyperkinetic loony have made a funnier monarch — say, a Steve Martin or Jonathan Winters or Martin Short? Maybe, but warmth and amiability have their place too, and even when Van Patten is a comic bad guy as in *Gus* or *The Shaggy D.A.*, it's easy to see why fans still like him.

While a far more abrasive personality, Joan Rivers does nice work as Dot Matrix too, and somehow "playing" a machine makes her more likable. Despite the off-color extras, *Spaceballs* radiates such a childlike, Disney-ish aura that Rivers' willingness to lend her distinctive voice to what amounts to a full-size wind-up toy softens her usual rude, crude talk show style. It's like casting Rodney Dangerfield as Tom Thumb, or Don Rickles as Winnie-the-Pooh. Despite her reputation for acid-tongued innuendo, furthermore, Brooks avoids making Dot some gold-plated potty-mouth, and we're glad of it; Rivers' lines need to be funnier, not dirtier, and having her play a loyal helper type wins the comedienne–talk show host astonishing new respect. We like her like this, and with a few dozen sharper lines, and if only her unique personality weren't hidden behind unblinking eyes and drive-in speaker mouth, Dot might have become a real breakout character.

The same goes for Dom DeLuise, heard but not seen voicing the literally greasy, cheesy (and, stereotypically, faintly Italian) felon Pizza the Hutt. Reliable as always, DeLuise handles Pizza's rather lazy dialogue just fine, but what a waste; here's one of the most sublimely malleable faces in film locked away doing studio voice-overs. A mere decade earlier, when his wild-man hysteria as Burt Reynolds' fruit-cake-nutty asylum mate in 1978's *The End* nearly stole the whole show, DeLuise might have played Barf, or Col. Sandurz or Yogurt or Dark Helmet, but who'd guess the arm-waving, head-banging maniac behind all that side-splitting physical comedy in *The Twelve Chairs* would end up spending so much of his later career unseen, taping cartoon parts in films like *The Secret of NIMH*, *An American Tale*, *Oliver & Co.*, and *All Dogs Go to Heaven*? Sure, the movies were mostly good ones, and animators were smart to use him, but we want to *see* DeLuise act crazy, not just hear him. Even if the older, heftier DeLuise of Brooks' later films couldn't recreate the bounce-off-the-walls energy of *The Twelve Chairs*' Father Fyodor, we'd still love to see him try, but a laid-back, stone-still sluggard like Pizza doesn't even give this funny, funny man a chance.

Spaceballs employs lots of talent it doesn't know quite what to do with. Lorene Yarnell, half of TV's 1977–78 *Shields and Yarnell* series with mime partner husband Robert Shields, stays nimble as ever inside her Dot Matrix getup, but beyond one or two mild bits isn't asked to do much the average stuntperson couldn't do. Michael Winslow, beloved by *Police Academy* fans, repeats his self-vocalized sound effects shtick here to fine success, but despite winning star treatment in Brooks' closing clip sequence, comes and goes so quickly he makes almost no impact at all on the actual story. *History of the World — Part I*'s John Hurt, an Oscar nominee for Brooksfilms' 1980 hit *The Elephant Man*, enjoys similar success in his stand-alone *Alien* takeoff, again mostly as a kind of one-shot stunt; like Winslow's, his entire performance, funny as it is, could have ended up cut and we'd have never been the wiser. With apologies to *Blazing Saddles*' Hedley Lamarr, "ditto" *The Bob Newhart Show*'s Jack Riley, back for his fourth Brooks role and watchable as ever, but hardly story-crucial as the anchorman reporting Pizza's death since even without Pizza's threats Lone Starr and Barf likely would rescue Princess Vespa for the right reward anyway.

Similarly underutilized, TV's JM J. Bullock brings more built-in comic flair to twice-jilted groom Prince Valium than Princess Vespa's more traditional-looking pick Bill Pullman, having just ended a scene-stealing half-decade on *Too Close For Comfort* and still enjoying spill-over popularity in a late–'80s update of *Hollywood Squares*. Bullock's funny, but ultimately even this vaguely Paul Lynde–ish young clown mostly just stands about yawning in a girly-looking pageboy wig, which at least allows him a few amusing close-ups but not much else. *Spaceballs* underuses another well-liked sitcom face too, *Soap*'s Sal Viscuso, whom Brooks' wife Anne Bancroft had directed in 1980's *Fatso* and whose Pollyanna perkiness as a *Spaceball I* radio man helps carry one scene that mostly just putters. Viscuso appears just long enough to brighten things up, then vanishes, as does Rudy DeLuca, in his fourth of seven Brooks films, seen briefly as Pizza's robot crony Vinnie. Like Pizza, Vinnie has potential, but cut his scene and the plot loss is near-zero.

Spaceballs co-writer Ronny Graham, in his third of five Brooks efforts, has only slightly more plot relevance, putting his intrinsically funny voice and visage to good use as an ill-tempered priest (he'd play another, off-screen, in *Life Stinks*). Even some of Graham's bits feel too forced to play all that well, though, especially his turn as impromptu sports reporter, and as sexy, sultry Commanderette Zircon, Leslie Bevis can't make much mark either, her carnal earnestness better suited to non-parody science fiction, as seen in *Alien Nation* the next year. She's a good actress, but deleting the double-entendres, Wyner, Winslow, Viscuso, or any "crewman" could deliver her military communiqués with equal relevance; beyond the innuendo, the role is nearly as expendable as those played by DeLuca and DeLuise, or those of Ira Miller (back in a second of three Brooks turns) as a diner cook; future *Star Trek: Voyager* actor Tim Russ as a Spaceballs trooper; or *The Addams Family* and *Buck Rogers in the Twenty-fifth Century* TV legend Felix Silla as one of Yogurt's Munchkin-like helpers, the Dinks. The parts are fun to watch for, but vital? Hardly.

Fittingly, Mel Brooks' best work may well come from Mel Brooks, who plays both bad guy Pres. Skroob and good guy Yogurt and uses both to play to his greatest strength as a writer: satirizing society's foibles, its defects, its corruption. Read backwards, Skroob's name suggests Brooks' own (or, uttered straight, Skroob's disregard for the voters), and while an interplanetary politico, at heart he's pure, or impure, Washington, D.C.— conning, philandering, mismanaging left and right. He's *Blazing Saddles'* penlight-dim Gov. Lepetomane turned Machiavellian conniver, a bureaucratic bumbler incapable of intelligent decision-making without top-level aid. Through Jewish-accented product-pitchman Yogurt, meanwhile (again, we're made uneasy by the ethnic stereotyping, but if Brooks doesn't worry, should we?), Brooks comes closest to "sticking it

to" George Lucas, whose untold millions marketing *Star Wars* items Brooks skewers all through the comedy's last half. Merchandising, says Yogurt, not ticket sales, is where the *real* money comes from (for Lucas, that is; Brooks had to promise not to hawk tie-ins too "*Star Wars*-y"), a point driven home just beautifully as gaudy, crassly conspicuous "*Spaceballs*"–emblazoned bedsheets, shaving cream, and toilet paper pop up around every turn. Yogurt, completely casual about all this Madison Avenue–ization of art, even hopes for a sequel, the better to further milk fans out of every last dime. *Spaceballs'* lesser gags notwithstanding, this is shrewd, shrewd writing.

Yes, it's here, when Brooks ignores mock-mimicking *Star Wars* and, *Get Smart*–style, lets D.C. politics and Hollywood smarminess have it like a Schwartz blast to the gut, that *Spaceballs* really hits its comic heights. In moments like these it reaches the satiric genius of Brooks' earliest triumphs, and if *Spaceballs'* happy-go-lucky slackness lacks *The Producers'* fever-pitch intellect or *The Twelve Chairs'* greed-of-humanity ferocity — well, he's still given the silly, nonsense-loving schoolkid inside each of us a grand old time at the fun park, a gloriously carefree day at the zoo. "When did we get to Disneyland?" wonders a desert-dazed Lone Starr in one scene. The instant Brooks first called "Action," that's when, and loose, limp, and lowbrow as it often is, *Spaceballs* contains just enough sunny, forget-all-your-troubles cheeriness to make us awfully glad he did.

CAST: Mel Brooks (President Skroob/Yogurt); John Candy (Barf); Rick Moranis (Dark Helmet); Bill Pullman (Lone Starr); Daphne Zuniga (Princess Vespa); Dick Van Patten (King Roland); George Wyner (Colonel Sandurz); Michael Winslow (Radar Technician); Joan Rivers (Voice of Dot Matrix); Lorene Yarnell (Dot Matrix); John Hurt (John Hurt); Sal

Viscuso (Radio Operator); Ronny Graham (Minister); JM J. Bullock (Prince Valium); Leslie Bevis (Commanderette Zircon); Jim Jackman (Major Asshole); Michael Pniewski (Laser Gunner); Sandy Helberg (Dr. Schlotkin); Stephen Tobolowsky (Captain of the Guard); Jeff MacGregor (Snotty); Henry Kaiser (Magnetic Beam Operator); Denise Gallup (Charlene); Dian Gallup (Marlene); Gail Earle, Dey Young (Waitresses); Rhonda Shear (Woman in Diner); Robert Prescott (Sand Cruiser Driver); Jack Riley (TV Newsman); Tom Dreesen (Megamaid Guard); Rudy DeLuca (Vinnie); Tony Griffin, Rick Ducommun (Prison Guards); Ken Olfson (Head Usher); Bryan O'Byrne (Organist); Wayne Wilson (Trucker in Cap); Ira Miller (Short Order Cook); Earl Finn (Guard with Captain); Mitchell Bock (Video Op.); Tommy Swerdlow (Troop Leader); Tim Russ (Trooper); Ed Gale, Felix Silla, Tony Cox, Antonio Hoyos, Arturo Gil, John Kennedy Hayden (The Dinks); Deanna Booker (Bearded Lady); Johnny Silver (Caddy); Brenda Strong (Nurse); Dom DeLuise (Voice of Pizza the Hutt).

Credits: Director: Mel Brooks; Producer: Mel Brooks; Co-Prod.: Ezra Swerdlow; Dir. of Photog.: Nick McLean; Prod. Dsgnr.: Terence Marsh; Ed.: Conrad Buff IV; Mus.: John Morris; "Spaceballs" Cmpsrs.: Jeff Prescetto, Clyde Lieberman, Mel Brooks/Prfmrs.: The Spinners; "My Heart Has a Mind of Its Own" Cmpsrs.: Gloria Sklerov, Lenny Macalusa/Prfmrs.: Kim Carnes, Jeffrey Osborne; "Heartstrings" Prfmr.: Berlin; "Good Enough" Prfmr.: Van Halen; "Raise Your Hands" Cmpsrs.: Jon Bon Jovi, Richie Sambora/Prfmr.: Bon Jovi; "Hot Together" Prfmrs.: The Pointer Sisters; "Wanna Be Loved By You" Prfmr.: Ladyfire; Mus. Ed.: Eugene Marks; Orchestrations: Jack Hayes; Scoring Mxr.: Armin Steiner; Spec. Vis. Effects: Apogee, Inc.; Cost. Dsgnr.: Donfeld; Casting: Lynn Stalmaster & Assoc., David Rubin; Casting: Bill Shepard; Prod. Mgr.: Robert Latham Brown; Assist. Dir.: Dan Kolsrud; 2nd Assist. Dir.: Mitchell Bock; Vis. Effects Supvr.: Peter Donen; Addnl. Editing: Nicholas C. Smith; Art Dir.: Harold Michelson; Set Dec.: John Franco, Jr.; Assist. Art Dir.: Diane Wager; Set Dsgnrs.: Peter Kelly, Richard McKenzie, Jacoues Valin; Illus.: Camille Abbott; Prop. Mstr.: Dennis Parrish; Cam. Ops.: Michael D. O'Shea, Steve Bridge; 1st Assist. Cam.: Michael A. Chavez, Steve McLean; 2nd Assist. Cam.: George Llerena; Ch. Lghtg. Tech.: Tom Stern; Key Grip: Wm. C. Young; Prod. Sound: Jeff Wexler, Don Coufal, Jim Steube; Script Supvr.: Julie Pitkanen; Assoc. Ed.: Jay Ignaszewski; Assist. Eds.: Clarinda Wong, Debra Goldfield; Locat. Mgr.: Michael J. Meehan; Prod. Coord.: Mary Courtney; Prod. Controller: K. Lenna Kunkel; Accntnts.: Allison Harstedt, Laurie Steube; Addnl. 2nd Assist. Dir.: Carol D. Bonnefil; Assist. to Mr. Brooks: Leah Zappy; Assist. to Mr. Swerdlow: Daren Hicks; Women's Wardrobe Supvr.: Charmaine N. Simmons; Men's Wardrobe Supvr.: Bruce Ericksen; Makeup Dsgnr./Creator: Ben Nye, Jr.; Makeup Artists: Ken Diaz, Melanie Elaine Levitt; Hair Stylist: Dione Taylor; Constr. Coord.: S. Bruce Wineinger; Genl. Frmn.: Guy Allan MacLaury; Constr. Frmn.: Ken Reed; Propmaker Frmn.: Steve Willis; Standby Painter: Jerry Cadette; Spec. Effects Supvr.: Peter Albiez; Spec. Effects: Richard Ratliff; Assist. Lghtg. Tech.: Victor Perez; Sec. Grips: Jerry King, Bruce Spellman; Video Playback Op.: Lindsay P. Hill; Assist. Prop. Mstr.: Bill King; Prop. Illus.: Arthur Gelb; Leadman: Wm. Maxwell III; Drapery Man: James J. Pickering; Prod. Assists.: JoAnne Wetzel Caverly, James Caverly, Charles Schlissel; Assist. to Mr. Candy: Nyna Cravens; Assists to Mr. Meehan/Mr. Graham: Ann Fisher, Karen D'Arc; Still Photog.: Peter Sorel; Publicist: Saul Kahan; Barf Ear Animatronics: Rick Lazzarini; Vis. Effects Coord.: Craig Boyajian; Vis. Effects Prod. Assist.: Peter Gruskoff; Craft Serv.: Ramon Pahoyd; Transp. Coord.: Jim Chesney; Transp. Capt.: Chet Brooks; Stunt Coord.: Richard Warlock; Exec. in Charge of Prod.: Robert Shepherd; Spec. Vis. Effects Prod.: Percy Angress; Mot. Cont. Cam. Ops.: Doug Smith, David Hardberger, John Sullivan, Mat Beck; Mot. Cont. Cam. Assists.: Stephen Brooks, Glenn Campbell, Ron Robinson, Mark Gredell; Opt. Supvr.: Roger Dorney; Opt. Cam. Op.: Jerry Pooler; Opt. Cam. Assists.: Cosmas Paul Bolger, Jr., Dennis Dorney, Richard Gilligan; Effects Anim. Supvr.: Clint Colver; Anim. Illus.: Harry Weinmann, John Shourt; Assist. Ed.: Joe Yanuzzi; Prod. Coord.: Michael Van Kimbergen; Ch. Model Maker: Grant McCune; Model Makers: Chris Ross, Cory Faucher, John Eaves, David Sosalla, David Beasley, Jay Roth, Tom Pahk, Suzy Schneider, Smokey Stover; Model Dpt. Spec. Dsgn.: Rae Burkland, Ron Thornton; Vis. Effects Art Dir.: Steven Dane; Ch. Set Lghtg. Tech.: Bob Jason; Vis. Effects Matte Tech.: Jonathan Erland; Mot. Cont. Elctrncs. Engr.: Alvah J. Miller; Vis. Effects Engr.: Don Trumbull; Effects Techs.: Richard Alexander,

Bill Shourt, Rod Goldstein; Mot. Cont. Prgmr.: Paul Johnson; Ch. Prod. Aud.: Debbi Nikkel; Effects Prod. Publicist: Susan McGuire; Post Prod. Sound Srvcs.: Sprockets Systems, a Div. of Lucasfilm Ltd.; Sound Dsgnrs.: Randy Thom, Gary Rydstrom; Rerecording Mxrs.: Randy Thom, Gary Summers, Richard Beggs; Vocal Effects Supvr.: Norman B. Schwartz; Spvsng. Dialogue Ed.: Michael John Bateman; Dialogue Eds.: Glad Pickering, Ronald Sinclair, George Simpson; Sound Effects Eds.: Ken Fischer, Ernie Fosselius, Ronald Jacobs, Sandina Bailo-Lape; Assist. Sound Eds.: Pamela J. Yuen, Sue Breitrose, David Slusser, David Bergad, Scott Chandler, Robert Bowman, Paige Sartorius; Foley Recordist: Tom Johnson; Foley Artist: Dennie Thorpe; Alien Monster Creator: Indus. Light & Magic; Matte Pntg. Effects: Sid Dutton, Bill Taylor, A.S.C., Illusion Arts, Inc.; Video/Grphc. Displays: Video Image, Rhonda C. Gunner, Richard F. Hollander, Gregory I. McMurray, John C. Wash; Addnl. Anim.: Available Light Ltd.; Title Dsgn.: Anthony Goldschmidt; Opticals: Pacific Title; Panaflex Cam./Lenses; Panavision; Metracolor; Special Thanks to: Jerry and Bob Greenberg, U.S. Dpt. of the Int., Bur. of Land Mgt., "Public Lands U.S.A., Use, Share and Appreciate," Winnebago Indstrs., Inc., Lark Luggage Co., Goody Prdcts., Inc., Calico M-100 Rifles by Calico Co.; A Brooksfilm Pres.; Metro-Goldwyn-Mayer; 1987; 97 minutes.

10

* * *

"We Have Reached Capacity!"

Life Stinks

★ ★ ★ ★ ★ ★

(1991)

Pitiless Los Angeles billionaire Goddard Bolt (Mel Brooks), meeting with his company lawyers Pritchard (Stuart Pankin), Knowles (Michael Ensign), and Stevens (Matthew Faison) in his posh office, unveils plans to turn a section of L.A. slums into ultra-flashy Bolt Center. Rich rival Vance Crasswell (Jeffrey Tambor), however, new owner of the half Bolt lacks, visits to pose a bet: If Bolt can survive, penniless and unrecognized, in these slums for thirty days, he will win Crasswell's half; if he can't, Crasswell wins Bolt's. Confident he can win, Bolt eagerly agrees, gives up his mustache, toupee, credit cards, and jewelry, and — wearing an anti-cheating electronic ankle device to monitor his whereabouts, is dropped off in the ghetto to get the bet underway.

After an eye-opening first night in which even priests deny him aid, Bolt wakes to the word *Pepto* smudged on his forehead from a Pepto-Bismol box and, briefly, friendly aging derelict Sailor (Howard Morris). Later, Bolt fails trying to earn food money, and even loses his shoes in an unprovoked run-in with nasty ghetto thugs Mean Victor (Brian Thompson) and Yo (Raymond O'Connor), who flee when territorial alley dweller Molly (Lesley Ann Warren) intervenes. Giving him a pair of spare shoes, Molly grudgingly escorts Bolt to a mission for a hot meal — where, known now as Pepto, Bolt dines with Sailor and his liquor-loving pal Fumes (Teddy Wilson).

Later, alone with Bolt, a bitter Molly discloses she was once a dancer who quit her job, wed a man who deserted her, then suffered a nervous breakdown, while Bolt shares how his wife divorced him over his endless money-chasing. After Mean Victor and Yo burn her few meager belongings, an angry Molly enlists Bolt, Sailor, and Fumes in a "hot soup on the head" revenge plot that, while successful, not only brings a briefly "out of bounds" Bolt seconds away from losing his bet but nearly gets him killed. Informed of his opponent's brush with death, Crasswell, hoping Bolt will die of exposure, closes the mission on a rainy night, but it is not Bolt but the sickly Sailor who is dead by next morning, and as a grieving Bolt, Molly, and Fumes give Sailor's ashes a "burial at sea" at a tiny viaduct trickle, the wind hurls the remains back in their faces.

On Bolt's bet-winning final day, he and Molly, quite close now, celebrate his victory with stolen champagne, a romantic dance in a rag warehouse, and a night of passion. Their jubilation ends at Bolt's estate, however, where they learn Crasswell has paid Bolt's lawyers to have him declared insane and rob him of all he owns. A broken man, Bolt flees alone into the night.

The next day, after wildly assaulting an infuriating bum who believes himself J. Paul Getty (Rudy DeLuca), Bolt is hospitalized, overmedicated, and left barely alive until Molly finds him, tenderly confessing her love. Bolt recovers, and later, at Crasswell's groundbreaking ceremony, Bolt and Molly turn the bulldozer-uprooted homeless into party-crashing protesters. Defeating Crasswell in a tyrannosaur-like earth-mover battle, Bolt dangles his terrified adversary in midair until Crasswell admits — on live TV — that Bolt, not he, has won the bet. Winning full legal control of the area, Bolt vows to turn it into a shelter and health care area for the poor, and weds Molly in a slum chapel, with only a return of the phony J. Paul Getty delaying the happy honeymoon.

★   ★   ★

Generally dismissed as the least successful of his post–1970s directorial efforts, Mel Brooks' *Life Stinks* has been struggling to pull free of the stigma of failure ever since it slid in and out of American theaters pretty much unnoticed during summer of 1991. Though a fair-sized hit overseas in the months that followed, at home *Life Stinks* caused barely a ripple, even in a movie season whose comic successes varied from *City Slickers* to *Hot Shots!*, from a

Father of the Bride remake to *What About Bob?* In a year in which Michael J. Fox scored hits with *Doc Hollywood*, Raul Julia with *The Addams Family*, and Leslie Nielsen with *The Naked Gun 2½: The Smell of Fear*, U.S. filmgoers in 1991 were clearly in a mood to laugh, yet until this touching little tale of a billionaire playing street bum on a bet hit video and TV, many weren't aware Brooks had shot a new film after *Spaceballs* at all. Even today the general assumption is that since *Life Stinks* didn't make big money in the U.S., it must not be very good — as if because *Friday the 13th*, *Police Academy* and *Revenge of the Nerds* made bigger first-release splashes that somehow makes them better movies than box office slow-starters like *Vertigo*, *It's a Wonderful Life*, and *Citizen Kane*!

Somewhat undeservedly, really, word that Brooks' latest was a dud accompanied *Life Stinks* before most fans even had a chance to see it. This writer himself recalls his disappointment upon being told one afternoon that his own neighborhood cineplex, up till then as Brooks-friendly as any movie house anywhere, wouldn't be booking *Life Stinks* that summer at all; the owner had screened it already, decided it held little of the mammoth box office appeal of a *Blazing Saddles* or *Young Frankenstein*, and just wasn't convinced he'd find much audience for it. From a strictly economic standpoint, he was probably right, too. Imagine *Life Stinks* and *Blazing Saddles* hitting theaters the same weekend, with fans given time and money enough to see just one; no matter how slickly edited the TV ads, which film would *anyone* most want to see? What's jab-to-the-gut funnier: one drab-looking Los Angeles derelict slapping around another beside a chainlink fence, or a King Kong cowboy swaggering up to a saloon punching the living daylights out of a horse?

No doubt about it, *Life Stinks* plays softer and more subtly than most Brooks movies, and popularity-wise that's both blessing and curse. Like *The Producers* and *The Twelve Chairs*, the project at least tries semi-original material instead of spoofing an already existing genre, so it wins high marks for risk-taking right off. On the other hand, how writers Brooks, Rudy DeLuca, Steve Haberman, and story contributor Ron Clark ever could have made such an uneasy mix of slapstick and sensitivity a box office smash like *Blazing Saddles* or *Young Frankenstein* is hard to say. *Life Stinks'* very premise is at odds with itself, really, demands Brooks somehow wear kid gloves and boxing gloves at the same time. Play the material too gently, nobody laughs; come on too strong, risk charges of blatant insensitivity. Indeed, finding laughs in a story populated by brain-feeble beggars, sickly seniors, and disabled dwarfs in the politically correct '90s was an idea so rife with pitfalls one can't imagine tackling it to start with; *Life Stinks'* entire foundation is as precarious as a house of cards, built at a time when an entire nation of table-shaking overreacters were blaming Disney's *Aladdin* for besmirching Arabs and *Jurassic Park* for vilifying the obese.

Precarious, yes — but courageous too. Though scene-for-scene less pricey than most of his post–'70s hits, marketing-wise *Life Stinks* may be Brooks' riskiest film since 1970's *The Twelve Chairs*, which may have looked too much like some Sergei Eisenstein historical epic to win over most fans. While *History of the World — Part I* and *Spaceballs*, with their fanciful costumes and sets, look so much like souped-up variety show sketches we're tempted to take a peek just for the sheer spectacle of it all, *Life Stinks'* drab L.A. streets and sidewalks look no more interesting than the ones we've seen over and over again on TV, on *Dragnet, Mannix, Adam-12, Emergency, Police Woman, Cannon, The Rockford Files, CHiPs, Hunter* — and that's just naming a handful.

Since *Life Stinks* isn't really a spoof, it can't benefit from the popularity of past movies, either. Its upbeat "nobility of the common man" sentiments recall those favored by '30s and '40s directors like Frank Capra and Preston Sturges, but Brooks doesn't "goof" on these men's film styles the way he did James Whale and Hitchcock. This *could* have been Mel Brooks' big Capra lampoon, poking fun at too-good-to-be-true James Stewart–Gary Cooper types with their stirring, faith-restoring oration, but Brooks more nearly plays the exact same notes as Capra than dreams up some loopy new mock–Capra sendup. With its winner-turned-loser named Goddard Bolt, *Life Stinks* echoes Gregory La Cava's 1936 hit *My Man Godfrey*, but even renamed *My Man Goddard* only the title would really qualify as spoof because so little gets exaggerated. If *Life Stinks* began as somebody's "Hey, let's parody Frank Capra!" idea, we'd never know it from what we see here.

Still, beyond the added expense involved, one wonders why Brooks doesn't just set the film in the 1930s, where, for all its "ancient history" feel, the Great Depression backdrop at least might have made his themes a bit easier to handle. In the post Stock Market Crash '30s, half the country was a hairbreadth away from the poorhouse, so with "Brother, Can You Spare a Dime?" the era's unofficial theme song, if some film hero played by Charlie Chaplin or Henry Fonda or William Powell hits the skids, nobody casts blame. Times are hard, we figure; he'd dig himself out if he could. Set in the Turner-and-Trump '90s, though, when even some street people wore castoff Nikes and Lakers caps *The Waltons'* kids' real-life barefoot, overalls-clad counterparts might envy, *Life Stinks* has a harder time convincing us society's victims are all that victimized. Nobody doubts the early '90s' recession's life-crippling severity, but from a strictly cinematic standpoint it leaves us skeptical, and can't offer the all-purpose excuse-all the Great Depression gives *To Kill a Mockingbird*, *The Grapes of Wrath*, and *Places in the Heart* right out of the box.

Life Stinks offers little explanation for its street dwellers' poverty, really, at times coming disquietingly close to implying the only reason its homeless remain so is because they're simply unlucky, just "dealt a bad hand"—a reasonable enough justification in the '30s, maybe, but just a little bit unconvincing even in the pre-recovery '90s. These folks aren't responsible for what's happened to them, the film suggests; *we* are, *society* is, if only for not helping them escape. Well, perhaps, but except

Brooks' rich-guy land baron, who's only passing through on a bet, we never really see anyone *trying* to escape all that hard, so how do we decide who's really "stuck" here with no way out and who's just avoiding the humdrum, everyday drudgery of time card–punching, nine-to-five work? Are they making any real effort toward self-improvement, or have they just "dropped out"? They're all homeless—but how many are genuinely helpless too? Have the rest of us secured employment only because we're "lucky"? Do the "less fortunate" get off with a pass?

Chicago Sun-Times critic Roger Ebert, one of *Life Stinks'* few early admirers, touches on this "accountability vs.

Dancer-turned-derelict Molly (Lesley Ann Warren) and street-slumming billionaire Goddard Bolt (Mel Brooks) enjoy a little good-natured camaraderie with homeless pals Fumes (Teddy Wilson) and Sailor (Howard Morris), as Sailor treats an injured Bolt's head wound, in director Mel Brooks' *Life Stinks*, a 1991 comedy reuniting producer and co-writer Brooks with his old *Your Show of Shows* buddy Howard Morris for their first movie together since 1981's *History of the World—Part I.*

inactivity" issue even while pinpointing the film's basic appeal: "Donald Trump can make millions selling condos to other millionaires, but could he make ten bucks in a day if he had to start from scratch?" Bolt thinks *he* can, certainly, especially with full control of a prime chunk of L.A. real estate as incentive, yet likable as most of them are, we see little evidence his slum pals are matching his efforts, and if, even with "no boots," as Ebert puts it, they won't try to "pull themselves up by their bootstraps," how deserving of Bolt's final-five-minutes financial rescue are they? Is Bolt giving these people what they'd gladly work for themselves if they could, or something they're unwilling to break a sweat for but will take when it's cost- and labor-free?

That last question sounds, admittedly, pretty pitiless, but *Life Stinks* deals with just such how-dare-we-even-doubt-it presuppositions. These days even *hinting* a homeless person might be less than saintly amounts to pulling the wings off butterflies or skinning puppies alive, but Brooks' street-dwellers aren't *all* unable to work, are they? Billy Barty's legless little person Willy might have job troubles, or Rudy DeLuca's spaced-out crank with the Larry Fine hair — but *all* these people? The implication is that homelessness is its own excuse for not trying, as if because minimum wage can't fully pay the rent and gas bill we'd be cruel asking anyone to put in regular hours anyway and save up. That lazy, "too cool for school" slack-off who sat behind us in tenth grade, the one who mooched homework answers, never studied, never trained himself for anything — logically, he might be right here, but saying so just isn't "P.C.," and the closest Brooks comes to accounting for him is with Johnny Cocktails as the Burrito-Eating Bum who, though looking fit as a fiddle and obviously well-fed, doesn't know where his "next meal is coming from."

That's a nice touch — but somehow it's not enough. Consider Bolt's romantic interest, for instance, Lesley Ann Warren's scrappy young bag lady Molly. We feel sorry for her, since she's been spouse-abandoned, nervous breakdown-afflicted, and all, but, eccentric as she is, she seems too active, clever, and pretty to be "trapped" here, marrying into money her only way out, and it's hard to believe anyone wily enough to fend off downpours, disease, and dope fiends can't find a job. Are we being unrealistic here? Uncharitable? Unfair? Absolutely, and if we really *were* in this same plight we'd eat all these words — but, even given that this is the eighth year of Molly's breakdown, shouldn't someone written this Lois Lane street-savvy and Ginger Rogers nimble at least be given bigger nervous tics or anxiety attacks or *something* to better explain why she isn't out hunting work? And what of Teddy Wilson's good-natured liquor-lover Fumes? How wise is it to script scenes in which poor, "ill-fated" Fumes wastes money on alcohol? If he's addicted, his sickness losing him job after job, that's one thing — but he's not really depicted that way, and it's a crucial omission in a character who, despite seeming, like Molly, still young and fit enough to work, has no trouble finding liquor but takes charity for meals. How should we feel about this?

Most U.S. filmgoers, exempting *Life Stinks* from their "must-see" lists that year, never felt anything, and unfair to him though it may be, perhaps they held higher expectations for Brooks than most other directors. Nobody minds much when other comic filmmakers develop a classier, more delicate touch — when Ivan Reitman drops the goofball irreverence of *Meatballs* and *Stripes* to give us *Dave*, or when Harold Ramis moves on from *Caddyshack* and *National Lampoon's Vacation* to head up *Groundhog Day* — but when Brooks tries too it's labeled a career misstep, as if Akira Kurosawa had suddenly tried helming teenage slasher flicks or Orson Welles shooting Jerry Lewis films. Whatever the case, however well-intentioned *Life Stinks* may have been, most U.S. audiences in 1991 just weren't buying, and while super-hyped, high-profile powerhouses like Oliver Stone's *JFK*, Barry Levinson's *Bugsy*, Ridley Scott's *Thelma & Louise*, John Singleton's *Boyz N The Hood*, Kevin Reynolds' *Robin Hood: Prince of Thieves*, Ron Howard's *Backdraft*, Steven Spielberg's *Hook*, and the Disney team's *Beauty and the Beast* raked in both untold millions and critical raves, *Life Stinks* barely got any serious attention at all. Indeed, how could it *not* get overlooked, in a movie year that included *My Girl*, *Fried Green Tomatoes*, *The Fisher King*, *The Rocketeer*, *Soapdish*, *Little Man Tate*, *Rambling Rose*, *Jungle Fever*, *Grand Canyon*, *The Doctor*, *L.A. Story*, and *Defending Your Life*—just to name a spotlight-grabbing few?

Ignored or not, though, *Life Stinks* is far from the crash-and-burn train wreck its nastiest reviews would have us believe, and all those critics who've ended up, like the *Washington Post*'s Hal Hinson, denouncing it in one fell swoop with a sniff and an easy pun ("The title of the new Mel Brooks comedy is *Life Stinks*, and brother, does it ever — the movie, that is") are just being clever at the expense of what is actually a nice little film. Yes, *Life Stinks* looks pretty ordinary beside a blast-all-expectations smash like *Young Frankenstein*, and we could do without the odd visual and verbal vulgarity, but however much some may have hated it, it's hardly the "bottom of the barrel" shower of "garbage" critics like Hinson imply. As property baron-turned-beggar Bolt, Brooks can't let fly the dodo bird madness of *Blazing Saddles*' Gov. Lepetomane or *Spaceballs*' Pres. Skroob, but isn't he at least as engaging as a film about the poor and infirm allows? Doesn't his fabulously gifted costar Lesley Ann Warren, fighting like a tigress, dancing like an angel, come off just dandy as Molly, the dancer-now-derelict who first rescues Bolt, then befriends him, then falls for and marries him? Doesn't Howard Morris endear himself yet again as dying alley-dweller Sailor, whose wind-blown ashes blanket his pallbearers like bug dust? And doesn't Rudy DeLuca make us grin a little as an out-of-his-head would-be J. Paul Getty? Absolutely they do, yet to hear some critics tell it *Life Stinks* is a flat-out flop, an unqualified disaster from Scene One to Scene None.

Those reviewers are wrong. Brooks would have been just plain balmy to start listing *Life Stinks* first on his resume, but it's hardly some cinematic *Titanic* or *Hindenberg* (the disasters — not the films), and here and there we can still see the old Mel Brooks genius peep through. We see it in the early office building scenes, in which, recalling the opening of Alfred Hitchcock's *Strangers on a Train*, he suggests the pre-poverty Bolt's cold corporate ruthlessness by focusing on his marching, high-priced leather shoes. That's an especially nice scene, given fine melodic backup from composer John Morris, with Bolt stepping on floor-cleaners' fingers, slipping on coffee, and kicking a subordinate for tapping his toes to some music. So is the "burial at sea" bit in which Brooks, having kept a real-life *Your Show of Shows*–era incident involving Howard Morris's late father percolating in the back of his mind for some forty years, has Bolt, Molly, and Fumes scatter the dead Sailor's ashes only to have the wind fling them back in their faces in a choking cloud. We see the old magic too in the post-bet Bolt's screwball desperation when, his mansion stolen by double-crossing employees, he tries making off with an armload of Chateau LaFit, Rodans, and Van Goghs; in Molly's rail-at-the-universe freak-out recalling her abandonment by her husband Tom; in the enchanting warehouse-of-rags waltz between Bolt and Molly, so beautifully stylized with colorful lighting, set props, and Morris's enticing adaptation of "Easy to Love"; in the Three Stooges–type slap fest between Bolt and "J. Paul Getty" and Bolt's crazed attack on this nut even as ambulance staffers drag him away; in the climactic monster-vs.-monster combat between Bolt and Crasswell aboard dinosaur-like backhoes; in a just-married Bolt's last-straw outrage as the phony Getty starts pestering him all over again. In scenes like these, in which Brooks' passion for camera tricks, song-and-dance, and rampant unpredictability get free rein, we happily say to ourselves, "Aha! That's the Mel Brooks we've been missing! Keep it coming! Keep it coming!"

Likable as they all are, though, it's of course doubtful any serious discussion of Brooks' greatest moments will ever start off with any of these scenes, not with prints of *The Producers* and *Blazing Saddles* and *Young Frankenstein* around, and there's no denying some of the material in between has about as much comic "oomph" as the dirt-drab cardboard Bolt has to sleep on. Still, what *do* we have here? Just Mel Brooks' best-scripted acting role in years, for one thing, arguably since heights-phobic Richard Thorndyke in 1977's *High Anxiety*, at the very least Polish stage hack Frederick Bronski in 1983's *To Be or Not to Be*; just, in Lesley Ann Warren's Molly, his best-scripted female part since Anne Bancroft reinvented Carole Lombard's old role for the same film; just Howard Morris and Rudy DeLuca given their juiciest Brooks roles since *High Anxiety*. Think *Life Stinks* isn't barrel-of-monkeys crazy enough after *Spaceballs*, with its tail-wagging dog-men and Winnebago spaceships and gangsters dripping pizza cheese? Maybe not, but just reweigh all the added character bonuses. Can anyone picture *Spaceballs*' Lone Starr hovering near death in a hospital bed after an overmedicated mental breakdown? Princess Vespa tearfully pleading with her comatose beloved to pull through? Barf, frail and sickly, leaving his only friends and dying alone? Of course not; the characters in *Spaceballs* simply aren't that deep.

Thus, *Life Stinks* satisfies more character-wise (perhaps *only* character-wise) than either *Spaceballs* or *Robin Hood: Men in Tights*, the two Brooks films it lies between, whose costumes look just glorious but can't make the people wearing them true-life, full-fledged personalities any more than the spaceship and castle sets they stride through. *Spaceballs*' attractive young lovers, while well-played by Bill Pullman and Daphne Zuniga, seem fated to pair up more because of paint-by-numbers fairy tale tradition than anything else (even after their initial frostiness starts melting they're still pretty shallow), and Brooks' Robin and Marian, for all Cary Elwes and Amy Yasbeck's style and charm, seem only slightly more fleshed-out than all those one-note, cel-drawn sweethearts from the old Disney films. With *Life Stinks*, though, Brooks can't dress '90s antihero Bolt in Prince Charming outfits or back-alley bag lady Molly as Snow White; dashing royal rescuers nearly always marry their fair young damsels in distress, but it's not every day super-rich real estate moguls wed castoff-clad riffraff from off the streets, so the sort of cinematic shorthand that lets Brooks cut a few storytelling corners in those other films won't quite work here. This time love must mature on its own, in steps and stages, through sheer scripting and performance.

In this respect, *Life Stinks* closely recalls Brooks' early works, most of which aren't love stories per se, yet do spend some ninety minutes forging bonds between two people who at first seem to have nothing in common. There bombastic troublemakers and timid wallflowers become bosom buddy business partners (*The Producers*), fallen nobles and born-poor commoners turn coin-begging allies (*The Twelve Chairs*), persecuted blacks and racist whites form a united front against evil land-grabbers (*Blazing Saddles*), and high-class scientists and grunting lab monsters become pals (*Young Frankenstein*). In a more strictly romantic sense, that occurs in *Spaceballs*, too, though that film has such a silly, cartoonish feel we can't identify with Lone Starr or Princess Vespa as if they were truly real people; we can see they're in love, in a fated-to-happen, Brothers Grimm/Hans Christian Andersen sort of way, but the quick trip from ill-tempered combatants to happy honeymooners seems awfully perfunctory, even after the speedy attraction between *High Anxiety*'s Thorndyke and Vicki, who at least begin their relationship on essentially the same side.

What develops between Bolt and Molly in *Life Stinks*, however, is just a little more artful. In a way, both start out caricatures almost as fully as the young lovers in *Spaceballs*—early on, Bolt stomps on fingers and stamps out rain forests with equal heartlessness, and chasing off thugs with a two-by-four Molly at first comes off half-charwoman, half-banshee — but in time we not only grow to care about these two crackpots, we feel we're truly starting to piece together who they are. Both Bolt and Molly confide to us lifelike, easy to relate to back-stories, and learning how both have been rejected by past spouses (Bolt because of his preoccupation with finance, Molly because her no-account husband had a roving eye) not only secures our sympathy but lets a fairly unlikely star-crossed love story evolve in a reasonably convincing, at least semi-believable way. Take away the rich/poor aspect, we might meet people very like these two in some support group somewhere, or spilling their souls in therapy. Unlike Brooks' Robin and Marian, or Lone Starr and Vespa, they're human beings, not cartoons. We *know* these people; they're "real."

Even after seeing the toupeed, mustached, pre-wager Bolt behave like some insensitive, cruel jerk, we still find a soft spot for him because, having pledged to business rival Crasswell to "make it" on the streets thirty days without cash or connections, he's as alone and vulnerable as some lost child, and because he shows a kind of panicky half-courage confronting the two toughs who've torched Molly's belongings. And Molly? Sure, she's cranky — after eight years on the streets, it's understandable — but both we and Bolt come to admire her because, besides being beautiful and a graceful dancer, she has survived a nervous breakdown (as will Bolt, before the movie is over) and braved life all alone for so long. They're kindred spirits, these two, former winners now fighting for survival, Bolt as part of a rich man's money game, Molly out of live-or-die necessity, and Brooks' surprisingly unhurried, leisurely manner of allowing plenty of quiet time to let their romance unfold makes *Life Stinks* his most human, personality-rich film in years.

That's not to say the film's themes themselves are all that new. We see quite a bit of *The Twelve Chairs*' gluttonous Ippolit Vorobyaninov in Goddard Bolt, particularly in the way both men discover a form of humility during their quest for wealth. We see Vorobyaninov reduced to a penniless vagrant, wolfing down all the food he can grab at a free buffet meant for hardworking rail workers, then learning to beg like lifelong pauper Ostap Bender — quite a long fall for a man who once employed servants and feasted atop elegant dining room furniture, and yet, personal growth–wise, quite a step up too. Likewise, in *Life Stinks* a half-starved Bolt, until now planning to replace an entire slum with his massive Bolt Center complex, savors every morsel of the free meal ladled out to him at a neighborhood soup kitchen (much as the piggish Vorobyaninov makes a spectacle of himself at the buffet, Bolt steals one extra ladle-ful meant for someone else), and he too learns to beg, if not too skillfully. Like the arrogant Vorobyaninov, who in his nobleman days might not stoop to help a fallen Bender out of the road, a somewhat more broad-minded Bolt acquires new friends too — Molly, Sailor, Fumes — of a sort he's never had much use for until now, after he's been reduced (and, like Vorobyaninov, spiritually built up) to their level.

In this regard Bolt reminds one of *The Producers'* Max Bialystock as well. That tiny little plastic "bum" a pre-humility Bolt flicks off his Bolt Center model like some worthless dirt speck represents real people, and Bolt's failure to see this recalls Bialystock's plan to wreck *Springtime for Hitler* by having nutty Franz Liebkind shoot all the actors. The one real difference: Bialystock is as self-servingly ruthless in *The Producers'* final stages as when he was one of Broadway's top movers and shakers, while Bolt does a moral about-face and turns poor man's champion after his fall from greatness. Impenitent windbag Bialystock makes room in his stone-cold spirit only for new "son" Bloom, while Bolt finds space enough for hundreds of sickly, unsightly derelicts he doesn't even know. Bolt too can "shoot the actors" if he wants — once the slums are his, he's well within his rights to drive these idlers off his land — but Bolt's heart, like that of Dr. Seuss's Grinch, has grown several sizes by now, while a *Prisoners of Love*–staging Bialystock is still duping away.

In a sense, Bolt is Bialystock in reverse, for where once well-to-do schemer Bialystock starts *The Producers* near-penniless, gets rich a second time through shameless greed, then loses everything all over again (and learns, in the end, absolutely nothing), Bolt's brush with poverty proves a real "wake-up call," making him yet another Brooks "hero"—*The Twelve Chairs'* Vorobyaninov again comes to mind, or *Spaceballs'* Princess Vespa — for whom a "walk on the wild side" is a blessing in disguise. For Vorobyaninov, being reduced to begging makes him face reality head-on: onetime nobleman or not, he'll have to live by his wits from now on. For Vespa, requiring help from an earthy, unrefined drifter softens her ego a little, changes her from proud, pampered prima donna into someone warmer, gentler, sweeter: true love, she realizes, may be worth more than social status after all. It's worth noting, though, that as much as Brooks' movies protest the evils of greed, the old "It's good to be the king" realities of *History of the World — Part I* still come through. Vorobyaninov still wants his lost riches even after he finds he can't have them; Vespa marries Lone Star, but only after she learns he's royalty; and while Bolt gives some of his money to charity and even weds one-time derelict Molly in a slum chapel, he drives off in his limo and tuxedo just the same. True humility, it seems, even in a Mel Brooks comedy, can only go so far.

Life Stinks has lots in common with *High Anxiety*, too, a film clearly more parody-based than this one but still bringing to mind *Life Stinks'* best elements. Both movies feature Brooks himself as a respected, business-suited professional in the big city; a too-trusting hero betrayed by his own colleagues and nearly losing his life through their machinations; harmless yet obviously mentally ill personalities suffering identity delusions; sizable stretches in which Brooks' character badly needs help but is cut off from outside aid; scenes in which he purposely "dresses down," at times teamed with an equally scruffy love interest quite lovely under better circumstances; scenes in which greedy profiteers prosper by accusing the well-off of madness; and even a daffy team-up between Brooks' character and a pretty, intelligent woman that leads to an end-of-story marriage. Of the two, *High Anxiety* is far more entertaining — it's funnier, faster, more colorfully cast, even better scored, and not even Howard Morris's heart-tugging old Sailor can quite overshadow the eccentric, dotty fun of *High Anxiety*'s animated, punch-swapping Prof. "Little-Old-Man" — but then *Life Stinks* also has more emotional warmth, more sensitivity, gives its characters more quiet moments in which to tenderly grieve over lost money, lost husbands, lost security, lost friends.

Perhaps its socially significant subtexts about destitution, infirmity, and malnutrition keep *Life Stinks* from really "cutting loose" and force its writers, cast, and even composer John Morris to keep the usual Brooksian irreverence in check. How can Brooks really feel free to make jokes or stage farce-heavy song-and-dance numbers about street people without mocking the very souls he's defending? Mel Brooks isn't anti-poor, just anti-poverty, has nothing against the homeless, just homelessness itself, the same way his old *Your Show of Shows* colleague Larry Gelbart's position writing TV's *M*A*S*H* wasn't anti-soldier but anti-waste, anti-stupidity, anti-war.

John Morris's score, his last for Brooks before Hummie Mann would take over, illustrates just this difficulty. His recurrent use of Cole Porter's "Easy to Love," first danced to by Eleanor Powell in 1936's *Born to Dance*, seems perfect for Brooks' softer tone (using it as the movie's ongoing musical motif was a stroke of genius, whoever's idea it was), but it's more romantic than funny, and not even mock-romantic at that. Morris's opening march for Bolt's no-mercy stomp to his office, the closest the

music ever comes to outright comedy, helps some, but in between *Life Stinks* falls silent uncomfortably often, and when the laughs aren't big enough the hush can be decidedly awkward. Are we meant to be having fun here? Is it okay to laugh? Since the film's semi-serious content sends out mixed messages, and Morris often sends none at all, we can't be sure. Of course the similarly textured *The Twelve Chairs* doesn't exactly brim with music either, but Morris finds richer uses for it there than here, matching a market's European hustle-bustle in one scene, creating a *Doctor Zhivago*–ish epic melancholy in another. True, filling *Life Stinks'* static blankness with *Silent Movie*–style whimsy risks throwing the tone all out of whack, but most comedies need music, especially if the dialogue doesn't let loose much high-speed crackle.

If the critics thought Morris's accompaniments too skimpy, most never said, but nearly everyone found *Life Stinks* itself nowhere near funny enough to suit them. Most weren't as kind as Roger Ebert, who admired Brooks' efforts to create a warmer, more intimate film here, one nearer in tone to heart-in-the-right-place comedies like *Gung Ho* or *Roxanne* than *History of the World — Part I* — sporadically manic, sure, but most of the time treading gingerly lest anyone accuse Brooks, DeLuca, Haberman, and Clark of insensitivity, of cruelly exploiting the less fortunate for a cheap laugh. Edited together just right, outtakes of Bolt fleeing street punks, falling in garbage, and dancing for pennies might make *Life Stinks* look pretty madcap, but an element of melancholy lurks beneath even these playful images. We're allowed to laugh at Bolt's predicament, yes, but how hard? At what point have we callously crossed the line? Evidently some felt Brooks himself crosses over just *making* a comedy with street people involved, and a few super-benevolent types, always charitable with others' money, even urged a happy-to-help Brooks and his studio reps in 1991 to set aside some of *Life Stinks*' profits to aid the homeless — by which cockeyed logic part of the tallies from Steve Gordon's *Arthur* belongs to Alcoholics Anonymous, Carl Reiner's *The Man with Two Brains* to head trauma research, and Larry Gelbart's *Oh, God!* to buying Gideon Bibles.

Defenders of life's ill-fated underdogs shouldn't complain too much, though. The entire cast comes to the project surprisingly subdued, with Brooks downplaying his usual wild-man shtick in favor of a low-key, semi-credible character closer in texture to *High Anxiety*'s Richard Thorndyke than *History of the World — Part I*'s skirt-chasing King Louis XVI, leaving only Rudy DeLuca, as the bogus J. Paul Getty, really free to blast loose. The doctors, lawyers, and vagrants of *Life Stinks* aren't goon-loony preposterous enough to give far-out characters like Mongo or Igor or Nurse Diesel much of a run for their comic money, but, unlike all those gremlin-green, sheepdog-shaggy carnival types Brooks gives us in *Spaceballs*, at least they're akin to real people this time and not troll-eared, tail-wagging cartoons. Indeed, it's quite a relief after nearly a decade-and-a-half of time-tripping chariot horses and robot gangsters to see Brooks can still tell an old-fashioned *people* story for a change. His *To Be or Not to Be* remake had revisited such climes as recently as 1983, of course, but Brooks neither directed nor wrote that one, recall, and if one labels *High Anxiety* just another genre spoof along the lines of *Young Frankenstein* and *Silent Movie*, *Life Stinks* marks the first time in over twenty years the word *satire* and not *sendup* is a Brooks comedy's most apt description. This time Brooks targets problems found in real life, not just reel life, goes after prey far more substantial then mere Hollywood motion picture clichés.

That's not to say the clichés don't get targeted too, if only indirectly. One could argue the scene in which Ronny Graham's off-camera priest threatens calling the police if Bolt doesn't stop annoying him spoofs the kind of unbelievably pious do-gooder pastors in films like *Boys Town* and *Going My Way*, or that Brooks' depicting medical types as angry, disorganized incompetents is his way of taking potshots at the super-capable likes of *Ben Casey* and *Dr. Kildare*—but that's really a bit of a stretch, isn't it? More likely, if Brooks is trying anything at all, he's just satirizing the idea that real priests and doctors are that much more self-sacrificing than we are. That's fine, though; after six genre parodies straight, it's high time Brooks returned to straight satire anyway, especially since that's so often what he's best at — though, again like *M*A*S*H*, which after Gelbart's departure went from attacking wartime atrocity and bureaucracy with razor-sharp wit to shooting deadly serious stories with little or even zero humor mixed in, sometimes the satire all but disappears and plain old drama takes charge. When actor Marvin Braverman's oblivious Dr. Kahahn, thinking Bolt someone new each time he sees him, pushes him closer to total catalepsy with more and more drugs, that's satire. When Sailor's sidewalk corpse goes barely noticed even as he's zipped into a bodybag and driven off, that might have been satire if depicted the way the dead, long-forgotten film star lies overlooked by all but his own dog in Blake Edwards' *S.O.B.*, but here it's pure drama. Small surprise, then, if some whose last dose of Brooks came from *History of the World — Part I* and *Spaceballs* saw *Life Stinks* and didn't know what to make of it.

Quite a lot of what appears in the film, in fact, could have been satire had Brooks intended it, but, as in *Young Frankenstein* and *High Anxiety*, his love affair with old movies prevents his poking too much fun. *Life Stinks* depends on just the sort of old-fashioned, sentimental images one finds in the musicals and romantic comedies of the '30s and '40s, and when Brooks stated in a 1991 *Later with Bob Costas* interview he and his co-writers had flirted with titling the picture something along the lines of *The Billionaire and the Bag Lady*, he wasn't kidding; it's that kind of movie. True, Fred Astaire and Ginger Rogers usually wore tuxedos and flowing gowns instead of shabby vagrant attire, and their backdrops tended to be much more lavish than Bolt and Molly's warehouse of rags, so from that angle it's parody—yet one notices that John Morris delivers "Easy to Love" exactly the way some straight-arrow '30s ballroom orchestra might have played it, and the choreography is strictly Hermes Pan. No funny dance moves here, no silly sendup tunes, no screwy Brooks lyrics along the lines of "The French Mistake" or "The Inquisition."

Quasi-serious intent or not, though, a harsh, body-slamming moniker like *Life Stinks* (it reminds one a little of Brooks' 1975 sitcom title *When Things Were Rotten*) suggests a Brooksian bitterness that the film itself, with its reverence for the underprivileged, only rarely lives up to; *The Producers*, *The Twelve Chairs*, and *History of the World—Part I* are all less Pollyanna-ish than his work here, in which good guys beat bad guys, sinner turns saint, cheaters never prosper, boy wins girl, and love conquers all. *Life Stinks* is Dickens' *Oliver Twist* magnified; not one Oliver gets adopted, but scores of them, rescued from the gutter by Fagin-tuned-philanthropist Goddard Bolt.

In fact, *Life Stinks* has a great deal in common with some of Dickens' other works as well, for, like Dickens' material, it so often concerns the contrast between greed and want, the power of money to both destroy and uplift. Goddard Bolt starts out as ruthlessly self-serving as Jeffrey Tambor's Vance Crasswell (even

more so, perhaps, since Bolt is the one born into money), yet it is also Bolt's wealth that finally rescues the homeless from the hunger, exposure, and disease his egotistical disinterest has only perpetuated before. Coolly chauffeured past refuse and rejects in his pearl-white limo, surveying grit and grime from rooftop alone, Bolt sees only real estate, not residents, and it takes hitting "rock bottom," seeing how "the other half" lives, to turn him from stone-souled capitalist into concerned caretaker. As with *A Christmas Carol's* Scrooge, only a descent into the abyss can convince Bolt mankind is indeed his business, and it takes the redemptive redistribution of some of his greed-won gains to make life better for those whose pain he's been blind to before. As always, Tiny Tim *can* live still, but only if Scrooge steps in.

Considering its sincerity of purpose, in fact, we're rather surprised how little respect *Life Stinks* still receives from media types, most of whom grumble incessantly about how too many setup-gag-setup-gag comedies lack "heart," are all about punchlines and not personality. Pointing to such oldfangled, sweet-natured classics as *My Man Godfrey* and *Sullivan's Travels*, reviewers forever complain today's filmmakers "don't make 'em like that anymore," yet given a quaint little love-and-riches romance that genuinely tries, many of these same critics attacked *Life Stinks* for not being Brooksian enough, for being too romantic comedy run-of-the-mill. Perhaps it had been so long since *The Producers* and *The Twelve Chairs* many had forgotten he had shot spoof-free films before, or couldn't accept Brooks outside his usual element, like Hitchcock lensing cowboy flicks or John Ford shooting sci-fi. Perhaps too his L.A. office and slum locales just felt too much like the sort of places viewers work at or drive through every day, places we go to the movies to forget, not confront all over again several times life size. Or perhaps critics simply felt the tempered P.C. gallantry of *Life Stinks* just wasn't the right place for Brooks, who couldn't resist the occasional shock word, lewd gesture, and body part gag no matter how old-fashioned the spirit and tone.

Then again, some of the problem may stem from the fact that, talented as they are, *Life Stinks* never quite rises above the overall colorlessness of its supporting cast. We can count on Brooks himself for plenty of swing-from-the-chandelier insanity no matter how semi-dramatic the material, and Warren at least brings a famous name to slap on theater marquees. Unfortunately, the film's got-to-go-see-it factor gets sabotaged elsewhere as its already mundane settings add in so many capable but unfunny-looking actors who wouldn't seem out of place playing lawyers, doctors, and such on *Law & Order, E.R.,* or *NYPD Blue*. It's great fun seeing Howard Morris again, and even (not that he's a household face or name by any means) co-writer Rudy DeLuca, both of whom have their best parts here since *High Anxiety*, but with the exception of Brooks, Morris, DeLuca, and a handful of bit players popping up briefly here and there, very few actors in *Life Stinks* have the sort of comically striking looks or voice one hopes for in Mel Brooks.

Does the more reserved, dignified casting evidenced in *Life Stinks* result from conscious design? Were the casting people worried that hiring too many conspicuously off-beat eccentrics might make its texture too jokey, like stripping *Bambi* of its painstakingly realistic animals and replacing them with buck-toothed, slack-jawed caricatures: Bambi with Bullwinkle, Thumper with Bugs Bunny, Flower the Skunk with Pepe LePew? If so, they certainly succeeded, leaving *Life Stinks* with Brooks' least interesting-looking cast list since *The Twelve Chairs* twenty-one years before.

Perhaps most clearly illustrating this point is co-star Lesley Ann Warren, who, having sung and danced in Rodgers and Hammerstein's 1966 *Cinderella* on TV at eighteen, makes such a splendid Molly, another fairy tale princess who leaves the ash heaps to wed born-rich royalty. Brooks' best casting surprise, Warren has a can't-take-your-eyes-off-her screen presence nearly as strong as his own, and maybe we should have expected this, given her song-and-dance work in Disney's *The Happiest Millionaire* (1967) and *The One and Only, Genuine, Original Family Band* (1968). Still, her '70–71 *Mission: Impossible* TV stint had mostly wasted her scene-stealing potential, and even her best miniseries and telefilms had tapped mostly only her dramatic skills, so not until '82's Oscar-nominated turn as a Judy Holliday–esque gangster's moll in Blake Edwards' *Victor/Victoria* would fans recall how focus-grabbing she can be. Since Molly dances, hiring Warren makes sense, too, though profit-wise the film might have needed someone whose very presence promises big laughs: Carol Burnett, Lily Tomlin, Penny Marshall, Rosie O'Donnell, Julie Hagerty, Shelley Long. Even at her daffiest, Warren looks so sensible, so real, her own normality limits how over-the-edge crazy she can be. Like his female leads in *History of the World — Part I, Robin Hood: Men in Tights,* and *Dracula: Dead and Loving It,* Warren is another superb actress for whom even the snappiest line readings can animate Brooks' weakest bits just so far. Warren can *act* zany, but even at her stressed-out, strung-out best she can't *personify* zaniness the way a Madeline Kahn or Cloris Leachman can, any more than, say, Irene Dunne, Jean Arthur, or Carole Lombard can match the natural-born nuttiness of a Gracie Allen or Phyllis Diller or Lucille Ball.

Sharing Warren's superb character-creating if somewhat too rational look and

Back on the streets after nearly dying at the hands of overmedicating hospital personnel, defrauded ex-billionaire Goddard Bolt (Mel Brooks) celebrates being alive and in love with his street-dweller girlfriend Molly (Lesley Ann Warren) in *Life Stinks*. This sweet, soft-hearted little comedy recalls both the "social responsibility" storylines of classic Frank Capra and the "greed-gone-wild" craziness of earlier Brooks pictures like *The Producers* and *The Twelve Chairs*.

sound is Jeffrey Tambor, an actor we've all enjoyed for years because his delivery is so first-rate (his years on HBO's *The Larry Sanders Show* won raves) — but not because of anything all that funny in his voice or face. We all recognize Tambor when we see him, like him on sight, know we can always count on him for an effective performance, but we really don't expect anyone this bank president average-looking to come across all that gooneybird weirdo — and, as sharp and slick as Tambor is, that's exactly the case here. Like Warren's, Tambor's acting never slips for even a second, and at times his pixyish charm as land tycoon Vance Crasswell is a real treat (the way his mock-guilty "I should leave"s so easily turn into "Can I

come in?"s in particular), but here again the casting is so grounded in reality, so straight-arrow judicious, we can't have much fun with it. Harvey Korman, Gene Wilder, Rick Moranis, John Candy — actors like these, named alongside Brooks on posters or marquees, just naturally lead us to expect laugh-riot hilarity — somehow all these guys have to do is show up and we're counting on something crazy — but, good as he is, who predicts big yuks from a comedy pitting Mel Brooks against Jeffrey Tambor? Dom DeLuise maybe — but Jeffrey Tambor?

Theoretically at least, casting comes closer to the mark with funnyman Howard Morris as elderly derelict Sailor, since we already associate Morris with kooky behavior after all those years on '50s and '60s TV. Once again, though, *Life Stinks'* underlying cultural sensitivity ends up getting in the way, its won't-somebody-please-lend-a-hand social consciousness not permitting making *too* much fun of a sickly, homeless senior citizen, so the spin-like-a-top Morris who's always so buzzsaw boisterous opposite TV's Sid Caesar and Andy Griffith won't quite work. A frail old man sleeping in a cardboard box can't be made a complete fool of, especially when he's going to die from exposure later on. Indeed, Morris couldn't logically make Sailor all *that* live-wire energetic no matter how desperately he might want to — not if we're seriously meant to believe this sweet, sentimental, expiration-wary sea-dreamer stands just a few shaky steps away from death's door.

Unlike Morris's situation, however, most performances in *Life Stinks* suffer both from too little comic freedom and because the casting itself feels so unremarkable from the get-go. Hiring vaguely sitcom-familiar Teddy Wilson as liquor-soaked derelict Fumes proves sound enough, and Wilson's good-humored, neighbor-down-the-street friendliness definitely plays just right. Still, instantly likable as Wilson is, as comic backup goes, Fumes can't possibly make the same impact as Marty Feldman's Igor or even Ron Carey's Brophy. Not only is the part too small, but Wilson, through absolutely no fault of his own, simply can't match Feldman's wonderfully way-out eyes and Silly Putty scarecrow legs, or Carey's lapdog yelp and bantam-cock hyperactivity. It's not lack of talent — just simple comic genetics. Wilson's warm, "average Joe" face is just perfect for what he's asked to do, but in Brooks, the lesser the humor, the greater need for funny faces. Impolite to laugh at alcoholism? Fine — but why can't the actor playing Fumes amuse us all on his own?

Still less satisfying, though, is the film's casting of its various attorneys, none given much more to do than James Van Patten as a wheelchair attendant and all looking shipped in direct from the sets of *Matlock* and *Perry Mason*. Sure, staid-seeming actors Stuart Pankin, Michael Ensign, Matthew Faison, Robert Ridgely, and John Welsh all *look* like lawyers, but, as with casting Cary Elwes as a straight-from-Central-Casting Robin Hood for what's meant to be a spoof, why does it matter? Even given *Life Stinks'* "help the homeless" subtext, why not apply the usual Mel Brooks rule of comic juxtaposition and outfit Bolt and Crasswell with the most colorful second bananas available? Of the actors selected, Stuart Pankin comes off funniest (not surprisingly, he's the one with the most comically expressive face), but overall these men all end up wasted, even Robert Ridgely, so memorable elsewhere in Brooks as spooky hangmen and sissy flashers but here little more than some soulless, suited cipher. Indeed, the usually hilarious Ridgely is so straitjacketed, and his fellow barristers right along with him, one wonders if the entire attorney roster shouldn't have been cast with faces more visibly eccentric — say, just about anybody from *Rowan & Martin's Laugh-In, Monty Python's Flying Circus, The Carol Burnett Show,* or *SCTV*. No offense, but even with minimal direction, just about anybody could fill these parts — somebody's dentist, even, or the catalog clerk at JC Penney, or the fellow who rubber stamps boxes at the post office.

As street punks Mean Victor and Yo, meanwhile, actors Brian Thompson and Raymond O'Connor are at least a trifle more colorfully offbeat — they remind one a little of Michael McKean and David L. Lander as *Laverne & Shirley's* spaced-out nitwits Lenny and Squiggy on TV — but, as with Brooks' virtually interchangeable lawyers, minimal screen time ends up working against them. Given better material, Brooks' co-writer Rudy DeLuca scores a surprisingly solid hit as the deluded derelict who insists he's really a down-on-his-luck J. Paul Getty. The part works for two simple reasons: one, complete with Marty Allen fright-wig hair and patchwork Emmett Kelly wardrobe, DeLuca plays the part for all the bubblebrain comic idiocy he can milk out of it; and two, his character is actually asked to step out of *Life Stinks*' no-nonsense P.C. realism and *do* something — something funnier, that is, than deliver dry-as-dirt financial reports and talk real estate.

Indeed, one knows something is amiss when so many comic attention-getters go to virtual unknowns: Frank Roman as a bawdily indelicate Spanish wedding interpreter; Marvin Braverman as an over-medicating doctor who mistakes Bolt for a new patient each time he sees him; and Angela Gordon as a bossy nurse who, in a joke lasting just seconds, blasts out a bull-moose bellow that her area has "reached capacity" patient-wise and can't take one more. Even film legend Billy Barty, so funny as a beaten-up Bible salesman in *Foul Play* (1978), is badly underused (playing a double amputee, he fakes being crushed by machinery so Bolt can commandeer an earth-mover — a variation on a gag first seen, more memorably, in *Silent Movie*), and Ira Miller, despite his years with Second City, is no better exploited here (as "Man at Fire") than in his roles for *High Anxiety* and *Spaceballs*— all that comic skill for a part so tiny the average repairman or meter reader could do it. Not even Ronny Graham, heard in voice-over as an ill-tempered mission priest, gets much to do; step out of the room for a glass of water and it's over. *Life Stinks* is just that kind of film.

Still, let's celebrate where a good cast goes right, not wrong. We've got Brooks' fantastic stone-faced cluelessness as Bolt's advisers try explaining why evicting hundreds of street people might bring bad P.R.; Warren's *When Harry Met Sally* scream-aloud breakdown reenactment; an expertly timed exchange between Brooks, Howard Morris, and Teddy Wilson involving Bolt's efforts to help Sailor wipe food from his face, wrapped up by a final-line intervention from Fumes; a clothes-shedding fever-frenzy involving Brooks and Warren in which Bolt and Molly's passions run wild (with Brooks admirably implying nudity, not showing it); Brooks and DeLuca's madness vs. logic conflict between a pauperized Bolt and DeLuca's lunatic J. Paul Getty, a too-brief tribute to Golden Age slapstick that breathes life into a tale that up till now has been only spottily funny; Brooks' bravura depiction, in just minutes, of a Bolt gone from elated exultation to anguished betrayal to crazed fury to drugged-out distraction to near-death insensibility; and a strikingly moving hospital scene, vastly different from the all-comedy version in *Silent Movie*, beautifully handled by Brooks and Warren, as an adoring Molly begs a seemingly dying Bolt to pull through.

As for Mel Brooks himself, this sublimely gifted comic performer just gets better and better, and *Life Stinks* makes clearer than ever that, if he'd wanted it, he might have made quite a distinguished serious actor. Like Jerry Lewis, who gained new respect after his dramatic turns in *The King of Comedy* and *Arizona Dream*, in the hands of directors like Martin Scorsese and Emir Kusturica, Brooks might have surprised us all with his flair for the dramatic. He's just that good.

Fans apparently weren't all that interested in a grimmer, or grimier, Mel Brooks, however, and so in the U.S., if less so overseas, *Life Stinks* is largely remembered even now as an admirable nonsuccess, a laudable effort that, for all its merits, just couldn't find enough fans interested in seeing it to make it an across-the-board hit. To really succeed as it might have, maybe *Life Stinks* just needed a zanier ad campaign, or a more message-friendly release date, or a more marketable supporting cast. Maybe it really needed all of these things. Thankfully, though, like so many Brooks movies, *Life Stinks* continues to find new fans on TV and video, where the contrast between financial success and failure, as in the film itself, proves just a little more indistinct. Like billionaires who come dressed as bums, or dancers decked out like derelicts, sometimes even the nicest of movies come disguised in failure. Slums are more interesting that way — and cinema too.

CAST: Mel Brooks (Goddard Bolt); Lesley Ann Warren (Molly); Jeffrey Tambor (Vance Crasswell); Stuart Pankin (Pritchard); Howard Morris (Sailor); Rudy DeLuca (J. Paul Getty); Teddy Wilson (Fumes); Michael Ensign (Knowles); Matthew Faison (Stevens); Billy Barty (Willy); Brian Thompson (Mean Victor); Raymond O'Connor (Yo); Carmine Caridi (Flophouse Dweller); Sammy Shore (Reverend at Wedding); Frank Roman (Spanish Interpreter); Marvin Braverman (Dr. Kahahn); Robert Ridgely (Fergueson); John Welsh (Dodd); Stanley Brock (Store Owner); James Van Patten (Wheelchair Attendant); Michael Phiewski (Male Nurse); Marianne Muellerleile (Head Nurse); Anne Betancourt, Kathryn Skatula, Robin Shephard (Nurses); Angela Gordon (Capacity Nurse); Mary Watson, Saida Pagan, Tamara Taylor, Henry Kaiser (Newscasters), Danny Wells (Mercedes Driver); Larry Cedar, Christopher Birt (Paramedics); Johnny Cocktails (Burrito-eating Bum); Clifton Wells (Taco Stand Owner); George Berkeley (Derelict Outside Flophouse); Anthony Messina, David Correia (Policeman); Helene Winston (Society Patron); Terrence Williams (Boy Dancing in Doorway); Joan Crosby (Woman at Fire); Ira Miller (Man at Fire); James Mapp (Blind Man); Sam Menning (Old Wino); Ralph Ahn (Chinese Cook); Stu Gilliam (Desmond); Darrow Igus (Maynard); James Martinez (Dancing Vagrant at Party); Rose D. Caine (Dancing Dowager at Party); Ralph Mauro (Hors d'oeuvres Vagrant at Party); Martin Charles Warner (Dirty-faced Vagrant at Party); Anthony Thomas Mitchell (Nibbler Driver); Patrick Valenzuela (Street Person in Fight); Carmen Filpi (Pops, "Elevens-Up"); Casey King (Shopping Cart Chauffeur); Ronny Graham (Priest's Voice); Jere Laird (Stock Market Reporter).

CREDITS: Director: Mel Brooks; Producer: Mel Brooks; Exec. Producer: Ezra Swerdlow; Screenplay: Mel Brooks, Rudy DeLuca, Steve Haberman; Story: Mel Brooks, Ron Clark, Rudy DeLuca, Steve Haberman; Assoc. Producer: Kim Kurumada; Prod. Mgr.: Kim Kurumada; 1st Assist. Dir.: Mitchell Bock; 2nd Assist. Dirs.: Martha Elcan, Albert Cho, Catherine Schlesinger; Casting: Bill Shephard, C.S.A., Todd Thaler; Costume Designer: Mary Malin; Editor: David Rawlins; Prod. Designer: Peter Larkin; Dir. of Photog.: Steven Poster, A.S.C.; Film Eds: Anthony Redman, A.C.E., Michael Mulconery; Art Dir.: Josan Russo; Set Decorator: Marvin March; Set Designer: Carroll Johnston; Camera Operator: George Kohut, S.D.C.; Additional Camera Operator: John C. Koester; 1st Assist. Camera: Norman Parker; 2nd Assist. Camera: Brian T. Pitts; Film Loader: Paul Plannette; Chief Lighting Tech.: Mike G. Moyer; Best Boy Electrician: Dave Burnett; Key Grip: Bob Gray; Best Boy Grip: Rick Rader; Sound Mixer: Willie D. Burton, C.A.S.; Boom Operator: Marvin F. Lewis; Sound Utility: Robert Harris; Prop. Master: Jack M. Marino; Script Supvr.: Judi Townsend; Assist. Eds.: Darren T. Holmes, Ben Williams, Albert Coleman, Dennis Newman; Music Ed.: Eugene Marks; Post Prod. Supvr.: Leah Zappy; Assist. to Mr. Swerdlow: Daren Hicks; Prod. Coordinator: Paula Benson-Himes; Prod. Accountant: Jan Garner; Assist. Accountants: Linden Wineland-Johnson, Kati Scharer; Location Mgr.: John Armstrong; Assist. Costume Designer: Paki Wolfe; Costumers: Carlane Passman, Roberto Carneird; Heade Makeup Artist: Fred Blau; Ms. Warren's Makeup: Eugenia Weston; Makeup: Mark Bussan; Ms. Warren's Hair Stylist: Barbara Lorenz; Hair Stylist: Carolyn Elias; Music: John Morris; "Easy to Love" Lyrics/Music: Cole Porter; Choreographer: Jeffrey Hornaday; Assist. Choreographer: Miranda Garrison; Orchestrations: Jack Hayes; Dance Orchestrations: Ralph Burns; Music Recorded at: Evergreen Recording Studios; Scoring Mixer: John Richards; Sound Re-recorded at: Todd-AO/Glen Glenn Studios; Re-recording Mixers: Andy Nelson, Steve Pederson, Tom Perry; Sound Supervision: Clancy's Sound Vibrations, Inc.;

Supervising Sound Ed.: Jim Troutman; Sound Eds.: Dwayne Avery, MPSE, Edward Hirsch, Alan Schultz, Adam Johnston, Greg Stacy; ADR Supvr.: Michael Goodman; Foley Artists: Casey Troutman, Bess Hopper; Video Playback: Lindsay P. Hill; Still Photographer: Peter Sorel; Publicist: Saul Kahan; Secretary to the Writers: Sarah McAnally; Assist. Prod. Coordinator: Leslie A. Tokunaga; Assist. Location Mgr.: Robert Dohan; Art Dpt. Coordinator: Kevin Constant; Assist. to Mr. Brooks: Dyan Austin Conway; Assist. to Ms. Warren: Gina E. Sforza; DGA Trainee: Bryan Dresden; Prod. Assists: Scott Rosencrans, Victoria Halboth, Sean King, Colleen O'Neill, Michael Kanter, Ron Chesney, J.T. Thayer, Stephen Joubert, Christopher B. Stone; Const. Coordinator: S. Bruce Wineinger; Const. Foreman: Steve Willis; Lead Man: Jack Eberhart; Assist. Properties: Roger Knight; Spec. Effects: Dave Kelsey, Ray Robinson, Curtis Decker; Spec. Effects Model Makers: Mark Stetson, Robert Spurlock; Standby Painter: Basil Lombardo; Stunt Coordinator: David Richard Ellis; Transportation Coordinator: Jim Chesney; Transportation Captain: Charles Renfroe; Craft Service: Richard W. Scarpone; Negative Cutter: Gary Burritt; Color Timer: Phil Hetos; Caterer: Angel Trujillo; First Aid: Barbara Lortie; Voice Casting: Barbara Harris; Stunts: Jesse Wayne, Denise Lynne Roberts, Steve Boyum, Steve Davison, Richard M. Ellis, Justin DeRosa, Bill Hooker, Gary McLarty, Don Pulford, Dick Ziker, Dennis Frick, Larry Frazier; Titles Design: Saxon/Ross Film Design; Titles/Opticals: Pacific Title; Cameras/Lenses: Panavision; Color: DeLuxe; Spec. Thanks: Piper-Heidsieck, Cole Haan Footwear, Kenneth Gordon New Orleans, Brioni Clothing, Heatling, Ruff Hewn, Los Angeles Mission; Cranes/Dollies: Chapman; Masco Light Techs.: Todd Braden, Brad Chelesvig; Lighting/Grip Equipment: Culver Studios Lighting and Grip Dpt., Hollywood Rental Company, Inc.; Filmed at Culver Studios; MGM Pathé Communications Company; A Brooksfilms Prod.; Metro-Goldwyn-Meyer; 1991; 93 minutes.

11

* * *

"LEAVE US ALONE, MEL BROOKS!"

Robin Hood: Men in Tights

* * * * * *

(1993)

In Medieval Jerusalem, a captured Robin of Loxley (Cary Elwes), having left England to fight in the Crusades, is locked in a prisoner-filled dungeon. Helped to escape by wise Moorish captive Asneeze (Isaac Hayes), however, Robin quickly frees all the prisoners and heads home.

Swimming back to England, Robin soon rescues Asneeze's hipster son Ahchoo (Dave Chappelle) from a police beating, then receives his late father's locket from blind family servant Blinkin (Mark Blankfield), who reveals that Robin's family is now dead and his lands stolen by the greedy Prince John in the absence of his brother King Richard, who is still off fighting in the Holy Land. Soon after, Robin rescues a panicky little boy from the pompous Sheriff of "Rottingham" (Roger Rees), whom Robin sends to Prince John with word Robin has vowed to fight on the side of the English poor. Hearing this, a worried Prince John (Richard Lewis) seeks counsel from Latrine (Tracey Ullman), an ugly, witch-like cook absorbed by a one-sided passion for the Sheriff.

Having enlisted in his Merry Men the shy but powerful Little John (Eric Allan Kramer) and wiry knife-hurler Will Scarlet O'Hara (Matthew Porretta), Robin appears at Prince John's castle, where he quickly humiliates the would-be king and the Sheriff with dazzling swordplay and a colorful escape. During this visit, Robin also wins the affections of the lovely Maid Marian (Amy Yasbeck), whose long-shielded virtue, though coveted by Rottingham, is guarded by both a keyless steel chastity belt and her overprotective maid Broomhilde (Megan Cavanagh).

The next day Robin begins training a group of none-too-bright English peasants to defend themselves against Prince John's army, and soon wins yet another new friend in circumcision- peddler Rabbi Tuckman (Mel Brooks), who happily shares sacramental wine with Robin's men. Unknown to Robin, however, the Sheriff of Rottingham has craftily hired Mafia-type gang boss Don Giovanni (Dom DeLuise) and his two "hired guns" Filthy Luca (Steve Tancora) and Dirty Ezio (Joe

Dimmick) to murder Robin during a big archery contest Robin seems sure to attend.

Overhearing this wicked plan, Marian sneaks away to warn Robin, who cannot resist the urge to show off and attends — and wins — the contest in disguise. The murder attempt is foiled by Blinkin, but a captured Robin, his neck in a hangman's noose, must watch helplessly as the lustful Sheriff prepares to wed Marian by force. Rescued by his followers once more, Robin delivers the Sheriff a fatal wound in a swordfight after the fiend flees with Marian to his bridal bed — and finds the key to Marian's chastity belt hidden in Robin's shattered locket — but a magical spell from a lovesick Latrine cures the dying Sheriff, who is dragged off in horror to his dreaded honeymoon.

Robin asks Rabbi Tuckman to wed him to Marian right away, but the ceremony is briefly interrupted by the return of Good King Richard (Patrick Stewart), who punishes John for his crimes, restores Robin's birthright, and attends the wedding as guest of honor. As the tale ends, Robin rules Sherwood, Ahchoo is named the kingdom's new sheriff, and all is well in Rottingham, with one small exception: the key does not fit Marian's chastity belt after all, thus necessitating an after-hours visit from a locksmith before the happy honeymoon can resume.

★   ★   ★

When Mel Brooks announced plans to follow 1991's rather subdued, low-key comedy Life Stinks with a madcap sendup of the ever-popular Robin Hood legend, longtime Brooks fans reacted with both upbeat enthusiasm and ill-at-ease surprise. On the one hand, the picturesque, near-fairy tale universe of Robin and His Merry Men, like the Wild West and Final Frontier of Brooks' riotous horse- and space-operas Blazing Saddles and Spaceballs, promised a far richer landscape than the dingy side streets of Life Stinks, a grander canvas for the master funnyman's bold comic strokes. On the other, since Brooks had already plundered Sherwood Forest's comic potential in his 1975 ABC-TV series When Things Were Rotten, his decision to try again so soon suggested the man who had previously spoofed everything from Hitler to Hitchcock might finally have run dry of ideas — understandable, if true, given the hundreds of hilarious comedy sketches pulled from Brooks' delightfully demented imagination on Sid Caesar's Your Show of Shows, but still pretty puzzling considering he had actually directed just ten movies in some twenty-five years.

Equally puzzling, of course, was Brooks' having a second go at a project that had never been much of a hit to begin with. When Things Were Rotten had featured a fine cast — Get Smart alumni Dick Gautier as Robin and Bernie Kopell as Alan-A-Dale; future Eight is Enough star Dick Van Patten as Friar Tuck; Hee Haw regular Misty Rowe as Maid Marian; David Sabin as Little John; versatile Richard Dimitri as Bertram and his evil twin Renaldo; Henry Polic II as the Sheriff of Nottingham; Ron Rifkin as Prince John; Jane A. Johnston as Princess Isabelle — but on-screen potential alone hadn't been enough to keep the show on the air. Appealing guest stars? The show ran only four months, but in just thirteen episodes welcomed such likable one-shot talents as Sid Caesar, Dudley Moore, John Byner, Steve Landesberg, Joe E. Ross, Paul Williams, and Ron Glass. Quality directors? Brooks had them, from actor/director pal Marty Feldman to TV actors-turned-directors Jerry Paris (The Dick Van Dyke Show) and Peter Bonerz (The Bob Newhart Show) to such ever-reliable TV helmsmen as Peter H. Hunt, Bruce Bilson, Cory Ruskin, and

Norman Abbott. Good writers? *When Things Were Rotten* had those too, from Norman Steinberg (*My Favorite Year*) to Pat Proft (*Hot Shots!*) to Tony Geiss (*An American Tail*).

Still, Brooks himself had never directed *When Things Were Rotten*, nor guest-starred on it, nor even so much as written for it after the first episode (with co-scripters John Boni and Norman Steinberg), so surely the concept stood a far better chance with Brooks taking on a larger role. The gamble worked too, since 1993's *Robin Hood: Men in Tights*, while artistically rarely more than "fair to middling" Brooks, did indeed become his biggest hit of the 1990s. If his sci-fi parody *Spaceballs* had straggled into theaters too long after *Star Wars* for its own comic good, this time Brooks clearly struck while the iron was, if not hot, at least still warm, trailing the huge box office impact of Kevin Reynolds' *Robin Hood: Prince of Thieves* (and John Irvin's less often seen *Robin Hood* feature shot about the same time) by just two years. What's more, this pleasant little gag-fest quickly became yet another Brooks comedy to fare well on video and TV, especially among the skateboards-and-sneakers set, who tittered unashamed at blatantly juvenile gags many older fans sneered at. Predictably, it won over few of Brooks' harshest critics, but fans whose idea of fun included relocated castles labeled "WIDE LOAD" and horses in "RENT-A-WRECK" signs didn't much care, ignored all the carping and caviling, and just had a fine old time anyway.

And, in fact, a fine old time is certainly to be had here, at least for less discriminating Brooks fans, even if only because *Robin Hood: Men in Tights* flat-out looks more fun than the average comedy just from its whimsical bedtime story atmosphere alone. The movie dazzles with its bright, charming fairy-tale shimmer, and paints for itself a quaint, colorful Walt Disney ambiance far prettier than anything *Life Stinks* could have turned up on the filthy side streets of urban L.A. Indeed, only Tracey Ullman's purposely hideous witch make-up, a few unavoidably drab castle interiors, and the requisite Brooksian sex gags and gross-out jokes dampen one's enthusiasm for the overall feel of the film, and some scenes are so storybook enchanting one half-wishes Brooks had gone all-out and tried spoofing Hans Christian Andersen or The Brothers Grimm instead. Can one just imagine Mel Brooks' take on Red Riding Hood? Rapunzel? Beauty and the Beast?

Robin Hood: Men in Tights is, in short, a pleasant, highly likable little film, one children in particular are sure to have fits over whenever it pops up on Saturday afternoon TV. They'll laugh when Robin's shadow puppet dog yelps after a bite from the Sheriff's shadow puppet duck, and when Brooks' big "Men in Tights" number gets rolling, they'll want to sing too. It's guaranteed.

Unfortunately, lovable as it is, *Robin Hood: Men in Tights* also remains one of Brooks' biggest missed opportunities, a tale so *Harvey*-esque easygoing and mild we can't help finding ourselves, as with many later Brooks movies, mentally "punching up" the material every time it starts to drag or sputter. We're charmed by its gentle, soft-touch pleasantness, its featherweight, lighter-than-air affability, but we can sense in five minutes Brooks' rhythm is off, that this isn't the next *Blazing Saddles* or *Young Frankenstein*, and we want another knock-us-for-a-loop, all-out Brooks comedy smash so badly it's all we can do to avoid yelling advice to him from off-screen: "Pick up the pace!"; "Trim that scene!"; "Move that camera!"; "Ask that actor for a second take!"

Among this amiable little film's shortcomings is a noticeable lack of tension, dramatic or comedic. Prince John's subjects are being overtaxed and ill-used, we're told, but for some reason none of them seem all that angry about it. Robin trains the peasants to fight, but we're given no real indication that either the film's heroes or villains are seriously plotting some kind of attack. Both Prince John and the Sheriff want Robin dead, but we're shown little proof either villain is in any hurry. And Maid Marian is, one assumes, in constant peril living in Prince John's castle, yet she doesn't seem the least bit afraid there. Where's the comic outrage, the fear, the desperation? If Nottingham — that is, Rottingham — really, truly is in such dire straits, why don't we sense it?

If this otherwise enjoyable little film suffers one major weakness, in fact, it may best be summed up in just one word: pas-

sivity. Neither Brooks nor his characters take Brooks' "right vs. might" scenario seriously enough, resulting in heroes who seem apathetic and villains uninvolved. When the tiny hamlet gets torched by Prince John's soldiers early on, where's the out-of-control, loopy chaos unleashed on *Blazing Saddles'* Rock Ridge, its men dragged through town by horse rope, its little old ladies taking fists to the stomach? Funny-lovable or not, *Robin Hood: Men in Tights* needs just this sort of free-for-all, comic confusion, but instead we get only a few dozen lazily aimed arrows and, later, one silly little boy chased, in no real hurry, by a few half-hearted horsemen with kazoos. When Marian and her friend sneak off to warn Robin, Broomhilde fears the penalty should Prince John take notice,

Surrounded by Medieval English soldiers taking their orders from Rottingham's corrupt sheriff and power-abusing prince, hipster student Ahchoo (Dave Chappelle) and heroic Crusades returnee Robin of Loxley (Cary Elwes) employ martial arts moves to make their escape, in director Mel Brooks' 1993 Sherwood Forest comedy *Robin Hood: Men in Tights*, a big-screen variation on Brooks' short-lived Robin Hood sitcom *When Things Were Rotten* from 1975.

but the Prince we've seen is such a bored, dispirited sluggard we can't see the threat, and when the Sheriff hires killers to "rub out" Robin, the fiendish laughter ending that scene helps, but the meeting itself is just too languid, too static, too dull.

Even the film's camerawork feels dispassionate compared to the spirited scene-painting of Brooks' best movies, so much so one half-wonders if Brooks hadn't spent so many years spinning madcap variations on the legend that for once he just couldn't, as Robin's pal Ahchoo puts it, "get pumped" enough to tackle it at top fervor. The two biggest flaws directing-wise: first, a baffling scarcity of good close-ups, a common failing of wide-screen releases but once rare in Brooks; and second, an unusual number of stationary, often even perfectly centered scenes that only accentuate the overall idleness of a "spoof" movie that never really twists the original very far out of shape.

One would think a film starring an actor as photogenic and likable as Cary Elwes would give its lead plenty of close-ups, but this one doesn't — not nearly as many as, say, *The Producers* gives Zero Mostel or *The Twelve Chairs* Ron Moody, and just why Brooks seems so standoffish this time is a real mystery. Likewise, since he is spoofing Robin Hood flicks — *if* that's what he's doing, which is questionable in itself given how deferentially he treats most of the material — one expects plenty of dazzling camerawork to capture all that soul-stirring, thrilling energy, yet here too (passivity again) we're kept at a distance and, left mostly just flat, rather bland shots of folks just standing about (on foot-bridges, on roadways, on gallows) or sitting (in stocks, on bleachers, on thrones). Heroes in *Robin Hood: Men in Tights* don't ride to the rescue but just lackadaisically shuffle up to it, don't leap from horses in mid-gallop but only trot slowly up to a crisis and just as casually climb off. Robin and

Moorish pal Asneeze free a whole dungeon-ful of prisoners, yet neither they nor Brooks attack the problem with any real style or spectacle; Robin rescues young pal Ahchoo from a brutal beating, but, in no bigger hurry than Brooks, trudges leisurely up to the emergency as if the poor lad has all the time in the world; Merry Men kick up their heels for a big dance number but move from their original formation only slightly more noticeably than Brooks moves his camera. The entire film feels jam-packed with chances for movement, for surprises, yet beyond two admittedly rousing swordfight scenes Brooks resists those chances at every turn.

Particularly puzzling is Brooks' increasing habit — again, rare in his early work — of keeping his camera in a fixed, near-dead center position for bits clearly crying out for something a bit more off-kilter. The story opens with a truly ingenious gag set-up as flaming arrows set a tiny village ablaze (the joke: the same unlucky little hamlet gets torched every time somebody shoots a new Robin Hood film!), but because Brooks photographs this rather phony-looking village only from the front, focusing mostly on just one shack and without any energy-building shots of panicked faces or scampering feet spliced in, all pretense that an entire village has been attacked — or that it is a real one, outdoors, and not just a semi-complete indoor set — is immediately undermined. The scene needs rapid-fire cutting, not visual inertia, but evidently editor Stephen E. Rivkin isn't given enough angles to put together the rip-roaring, world-gone-mad montage we're all so eager to see.

The movie's energy also sags at times, like so many post–'70s Brooks films, from a little unaccountably slack scene-cutting, a curious reluctance (from Brooks? from Rivkin?) to trim the "down time" between laughs. This sort of editing-room hesitation rarely does any comedy much good, but Brooks' latest suffers even more because so much of its dialogue is unnecessary and its rhythm so saggy. When Brooks' camera slowly scans the archery contest crowd's "Tomahawk Chop," must we hear the entire chant to get the joke? And must we have an onlooker announce it by name? Prince John insists the Sheriff sugarcoat his bad news, and after the poor Sheriff tries at great length, he explains why he's doing it — again, at length — after Prince John objects. Surely a quick "Sorry, Sire" would do. A bluebird relieves itself on our heroine's hand, but instead of just one quick, wordless grimace from Marian, slow-talking Broomhilde spells out for us what we've just "seen." Palace witch-cook Latrine reveals what her family name used to be, but Prince John still has to verify for us, with painful slowness, twice, what a "good change" it is. And so on.

Sometimes entire scenes — potentially really funny scenes, too — suffer from such overkill. While well acted, Dom DeLuise's *Godfather* bit lasts far too long, with DeLuise's slow, Brando-voiced Don Giovanni, Steve Tancora's monotoned Filthy Luca, and Joe Dimmick's stone-silent Dirty Ezio pushing our patience for this mostly stationary across-the-table meeting scene to the breaking point. Beyond the occasional "Good grief!" or "Wow-ee!" (and thank goodness for those), even Roger Rees' frequently amusing Sheriff exudes mostly just earnest, low-key gravity here, and Brooks lingers on this tedious business some four-and-a-half minutes — four-and-a-half minutes of actors just sitting or standing about a table, shot not nearly close enough, dragging out sixty seconds' worth of comedy to nearly five times that. To put the matter into perspective, consider this: That exhilarating castle battle between Robin and Prince John's guards, the one that delivers so much long-needed energy so long into the film? That whole fast-paced extravaganza,

the one really invigorating part of the movie's entire first hour, runs only a quarter-minute longer!

Again and again, Brooks' otherwise highly enjoyable little film suffers from such dramatic slackness. Robin frees himself, Asneeze, and others from a presumably barbaric Jerusalem prison, and while we should find the feat absolutely electrifying (or at least funny), we're thinking instead only that the escape happens much, much too easily — that liberating a dungeon-ful of prisoners looks about as difficult as untying the family puppy from a chain in the backyard. Robin shoves open the heavy double doors at Prince John's castle, and laughing at the two guards knocked cold should be automatic, but we're just too aware the doors haven't swung hard enough to make that much impact. A catapult sends the Sheriff flailing into space, but we can't enjoy the joke because it's just too obvious the device has been fired too slowly to fling a man more than five or six feet.

Surprisingly, the movie's overall languorousness becomes most apparent in scenes with funnyman Richard Lewis as Prince John, a part so rife with comic potential Lewis's "stressed-out neurotic" comedy club persona should have stolen the film. The usually manic, angst-rattled Lewis, so hilarious on stage, here seems less frantic than just bored; in press releases, he called Prince John "a screaming worry wart" who "needs therapy," "always looking over his shoulder, frightened to death that his big brother might come back from the Crusades any minute," yet instead of panicky and agitated, which surely would have been funnier (think Gene Wilder in *The Producers*), he mostly seems sluggish and dispirited. This man doesn't need therapy; he needs vitamins! Part of the problem, no doubt, is script- and editing-related (many of Lewis's lines need cutting anyway), but it's also true

Lewis is mostly kept seated or just standing around instead of allowed to run around wild, and his inability to really cut loose remains one of the movie's biggest letdowns. Like Brooks himself, Lewis is simply much, much too funny to come across this bland.

Though amply endearing as Robin's sidekick Ahchoo, co-star Dave Chappelle, easily one of the best things in the film, can't pep up Brooks' comic tempo either. Like fellow stand-up Lewis, Chappelle can be hilarious given zingier, zestier material (his high-energy supporting work in 1999's *Blue Streak*, for example), but Ahchoo is so mellow and laid-back adjectives like *zany* and *madcap*, traits one longs for in Brooks, don't much apply. Ahchoo's unperturbed ghetto cool *is* mildly funny, of course — one can't very well watch a very 1990s L.A. street youth "chill" his way through twelfth-century England in turban and sneakers without grinning a little — but beyond the rare Bob Newhart or Jack Benny, unruffled calm and sidesplitting comedy seldom go hand in hand. If Chappelle still manages to make Ahchoo lovable just the same, it's less because Ahchoo is funny than because Chappelle himself is so winning and Ahchoo so faithful, polite, obliging, and friendly — as Brooks might put it, "a nice boy," a good kid. We *like* Ahchoo, smile fondly when he is on-screen, but, like so much in the film, he's far too low-key to break loose for the big laughs.

Robin Hood: Men in Tights remains great fun, yet it abounds with such self-restraint, and at times the results can be maddening, like viewing some lackluster old *Andy Griffith Show* filled to the rim with stable, sedentary Helens, Howards, and Emmetts but nary a cuckoo-crazy Barney, Gomer, or Ernest T. Bass in sight. Like Lewis and Chappelle, musician/actor Isaac Hayes (as philosophical, sober Asneeze), Megan Cavanagh (as slow-shuffling, corpulent Broomhilde), and Dom DeLuise (as lazy, leaden Don Giovanni) all have roles whose emotional languor or physical immobility work against the idea of madcap comedy to begin with, yet Brooks just keeps giving them padded, go-nowhere material that either slows the film's rhythm or virtually stops it dead. The actors are all superbly cast — Hayes has done quality work in several comedies, Cavanagh did a fantastic job in *A League of Their Own*, and the inimitable DeLuise would be funny reading tax returns — but must the film test our patience having Hayes mull matters over with so much relaxed, all-the-time-in-the-world passivity? A seated, near-motionless DeLuise strain over the meaning of the word *succinctly*? Cavanagh waste precious narrative seconds scolding a disobedient horse?

Furthermore, lacking any of Brooks' best bigger-than-life comic wackos in key roles, the film contains no real breakout performance, no character over-the-top enough to rival the Freddy Frankensteins, Nurse Diesels, or Lili Von Shtupps of the past. A really terrific Brooks film needs not just good acting but madness, and however many comedies its star may have done, the name "Cary Elwes" as likely suggests *Glory* or *Days of Thunder* as *Hot Shots!* to most fans, and the names "Amy Yasbeck," "Mark Blankfield," "Eric Allan Kramer," "Matthew Porretta," and (for some) perhaps even "Dave Chappelle" or "Roger Rees" may not suggest anything at all. Even if they do know these gifted actors for their comedy credits — say, recall Yasbeck, Kramer, and Rees from TV's *Wings*, *Down Home*, and *Cheers*— one can't imagine many fans seeing them on-screen, sitting up suddenly, and saying, "Hey, that guy's *always* funny! This picture ought to be a riot!"

The delightful Cary Elwes, for instance, has superb comic instincts — his Robin might have been a real show-stopper written zanier, quirkier — but because he seems so sensible, so sane, he's never far enough "out there" to make much impact. The same holds for Amy Yasbeck, a hugely talented, strikingly beautiful actress who likewise looks far too rational for the way-out absurdity spoof comedy requires. Like Elwes, Yasbeck can be sublimely funny — her "veddy British" accent wins us over right away, and her vibrating cries as the Sheriff jackhammer-attacks her chastity belt is one of Brooks' looniest bits — but she ultimately has to reach much, much deeper for the sort of built-in comic madness stars like Madeline Kahn and Cloris Leachman seem practically born with.

The whole film is like that: expertly cast but rather unfunny-looking actors unleashing not nearly enough comic craziness to make anyone really stand out. Eric Allan Kramer makes a more endearing Little John than *When Things Were Rotten*'s more adult David Sabin, but even with his little-boy shyness going for him Kramer both looks and acts, like his costars, so man-on-the-street average we can't help wishing for something a little loonier. He definitely strikes gold with his ditzy drowning-in-six-inches-of-water anxiety attack (like Leo Bloom in *The Producers*, he's both hysterical and wet), but aside from his sweetness the rest of the time Little John is written pretty much like any other Little John — except far less energetic, as if the character were some big, slow-moving panda bear. Like his costars, Kramer amuses in his own quiet way — we do like him — but why not a Little John as boisterous as Zero Mostel's Max Bialystock in *The Producers* or Dom DeLuise's Father Fyodor in *The Twelve Chairs*? For that matter, since Patrick Stewart plays King Richard very nearly as stalwart, stately, and true as Sean Connery in Reynolds' film (oddly, Connery once played Robin in Richard Lester's *Robin*

and Marian, and Stewart tried the role too in the "Q-pid" episode of *Star Trek: The Next Generation*), where's the parody in that? Remove one or two lines, and Stewart's king could fit into any "real" Robin Hood movie just fine.

Brooks comes closer with Roger Rees, who, vaguely resembling the series' Henry Polic II, has some truly brilliant bits as the sputtering, sentence-garbling Sheriff (a nutty reinterpretation of Alan Rickman's *Robin Hood: Prince of Thieves* villain, and another otherwise fine acting job played just a tad too slowly), and with comic Mark Blankfield's Blinkin, whose incongruous dark glasses, broad British accent, and kooky blind man shtick draw several big laughs. His part isn't exactly politically correct, no (neither is Rees', actually, if the speech-impaired wanted to kick up enough fuss about it), but at least the more exaggerated Blankfield looks and acts zanier than, say, Matthew Porretta (as Will Scarlet O'Hara), a gifted actor whose virile, slice-of-life earnestness feels better suited to a non-comedy Robin Hood story (Porretta would, in fact, play Robin himself in a semi-"straight" Robin Hood TV series a few years later) than a kooky, crazy Brooks movie.

Similarly, one applauds Brooks for restoring Prince John, sorely missed in Reynolds' film, to his rightful place in the legend, but his inclusion of a Reynolds-inspired witch figure, Tracey Ullman's Latrine, seems like just asking for trouble. Latrine's obsession with wedding the Sheriff lends the skirt-chasing rogue a fitting penalty in the finale, yes, but it also directly triggers one of the film's worst jokes when he ends up flung by catapult through a roof into her bed. Never mind that the device never does get used against Robin; we're really expected to believe Rees's Sheriff would invite disaster by sitting in it while unveiling it to Prince John? Jokes this predictable aren't merely telegraphed ahead; they're practically phoned in. Then too, the scene between Prince John and Latrine, beyond revealing the grizzled old hag loves the Sheriff, ends up taking us absolutely nowhere, since Latrine's offer to help destroy Robin via magic potion is never alluded to again.

Catapults and potions aren't the only plot points the final cut brings up and then drops, either. For all the talk of teaching the peasants to fight Robin Hood–style (archery, jousting, that sort of thing) the villagers rescue Robin using few of the skills we've actually seen them practice, and, having left its commoner types nondescript from the start, the film makes no real attempt to individualize them in their big battle, nor even to bring to the conflict a genuine sense of *Blazing Saddles* common man pride. Not even Ahchoo's half-joking notion about taking the training dummies, not the villagers, into battle has any real pay-off; the suggestion at first seems to give Robin a bright idea (something akin to Sheriff Bart's "fake Rock Ridge" ploy, maybe?), but whatever clever, Bart-style trickery he might be planning, if any, remains unspoken and untried.

Indeed, even the film's minor mystery about the locket left Robin by his father— the one containing the "key to the greatest treasure in the land"—fails to resolve itself all that well. Even ignoring the question of why Robin's father had this key or who put Marian in her chastity belt to begin with, are we meant to know right off that a *literal* key is inside? Presumably not, since the locket eventually shatters and a real key tumbles out—and yet earlier, when Robin first slips the ornament about his neck, Elwes' prop locket accidentally (?) pops open and we glimpse an actual key inside. Elwes casually snaps the locket shut again and moves right on (as directed? saving the scene?), yet later this same spur-of-the-moment little cover-up proves baffling. Obviously Elwes the actor knows

the pendant has an easy-to-open latch and houses a real key, but does Robin? Is he genuinely surprised to see the key at film's end— or just that it fits Marian's chastity belt?

Come to think of it, other than one line from Brooks' "Men in Tights" number, Little John's goofy footbridge scam (echoing the desert tollbooth gag in *Blazing Saddles*), and Robin's highwayman-type encounter with ally-to-be Rabbi Tuckman, the film offers little evidence Robin's men are even outlaws. We never do see them rob from the rich and give to the poor, and beyond "crashing" Prince John's party and poaching a wild boar, Robin doesn't do much illegal at all!

Causing the film further, if minor, injury: a rash of verbal jokes either too corny or too ill-paced for the Brooks of the '60s and '70s but, post–*Spaceballs*, increasingly common. The less said of Brooks' *Julius Caesar* gag the better, the *White Men Can't Jump* feels pretty lame too, and Ahchoo's anachronistic inflatable sneakers bit only slows up a potentially exciting fight scene for no good reason. If Brooks wants Ahchoo in sneakers, fine, but why waste dialogue over it?

One hates to sound so negative, especially when one actually likes the picture he's finding fault with (let's face it: the movie's still pretty much irresistible), but while we're at it one may as well say a bit about the film as parody, too. The very first joke, in which peasants protest the fact that nearly every Robin Hood film includes a burning-down-the-village scene, is a terrific slam on "Prince John vs. Nottingham" movie clichés, as are Robin's orders that the requisite "Training Sequence," "Fight Scene," and love song get underway, and the "Robin Hood Rappers" and chastity belt bits nicely mock-mimic all those Alan-a-Dale-type forest warblers and Maid Marian-style monastic maidens forever turning up in medieval romance—

yet so few of Brooks' other jabs are Sherwood-specific it's difficult to think of them as spoofing Robin Hood at all. Surely putting Tracey Ullman into witch makeup, casting Isaac Hayes and Dave Chappelle as likable Moors, or having Roger Rees' Sheriff try to deflower Marian—'90s-trendy concepts more or less originated in Reynolds' film just two years before—can't qualify as longtime, worn-out genre clichés already!

Either way, *Robin Hood: Men in Tights* isn't half so take-no-prisoners cheeky as its "The Legend Had It Coming" lobby posters promise, never so much explodes the Robin Hood myth as merely revisits it, tourist-like, smiling uncritically all the way. *Blazing Saddles'* ads sport a similar tagline—"Never Give a Saga an Even Break"—but that film better lives up to its claim, deflates its genre's conventions much more overtly. Bean-eating cowboys; sultry saloon singers; folksinging railworkers—*Blazing Saddles* turns each of these old stand-bys on its ear, practically daring future shoot-'em-ups to play the material "straight" again. *Robin Hood: Men in Tights* makes us laugh, yes, but at gags we'd laugh at anywhere, rarely at the concept itself, the idea. It's a Robin Hood comedy, sure, but is just putting funny lines in the mouths of men in the same old nylons and chainmail enough to make it a spoof? Do sight gags and silly puns really a parody make?

Indeed, if at times the film barely feels like parody at all (an acceptable loss, since Brooks' goal seems less to laugh at the legend as laugh with it), it resembles satire even less—a far more disappointing situation, really, since Brooks' least satirical works also tend to be his least witty. As always, Brooks clearly loves the original material he targets (John Ford, James Whale, Alfred Hitchcock, George Lucas—none had bigger admirers than Brooks), yet for once that love seems to temper his satiri-cal intensity, softens his attacks. *Blazing Saddles* says racists are "morons," *Young Frankenstein* that hate-riots are "ugly," *High Anxiety* that psychiatrists are out for "the big bucks," *Spaceballs* that presidents "can't make decisions," but what *Robin Hood: Men in Tights* says—about hypocrisy, greed, incompetence, hate—is a little less clear. That power corrupts—that's certainly implied. That fair maidens, chaste or not, still crave men—that's implied too. For the most part, though, Brooks' tenth film is among his least outwardly satiric: no Nazi armbands spat upon in disgust as in *The Producers*; no priests turned money-hungry madmen as in *The Twelve Chairs*; no foaming-at-the-mouth corporate raiders as in *Silent Movie*; no cash-grabbing senators as in *History of the World—Part I*; no over-medicating doctors as in *Life Stinks*.

One recalls Brooks' and Carl Reiner's delightfully subversive "2,000 Year Old Man" bit about how the "real" Robin, far from the selfless, squeaky-clean hero depicted here, gave nothing at all to the poor but instead "stole from everybody and kept everything"—and how Robin's press agent Marty played up the old "robbed from the rich and gave to the poor" bit for the good P.R.. Though set on "not trashing the legend," on "having fun *with* it, not making fun *of* it" (that's how Brooks put it promoting the movie), the film might have played better pushed in that irreverent direction, giving us, at least at first, a greedy, corrupt Robin who, like *Life Stinks'* Goddard Bolt, only gradually decides to defend the poor rather than abuse them. Yet Brooks doesn't explore the myth's "greed vs. charity" subtext much at all, instead just sprinkling in more *Airplane!*-type puns, sight gags, and other groaners, few of them even half so slyly sophisticated as the sort of thing *The Producers* gave us with, say, its no-taste director so aptly named Roger DeBris.

Traveling by wagon dispensing Jewish sagacity, circumcisions, and sacramental wine, kind-hearted old wayfarer Rabbi Tuckman (Mel Brooks) wins over would-be highway bandits Robin and his Merry Men, in *Robin Hood: Men in Tights.* Brooks' clever reinvention of English legend's classic Friar Tuck character provides the film with its wittiest, most unexpected twist.

Perhaps celebrating what more or less amounts to his twenty-fifth anniversary behind the camera, Brooks also relies more than ever upon allusions to his own films, freely reprising favorite old sight gags (the crew-menacing sword-swipe in *Spaceballs*; the side-shifting infirmity, doggy treat reward, face-changing painting, and "walk this way" bits from *Young Frankenstein*, the last re-used in *History of the World — Part I*), characters (Robert Ridgely's *Blazing Saddles* hangman), and dialogue (*History of the World — Part I*'s "It's good to be the king") with considerable relish but usually lesser effect. Even warmed over the jokes remain pretty funny, but it's odd Brooks thought fans preferred know-it-by-heart old gags to fresh, funnier new ones. Why not reward fans with novelty instead of nostalgia? Even when shocked lily-white

villagers gasp as Robin names black pal Ahchoo their new sheriff—a genuinely witty reference to *Blazing Saddles*—we're none-too-wisely reminded how much funnier that film still seems even two decades later.

The movie *should* have rivaled *Blazing Saddles* too, since the basic premise of both films — heroic, quick-thinking underdog defends slow-witted commoners against corrupt government oppressors — is virtually the same. What are the badgered, over-taxed villagers of Rottingham but twelfth-century versions of the bullied, persecuted citizens of *Blazing Saddles'* Rock Ridge? Who are money-chasing Prince John and the Sheriff but Medieval variations on land-grabbing Hedley Lamarr and lapdog mob leader Taggart? For that matter, isn't the long-absent, power-usurped King Richard, ignorant of his brother's corruption until his return from the Crusades, just a more "serious" version of naive, more easily duped Gov. Lepetomane? Robin a more revered, more action-oriented Sheriff Bart? Ahchoo (or, given his weaponry skills, perhaps Will Scarlet O'Hara) a smoother, soberer Waco Kid?

Accordingly, *Robin Hood: Men in Tights* offers Brooks his best opportunity yet to one-up the shrewd, sacred cow-killing social commentary found in his finest films, but Brooks doesn't seem much interested this go-around, and it's really too bad. Show biz smarminess, upper-crust snobbery, predatory capitalism, mob violence, mindless racism, celebrity egotism, political corruption, bureaucratic incompetence, religious hypocrisy: ridicule-ready targets like these are what give Brooks' best work its heart and soul, yet *Robin Hood: Men in Tights*, clearly the ideal place for it, never takes full advantage of the legend's inherent room for social criticism. Greedy government types who line their own pockets at the taxpayers' expense? Corrupt police who beat and bully the very citizens whose well-being they are sworn to protect? The potential for razor-sharp satire seems obvious, yet for some reason Brooks this time largely prefers puerile, grade school-ish gags about hurled body parts ("Lend me your ears") and sophomoric, "kid joke" wordplay. ("No noose is good noose"? "H. & R. Blockhead"? Please!)

Of course, satire isn't entirely lacking in any Brooks film, and the Robin Hood saga carries just enough anti-corruption, pro-common man reproachfulness built-in to ensure at least a little of the old Brooksian vitriol. Crusades veteran Robin's richest line in this vein — "Unfortunately, *my* father couldn't get *me* into the National Guard" — has a deliciously devious Clintonian sting, and Ahchoo's barely audible Rodney King–like "Man, I hope someone's gettin' a video of this thing!" during his beating by the Sheriff's men is just the sort of biting social commentary the film really needs. Nevertheless, beyond one final swipe at *Blazing Saddles*–style racism and depiction of the crown as an institution easily breeding decadence and abuse of power (a valid enough barb surely cutting still deeper had replacing "evil" Prince John for "good" King Richard meant but losing one bad king for another), little else in the film comes close to that same sharp, satirical edge. Robin's grandiloquent speeches about bringing justice to England do take some ribbing a time or two — the instant he starts prattling on too long, someone either cuts him short or just plain dozes off — but one suspects Brooks isn't so much upending the idea of true gallantry in this dirty, dirty world as just poking fun at long-winded speeches. When Sheriff Bart delivers similar high-blown oratory in *Blazing Saddles*, the message is clear: Bart is full of hot air, his selfless nobility just a prettified Western hero sham. When Robin speaks, he means it; he fully intends to follow through. Satirically speaking, the joke might have hit harder pushed the other direction — ridiculed, say, not Robin's speeches but the impatient little boy or sleepy villagers for their '90s-style short attention spans or political disinterest. Would a child this fidgety listen to any hero who doesn't play pro basketball or cut rap CDs? Would grown-ups this shallow turn out for a free election like the one Robin promises even if he gave it to them? Suppose the peasants he has such high hopes for prove not worth saving to begin with, are nothing but a bunch of lazy, shiftless good-for-nothings after all?

Such larger issues aside, however, the film would be stronger too had co-writers Brooks, Evan Chandler, and J. David Shapiro made Robin himself a more complex hero, more flawed, more human. Brooks might have written Robin as a stressed-out worrier like *The Producers'* Leo Bloom, a pretentious social-climber like *The Twelve Chairs'* Ippolit Vorobyani-nov, a glory-grabbing egotist like *Young Frankenstein's* Dr. Freddy Frankenstein, a recovering addict like *Silent Movie's* Mel Funn, a trauma-haunted neurotic like *High Anxiety's* Dr. Richard Thorndyke — yet all he really asks is that star Cary Elwes play Robin pretty much the same way Errol Flynn or Douglas Fairbanks or even Richard Todd might have played him — suave, heroic, noble, and true.

One appreciates the fact that Brooks cherishes the Robin Hood legend too much to smash it to smithereens — *Young Frankenstein* certainly doesn't set out to humiliate Mary Shelley and James Whale, either — but it's hard to spoof something without re-inventing it a little, and Brooks never really mock-exaggerates Robin's true-blue magnificence (Robin as Super-man) nor seriously calls it into question (Robin as Inspector Clouseau). Elwes' Robin has near-perfect aim — fires six ar-rows at once, even — but we've seen "real" movie heroes shoot almost this well, and even when he falls off his horse he never blunders so badly he looks like a fool. After the horse bit, we don't even know how he reacts. Laugh it off? Rationalize? Try to cover up? We know what Freddy Frankenstein would do, but what about Robin? Imprisoned, tortured, facing exe-cution, our hero never explodes his own myth in a crisis — never panics, never whimpers, never tries a desperate *Get Smart* bluff, all of which might have hilar-ious — yet Robin's *not* turning 'fraidy-cat doesn't seem comical either. Ironically, Elwes' Robin is funniest when he's either overconfident (cutting the wrong rope and dropping a chandelier on his head) or dev-astated (losing family, property, pets, and, seemingly, an archery win), and we really

like these scenes too — who knows what wild comic heights Elwes might have scaled falling apart completely every time someone mentions Mumsy, or Daddums, or Robin's beloved dead cat? — but this Robin is far too "together," too solid, too wise. Elwes looks and sounds the part to perfection (promoting the film on *Larry King Live*, Brooks called him "the best young Robin Hood since Errol Flynn," and he'll get no argument here), but why is that so important in a comic Robin? If Brooks wants him played so nearly "for real," doesn't want him "exposed" or humiliated, why make a so-called Robin Hood "spoof" at all?

Other characters in the film get short-shrift too. Leo Bloom's gradual transfor-mation from chronic worrier to happy, self-confident risk-taker in *The Producers*; Ippolit Vorobyaninov's reluctant shift from embittered fallen nobleman to hum-bled commoner in *The Twelve Chairs*; Freddy Frankenstein's steady evolution from heartless braggart to selfless father figure in *Young Frankenstein* — that brand of rich, multi-layered character develop-ment once so vital in Brooks is harder to find here, and it's sorely missed. Robin and Marian fall in love, but not in any com-plex, semi-believable way, like Richard and Vicki in *High Anxiety* or "Pepto" and Molly in *Life Stinks*; they end up together simply because it's expected in tales like this, because Robin and Marian always do. The dull-witted peasants Robin trains to fight, meanwhile, reveal none of the vivid distinctiveness of *Blazing Saddles'* Rock Ridge folk, who, even all last-named John-son, still reveal more individuality — and, slowly accepting Bart, character growth — than any of Brooks' villagers here. Surely the movie would be more emotionally en-gaging if Robin and Marian likewise grew a little in the film, if these peasants too had separate personalities, some gradual change of heart.

Having said all this, then, can a comedy as riddled with shortcomings as *Robin Hood: Men in Tights* really be worth recommending? Is a film this disappointing even worth watching at all?

The obvious answer: Yes, indeed; of course it is. This is no cheap Hollywood hack at work here, after all, no rank comic amateur who doesn't understand how comedy works; this is Mel Brooks, for goodness' sake, one of the funniest men in the world. Mel Brooks couldn't be Mel Brooks without taking a sure-fire idea like this one and making *something* memorable out of it, and, in fits and starts at least, with *Robin Hood: Men in Tights* that's exactly what he does.

If, for instance, TV's *When Things Were Rotten* proves scene-for-scene funnier simply by squeezing in so many gags per half-hour — certainly the series is better paced than the movie, which often seems to need a good kick in the pants to keep it from stopping entirely — the film at least remains more openly romantic, more richly old-fashioned and sentimental. Robin Hood isn't just Robin Hood here but Prince Charming, and Marian, doe-eyed friend to the "happy little bluebird," lovelorn prisoner of her keyless steel chastity belt, is his Snow White, his Sleeping Beauty, his Cinderella. By contrast, all rat-a-tat-tat puns, takeoffs, and sight gags, *When Things Were Rotten* was the *Police Squad!* of its day, mile-a-minute nonsensical fun but without much warmth, and on this score the film easily "one-ups" the original. It's doubtful a Marian-enamored Robin ever would have serenaded his lady love with a tune as traditional and romantic as "The Night Is Young And You're So Beautiful" on TV (not in its entirety, anyway), and for the film's sweeter, softer spirit one simply must credit Brooks, who, always a fan of a really great love song (remember *Life Stinks*' terrific use of Cole Porter's "Easy to Love"?), knows a great

tune when he hears one and wisely dusts off this magnificent old melody here. Indeed, Brooks not only gives Robin a love interest this time but Little John as well (Latrine too, though it's questionable how good a catch he is), and he even lets Marian, like the pretty, lovesick heroine of some passion-rich Broadway or Disney musical, warble one of those beautifully soul-searching, character-defining "What I want" songs (Brooks' "Marian," of course) so deservedly popular in Lerner/Loewe or Ashman/Menkin — sort of the Mel Brooks equivalent of "Wouldn't It Be Loverly" and "Someday My Prince Will Come" and, to Brooks' considerable credit, quite a nice little tune in its own right.

Frequently filming outdoors on gorgeously grassy, rain-nourished California locales, the film has a remarkably authentic British look in many scenes, not only superbly duplicating the lush pastoral greenery of Merry Olde England but visually outclassing the film's small screen foregoer as well. While *When Things Were Rotten* shot almost solely on sitcom-obvious indoor sets, the movie steps outside the studio for a breath of fresh air where it can, and it benefits immensely, especially when the emerald boughs atop Brooks' makeshift Sherwood part just enough so a few warm beams of tree-filtered sunlight trickle though. The actors' costumes, likewise, with all their vivid high school Madrigal reds and greens, also give the tale a nice fairy tale lift, and while they may not look all that different from those worn by Dick Gautier and pals on TV, that's actually to its credit. After the earth-drab, visually subdued world of Reynolds' film its a real joy just seeing Robin *look* like Robin again, right down to the green tights and feather in the cap. Historically accurate or not, this is how the legend should look — bright, bold, and bigger-than-life, just the way fans imagined it in childhood, in backyard tree forts, with plastic swords and cardboard hats.

Furthermore, Brooks certainly hasn't lost his touch directing-wise, even if *Robin Hood: Men in Tights isn't* his most visually interesting film. For all his odd new fondness for shooting his actors from afar off, after all, for all his out-of-character passion for keeping his camera in one spot longer than any good comedy should, Brooks' scene set-ups are never really disastrous. It's not as if he cuts off the actors' heads, or has them posing with objects he's pushed out of frame, like Great-Grandma with her bad vacation pictures; the camerawork just isn't particularly cinematic, that's all, takes too little advantage of the medium's ability to make us flinch, gasp, laugh, cry. Too often actors whose expressions alone — a raised eyebrow, an impatient smirk, a baffled stare — might have had us laughing out loud (and made up considerably for the movie's drowsy pace) get lost in the landscape, and material that should be sure-fire leaves perfectly good gags flat on the floor when it should be bouncing, flubber-like, right off the walls.

When Brooks *is* in top form, though, it's another matter. The opening images of rows of archers firing flaming arrows before a twilight sky are splendidly picturesque (so "artsy" looking, in fact, one half-expects a serious Robin Hood film, but it's worth being misled a little for such a fabulous opening joke), and the movie boasts several admirably fluid zoom-ins and zoom-outs, including one truly distinctive end-of-film effects shot, a real eye-dazzler, pulling back from Robin and Marian's honeymoon window to reveal all Rottingham, then England, then the entire British Isles. Brooks also delivers an exquisitely atmospheric build-up to Robin's first meeting with Little John as, reflecting Robin's perspective, the camera slowly, warily moves in on the towering man; a superbly assured pan tracking

"camel jockeys" across a sandy beach until Robin and Asneeze appear in the distance; a fine from-the-footbridge look at Ah-choo's playful hops between the tiny brook's east and west banks; some appealing camera pans as Brooks sets up series of visual jokes scanned in one take; some effective over-the-shoulder views as characters speak face-to-face; a hauntingly lyrical bathtub scene in which Marian is slowly zoomed in on and, in all her beauty, glimpsed twice in breathtaking close-up (true close-ups, too — not just medium close shots); some well-staged bits as Robin, seen only in shadow, first regales Marian with "The Night Is Young and You're So Beautiful," then (in a nod to a beautifully photographed moment from 1938's *The Adventures of Robin Hood*) battles the Sheriff's shadow puppet duck with a shadow puppet dog; an excellent slow-motion effect involving Robin's locket shattering and the key inside landing in Marian's chastity belt's lock; a few tree-level looks at Robin and Blinkin during Blinkin's blind lookout bit; and two particularly satisfying glimpses of a sword-wielding Robin from the Sheriff's view as he hangs upside-down from his horse just before Robin sends the animal galloping away.

Brooks' camera comes alive most successfully in the big battle between Robin and the castle guards during Prince John's banquet. In just under five minutes, Brooks serves up a truly smashing view of the battle as seen above the combatants' heads; a few quick pans indicating on-the-spot battle planning through Robin's eyes; through-the-slats shots of characters watching the battle (and leering at one another) from behind stairs; shots of swords crashing down atop staircase railings; knee-level shots of Robin and Marian getting acquainted under a banquet table; glimpses of the battle shot from staircases; rows of armored knights stomping toward the camera, then charging past it on either side; a high-speed bit in which Blinkin, like some sightless human pencil-sharpener, shears a wooden column to splinters with his sword; shots of steel-booted feet clanking noisily over stone and wood; and an incredibly complex set-up featuring lined-up knights tumbling like dominos as Brooks' camera expertly traces their noisy collapse. One senses Brooks worked really, really hard staging all this, and while one deftly orchestrated battle sequence can't make up for so many aimless minutes of tiresome long shots and cameras mired in cement, it's still sensational, sensational fun. Just imagine if the whole movie were filmed and paced this well.

Moreover, even without a naturally farcical big-screen personality the film's biggest asset is still star Cary Elwes, a perfectly splendid Robin whose comic instincts work wonders for a film whose rather tired premise Brooks had already strung out into an entire TV show. Cheerfully replacing Dick Gautier's clean-shaven, Beatle-wigged look with a debonair Errol Flynn mustache and goatee, Elwes (co-starring that same year in Francis Ford Coppola's *Bram Stoker's Dracula*, the tale inspiring Brooks' next film) looks more Robin Hood-ish than Gautier, and this heightened realism should sink the movie completely, but it doesn't because Elwes' delightfully witty silliness (lisp-"thpeaking" through a tong-tortured tongue, spitting out beach sand, etc.), while underused, make up for so much. Sometimes all Elwes need say is a mere "Uh, uh" and we grin, just because he puts such an idiosyncratic, goofy spin on it, and when the line is funny on its own he comes off better still. The film might win more yuks with a less heroic-looking lead (Gene Wilder? Rick Moranis? John Candy?), but Elwes handles the derring-do with exceptional swashbuckling dash, and, as a favorite line from the picture so

slyly observes, even makes a more convincing Robin than American-accented Kevin Costner in *Robin Hood: Prince of Thieves*. If only Brooks could have somehow combined Elwes' showmanship with Costner's huge fan following, the film might have been his biggest smash yet — *if*, that is, it also had Brooks' sharpest, funniest script too.

Indeed, for all the complaints here about the film's less than wacky characterizations, not one actor in it fails to win us over. Amy Yasbeck may not be the world's kookiest Maid Marian, but she's so disarmingly perky and pretty we can't help liking her. Small wonder Brooks used her again. He might have found loonier Merry Men than Eric Allan Kramer, Dave Chappelle, Mark Blankfield, and Matthew Porretta too, but he'd be hard-put to find anyone more personable; only Kramer and Porretta's characters know each at first, but they soon feel like old friends — theirs *and* ours — the second Brooks puts them together. (Blankfield had already played a near-blind elevator operator in Brooks' 1989 NBC Harvey Korman–Cloris Leachman sitcom *The Nutt House*, and a clumsy blind psychologist in CBS's 1991 sitcom *Good and Evil*, with Teri Garr. Both Blankfield and Porretta, like Yasbeck, would appear in Brooks' next film.) As a far too serious-looking but drolly debonair King Richard, Patrick Stewart is a solid choice too — not asked to do much beyond mimic Sean Connery and look regal, really, but easily up to what little humor the role demands.

As the film's villains, meanwhile, Roger Rees and Richard Lewis (the latter of whose 1995 Fox sitcom *Daddy Dearest*, coincidentally, Brooks' son Max served as production assistant near the time of this film) don't exactly ooze menace, no, but Rees' limitless enthusiasm and daffy verbal gymnastics superbly counterbalance Lewis's softer, more downbeat approach, and it's easy to see why Brooks teamed them. Playing soft-spoken, pious types, Megan Cavanagh and Dick Van Patten (Friar Tuck in the TV show, here the Abbot who nearly weds the Sheriff to a helpless Marian) can't go really crazy on screen, but Cavanagh somehow seems lovable without saying a word (having worked with Eric Allan Kramer for the revamped second year of Bob Newhart's 1992–93 CBS sitcom *Bob*, she too would return for *Dracula: Dead and Loving It*), and it's hard to think of anyone fans feel more comfortable with than Brooks' old pal Dick Van Patten. Tracey Ullman? Her role may sidetrack matters with plot points the film never makes good on, but she's still the best sketch comedienne post–*Carol Burnett* that TV has ever produced, and Brooks, having guested on her Fox variety show in 1987, was smart to take note of her. And Dom DeLuise? True, his mobster bit runs too long, but this masterful loony does a top-of-the-line Brando, and the screen — like our eyes — lights up the instant we see him working for Brooks again. If only Brooks would stop putting his old buddy in "sit-down" parts and let him run around wild again!

And, of course, it's always fun picking out longtime Brooks standbys as they pop up in each new film, and naturally this time proves no exception. Besides Dom DeLuise (in his sixth Brooks role), Dick Van Patten (his third), and Robert Ridgely (his fourth), fans might also spot familiar TV comic Chuck McCann, seen before in *Silent Movie* and here as an archery-training villager; longtime Brooks writer-actor Rudy De Luca (in his sixth appearance) as a lustful guest at Prince John's party-turned-swordfight; in his fourth Brooks-directed role (as a villager this time), ever-present Brooks writer-actor Ronny Graham, a Brooks co-writer and performer in 1952's *New Faces*, the film version of their Broadway revue *New Faces of*

1952, and co-scripter (without Brooks) of the Brooks-starring remake of *To Be or Not to Be*; actor Ira Miller, here making his third Brooks appearance, this time as a villager; and actor Johnny Cocktails, returning to the fold as a wedding guest after a small role in *Life Stinks*. Sharp-eyed observers might also pick out such Brooks family friends as James Van Patten and David DeLuise among the various wedding guests and villagers, and at least one up-and-coming actress, "Giggling Court Lady" Chase Masterson, who soon after this role achieved something of a cult following for her ongoing role as "Dabo girl" Leeta in the syndicated sci-fi series *Star Trek: Deep Space Nine*.

And Brooks himself? He's visible too, of course, and though it may sound like fawning, his re-interpretation of Friar Tuck as a very Jewish Rabbi Tuckman is real genius, perhaps the one conceptual change in the entire movie that comes so completely out-of-the-blue the rest of the film, most of it pretty much by-the-book Robin Hood, actually suffers by comparison. Brooks' acting itself is fairly low-key (funny, but nothing showy), but this entirely unexpected re-invention of the familiar instantly points out just how routine the rest of the film really is. If changing just one little character could make this much difference, one wonders, what if the script had taken similar risks with Robin? Marian? Little John? The result, surely: a much, much funnier film.

That's not to say, of course, that the script is all that bad, either. Some of the Brooks/Chandler/Shapiro material is quite strong, if too quickly dated (the Kevin Costner barb; the Rodney King bit; the Bill Clinton gag — anything remotely satirical), and several bits that seemingly shouldn't work at all play amazingly well. Just why we laugh at, say, Robin's nonsensical reply when grilled on the whereabouts of his king is hard to pin down exactly — the persistent repetition? the increasing absurdity of the anachronisms? the singsong playfulness of Elwes' delivery? — but laugh we do, and it's hard to imagine even the most stone-faced movie fan not grinning at it.

Better still, though, is a wonderfully funny bit between Elwes and Mark Blankfield after Robin returns from the Crusades to find his estate stolen by Prince John — and his whole family and even his pets all long dead. In a more serious film, such a ghastly chain of catastrophes might sound utterly horrific, but the final punchline gets such a hilarious build-up we just can't help laughing. A comedy historian could probably trace this gag all the way back to vaudeville if he looked far enough, but who cares? It's all performed so perfectly here — Blankfield's exaggerated British increasingly laced with pity, Elwes' upper-crust eloquence quaking with waggish horror — it utterly crackles with Abbott and Costello–style comic energy. Or, speaking of that famous team, consider the way several cheery well-wishers greet Dick Van Patten's pious-looking Abbot as he arrives for poor Marian's forced wedding. Fans too young to remember old-time radio or who have yet to stumble across Bud and Lou's old movies on TV may not "get" that one at all — but for anyone else, the joke's big payoff is music to the ears. Come to think of it, both setup and joke are handled so flawlessly, and the lines delivered so well, children just might laugh anyway.

Additionally fun — even if the scene does linger a few seconds too long after the joke — is Robin's triumphant first official act as new ruler of Sherwood: naming black Ahchoo the new sheriff of all-white Rottingham, much to the shock of the locals. Not many of Brooks' in-joke references to his own films work this well — Chappelle's Ahchoo even alludes to Blazing Saddles by name, another first for Brooks — but this one succeeds at least in part because Blinkin, in some out-of-nowhere stroke of genius (Blankfield's? Brooks'?), drops his English accent for just this one line ("He's black?") — and the semi-satirical "Yankee racist" effect is so unexpectedly jarring it's instinctively funny. Is Brooks indicting American bigotry here? If so, bravo.

The film boasts scores of other good bits, too, among them a truly amazing, if comically over-extended, nod to The Godfather, The Freshman, On the Waterfront, A Fistful of Dollars, and Dirty Harry in the same scene, and a Dirty Ezio Dallas–style attempt to shoot Robin from the "Royal Folio Depository" that becomes even funnier knowing Dirty Harry himself, actor Clint Eastwood, was that same summer playing a former JFK Secret Service agent in In the Line of Fire. Clearly, the real problem with the movie isn't that it lacks enough wit, but that (remember Shakespeare's line about brevity?) it lacks enough wit to sustain a film of its length and narrative stodginess. TV comedy shows don't usually run shorter than drama series by mere accident, and knock-knock jokes aren't called knock-knock-knock-knock-knock jokes for no reason.

Another of Brooks' big victories with the film stems from hiring composer Hummie Mann (City Slickers, The Addams Family) to take over the position vacated by longtime contributor John Morris. While Mann's melodies never rise to the level of Morris's best work of the late '60s and early '70s — the film's lyric-less main theme isn't one-tenth as memorable as Morris's rollicking title composition for Blazing Saddles, and the tale would surely benefit from a rousing "Robin Hood, Robin Hood, Riding Through the Glen"–type parody (the old Richard Greene TV show, remember?) — once or twice he comes so close one might swear

Multi-talented performer-filmmaker Mel Brooks (center), helming his tenth movie, directs Eric Allan Kramer (far left) as Little John, Cary Elwes as Robin Hood, and other members of the cast and crew during the climactic outdoor battle scene from *Robin Hood: Men in Tights.*

it's still Morris. The closing "Men in Tights" reprise, in particular — the spirited, happy-go-lucky version heard over the end credits — sounds astonishingly Morris-like (as, logically, it should, since Brooks' tune is largely a variation of his own "Jews in Space" melody in Morris's *History of the World — Part I*). Mann's "Marian," meanwhile, is easily the most beautiful tune to come from a Brooks film since *High Anxiety*—both times it turns up, it's a real winner — and his version of the Billy Rose/Irving Kahal/Dana Suesse classic "The Night Is Young and You're So Beautiful" sounds better than ever, particularly with Brooks' "Merry Men Singers" as backup. Even Mann's lively, bouncing version of "Row, Row, Row Your Boat," heard as Robin swims (yes, swims!) all the

way from Africa to England, is a real treat; a tune this silly shouldn't work at all, yet somehow, thanks to Mann, work it does. One wishes this sort of whimsy had popped up more often, in fact, and that Mann had written more music; the less fast and furious Brooks' material, the more good songs help take up the slack.

Consider all these triumphs, then, and one quickly realizes just how much tremendous potential *Robin Hood: Men in Tights* had going for it, and what a top-of-the-line comedy classic the movie, certainly an enjoyable but never an exceptional Mel Brooks film, might very well have become. Given a tad more dramatic tension, a touch more actor-oriented camerawork, a slightly more saucy attitude, and perhaps a bit more emotional depth, the film might well be cited in the same breath as *The Producers*, *Blazing Saddles*, and *Young Frankenstein*. Mild as it is, however, Brooks' tenth stint as writer-director boasts more than enough highlights to keep it, like Brooks' very best comedies, playing on TV and video for years. It may not, like Marian's chastity belt, be an "Everlast" exactly, but as long as film fans enjoy a little good silly fun, it certainly should keep popping up on the small screen for years to come. Let's hope so, anyway; it's a nice little film.

CAST: Cary Elwes (Robin Hood); Richard Lewis (Prince John); Roger Rees (Sheriff of Rottingham); Amy Yasbeck (Marian); Mark Blankfield (Blinkin); Dave Chappelle (Ahchoo); Isaac Hayes (Asneeze); Megan Cavanagh (Broomhilde); Eric Allan Kramer (Little John); Matthew Porretta (Will Scarlet O'Hara); Tracey Ullman (Latrine); Patrick Stewart (King Richard); Dom DeLuise (Don Giovanni); Dick Van Patten (The Abbot); Robert Ridgely (The Hangman); Mel Brooks (Rabbi Tuckman); Steve Tancora (Filthy Luca); Joe Dimmick (Dirty Ezio); Avery Schreiber (Tax Assessor); Chuck McCann (Villager); Brian George (Dungeon Maitre d'); Zitto Kazann (Head Saracen Guard); Richard Assad (Assistant Saracen Guard); Herman Poppe (Sheriff's Guard); Clive Revill (Fire Marshall); Joe Baker (Angry Villager); Carol Arthur (Complaining Villager); Kelly Jones (Buxom Lass); Clement Von Franckenstein (Royal Announcer); Corbin Allred (Young Lad); Chase Masterson (Giggling Court Lady); Don Lewis (Mime); Roger Owens (Peanut Vendor); Patrick Valenzuela (Lead Camel Jockey); Steffon, Dante Henderson, Bryant Baldwin, Diesko Boyland, Jr., Edgar Godineaux, Jr. (Sherwood Forest Rapper-Dancers); Johnny Dean Harvey, Keith Diorio, Joseph R. McKee, Nathan Prevost, Don Hesser, Bill Bohl, Chris Childers, Raymond Del Barrio (Merry Men Dancers); Malcolm Danare, Edwin Hale, Nick Jameson, Peter Pitofsky, Nicholas Rempel (Inept Archers); Rudy DeLuca, Matthew Saks, Robin Shepard, Dee Gubin (Party Guests); Johnny Cocktails, Lisa Cordray, Laurie Main, Elaine Ballace, Stuart Schreiber (Wedding Guests); James Van Patten, Ira Miller, David DeLuise, Lillian D'Arc, Patrick Brymer, Robert Noble, Henry Kaiser, Tony Tanner, Diana Chesney, James Glaser, Ronny Graham (Villagers); Dan Barringer, Blair Burrows, Erik Cord, Danny Costa, Kiante Elam, George Fisher, Lance Gilbert, Troy Gilbert, Larry Holt, Loren Janes, Robert J. Jauregui, Clint Lilley, William James Madden, John Phillip, Charles Picerni, Jr., Steve Picerni, Jim Pratt, Philip J. Romano, George Marshall Ruge, Ben R. Scott, Paul G. Stalone, R.L. Tolbert, Richard Warlock, Ted White, Bob Yerkes (Stunt Players).

CREDITS: Director: Mel Brooks; Producer: Mel Brooks; Screenplay: Mel Brooks, Evan Chandler, J. David Shapiro; Story: J. David Shapiro, Evan Chandler; Executive Producer: Peter Schindler; Director of Photography: Michael D. O'Shea; Production Designer: Roy Forge Smith; Film Editor: Stephen E. Rivkin; Costume Designer: Dodie Shepard; Music: Hummie Mann; Associate Producer: Evan Chandler; Casting: Lindsay D. Chag and Bill Shepard, C.S.A.; Production Manager: Robert Latham Brown; First Assistant Director: Gregg Goldstone; Second Assistant Director: Kenneth J. Silverstein; Executive in Charge of Production: Robert Latham Brown; 2nd Unit Director: Peter Schindler; Additional Photography: Lloyd Ahern II; Associate Editor: Darren T. Holmes; Brooksfilms Production Executive: Leah Zappy; Art Directo0r: Stephen Myles Berger; Set Decorator: Ronald R. Reiss; Senior Set Designers: David M. Haber, Cate Bangs; Set Designers: Bruce Robert Hill, Gary A. Lee; Leadman: Chuck Lipscomb; Script Supervisor: Marshall I. Schlom; Choreographer: Cindy Montoya-Picker; 2nd 2nd Assistant Director: Judith Moore; Camera Operator: Michael Genne; First Assistant Camera: Michael Chavez; 2nd Camera Operator: Steven H. Smith; First Assistant 2nd Camera: Kenneth Kenny Nishino; Second Assistant Cameras: Sean J. O'Shea, Vincent Mata; Film Loader: Martin Glover; Production Sound: Jeff Wexler, Don Coufal; Gary Holland; Videotape Operator: Lindsay P. Hill; Assistant Editors: Gina Lombardo Silano, Cynthia E. Thornton, Ewa Zbroniec; Location Manager: Bill Bowling; Property Master: Jack M. Marino; Assistant Property Masters: Jennifer Dawson, Glen Kennedy; Gaffer: Gary Tandrow; Best Boy Electric: James M. Cox; Rigging Gaffer: Jerry Enright; Set Lighting: Michael J. Bailey, William T. McKane, Norm Berens, James Krattiger, Thomas P. Powell; Key Grip: Scott M. Robinson; Best Boy Grip: Richard Redlin; Dolly Grip: Albert Ramos; 2nd Dolly Grip: Dave Canestro; Grips: James D. Doherty, Laszlo Horvath; Rigging Key Grip: Robert Duggan; 2nd Unit Key

Grip: Tom Prophet, Jr.; Costume Supervisors: Christine Heinz, Charles DeMuth; Key Costumer: Robert Q. Mathews; Make-up Department Head: Bari Dreiband-Burman; Special Make-up Effects: Thomas R. Burman; Cary Elwes' Make-up: Carol Schwartz; Make-up Artists: Todd A. McIntosh, Blake Shephard; Key Hair Stylist: Linle White; Hair Stylists: Susan Kietlow-Maust, Judith Tiedemann; Production Coordinator: Alyson Evans; Assistant Production Coordinator: Steve Kornacki; Production Accountant: Cynthia Quan; Assistant Accountant: Josh Ornstein; Post Production Accountant: Linden Windeland Johnson; Still Photographers: Peter Sorel, Robert Isenberg; Publicity: Saul Kahan; Extras Casting: Charlie Messenger; Special Effects Coordinator: Richard Ratliff; Special Effects: Wayne Rose, Fred Tessaro, R. Michael Bisetti, Roger W. Lifsey, Terry P. Chapman, Mark R. Lilienthal; Stunt Coordinator: Brian Burrows; Sword and Fight Coordinator: Victor Paul; Archery Master: Jack Verbois; Wrangler Ramrod: Corky Randall; Dialogue Coach: Julie Adams; Orchestrations: Brad Dechter; Additional Orchestrations: Frank Bennett, Don Nemitz; Music Editor: Chris Ledesma; Assistant Music Editor: Gary Wasserman; Scoring Mixer: Armin Steiner; Music Mixer: Rick Riccio; Music Contractor: Steve Liveley; Music Preparation: Joann Kane Music Services; Sound Effects: Visiontrax Inc.; Supervising Sound Editors: Gregory M. Gerlich, Gary S. Gerlich; Sound Editors: William Jacobs, Richard M. LeGrand, Jr., Bruce Lacey, Andy Kopetzky; Sound Designer: Harry E. Snodgrass; Supervising ADR Editor: Petra Bach; ADR Editor: Rober Ulrich; Assistant Sound Editors: Michelle Pleis-Stirber, Samuel L. Webb; ADR Assistant Editor: Kelly J. Quinn; Foley Editors: David L. Horton, Jr., Scot A. Tinsley; Post Production Services: Skywalker Sound, a division of Lucas Digital, Ltd.; Re-recording Mixers: Steve Maslow, Gregg Landaker; Recordist: Mark "Frito" Long; Loaders: Chris Minkler, Brian Fowler; Stage Engineer: Joe Brennan; ADR Mixers: Charleen Richards, Robert Deschaine, C.A.S.; ADR Recordists: Greg Steele, David Jobe; Foley Artists: Dan O'Connell, Gary "Wrecker" Heckler; Foley Mixer: James Ashwill; Foley Recordist: Nerses Gezalyan; ADR Group: L.A. MadDogs; Assistant to Mel Brooks: Jeff Bye; Assistants to the Producers: Tessa Francis, Lisann M. Karmiol, Christine Coates; Additional 2nd 2nd Assistant Director: Mark Tobey; DGA Trainees: Suzanne C. Geiger, David McWhirter; Assistant to Cary Elwes: Ken Bellanca; Production Assistants: Tricia Miles, Kurt Valles, Ron Chesney, Chris Armstrong; Casting Assistants: Caryn Richmond, Arlane J. Crawford; Clearance Research: Valerie O'Brien; Art Department Coordinator: Jacqueline C. English; Art Department Production Assistant: Dennis M. Brown; Set Dressing: Mark Boucher, Nigel A. Boucher, Philip Calhoun; Drapery: Terry A. Sheffield; Greens Foreman: David R. Newhouse; Construction Coordinator: W. Wayne Walser; General Construction Foreman: Tim Lafferty; Construction Foremen: Karl Walser, Terry Kempf; Propmaker Foreman: C. Jonas Kirk; Supervising Labor Foreman: Larry Wise; Paint Foreman: Paul A. Minitello; Standby Painter: Al Kenders; Transportation Coordinator: Jim Chesney; Transportation Captains: Charles Renfro, John Armstrong; Caterer: Michelson Food Services, Inc., Chef — Antoine Mascaro; Craft Service: John S. Moy; First Aid: Jonas C. Matz; Negative Cutter: Gary Burritt; Color Timer: Dale Caldwell; "Men in Tights" Words/Music: Mel Brooks, Performed by the Merry Men Singers (Steve Lively, Randy Crenshaw, Kerry Katz, Geoff Koch, Rick Logan); "Marian" Words: Mel Brooks/Music: Hummie Mann, Maid Marian's Singing Voice Performed by Debbie James, End Credit Duet Performed by Cathy Dennis and Lance Ellington, Cathy Dennis Courtesy of Polydor Records; "Sherwood Forest Rap" Words: Mel Brooks/Music: Hummie Mann, Performed by Kevin Dorsey and the Merry Men Singers; "The Night Is Young and You're So Beautiful" Words: Billy Rose and Irving Kahal/Music: Dan Suesse, Courtesy of Pic Corporation, Chappell Music Co., Inc., and Words and Music, Inc., Performed by Arthur Rubin and the Merry Men Singers; Main Title Design: VCE/Peter Kuran; Supervisor: Kevin O'Neill; Titles and Opticals: Cinema Research Corporation; Matte Paintings and Patriot Arrow Effects: Illusion Arts, Inc., Syd Dutton and Bill Taylor, A.S.C.; Visual Effects: Dream Quest Images; Visual Effects Supervisor: Mat Beck; Animatronix: Optic Nerve; Cranes and Dollies: Chapman; Location Lighting Equipment: Hollywood Rental Co., Inc./Matthews Group; Ranch Location: Frank and Vera Vacek's Rancho Maria, Canyon Country, CA.; Filmed at the Warner Hollywood Studios in Hollywood; Filmed with Panavision Cameras & Lenses; Color: Deluxe; 1993; Released by 20th Century–Fox; A Brooks-films Production in association with Gaumont; 1993, 20th Century–Fox Film Corporation; 102 minutes.

12

★ ★ ★

"AND YOU WILL REMEMBER NOTHING!"

Dracula: Dead and Loving It

★ ★ ★ ★ ★ ★

(1995)

In 1893 Transylvania, English solicitor Thomas Renfield (Peter MacNicol) endures a wild stagecoach ride when his superstitious coach driver tries outracing the setting sun. Deposited in a tiny mountain village, Renfield is urged to forsake his appointment at vampire-inhabited Castle Dracula, but the skeptical Londoner insists on arriving as expected and sets off on foot alone.

Arriving, Renfield meets Count Dracula (Leslie Nielson), who eerily walks through spider webs untouched, casts a shadow possessing a will of its own, and smacks his lips at the sight of blood. A naive Renfield, however, suspects nothing, and smilingly helps his new client complete paperwork granting the Count legal ownership of long-vacant London property Carfax Abbey.

That night, Dracula hypnotizes Renfield, giving him a sick craving for insects and other vermin and securing his loyalty in seeking fresh blood. Soon a ship arrives in London, crew missing and captain dead, and Renfield is locked in a mad-house run by stuffy Dr. Seward (Harvey Korman), Dracula's new neighbor. At an opera, Dracula introduces himself to Dr. Seward, his gorgeous daughter Mina (Amy Yasbeck), intended son-in-law Jonathan Harker (Steven Weber), and sensual ward Lucy Westenra (Lysette Anthony), who finds the Count instantly alluring.

At sunset, Dracula enters a sleeping Lucy's bedroom in bat form and drinks her blood. Baffled by Lucy's weakened state, Dr. Seward calls in Prof. Abraham Van Helsing (Mel Brooks), who thinks the punctures on Lucy's throat are of vampire origin and fears a new attack may cost both her life and soul. Foul-smelling garlic repels the fiend the next time, and when Dracula frees Renfield to remove it Renfield is recaptured peeking under Lucy's covers. Undaunted, Dracula lures a sleepwalking Lucy outside, where he is glimpsed but unrecognized by Mina while feasting.

Sadly, Lucy dies this time, and Van Helsing, who detests the Count's "always have the last word" arrogance, believes

Dracula responsible. Lucy, now a vampire, murders a caretaker (Clive Revill) in her crypt the next night, and Van Helsing forces her back to her coffin with a crucifix before she can attack Jonathan — who ends up drenched with blood driving a stake into her heart. Dracula, out to make a hypnotized Mina his vampire bride, takes her to Carfax Abbey and drinks her blood, calling up carnal impulses in her that shocked an appalled Jonathan at home the next day.

Proving Mina too is now in the monster's power, Van Helsing invites suspects Dracula and Renfield to a dress ball, where he reveals Dracula casts no reflection. Enraged, Dracula flees with Mina to the deserted cliffside chapel where he has moved his coffin, but Renfield foolishly leads Van Helsing, Dr. Seward, and Jonathan right to him. Before the Count can deliver Mina's soul-stealing final bite, the three rescuers storm the chapel attic, destroying him only when Van Helsing — and, accidentally, Renfield — admit morning sunlight reducing the scoundrel to dust. At the creature's demise, Mina reawakens and is swept away by a devoted Jonathan; Dr. Seward tries, and fails, to convince a grieving Renfield he no longer needs a master; and Van Helsing exits having what he thinks — *thinks* — is the last word to the arrogant, seemingly expired Count.

★　★　★

The big-screen accomplishments of writer-director Mel Brooks during the 1990s may not be every movie fan's cup of cinematic tea, but criticize the filmmaker's later works however one likes, one still has to admit at least one thing: if only for taking on *Dracula: Dead and Loving It* so many years after the stellar success of 1974's *Young Frankenstein*, Mel Brooks in 1995 was one brave, brave man. Sheriff Bart may show true grit bringing down a horse-punching Mongo in *Blazing Saddles*, and *High Anxiety*'s Dr. Richard Thorndyke real daring facing his fear of heights head-on, but spoofing a second horror classic more than two decades after the first one? Hoping against hope Transylvanian lightning can strike not once but twice? Now *that* takes courage.

To start with, expecting viewers not to compare *Dracula: Dead and Loving It* to *Young Frankenstein* — and don't think for a minute anyone as clever as Brooks ever once imagined they wouldn't — was utterly inconceivable, even if its ballroom and opera house settings were markedly more high-class, and even if its none-too-original story line was shot in blood-vivid Hammer-style color and not Universal-gothic black-and-white. Had *Young Frankenstein* been a colossal failure, a second Universal horror spoof might have stood some small chance at critical raves, but since *Young Frankenstein* remains to this day the single most admired monster comedy since *Abbott and Costello Meet Frankenstein*, the Film Critics' Law of Diminishing Returns all but guaranteed this latest try wouldn't steal away anyone's affections from Brooks' still popular-as-ever original.

Making matters stickier still, writer Robert Kaufman's Stan Dragoti–directed *Dracula* takeoff *Love at First Bite* (1978), starring an ultra-sophisticated George Hamilton as the vampire count in blackout-'70s New York, had already targeted essentially the same material nearly two decades earlier — and had, arguably, turned out loonier and more off-the-beaten-path inventive than most Brooks films going back at least that far. Riding the then-current disco craze, the movie had included a Brooksian musical number, too, and that *Saturday Night Fever*-style bit — dance floor dynamos Hamilton and Susan St. James setting the Big Apple strobelight scene ablaze to the driving beat of "I Love the Night Life"—came out so nicely that outclassing it with yet another vampire passion dance seemed unimaginable. Then too, Dragoti had even secured one of Brooks' best players, *The Producers'* Dick Shawn (such a funny man—what a shame Brooks never re-used him), not to mention the always watchable Richard Benjamin and Arte Johnson—just the sort of surefire comic winners Brooks might have used to great effect in his own films. Even more astonishing: it's Benjamin's "nice Jewish boy" Van Helsing figure, not Brooks', who attacks his blood-sucking nemesis with a Star of David instead of a crucifix: the absolutely perfect Mel Brooks Dracula joke, already snatched up by savvy scriptwriters beating him to the punch by almost twenty years!

Love at First Bite one-ups *Dracula: Dead and Loving It* in other ways, too, among them a sort of risk-taking *Blazing Saddles* hipness that was at one time Brooks' stock in trade. Remarkably, it's Dragoti's tuxedoed Count, not juxtaposition king Brooks', who glides, Travolta-like, across a '70s-flashy disco floor; whose coffin, like ordinary traveler's luggage, ends up misdirected by airport baggage handlers; who traumatizes a cocky minister by popping out of a closed casket at an all-black funeral; who is mistaken, in bat form, for a chicken by hungry foreigners; who pits ancient Transylvanian magic against switchblade-wielding street punks; who wakes up hung over after feasting on a drunken wino; who must flee New York City in mid-blackout; who, robbing a blood bank, marvels at its convenient "plastic disposable bodies." Considering *Blazing Saddles'* "fish out of water" shrewdness, slyly exposing white churchgoers' hypocrisy by dropping an urban black sheriff into the mix, it's Brooks from whom one expects a Dracula knocked silly by culture shock, a vampire-hunting Van

Helsing less worried about public safety than afraid this roguish lady-killer is trying to steal his girl—yet it's *Love at First Bite* that takes all the big chances, turns Bram Stoker's grim original inside-out and gives us something unexpectedly offbeat and new.

Perhaps the most surprising aspect of Brooks' film, in fact, is how utterly *unsurprising* it is, following, if not Stoker's 1897 novel exactly, the familiar old Hamilton Deane/John Balderston stage play and director Tod Browning's 1931 adaptation so faithfully, and with such oddly muted humor, it almost qualifies as a non-comic Browning remake, with bits and pieces of films like F. W. Murnau's *Nosferatu* (1922), Terence Fisher's *The Horror of Dracula* (1958), John Badham's *Dracula* (1979), and Francis Ford Coppola's *Bram Stoker's Dracula* (1992) thrown in. It's a pretty good remake too, hardly whiz-bang exciting, certainly, yet arguably better paced than the '31 film, which, classic though it is, feels awfully stagy and slow given its seventy-five-minute length, especially compared to Universal's *Frankenstein* or *The Wolf Man* shot a few years later. Indeed, though Brooks' movie runs a full quarter-hour longer than Browning's, that's including five-plus minutes of closing credits crawl, actually making this one of Mel Brooks' shortest pictures.

This pleasant little comedy has far more going for it than just brevity, though, including some surprisingly well-directed visuals: a coach wending its way through grim Transylvanian terrain; a carriage wheel, seen in close-up, crushing some long-neglected human skull; a candle- and fireplace-lit castle dance shot through fingers of flame in the foreground; a fancy-dress ball in which Dracula's otherworldly evil reveals itself (or rather, doesn't) in a gigantic wall mirror; a beautiful long shot of heroes Prof. Van Helsing, Dr. Seward, and Jonathan Harker, in haunting silhouette, chasing Dracula-enslaved solicitor Thomas Renfield up a hill hung heavy in sumptuous moonlit blue. Brooks also does a fine job using what passes for natural sunlight in several key scenes (during Dracula's death in particular, the sun's energy looks almost as lethal as A-bomb radiation), and it's amazing how well he's given a film shot solely in California such uncanny fog-on-the-moors English-ness. Best of all, however, is the director's expert handling of the final battle between Van Helsing, Seward, and Harker and the evil Count; all that crisp, quick cutting between tight shots of gripped forearms, flung beams, and upraised stakes reminds us more than a little of Alfred Hitchcock's fight scenes: minimal maneuvering space, maximum excitement.

Brooks pulls his camera in tighter when shooting his actors this go-around too, and if any one decision saves the movie, this is it. This time if one of his stars hits upon some particularly inspired grin, smirk, or eye-roll we usually see it up-close, and though every once in a while it's instantly apparent Brooks' camera is in the wrong place (the most obvious: Dracula's flat-looking left-profile, left-of-screen debut, atop a staircase shot drably from one side), his renewed "actors first, backdrops second" outlook marks a real cinematic step up after *Robin Hood: Men in Tights.* Yes, many of his exteriors are all too clearly just indoor sets, and yes, it's a shame some of that high-energy desperation from his big stalkers-and-stakers showdown couldn't spill over to the rest of

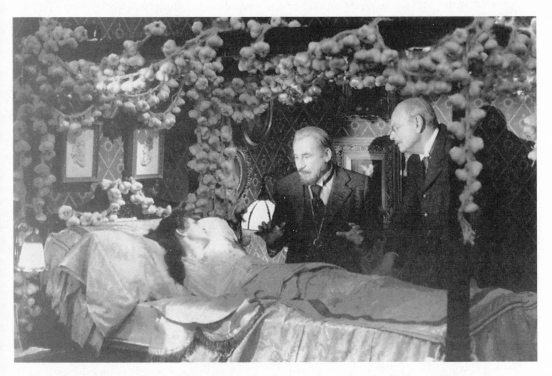

Unaware that her charming new neighbor Count Dracula is an undead monster who has attacked her in her sleep, blood-drained Victorian Lucy Westenra (Lysette Anthony) recuperates in a bedroom surrounded by garlic and watched over by vampire expert Prof. Abraham Van Helsing (Mel Brooks) and blustery madhouse physician Dr. Seward (Harvey Korman), in Mel Brooks' eleventh film as director, *Dracula: Dead and Loving It* (1995), which Brooks also produced and co-scripted.

the film, but at least this over-chatty, set-bound inaction seems in tune with the movies he's imitating. Brooks is right; vampire films often *do* look a lot like stage plays, so why shoot this one all earthy-outdoorsy lifelike when the genre's very night-at-the-opera phoniness accounts for so much of its appeal? And as for the pacing, even with the added sex and gore Hammer's best fright films can feel pretty sluggish — lots of stiff, stuffy Englishmen standing about drawing rooms, bedrooms, and bookrooms, all disputing and debating but otherwise doing fairly little — and, sure enough, this movie reflects that. In vampire flicks, a little theatricality isn't always a bad thing.

What's more, the *Dracula* everyone recalls from Stoker, Deane/Balderston, and Browning never did pack much narrative thrust to begin with, and the movies have rewritten it so often its English characters, none of them all that multi-dimensional to begin with, have become almost interchangeable in the public imagination. Is it Lucy or Mina to whom Harker is engaged? Harker or Renfield (or both) who visits Dracula's castle? Seward or Van Helsing who's Mina's father? Lucy or Mina who dies from Dracula's attacks? Frankly, Stoker's story has gotten so muddled on film over the years fans have difficulty sorting *any* of it out, and Brooks doesn't help much. This Harker never does visit Transylvania, neither as solicitor nor anything else; Dracula's move to London, presumably to seek fresh victims, never gets explained; and while the Count at first focuses solely on Lucy, it's the previously all but ignored Mina he plans to make his bride.

Keeping in mind Brooks' longtime distaste for critical fence-straddling (has the poor man ever received even one review that didn't include the words *on the other hand*, *but*, *nevertheless*, or *still*?), it's tempting to either flat-out gush over the picture or just slap-in-the-face condemn it, but once again adequately assessing Brooks' work just isn't that easy. No, the movie never does come up with anything really out-of-the-blue ingenious, so that's one strike against it — certainly nothing to rival *The Producers'* "Springtime for Hitler" bit, anyway, or the big through-the-set finale in *Blazing Saddles*—and since the whole picture feels pretty much the same as the 1931 film just reshot in color with a little light sitcom-style humor thrown in, that's Strike Two right there.

Then again, though (here we go again), Brooks' vampire comedy doesn't lose itself in its own detours as often as his last one either, and dramatically speaking that's a real plus. All that aimless, Hakuna Matata–style puttering about in mid-crisis that slows down *Robin Hood: Men in Tights* doesn't feel nearly as irritating here — these aren't action hero renegades with swords and scabbards, realize; they're just a bunch of tea-drinking aristocrats in well-tailored tweeds — and it's also a story without nearly as many pointless dead ends. Remember, in Brooks' Robin Hood film, the Robin-disabling potion that witch-cook Latrine proposes — then never mixes? The catapult the Sheriff hails as his new secret weapon — then never uses? Brooks employs few such red herrings here, if only because, given just ninety minutes, his new film simply hasn't time for them. He does raise a few unanswered questions about his characters' psychology (whether Dracula's bad dream proves he misses sunlight or just lives in fear of it; why he takes Mina, but not Lucy, for a secret dance; etc.), but where Brooks seems to forget the whole rob-from-the-rich-and-give-to-the-poor bit (honestly — the only character stick-up man Robin tries stealing from is Brooks' rabbi rendition of Friar Tuck?), his Dracula still snacks on his London neighbors just the way we remember him. This Dracula isn't, admittedly, very good at covering his own trail (besides his new neighbors, the '31 Count rather wisely attacks strangers on the streets too), but at least Brooks isn't losing Dracula's essence in mid-film.

Now if only Brooks had included as many solid laughs as in his Robin Hood picture, he'd really have something. Regrettably, though, most of the humor here feels pretty subdued — second for second, even that silly *Gilligan's Island* dream sequence spoofing *Dracula*, TV's *Batman*, and Sherlock Holmes makes better use of its running time — leaving it feeling only slightly funnier than such low-key efforts as *The Twelve Chairs* and *Life Stinks* and paling markedly alongside *The Producers*, *Blazing Saddles*, or *Young Frankenstein*. We do smile pretty often, and we admire the way Brooks, despite the PG-13 rating, keeps all but about sixty seconds so squeaky-clean, but while *Dracula: Dead and Loving It* needs repeat viewings to really convince us it's not a bad little film, an instant winner like *Blazing Saddles* just plain knocks us for a loop the first time we see it.

Perhaps one problem is that, adhering so strongly to Browning, Brooks gives himself too little room to maneuver — a problem critic Leonard Maltin noted when he observed that the film "spends so much time retelling the familiar Transylvanian's story it forgets to be funny." *Young Frankenstein*, by contrast, is more a comic sequel to James Whale's masterpiece than a comic remake, leaving Brooks freer to push the material into plenty of loony new directions. Freddy Frankenstein is *like* his infamous grandfather, but he *isn't* his grandfather, so Brooks can give him goofy-rhymed nightmares, an eye for his pretty lab assistant, a gift for singing, dancing, the violin. Freddy's Monster can stomp and shuffle to Irving Berlin because he's not Whale's creature but Brooks', yet because *Dracula: Dead and Loving It* is set in Stoker-era 1893 he can choose songs

only from back then — and how many funny-to-dance-to 1800s European song hits do *you* know?

Still, any film giving Harvey Korman a line as sublimely silly as "Yes, we have *Nosferatu*! We have *Nosferatu* today!" has something going for it, and when Brooks' "zick-ach-zented" Van Helsing really gets wound up, or a spellbound Lucy or Mina's seduction hits Harker's Victorian prudery head-on, the movie really takes off. The only real problem with gags like these is that we need more of them (as Janet Maslin hinted, in her mostly favorable *New York Times* review, in noting "a lot of dead air") — that and the fact that, unlike those in *Young Frankenstein*, Brooks' strait-laced, never-lose-composure heroes and pretty-but-placid settings can't really cut loose. Is madcap comedy achievable from people and places who by their very nature resist acting madcap? Compared with crack-and-crackle lab equipment, out-for-blood lynch mobs, and stage shows turned "string-him-up!" riots, can proper English libraries, picnics, and tea-tables really compete?

Perhaps not, but *Dracula: Dead and Loving It* still animates its tea-and-crumpets types the best it can, and if nobody's likely to mistake staid, settled Van Helsing, Seward, and Harker for Larry, Moe, and Curly (even if Harker does once give Dracula a Three Stooges eye-poke), Dracula and Renfield for Abbott and Costello, or Mina for Fanny Brice, they're still pretty likable in a controlled, low-key sort of way, largely because Brooks, Korman, Steven Weber, Leslie Nielsen, Peter MacNicol, Amy Yasbeck, and the rest voice their lines with such queer-to-the-ear, off-kilter quirkiness. Few Brooks films rely quite so much on outlandish accents and off-the-wall inflections to find laughs, and were Brooks stripped of his foreign "ech-zpert doch-ta" urgency, Korman his flabbergasted Britisher sputter, and so on, we might find many scenes barely funny at all. Even when the humor feels a little thin, Brooks and his costars give their lines a nice boost just with the way they're said: "Rahsp-berry?" "An e-mehr-genc-y?"; "*No one* can explain zat!"

That sort of thing is more crucial than it sounds, too, especially since the film's poignancy quotient feels pretty thin as well. All those scenes in which characters grieve for poor ailing, then dead, then "undead" Lucy help, but otherwise the movie rarely strives for real warmth, and keeps its tug-at-the-heart emotionalism fairly low-key. When *Young Frankenstein*'s creature speaks for the first time, pours out his soul like some scholar or wise man or poet, only fans without an ounce of sentiment remain unmoved, but for all Leslie Nielsen's talent his haughty, above-it-all Count feels more plastic, less "deep," as if Nielsen is guesting in some old Halloween skit on TV's *Tony Orlando and Dawn*. Less character than caricature, even when Dracula plots to make Mina his bride, he seems less in love with her than kidnapping her because Brooks' script *says* he should.

Maybe one reason we can't feel too involved emotionally is because we're given too many heroes to focus on. With three "good guys" dividing our attention (Harker, Seward, and Von Helsing), we can't commit emotionally to any one, and it can't help either that most of Brooks' characters seem so undefined and obscure. We feel sorry for Lysette Anthony's Lucy, but her pre-vampire personality is so cryptic we can't feel *too* sorry (she's a gorgeous flirt — but what else is she, really?), and even Amy Yasbeck's Mina stays oddly depthless for someone whose rescue dominates the entire last scene. Truth be told, Stoker's characters have never been developed all that well on film (Lucy and Mina are nearly always as indistinguishable as bookends), but unless we can "break the

ice" with these people, why should any of us worry what happens to them?

Maybe it hurts too that vampires — Stoker's, anyway, before Dan Curtis, Anne Rice, and others started humanizing them — can't inspire sympathy like Mary Shelley's monster, who craves love and acceptance while Dracula only really craves blood. Shelley's creature is the friendless, unhappy schoolboy the bullies all pick on, but in most adaptations Stoker's bloodsucker *is* that bully, and beyond that one fantasy-phobic "daymare" (and snagging fan-friendly Nielsen to play him), coscripters Brooks, Rudy DeLuca, and Steve Haberman don't do much to soften him up. He's less spacy than most Nielsen bunglers — usually Nielsen is the literal-minded simpleton, where here he's more *surrounded* by simpletons — but somehow even with all these foils for him to play against we have only slightly more emotional investment in Dracula than Nielsen's Det. Frank Drebin in TV's *Police Squad!* and its *Naked Gun* spin-off films; we love Nielsen himself, but an invisible wall between us and Dracula keeps emotion at arm's length. Is Nielsen's Dracula lonely? Is that why he wants Mina? Brooks doesn't say. Does Dracula's outside-in-daylight dream mean he dislikes being dead? Or is he "loving it" *Get Smart*–style as the title implies? Again, Brooks never tells. No doubt Nielsen could have played a disconsolate, long-suffering Dracula if asked to, but in every scene opposite Mina, Renfield, Van Helsing, and the rest he exudes mostly just the usual vampire arrogance, blazoning his intentions to marry or bewitch or control or defeat but never really dropping his guard, Frankenstein Monster style, to show us the frailty underneath.

Underdeveloped as the role is, though, Brooks' smartest move by far is hiring Nielsen to play it (Mel Brooks and Leslie Nielsen in the same movie? Pure comic bliss!), and while hardly anyone would ever see Nielsen as a dead ringer for Bela Lugosi, somehow that snow-white hair and tall, commanding frame seem just perfect all the same. Even Nielsen's Lugosi-type accent is considerable fun (especially the way he says the word "chick'n"), though it does, admittedly, raise the usual issues, or non-issues, about what's "true spoof" and what's "near-spoof." Is Nielsen's accent still parody even if it isn't all that wilder than Lugosi's? Are all those schoolkids who do Lugosi imitations parodists too — or just gifted impressionists, like Frank Gorshin or Rich Little?

So it goes too with Peter MacNicol, whose wild-eyed madman shtick gives us such a deliriously daffy Renfield. Even before he succumbs to Dracula's spell we're snickering at his stereotyped, proper-to-the-*n*th-power Englishness, but since MacNicol's loon-giggly post-hex Renfield plays only slightly more broadly than Dwight Frye's '31 version, it's hard to see his take on the part as much of an exaggeration. It's a terrific Dwight Frye impression, is definitely funny (especially his bug-eating scene opposite Harvey Korman's Dr. Seward — fantastic!), and all that tumbling about in ship holds and falling out windows puts a wonderful new spin on things (we are indeed "fortunate," as Brooks' Van Helsing puts it, that this Renfield is an "imbecile"). Yet again one wonders: beyond the expected Brooksian foul-ups and pratfalls, if the two Renfields look and sound so nearly the same, how much actual *Dracula* spoofing — parody — can really be going on?

Muddying the waters still further, Brooks' own work as vampire expert Prof. Van Helsing falls into much the same camp — marvelously lovable, frequently funny, yet ultimately so respectful of "serious" Van Helsings like Peter Cushing and Laurence Olivier it rarely seems loony enough to label a true lampoon. Though

arguably a spoof of all those staid, strong-stomached scientists played by *Dracula*'s Edward Van Sloan and others, Brooks' quaint, "kindly uncle" approach feels fairly mild after Anthony Hopkins' floppy-hatted Hemingway-Capote *Bram Stoker's Dracula* hybrid. It's actually a far richer role dialogue-wise than Nielsen's, and it does give Browning a nice comic twist, but is it really parody? Again, maybe — but only if we're not being too picky.

Infinitely less "spoof-ish" still is the work of co-stars Amy Yasbeck and Lysette Anthony, two real talents who, like Matthew Porretta in *Robin Hood: Men in Tights*, at times look and sound so serious they seem to have drifted in from some Merchant-Ivory adaptation of Thomas Hardy or Henry James. Yasbeck and Anthony's line readings couldn't be better, but neither plays much comedy at all until, like Gomez Addams at a word in French, Mina and Lucy drop their usual English reserve and start flinging themselves at Harker — funny stuff, but a far cry from the all-out nuttiness Madeline Kahn and Cloris Leachman give *Young Frankenstein* all the way through. In the end, Yasbeck fares better than Anthony, dropping in a few of those "veddy British" inflections done so well in Brooks' last film and even taking a loopy pratfall or two, but overall both roles exude such *Masterpiece Theater* earnestness one could omit just one or two scenes and either part could be swapped with a Mina or Lucy from any serious *Dracula* film.

Part-straight, part-sendup, *Dracula: Dead and Loving It* struggles with this same identity crisis nearly the whole way, unveiling its opening credits atop a handsome, red-leather volume of Stoker's masterwork and photographing each illustration so lovingly that, minus the twinkle-eyed in-jokes comparing the names on-screen with the ghouls in the book, we'd swear we're about to see the true, authentic *Dracula*, told straightforward and joke-free. The sequence is so luxurious and classy it's easy to imagine a "real" adaptation starting just this way, and Hummie Mann's exquisite music, like John Morris's in *Young Frankenstein*, follows Brooks' comic juxtaposition policy by deliberately resisting trying to sound funny—a solid idea, in theory (even if several truly funny comedies, from *It's a Mad Mad Mad Mad World* to *The Pink Panther*, do manage to let fly some pretty unapologetically crazy melodies for their big slapstick-packed finales at least), though *Dracula: Dead and Loving It* doesn't give us nearly as many funny lines and visuals as Brooks' first monster comedy anyway. Indeed, so much of the film seems so Stoker-reverent and Mann's compositions so sincere (only with the sight gags about Dracula's mind-of-its-own shadow do the melodies really turn playful) that anyone who doesn't know going in that this is a Mel Brooks comedy might not have a clue until Peter MacNicol launches his stuffy English gentleman shtick early on.

We're also pretty surprised by Brooks' welcome return to the semi-rational, quasi-realistic tone of *The Producers*, *The Twelve Chairs*, *High Anxiety*, *Life Stinks*, and, to a lesser extent, *Silent Movie* and even *Young Frankenstein*. Where in several of his biggest hits Brooks doesn't think twice about playing fast and loose with time and space for a good laugh (Count Basie jazz in the Old West in *Blazing Saddles*; fifteenth-century painters at the Last Supper in *History of the World — Part I*; interstellar Winnebagos in *Spaceballs*; twelfth-century Larry King gags in *Robin Hood: Men in Tights*), here he largely resists his passion for anachronism-type reality benders to pretty much focus on characters and plot. True, the notion of a bloodsucking undead monster is pretty farfetched to begin with, but once one "buys" this one central absurdity (men

turning into bats, sunlight dissolving people into dust, and all that), just about all else is strictly no-nonsense: no Gucci-logoed vampire capes, no Mr. Coffee machines in opera house lobbies, no electric EXIT signs in Dracula's castle. It isn't that Brooks' monkeying around with all the *wheres* and *whens* makes pictures like *Blazing Saddles*, *History of the World — Part I*, *Spaceballs*, or *Robin Hood: Men in Tights* bad films, but let's just say it: Brooks has already tried the old history-smashing bit four times, on each occasion just a little less successfully than the last. Been there, done that.

Of course, it's also true Brooks sidelines his anachronisms without really *replacing* them with anything (except more satire maybe, surely a good move), and perhaps precisely because its loyalty to Stoker, Browning, et al. holds so steadfast the laughs feel pretty tame after the raucous likes of a *Blazing Saddles* or *Spaceballs*. Where *Love at First Bite* at least gives Dracula a witty new spin shipping him to disco-flashy New York, Brooks seems even less interested in radically re-conceiving Stoker than in deconstructing Robin Hood for his last film. In fact, *Dracula: Dead and Loving It* sticks so closely to the white gloves-and-hoop skirts original it ends up pretty much as *Robin Hood: Men in Tights* might have, had Brooks tossed out everything not specifically Sherwood — no Vincent Price cracks, no Macaulay Culkin gags, no *Dirty Harry* or Mark Twain or *Godfather* jokes: a pretty fair Robin Hood film that might just as well have been played gag-free.

Brooks surely could have turned *Dracula* on its ear had he wanted to, subverted the entire genre the same way *Blazing Saddles* rips apart the whole business of cowboy film make-believe, but he instead seems contented to more or less re-shoot the old *Dracula* stage play with its usual Renfields, Harkers, Minas, and all that, and then just mildly silly it up a little. Nielsen's Dracula slips on bat dung, flies into a glass pane, and falls flat on his face, yes (certainly Lugosi's Count never did any of *that*), but, as in *Robin Hood: Men in Tights*, in which, beyond the anachronisms, Friar Tuck's new image as lovable old rabbi marks the only really major departure from its source, most of the same old starched-collared, cape-draped, bowler-hatted universe of old is here again exactly as before. Where *Young Frankenstein* keeps us always a little off-balance with its playboy hunchbacks and brain-shop drop-slots, here Brooks for the second time running helms a so-called "genre spoof" (others' term, recall — not Brooks', necessarily) that finally tweaks its source with so much reverence it feels less like parody than a by-the-book reiteration (well, by-the-play, anyway) with just a little light comedy sprinkled in. Perfectly fine, yes — just an odd decision, that's all.

Then again, a little semi-sobriety isn't necessarily a bad thing, and the film might play better told just a little scarier, if only because it includes so few really big laughs. *Young Frankenstein* feels pretty serious too, early on, what with John Morris's poignant music and that slow camera creep toward Frankenstein's castle, but once it finally gets moving that film works harder to forge its own identity, really goes all out thinking up something new. It's sheer Brooksian madness that transforms Whale's monster-sedating into a nutty "Charades" game; paints the hero's fiancee as an uptight, smudge-wary china doll; turns the one-armed policeman in *Son of Frankenstein* into a monocled, eyepatched mush-mouth; rewrites *Bride of Frankenstein*'s blind man as a soup-spilling one-man accident; adds a goofy brain-switch ending leaving our title scientist a zombie-eyed wild man and his creation a settled-down house-hubby; and so on. Even when they don't stray far from the original, writ-

ers Brooks and Gene Wilder keep pouring wackier and wackier dialogue on top of it in an effort to keep us laughing: "Pardon me, boy!" "What knockers!"; "Call it a — hunch!"

Compare all this to Brooks' Dracula film and one quickly sees how little actual risk-taking Brooks really tries for this time. Mina and Lucy, a third of the main cast, are such near-duplicates of their usual selves at times we barely notice the difference, and Dracula himself, klutziness aside, remains as ruthless and regal as ever. The eagerly awaited song-and-dance stays pretty traditional too; a stitched-up, floor-stomping monster hoofing "the dance of love" might have been hilarious, but high-class Romanian royalty? Dracula *always* comes attired for the ballroom, so when it turns out he's a hemoglobin-hobgoblin Fred Astaire, what's the big surprise? In *Love at First Bite*, at least, the twist comes from seeing Dracula *disco*-dancing — besides which, for both of Brooks' two dances, however well-choreographed by Brooks favorite Alan Johnson, Mann's music is lyric-free ("I Love the Night Life" isn't funny, but it is ironically titled), and Villoldo and Liszt classical. Even when Van Helsing, Harker, and Seward fight Dracula to save Mina, beyond the Stooge eye-jab and Renfield's accidentally effecting his master's demise, the ending might easily fit any number of "real" vampire films — a marked contrast to the wrap-up on *Young Frankenstein*, surely the first time ever scientist and monster end on such good terms they're practically lodge buddies.

Yet somehow, amazingly, all Stoker-worship aside, the film still holds up better as parody than *Robin Hood: Men in Tights*. Brooks' Sherwood Forest flick is funnier overall, but its laughs rely more on anachronism than acumen, while here, even when he's mostly just repeating vampire clichés, he's taking a few potshots at them as well, craftily exposing their absurdities to reality's cruel glare. The old "children of the night" bit, in which Dracula waxes poetic over the "music" of howling wolves? It's back, this time twisted into an ironic comment on the "mess" the night's *other* children make. Bats romantic? Flying around indoors, defecating on everything in sight? Nonsense. Just unsanitary, that's all. With one quick close-up of Dracula's staircase, Brooks subverts one of Stoker's best lines and strips it of all sentiment — exactly what parody is designed for. Could a Lugosi-type vampire *really* glide so silently and smoothly down all those castle steps? Even with filthy bat droppings spattered in his path? Ridiculous, hints Brooks. He'd either keep a close eye on where he's stepping (hard to do and still look dashing and stately) or go tumbling headlong — again, real parody for a change, a debunking, a deflating, very much akin to Brooks' *Blazing Saddles'* disclosure of what would *really* happen if campfire cowboys ate all those beans.

Those storm-tossed ships always conveying film vampires from Transylvania to London? Mightn't a coffin in a ship's hold do a little sliding around down there? All that flying through open windows vampires are always doing? Suppose the window isn't open? And how about that eerie hypnosis vampires use to make mortals their slaves? That's fine if the victim's clever, but suppose he's some simpleminded nincompoop who, warned to "remember nothing," forgets his instructions with everything else? Oh, and those stakings — Hammer vampire slayings often leave their targets covered in blood, but shouldn't the chap actually aiming the mallet get messy too? Brooks thinks so, leaving Weber's poor Jonathan Harker so blood-soaked he's practically swimming in it!

Could Brooks have done more in this regard? Absolutely. The vampire genre teems with opportunities for parody, yet where Brooks once very nearly consigned the Hollywood Western to Boot Hill, his stake-attack on *Dracula*'s legend-cluttered heart feels nowhere near as ruthless. The fact that vampire tales have no set-in-stone, agreed upon rules, for instance — the way some say one bite creates new vampires, others three, others death itself, and so on; the way some heroes battle vampires with crosses, others garlic, others mirrors, others wolfsbane; the way some vampires need homeland soil in their coffins, others nothing; etc. — annoys to no end, yet Brooks lets decades of make-it-up-as-we-go moviemaking off scott free. Nor does he ask why vampires, who could surely rob victims as easily as siphon them, live in such dust-cloaked squalor, or why so many stay dressed up when, living in such vast cultural wastelands, they clearly have nowhere tux-and-tails classy to go. Still, even if he does treat "vampire comedy" and "vampire spoof" too nearly the same, Brooks clearly tries harder at genre-shattering here than in his last film, in which he seemed too much in love with the whole Sherwood saga to upset Robin's apple cart at all.

The movie one-ups its predecessor satirically too, sly-wittedly littering the Transylvanian and English landscapes with dead sacred cows. Even on TV Brooks' richest influence was as a satirist — *Get Smart* was never funnier than when Max, Agent 99, and crew deadpanned something cut-to-the-quick candid about D.C. politics or nuclear buildup or network TV — and some of his swipes here are first-rate. Among his targets: medical ineptitude (Dr. Seward means well, but he'd fit right in at the ill-run hospital of *Life Stinks*); greed (a gypsy woman "gives" Renfield a protective crucifix, then charges him; a hypnotized usherette recalls nothing Dracula says except that she'll get no tip); even French culture (Renfield compares his lewd "nightmare" about female vampires to a trip to Paris). It's not exactly Jonathan Swift, but it's pretty impressive considering the potential for cut-'em-down-to-size satire was so much greater in *Robin Hood: Men in Tights*.

Most of the best barbs, though, are — pardon the pun — reserved for the reserved, poking a little good-natured fun at the English, especially the upper-class English, either for their celebrated to-the-extreme British politeness or their once-legendary oh-so proper Victorian prudery. Peter MacNicol's Renfield especially inspires laughs with all his extra-formal introductions, hat-tipping "Ta!" good-byes, dutiful insistence on punctuality, ultra-gracious apologies for mishaps entirely beyond his control — even his amusing pronunciation of "scheduled" with a precise British *sh*. The film's other British elite — Harvey Korman's Seward, Steven Weber's Harker, Amy Yasbeck's Mina, Lysette Anthony's Lucy — prove similarly ceremonial, their speech peppered with plenty of fancy-schmancy *jolly good*s, *ghastly*s, and *poppycock*s along the way. More Brooksian cultural stereotyping? Oh, sure. Is it still funny, though? Quite right! Wizard! Ripping! Right-o!

It's Brooks' hilarious skewering of Victorian virtue that gets the biggest laughs, though. Playing up vampirism's sensual, seductive side, Brooks craftily dive-bombs the straitjacket-strict moral code that, while postponing the West's spiritual near-collapse a few more years, also kept polite British society "talking on tiptoe" for ages, as if each word were some prude-planted moral landmine just waiting to go off. Knowing how much fun Brooks has blasting life-stifling rigidity into oblivion (again, just think *Blazing Saddles*, cowboys, and beans), it's amazing he didn't push the gag even farther, having horrified, Three Wise Monkey Britons clapping hands over their ears, dropping

trays at their feet, and fainting dead away every time someone dares even breathe such depraved, never-to-be-uttered articulations as *flesh* (GASP!), *lust* (CRASH!), or (THUD!) *naked*!

Even so, the amount of cheery comedy Brooks pulls from just this one idea isn't to be sniffed at. Several of a shocked Renfield's lines when Dracula's vampire "brides" try to seduce him draw big laughs, but the real humor comes from how quickly young Solicitor Pureheart gives in. The implication is obvious: like *Robin Hood: Men in Tights*' chastity belt–clad Maid Marian, unwilling to give herself unwed to a man unless he is "really, really cute," Renfield stays self-disciplined more by decree than by choice; like him, we behave ourselves more because preachers, parents, and police demand it than because we're naturally or willingly good. Small wonder Lucy's demure concealment behind pulled-up bedclothes, when Seward and Harker burst in seeking a prowler, rings so paradoxical; just before, alone, Lucy purrs her way through a Victorian-proper semi-striptease as, charmed by mysterious new neighbor Dracula's good looks, she half-invites his first visit. The private Lucy craves passion; the public Lucy, a good girl, must reject it.

This same "vampirism vs. Victorianism" battle yields similar fun via Harker's deliciously naive line about the forbidden joys of opera — music laden with the very "love, hate, sensuality, and unbridled passion" he's always suppressed. Later, when a now-vampiric Lucy offers to unleash on him "the deep, raw passion of unbridled sexual frenzy," we admire Harker's upright loyalty to fiancee Mina, but his near-neurotic response — "But Lucy — I'm British!" — suggests 1890s rigid super-conservatism has already made him very nearly as "undead" as she. "Who *really* lives a kind of living death?" Brooks seems to be asking. "Real" vampires like Lucy and Dracula, who, as the title suggests, though "dead" are "loving it" as best they can — or straitlaced, strait*jacketed* Victorians like Harker, so convinced *emotion* and *sin* are near-synonyms? One wishes Brooks had scripted a few lines directly stating the matter just that way, addressed this joyless life/joyful death, "stiffs vs. stiffs" idea more overtly, for while *Dead and Loving It* at first seems a botched subtitle given the usual depiction of vampires as foul but pitiable, closer analysis makes clear how fitting it really is. Given more push in this direction, the film would have won far kinder reviews.

Harker's uptightness surfaces too when Mina, a vampire-in-training after one of Dracula's attacks, literally lets her hair down and, like Lucy, preys openly on Harker's impulses. When she entices Harker with a reminder they have "never really explored" each other, his relief-loaded "Thank God!" speaks comic volumes, as does his Leo Bloom–ish squeamishness when she insists he sit by her on her bed. We're proud of Harker for sticking to his morals (we may laugh at the Victorians, yet still we wonder if all that chilly self-consciousness wasn't better than today's say-all, do-all shamelessness), but it's still funny seeing him squirm, just as it is seeing Mina's father's horrified reaction finding the two in a compromising position — both fully dressed — after a mere five-year engagement. It's a spectacularly witty scene, partly because poor Harker's done everything short of strapping on Maid Marian's chastity belt to keep Mina at bay, partly because Dr. Seward's reaction marks just the sort of over-the-edge Puritanism that, a half-century later, kept bathroom toilets hidden and married couples in double beds on American TV for years.

Even without such deeper subtexts, however, *Dracula: Dead and Loving It* makes a nice little film, with one of Brooks'

strongest casts in quite some time. The inimitable Gene Wilder isn't back, sadly, nor Madeline Kahn, nor Kenneth Mars, nor Cloris Leachman, and they're all greatly missed, but re-hiring the cast of *Young Frankenstein* could only invite undue comparison anyway, so maybe it's just as well. Dom DeLuise isn't back either, nor Howard Morris, nor Ron Carey, nor many of Brooks' best classic co-stars, but two of fans' long-time favorites actually do return: Mel Brooks himself, back for his ninth appearance before his own camera, and Harvey Korman, a three-timer back for his first Brooks movie since 1981's *History of the World — Part I.*

Just as his turn as Rabbi Tuckman was for *Robin Hood: Men in Tights*, Brooks' Prof. Abraham Van Helsing proves one of this more recent movie's best elements — not a particularly original characterization, admittedly, but easily one of the film's greatest assets. Like so many of the characters around him, Van Helsing is perhaps too gentlemanly and genial to really stand out after the movie is over, but he's vastly more animated than, say, Edward Van Sloan, and of course also a lot more fun. Indeed, Brooks makes such a great impression in the big Lucy-staking scene probably no one except *High Anxiety* "little old man" Howard Morris could have outdone him in the part. Just think how different Van Helsing is from, say, *The Twelve Chairs*' Tikon or *Blazing Saddles*' Gov. Lepetomane, and one gets the idea there's just about nothing Mel Brooks can't do.

Equally pleasing is the fact that Brooks gives Harvey Korman, who had played essentially the same snide, sneaky villain type in his three previous Brooks outings, a role entirely unlike any he had played before. One of those blustery, sputtering old English sorts so common to movies of the '30s and '40s, Dr. Seward is Korman's best part in years — something of a tribute, as several critics noted, to Nigel Bruce's flabbergasted, blathering Dr. Watson opposite Basil Rathbone's Sherlock Holmes. Every once in a while the good doctor slips into a tailspin stammer so sublimely out-of-control one swears he'll never pull out of it, and at such times Korman gives the film a comic "leg up" as solid as anything we could ask for. Such deliberate sketch-show over-emoting might be all wrong for a *When Harry Met Sally* or *Annie Hall*, but it fits here, so Korman clearly knows what he's doing, just as Brooks knew what he was doing rehiring him. "Capital thinking," Seward might say, or "Jolly good show" — and he'd be right, too.

A far, far bigger surprise comes from Brooks newcomer (and future replacement for Matthew Broderick in Broadway's *The Producers*) Steven Weber, a not especially funny-looking actor from whom we don't expect as much as Korman going in. Like *Robin Hood: Men in Tights'* Cary Elwes, though, Weber's clothes-model good looks barely hint at his comic talent, and not even his career-making TV stint on *Wings* (some spent bouncing lines off Brooks two-timer Amy Yasbeck) prepares us for how funny he is here. Oh, sure, he may display a tad too much self-awareness for some — once or twice his priggish Londoner rigidity is so over-the-top affected he might be lark-guesting on *Sonny and Cher* or *Donnie and Marie*— but Weber takes a potentially dead-end part and really runs with it, earning a fair-sized grin with his uptight British bachelor routine just about every time he opens his mouth. Filmdom's last major Harker, Keanu Reeves, had endured such bad press for his ill-fitting English accent in *Bram Stoker's Dracula* it's possible Weber is simply taking Reeves' self-conscious artlessness to even funnier extremes, but even if he isn't it hardly matters. Whatever drives the performance, it works like a gypsy charm.

Fellow rookie Peter MacNicol, whose lunatic Renfield ends up every bit the gig-gly scene-stealer as Dwight Frye's, may be even funnier. A kind of cross of Michael Palin, Peter Lorre, and Jerry Lewis (whom he even imitates once), MacNicol's Renfield starts off even more ultra-British fastidious than Harker, and it's hard to say who's funnier: the pre-hex Renfield with his "I say"s and "Ta"s or the post-hex version, all cackles and creepy-crawlies. One can only guess what led Brooks' team to think of MacNicol to begin with — his kooky turn as a demon-driven museum worker in 1989's *Ghost-busters II*, perhaps? — but what a fantastic idea it was. Not only does smallish, shrill MacNicol look and sound uncannily like Frye, physically he's so delightfully Silly Putty pliable we're left laughing at his every move. Trying to elude vampire slayers trailing Renfield to his master's lair, MacNicol's squirrel scamper zigzag provides one of the film's best laughs; he's like Martin Short's Ed Grimley sprinting on tiptoe!

As for the Lucy and Mina situation — the fact that, until Dracula's spell takes hold, these two characters just aren't funny — one certainly can't blame Amy Yasbeck and Lysette Anthony, both of whom breathe new life into the parts the second they start chasing after Weber's Harker. Still, why Brooks kept casting such lovely but serious-looking actresses in his post–'70s comedies is hard to say. Maybe, as he often argued, he believed even silliness needs an anchor of realism, or maybe he just found these two ladies so delightful in person it just didn't seem feasible it might not come through in the "straight" scenes. Still, Yasbeck clearly knows comedy (*Problem Child*, *Pretty Woman*, *The Mask*), and once Brooks finally lets her run wild, the then-new addition to Weber's *Wings* really takes her scenes by storm. Anthony makes a pretty funny Lucy too, the vampire-vamp Lucy, that is, despite bringing with her so few comic associations nobody could possibly expect much seeing her name in the credits. Were the casting folks influenced by Anthony's turn as sorceress-seductress Angelique on the '90s TV revival of *Dark Shadows*? If so, well and good — Madeline Kahn wasn't exactly world-famous funny when Brooks hired her, either, *What's Up Doc?* notwithstanding — but surely Yasbeck and Anthony's serious lines would at least *seem* funny with a pair of full-blown comics behind them. These two ladies handle every last gag just right, but only a Cloris Leachman or a Madeline Kahn can pull a laugh out of thin air.

Brooks' bit players also deserve sillier material to play with. As madhouse worker Martin, *The Nutt House* TV alum Mark Blankfield plays a smaller part here than in *Robin Hood: Men in Tights*, but he again uses his Cockney accent to fine effect, so much so we'd love to see more of him. Like Yasbeck and Anthony's, Blankfield's is another straight-from-Browning role that calls the old parody issue into question — actor Charles Gerrard played Martin for comic relief too, so how is Blankfield's near-identical performance a lampoon? — but Blankfield's instincts are dead-on, as are those of fellow returnee Megan Cavanagh, who doesn't play English maid Essie that far removed from Joan Standing's role either. Her part isn't as big as her last one for Brooks, but she does get some pretty fair "Simon Says"-type sleepwalking gags. She's a talented lady, Cavanagh, and we like her; it's a shame Brooks couldn't find her a bigger part.

Back too are Matthew Porretta — who in one brief drink-flinging scene shows more comic sparkle than his Will Scarlet O'Hara permitted in Brooks' last film — and co-writer Rudy DeLuca as a madhouse guard gone buggy. Avery Shrieber returns too, as a villager with a mannish wife (Cherie Franklin, given one fleeting but funny grunt-shrug), as do Chuck McCann

(*Silent Movie, Robin Hood: Men in Tights*) as a walrus-mustached innkeeper; Clive Revill (of Brooks' last film) in a straight part as doomed crypt-keeper Sykes; long-absent *Silent Movie* and *High Anxiety* actor Charlie Callas (a mental patient in *High Anxiety*), only glimpsed as Man in Strait-jacket; and Mrs. Brooks, Anne Bancroft, as a Gypsy whose self-created echo recalls all those voice-of-doom types in films like *The Wolf Man*. Other returnees appear too, like "interns" David DeLuise and Johnny Cocktails (both of Brooks' Robin Hood film, Cocktails also in *Life Stinks*), villagers Carol "Mrs. Dom DeLuise" Arthur (*Blazing Saddles, Silent Movie*), Ira Miller (*High Anxiety, Spaceballs, Life Stinks*), and Loraine Yarnell Shields (*Spaceballs*). Better used, debut actors Leslie Sachs (as the usherette) and actor Brooks' *Silence of the Hams* and *Screwloose* director Ezio Greggio (as a panicky coachman) get brief but nice results too.

Which brings us at last to Leslie Nielsen, the first Brooks star since *Young Frankenstein*'s Gene Wilder who probably inspired quite a few non–Brooks fans to buy a ticket. Cary Elwes had his admirers prior to *Robin Hood: Men in Tights*, yes, but it's doubtful his name alone filled many seats, and probably *Spaceballs'* Bill Pullman, still far from *Independence Day*, sold far fewer. Longtime dramatic actor Nielsen, however, was in a different league entirely, having spent the last fifteen years having a blast playing non sequitur-spouting nitwits in films like *Airplane!* and *The Naked Gun*. For fans of those films, Nielsen virtually guaranteed laughs, so for the first time in years — not that U.S. box office tallies provided much proof — Brooks seemed to have found just the right name for a big ad campaign. Leslie Nielsen as Dracula by way of Mel Brooks? Fantastic!

He delivers, too, not because his stumbling, fumbling Dracula offers much we haven't seen before (Al Lewis's *The*

Supposedly calling upon his neighbors to express his regrets over Lucy's bizarre death, Transylvanian vampire Count Dracula (Leslie Nielsen) meets consulting physician Prof. Abraham Van Helsing (Mel Brooks), who finds the Count's insistence on having the last word insufferable and his recent relocation to London suspicious, in *Dracula: Dead and Loving It.*

Munsters gig alone ran for two years), but because by now he's funnier in our own minds than the material itself. Nielsen's lines aren't half as witty as George Hamilton's in *Love at First Bite*, yet we *think* they are because he's spent decades reinventing himself as a sort of combination Ed Wynn, Groucho Marx, and W.C. Fields. We expect this man to make us laugh, and so inevitably he does, even more now that he's allied with Brooks, who couldn't have been more lucky than to snare such a wonderfully beloved goof ball to play on his team.

Sadly, no matter how good Nielsen, Brooks, and all the others might be, the critics hardly seemed to care, their once vast interest in Brooks seeming, like Dracula in Brooks' finale, to have turned to dust almost entirely by now. Many major critics, including those for *The New Yorker*, *Time*, and *Newsweek*, all of whom in the

mid–'70s had seen the release of a new Brooks comedy as a big event, had by now so lost interest they didn't even give the picture a review. Perhaps Brooks himself didn't much care — he'd complained for years about reviewers' wishy-washiness, the way they'd confess to laughing at his movies yet not admit to liking them — but if the old "It's when they *stop* talking about you" philosophy has any truth to it, this sort of critical neglect still has to hurt. Granted, Brooks hadn't been at the top of his form for some time, but surely even in 1995 the man's work was still reviewable. This isn't some nobody, people; this is Mel Brooks!

Dracula: Dead and Loving It isn't Brooks' finest or funniest film, but whenever it shows up on TV, which is often, fans and even non-fans find it just about impossible not to hang around at least a few minutes to watch. Excepting one or two bits assuring its '90s-naughty PG-13, the movie feels like a throwback to another time, back to the good old days when comics like Bob Hope, Martin and Lewis, and Abbott and Costello starred in grandly goofy little romps with titles like *The Ghost Breakers*, *Scared Stiff*, and *Hold That Ghost* at least once or twice in every career. *Dracula: Dead and Loving It* isn't high art, but a movie this sweet, sentimental, and silly will be playing from now till forever. For all of us who love Mel Brooks, that's great, great news.

CAST: Leslie Nielsen (Count Dracula); Peter MacNicol (Thomas Renfield); Steven Weber (Jonathan Harker); Amy Yasbeck (Mina Seward); Lysette Anthony (Lucy Westenra); Harvey Korman (Dr. Seward); Mel Brooks (Prof. Van Helsing); Mark Blankfield (Martin); Megan Cavanagh (Essie); Clive Revill (Sykes); Chuck McCann (Innkeeper); Avery Shreiber (Peasant Husband in Coach); Cherie Franklin (Peasant Wife in Coach); Ezio Greggio (Coach Driver); Leslie Sachs (Usherette); Matthew Porretta (Handsome Lieutenant at Ball); Rudy DeLuca (Guard); Jennifer Crystal (Nurse); Darla Haun (Brunette Vampire); Karen Roe (Blond Vampire); Charlie Callas (Man in Straitjacket); Phillip Connery (Ship Captain); Tony Griffin, Casey King, Rick Rempel (Crewmen); Zale Kessler (Orchestra Leader); Barbaree Earl, Maura Nielsen, Thea Nielsen, Robin Shepard, Elaine Ballace, Maude Winchester (Ballroom Guests); Lisa Cordray (Hat Check Girl); Cindy Marshall-Day, Benjamin Livingston (Young Lovers at Picnic); Gregg Binkley (Woodbridge); Anne Bancroft (Gypsy Woman); David DeLuise, Tommy Koenig, Grinnell Morris, Vince Grant, Ric Coy, Michael Connors, Stephen Wolfe Smith, Richard Alan Stewart, Johnny Cocktails (Interns); Carol Arthur, Sonje Fortag, Henry Kaiser, Derek Mark Lochran, Ira Miller, Kathleen Kane, Loraine Shields (Villagers).

CREDITS: Director: Mel Brooks; Producer: Mel Brooks; Screenplay: Mel Brooks, Rudy DeLuca, Steve Haberman; Story: Rudy DeLuca, Steve Haberman, based on the novel *Dracula* by Bram Stoker; Exec. Prod: Peter Schindler; Assoc. Prods.: Robert Latham Brown, Leah

Zappy; Editor: Adam Weiss; Music: Hummie Mann; Prod. Designer: Roy Forge Smith; Dir. of Photog.: Michael D. O'Shea; Casting: Lindsay D. Chag, Bill Shepard, C.S.A.; Costume Designer: Dodie Shepard; Prod. Mgr.: Robert Latham Brown; 1st Asst. Dir.: Gregg Goldstone; 2nd Asst. Dir.: Kenneth Silverstein; Choreographer: Alan Johnson; 2nd Unit Dir.: Peter Schindler; Addnl. Photog.: Gary B. Kibbe; Art Dir.: Bruce Robert Hill; Set Decorator: Jan Pascale, S.D.S.A.; Lead Set Designer: Joseph G. Pacelli, Jr.; Leadperson: Louise del Araujo; Script Supvr.: Marshall I. Schlom; Camera Op.: Steven H. Smith; 1st Asst. Camera: Alan Blauvelt; 2nd Asst. Camera: Sean O'Shea; 2nd Camera Op.: Norman G. Langley, S.O.C.; 1st Assts. 2nd Camera: Michael May, Clyde E. Bryan; Camera Loaders: Christopher D. Thompson, Daniel B. Nix; Prod. Sound: Jeff Wexler, Don Coufal, Gary Holland; Prop. Master: Jack Marino; Asst. Prop. Masters: Jennifer E. Dawson, Tom Altobello; Chief Lighting Tech.: Jack S. Shlosser; Key Grip: Marlin Hall; 2nd 2nd Asst. Dir.: Robert Scott; Asst. Eds.: Chris Jackson, David Crowther, Dana B. Wilson; Music Ed.: Chris LeDesma; Asst. Music Ed.: Gary Wasserman; Video Assist Op.: Charles May II; Music Playback: Bryan L. McCarty, C.A.S.; Asst. Choreographer: Charlene Painter; Costume Supvrs.: Charles DeMuth, Christine Heinz; Key Set Costumer: Marcie Olivi; Costumers: Paul DeLucca, Mike Evans, Bill Smith, Paul St. John, Andrea Weaver; Costumer for Mr. Nielsen: Gary Sampson; Makeup Design/Dep. Head: Todd A. McIntosh; Key Makeup Artist: Alan "Doc" Friedman; Makeup Artist: Carol Schwartz; Key Body Makeup Artist: Jane English; Key Hair Stylist: Dorothy D. Fox; Hair Stylist: Carol Pershing; Wig Maker: Erwin H. Kupitz; Prod. Coord.: Daren Hicks; Asst. Prod. Coord.: Janet Campolito; Prod. Accountant: K. Lenna Katich; 1st Asst. Accountant: Suzanne DeGrandis; Asst. Accountants: Robin Cross, John Semedik; Set Estimator: Johnnie Jenkins; Transp. Coord.: Jim Chesney; Transp. Capt.: Kenneth J. Moore; Publicity: Saul Kahan; Still Photog.: Peter Sorel; Location Mgr.: Bill Bowling; Extras Casting: Messenger and Associates; Set Designers: Lauren Cory, Barbara Ann Jaeckel; Senior Model Maker: Phil Dagort; Set Decorating Buyer: Heidi Baumgarten; On Set Dresser: Kristin Frances Jones; Drapery: Michael J. Miller; Set Dressers: Deborah Harman, Tim Bowen, Curtis Gutierrez, Gary H. Rizzo; Asst. Chief Lighting Tech.: Steve Shaver; Set

Lighting Techs.: David Dunbar, Kimo Easterwood, Jeffrey G. Hunt, Scott C. Keys; Rigging Gaffer: Blaise R. Dahlquist; Rigging Electricians: Dustin Huber, James J. Keys, Joe McKenzie; Best Boy Grip: Robert Nelson; Dolly Grip: Alberto S. Ramos; Grips: Edmond C. Wright, Raymond Michels, Jon Falkengren, Dennis L. Harper, Robert C. Crockett; Key Rigging Grip: John P. Cleveland; Rigging Grips: George D. Knight, Ron W. Peebles, Kevin B. Dean, John Lubin; Spec. Effects Coord.: Richard Ratliff; Spec. Effects Foremen: Danny Cangemi, Greg C. Jensen; Spec. Effects: Lambert Powell, Robert A. Phillips, Conrad Krumm, Paul Vigil, Doyle Smiley, Peter Albiez, Larz Anderson, Gary Schaedler, Terry P. Chapman; Sound Effects: Visiontrax; Supervising Sound Eds.: Gregory M. Gerlich, Gary S. Gerlich; Sound Eds.: Elliott L. Koretz, M.P.S.E., Hal Sanders, John M. Phillips, Colin C. Mouat; Foley Ed.: Jerry Pirozzi; Supervising ADR Ed.: Jerelyn Harding; Asst. Sound Eds.: Sonny Pettijohn, Craig Weintraub; Apprentice Ed.: Anne Laing; Music Recorded at: Todd-AO Scoring; Scoring Mixer: Rick Riccio; Recordist: David Marquette; Scoring Crew: Jay Selvester, Andy Bass, Marc Gebauer; Orchestrations: Brad Dechter, Frank Bennett, Don Nemitz; Music Contractor: Sandy DeCrescent; Vocal Contractor: Steve Lively; Music Preparation: Sheldon Music Service; Player Organ Roll Created by: Robbie Rhodes; Assts. to Mr. Brooks: Tricia Lewis, Katy Pacitti, David Schreiber; Asst. to Mr. Schindler: Michael Cavette; Addnl. 2nd Asst. Dir.: Darrell Woodward; DGA Trainee: Ken Wada; Prod. Assts.: Wayne A. Lamkay, Michael Anzalone, Woody Schultz, Tiffany Shine, Dianne Chadwick, Ronald Chesney; Art Dep. Coord.: Diane O'Connor; Casting Assts.: Tami Tirgrath, Belinda Gardea; Stand-ins: Roy Goldman, Ken Vils, Rany Harrington, Cheryl Henry, Betty Kibbe, Monty McKee; Specialty Dancers: David and Sharon Savoy; Ballroom Dancers: Audrey Baranishyn, Jeffrey Broadhurst, Kevin Crawford, John Frayer, Sandi Johnson, Shirley Kirkes, Manette LaChance, Stan Mazin, Tricia McFarlin-Matison, Anne McVey, Delores Nemiro, Jim Peace, Jody Peterson, Dennon Rawles, Sandra Rovetta, Alton Ruff, Blane Savage, Ted Sprague, Jude Van Wormer, Alan Walls; Stunt Coord.: Gary Combs; Dracula Double: Bruce Barbour; Renfield Double: Michael Washlake; Coach Driver Double: R.L. Tolbert; Sound Re-recorded at: Sony Pictures Studios; Re-recording Mixers: Greg Watkins, Carols DeLarios, Rick Kline; Recordists: Michael Reale, David Cunningham; Engineer: Bill Banyai; ADR Mixer: Jeff Gomillion; ADR Recordist: Louis Countee; ADR Voice Casting: L.A. MadDogs; Foley Recorded at: Joseph Luitly's and Steven Schear's Sound World; Foley Artists: Dan O'Connell, John Cucci; Foley Mixer: Jim Ashwill; Foley Recordist: Dennis Sager; Foley Asst.: Ryan Luithly; Visual Effects: Dream Quest Images; Visual Effects Supvr.: Mike Shea; Exec. Producer: Mark M. Galvin; Digital Effects Supvr.: Dan DeLeeuw; Prod. Mgr.: Chrys Forsyth-Smith; Prod. Coord.: Debbi Nikkel; Motion Control Op.: Scott Beattie; Assistant Camera Op.: Kevin Fitzgerald; Motion Control Tech.: Joseph Hagey; Computer Graphics Artists: Rob Dressel, Matt Hightower, Darin Hollings, John Murrah; Digital Compositing Techs.: Blaine Kennison, Marlo Pabon, David Lauer; Digital Matte Painters: Wendy Dobrowner, Carlin Kmetz; Film Scanning/Recording: Rick Lopez; Data Mgt.: Mark Dawson; Visual Effects Ed.: Jeff Beattie; Asst. Ed.: Daniel Arkin; Animatronics/Spec. Props: Optic Nerve Studios; Supvrs.: John Vulich, Everett Burrell; Assts.: Mark Garbarino, Larry O'Dien, Chris Heeter, Mario Torres; Greens Coord.: David R. Newhouse; Greens Standby: Robert G. Newhouse; Greens Foreman: Rene Van Den Berghe; Standby Painter: Al Kenders; Constr. Coord.: W. Wayne Walser; General Foreman: Tim Lafferty; Labor Foreman: Larry Wise; Foremen: Terry Kempf, Allen Lafferty, Neil A. Gahm, Steve Thayer; Plaster Foreman: Douglas R. Miller, Jr.; Plasterer: Tracy Stockwell; Mold Maker: Carl Robarge; Sculptor: Gene Cooper; Head Paint Foreperson: Jo Lumpkin Brown; Paint Foreperson: Rick Bernos; First Aid: Ahmed Saker; Craft Service: Clark "Cajun" Davis; Livestock Coord.: Corky Randall; Dolby Stereo Consultant: Douglas Greenfield; Negative Cutter: Mo Henry; Color Timer: Linda DeMarco; Main Title Design: Wayne Fitzgerald; Titles/Opticals: Pacific Title; Title Bkgds. from: Carousel Research, Fortean Picture Library, The Granger Collection, Simon Marsden/The Marsden Archive; *Mutiny on the Bounty* Clip: Turner Entertainment Co.; *The Premature Burial* Clip: Orion Pictures Corp.; Camera Cranes/Dollies: Chapman; Lighting/Grip Equip.: The Culver Studios Lighting and Grip Dep.; Filmed at the Culver Studios; Cameras/Lenses: Panavision; Color/Prints: Technicolor; Castle Rock Entertainment; A Brooksfilms Production; Columbia Pictures, 1995; 90 minutes.

13

* * *

Appendix:
Other Works by Brooks

* * * * * *

Despite including more than enough material for any ten careers, by no means is this list all-inclusive. Finding out precisely when Mel Brooks had appeared on *Today* or *Larry King Live* proved difficult enough in itself, but what of all those lesser-known shows? All those interviews given to magazines? Newspapers? Radio? The Internet?

And that's just *interviews*. Documentation of Brooks' audio, video, literary, and other creative output also remains sketchy at best, and some of Brooks' work — including his priceless appearance on NBC-TV's very first *Tonight Show Starring Johnny Carson* way back in 1962 — has been long erased, discarded, or just plain lost.

Ah, if they'd only known then what we all know now...

Nevertheless, the following list is offered in an attempt to preserve as much of the record as possible. In a career spanning more years than some lifetimes, especially a career as entertaining as Mel Brooks', it's a shame to lose even a moment.

Admiral Broadway Review. Live television comedy/variety series. NBC, DuMont, Jan. 28–June 3, 1949. Co-writer.

Your Show of Shows. Live television comedy/variety series. NBC, Feb. 25 1950–June 5, 1954. Co-writer.

New Faces of 1952. Stage revue, 1952. Co-writer.

The Imogene Coca Show. Live television comedy/variety series. NBC, Oct. 2, 1954–June 25, 1955. Co-writer.

Caesar's Hour. Live television comedy/variety series. NBC, Sept. 27, 1954–May 25, 1957. Co-writer.

New Faces. Movie adaptation; subsequent video release. 1954. Co-writer.

shinbone alley. Stage musical, from *Back Alley Opera* and the writings of Don Marquis. 1957. Co-writer.

The Polly Bergen Show. Television musical/variety series. NBC. Sept. 21 1957– May 31, 1958. Co-writer, co-producer.

Sid Caesar Invites You. Television comedy/variety series. ABC, Jan. 26–May 25, 1958. Co-writer.

At the Movies. Television comedy/variety special. NBC, May 3, 1959. Co-writer.

Marriage — Handle with Care. Television comedy/variety special. CBS, Dec. 2, 1959. Co-writer.

The Jerry Lewis Show. Television comedy/variety special. NBC, Dec. 10, 1959. Co-writer.

Tiptoe Through TV. Television comedy/variety special. CBS, May 5, 1960. Co-writer.

Variety: World of Show Biz. Television comedy/variety special. CBS, June 2, 1960 co-writer.

Play of the Week. Television dramatic series: *archie and mehitabel* presentation, based on *shinbone alley.* PBS, June 16, 1960. Co-writer.

2,000 Years with Carl Reiner and Mel Brooks. Audiorecording. 1960. Co-writer, performer.

The Comedians. Audiorecording. 1960. Performer, co-writer of previous material.

2,001 Years with Carl Reiner and Mel Brooks. Audiorecording. 1961. Co-writer, performer.

Excerpts from the New Albums for May 1961. Audiorecording. 1961. Performer, co-writer of previous material.

The Steve Allen Show. Television comedy/variety series. ABC, 1961. Guest performer, co-writer of previous material.

The Ed Sullivan Show. Television variety series. CBS, Feb. 12, 1961. Guest performer, co-writer of previous material.

The Connie Francis Show. Television comedy/variety special. ABC, Sept. 13, 1961. Co-writer.

The 2,000 Year Old Man: Origin of the Riviera. Television comedy insert following *On the Riviera* motion picture broadcast. NBC, Dec. 30, 1961. Performer, co-writer of previous material.

Remember How Great. Audiorecording. 1962. Performer, co-writer of previous material.

The Timex All-Star Comedy Show. Television comedy/variety special; subsequent video release. NBC, April 6, 1962. Performer, co-writer of previous material.

The 2,000 Year Old Man: Origin of Games. Television comedy insert following *It Happens Every Spring* motion picture broadcast. NBC, April 7, 1962. Performer, co-writer of previous material.

The Tonight Show Starring Johnny Carson. Television talk/variety series. NBC, Oct. 2, 1962. Interview participant.

"Ballantine Beer." Radio advertising series. 1962. Co-writer, performer.

All-American. Stage musical, from the Robert Lewis Taylor novel *Professor Fodorski.* 1962. Writer.

As Caesar Sees It. Monthly television comedy/variety specials. NBC, 1962–63. Co-writer.

The Steve Allen Show. Television comedy/variety series. Syndication, July 24, 1962. Guest performer, co-writer of previous material.

The Steve Allen Show. Television comedy/variety series. Syndication, March 21–22, 1963. Guest performer, co-writer of previous material.

Inside Danny Baker. Unsold television sitcom pilot; subsequent video release. 1963. Writer.

The Critic. Animated motion picture short. 1963. Co-writer, voice-over performer.

My Son, The Hero. Motion picture theatrical "trailer" only. 1963. Writer, director, performer.

Steve Allen's Funny Fone Calls: Excerpts from The Steve Allen Show. Audiorecording. 1963. Performer, co-writer of previous material.

Comedy Hits. Audiorecording. 1963. Performer, co-writer of previous material.

The Hollywood Palace. Television comedy/variety series. ABC, Jan. 15, 1964. Guest performer, co-writer of previous material.

Open End (a.k.a. *The David Susskind Show*). Television talk/discussion series. Syndication, March 25, 1964. Guest/participant.

ABC's Nightlife (a.k.a. *The Les Crane Show*). Television talk/discussion series. ABC, Aug. 5, 1964. Guest/participant.

The Hollywood Palace. Television comedy/variety series. ABC, Nov. 7, 1964. Guest performer, co-writer of previous material.

The Celebrity Game. Television game show. CBS, 1964. Guest/participant.

The Danny Thomas Show. Television variety special. NBC, April 23, 1965. Guest performer, co-writer of previous material.

Get Smart. Television sitcom. NBC, 1965–69, CBS, 1969–70; subsequent video release. Co-creator.

Get Smart. Television sitcom: "Mr. Big" pilot episode. NBC, Sept. 18, 1965. Co-writer.

Get Smart. Television sitcom: "Our Man in Leotards" episode. NBC, Nov. 20, 1965. Co-writer.

Get Smart. Television sitcom: "Survival of the Fattest" episode. NBC, Dec. 25, 1965. Co-writer.

Get Smart! Novel by William Johnston. 1965. Co-creator of *Get Smart* television source material.

Fly Buttons and Other Comedy Favorites. Audiorecording. 1966. Performer, co-writer of previous material.

The Sid Caesar, Imogene Coca, Carl Reiner, Howard Morris Special. Television comedy/variety special, subsequent video release. CBS, April 12, 1966. Co-writer.

The Face Is Familiar. Television game show. CBS, 1966. Guest/participant.

Playboy. Magazine: "Mel Brooks" interview. Oct. 1966. Interview participant.

The Andy Williams Show. Television comedy/variety special. NBC, Nov. 27, 1966. Guest performer, co-writer of previous material.

Sorry, Chief! Novel by William Johnston. 1966. Co-creator of *Get Smart* television source material.

Get Smart Once Again! Novel by William Johnston. 1966. Co-creator of *Get Smart* television source material.

Max Smart and the Perilous Pellets. Novel by William Johnston. 1966. Co-creator of *Get Smart* television source material.

The Colgate Comedy Hour. Television comedy/variety series pilot. NBC, May 11, 1967; subsequent video release. Guest performer, co-writer of previous material.

Missed It By That Much! Novel by William Johnston. 1967. Co-creator of *Get Smart* television source material.

And Loving It! Novel by William Johnston. 1967. Co-creator of *Get Smart* television source material.

The Producers. Motion picture; subsequent video release. 1968. Writer, director, voice-over performer, lyricist.

The Producers: The Original Soundtrack Recording. Soundtrack audiorecording. 1968. Lyricist, vocal performer, creator of original motion picture source material.

Best of The 2,000 Year Old Man. Audiorecording. 1968. Performer, co-writer of previous material.

Max Smart— The Spy Who Went Out to the Cold! Novel by William Johnston. 1968. Co-creator of *Get Smart* television source material.

Max Smart Loses Control. Novel by William Johnston. 1968. Co-creator of *Get Smart* television source material.

Max Smart and the Ghastly Ghost Affair. Novel by William Johnston. 1969. Co-creator of *Get Smart* television source material.

Caesar's Hour, Vols. 1–2. Video release. 1969. Co-writer of previous material.

Caesar's Hour (1956). Video release. 1969. Co-writer of previous material.

Caesar's Hour (1957). Video release. 1969. Co-writer of previous material.

The Mike Douglas Show. Television talk/variety show. 1970s. Interview participant/guest host.

Annie, the Women in the Life of a Man. Television comedy/variety special. CBS, Feb. 18, 1970. Co-writer, performer.

The Dick Cavett Show. Television talk/variety show. ABC, April 6, 1970. Interview participant.

The Tonight Show Starring Johnny Carson. Television talk show. NBC, Oct. 27, 1970. Interview participant.

The Twelve Chairs. Motion picture from the Ilya Ilf and Yevgenii Petrov novel *The Twelve Chairs*; subsequent video release. 1970. Writer, director, performer, lyricist.

Today. Television morning news/interview show. NBC, Feb. 10, 1971. Interview participant.

shinbone alley. Animated motion picture; subsequent video release. 1971. Co-writer of earlier stage material.

The Electric Company. Television children's series: 1971 episodes. PBS, 1971–76. Voice-over performer.

The Electric Company. Soundtrack audiorecording. 1972. Voice-over performer.

The Dick Cavett Show. Television talk/variety show. ABC, Jan. 21, 1972. Interview participant.

Jeopardy! Television game show. NBC, Feb. 21, 1972. Guest performer.

The Incomplete Works of Carl Reiner and Mel Brooks. Compilation audiorecording. 1973. Co-writer, performer of previous material.

2,000 and Thirteen. Audiorecording. 1973. Co-writer, performer.

Ten from Your Show of Shows. Motion picture; subsequent video release. 1971. Co-writer of *Your Show of Shows* television source material.

Blazing Saddles. Motion picture; subsequent video release. 1974. Co-writer, director, performer, lyricist.

Marlo Thomas and Friends in Free to Be ... You and Me. Television educational/variety special. ABC, March 11, 1974. Performer.

Marlo Thomas and Friends in Free to Be ... You and Me. Audiorecording. 1974. Vocal performer.

Young Frankenstein. Motion picture from characters in the Mary Shelley novel *Frankenstein*; subsequent video release. 1974. Co-writer, director, voice-over performer, theatrical "trailer" voice-over performer.

Young Frankenstein. Novelization by Gilbert Pearlman. 1974. Co-writer of *Young Frankenstein* motion picture source material.

Annie & The Hoods. Television comedy/variety special. ABC, Nov. 23, 1974. Performer.

Young Frankenstein: Music & Dialogue from the Soundtrack. Soundtrack audiorecording. 1975. Co-creator of original motion picture source material.

The 2,000 Year Old Man. Animated television special; subsequent video release. CBS, Jan. 11, 1975. Co-writer, voice-over performer.

Playboy. Magazine: "Mel Brooks Interview" by Larry Siegel. Feb. 1975. Interview participant.

The Tonight Show Starring Johnny Carson. Television talk show. NBC, Feb. 13, 1975. Interview participant.

Film Comment. Magazine: "Mel Brooks Interview." March–April 1975. Interview participant.

Today. Television morning news/interview show. NBC, April 3, 1975. Interview participant.

Black Bart. Television sitcom pilot. CBS, April 4, 1975. Co-writer of *Blazing Saddles* motion picture source material.

"Bic Pens." Television advertisements. 1975. Voice-over performer.

Today. Television morning news/interview show. NBC, April 23, 1975. Interview participant.

Today. Television morning news/interview show. NBC, May 17, 1975. Interview participant.

Don Adams' Screen Test. Television comedy/audience participant series. Syndication, 1975. Guest/participant.

When Things Were Rotten. Television sit-com; subsequent video release. CBS, 1975. Co-creator.

When Things Were Rotten. Television sit-com: "The Capture of Robin Hood" pilot episode. Sept. 10, 1975. Co-writer.

The Tonight Show Starring Johnny Carson. Television talk show. NBC, Dec. 15, 1975. Interview participant.

Breaking It Up! The Best Routines of the Stand-Up Comics. Nonfiction book edited by Ross Firestone. 1975. Co-writer of comedy material.

Second Annual Comedy Awards. Television awards special. ABC, April 10, 1976. Award recipient.

Today. Television morning news/interview show. NBC, July 6, 1976. Interview participant.

Today. Television morning news/interview show. NBC, July 28, 1976. Interview participant.

The Tonight Show Starring Johnny Carson. Television talk show. NBC, July 29, 1976. Interview participant.

Mel Brooks Movie Music. Soundtrack audiorecording. 1976. Lyricist, composer of previous material.

Silent Movie. Motion picture; subsequent video release. 1976. Co-writer, director, performer.

Silent Movie: Original Motion Picture Score. Soundtrack audiorecording by John Morris. 1976. Co-creator of original motion picture source material.

Silent Movie. Novelization. 1976. Co-writer of *Silent Movie* motion picture source material.

How the Great Comedy Writers Create Laughter. Nonfiction book by Larry Wilde. 1976. Interview participant.

Today. Television morning news/interview show. NBC, Dec. 2, 1977. Interview participant.

Twenty-five Years of Recorded Comedy. Audiorecording. 1977. Performer, co-writer of previous material.

High Anxiety. Motion picture; subsequent video release. 1977. Co-writer, director, performer, lyricist.

High Anxiety. Novelization by Robert H. Pilpel. 1977. Co-creator of *High Anxiety* motion picture source material.

The Star Treatment. Nonfiction book edited by Dick Stelzer. 1977. Essay contributor.

Leo Tolstoy's War and Peace. Radio reading. WBAI New York, 1977. Reader/performer.

Today. Television morning news/interview show. NBC, Feb. 9, 1978. Interview participant.

The Tonight Show Starring Johnny Carson. Television talk show. March 16, 1978. Interview participant.

The Hollywood Squares. Television game show. April 1978. Guest performer.

High Anxiety/Mel Brooks' Greatest Hits Featuring the Fabulous Film Scores of John Morris. Soundtrack audiorecording. 1978. Lyricist, composer, voice-over performer of original motion picture material.

Omnivores: They Said They Would Eat Anything — and They Did! Nonfiction book by Alfa-Betty Olsen and Marshall Efron. 1979. Introduction author.

The Muppet Movie. Motion picture; subsequent video release. 1979. Performer.

Fatso. Motion picture; subsequent video release. 1980. Executive producer.

The Elephant Man. Motion picture; subsequent video release. 1980. Executive producer.

The Nude Bomb (a.k.a. The Return of Maxwell Smart). Motion picture; subsequent video release. 1980. Co-creator of *Get Smart* television source material.

History of the World — Part I. Motion picture; subsequent video release. 1981. Writer, director, producer, performer, co-lyricist.

History of the World — Part I. Picture book

adaptation. 1981. Writer, co-lyricist for insert audiorecording.

History of the World — Part I: Dialogue and Music from the Original Motion Picture. Soundtrack audiorecording. 1981. Performer, co-lyricist, creator of original motion picture source material.

The 2,000 Year Old Man. Book adaptation of earlier audiorecordings. 1981. Co-writer.

"It's Good to Be the King." Audiorecording. 1981. Performer, lyricist, composer.

Tomorrow Coast-to-Coast. Television talk show. NBC, July 8, 1981. Interview participant.

Today. Television morning news/interview show. NBC, July 13–16, 1981. Interview participant.

Frances. Motion picture; subsequent video release. 1982. Executive producer.

My Favorite Year. Motion picture; subsequent video release. 1982. Executive producer.

To Be or Not to Be. Motion picture; subsequent video release. 1982. Performer, producer, lyricist.

Bonjour, Monsieur Lewis. French TV Jerry Lewis documentary. 1982. Interview participant.

The Dr. Demento Show. Radio series. March 14, 1982. Interview participant, co-writer, co-performer, co-lyricist of previous material.

"To Be or Not to Be" ("The Hitler Rap"). Audiorecording. 1983. Performer, lyricist. composer.

"To Be or Not to Be" ("The Hitler Rap"). Music video. 1983. Performer, lyricist, composer.

Dom DeLuise & Friends. Television comedy/variety special. ABC, Feb. 16, 1983. Performer.

Nightcap: Conversations on the Arts and Letters with Studs Terkel and Calvin Trillin. Interview series. Arts TV, Oct. 29, 1983.

Today. Television morning news/interview show. NBC, Nov. 2, 1983. Interview participant.

Today. Television morning news/interview show. NBC, Dec. 12–16, 1983. Interview participant.

The Tonight Show Starring Johnny Carson. Television talk show. NBC, Dec. 15, 1983. Interview participant.

The Twelve Chairs: Original Motion Picture Soundtrack. Soundtrack audiorecording. 1983. Lyricist, creator of original motion picture source material.

The Movie Business Book. Nonfiction book by Jason E. Squire. 1983. Essay contributor.

To Be or Not to Be. Soundtrack audiorecording. 1984. Performer, co-lyricist, co-composer.

An Audience with Mel Brooks. London-taped video. 1984. Live-audience performer.

Sunset People. Documentary motion picture. 1984. On-screen participant.

The Comedy Corner: The All-Time Best of Recorded Comedy. Audiorecording. 1984. Performer, co-writer of previous material.

The Great Standups: Sixty Years of Laughter. Television documentary/comedy special. HBO, 1984. Performer, co-writer of previous material.

The Television Academy Hall of Fame. Television awards special. NBC, April 22, 1985. Tribute recipient.

The Doctor and the Devils. Motion picture; subsequent video release. 1985. Executive producer.

Mel Brooks Hails Sid Caesar. Television documentary/variety special. 1985. BBC Channel 4-LWT. On-screen participant.

The Late Show Starring Joan Rivers. Television talk show. Fox, 1986. Interview participant.

Comedy Music Videos. Video release. 1986. Writer, composer, performer of previous material.

The Fly. Motion picture; subsequent video release. 1986. Executive producer.

Steve Allen's Golden Age of Comedy. Video release. 1986. Performer in previous material.

Today. Television morning news/interview show. NBC, March 11–12, 1987. Interview participant.

The Tonight Show Starring Johnny Carson. Television talk show. NBC, June 23, 1987. Interview participant.

Today. Television morning news/interview show. NBC, June 24–25, 1987. Interview participant.

Solarbabies. Motion picture; subsequent video release. 1987. Executive producer.

84 Charing Cross Road. Motion picture; subsequent video release. 1987. Executive producer.

Spaceballs. Motion picture; subsequent video release. 1987. Co-writer, director, performer, producer, co-lyricist.

Spaceballs: The Soundtrack. Soundtrack audiorecording. 1987. Co-lyricist, co-creator of original motion picture source material.

Get Smart Again! Made-for-television motion picture; subsequent video release. ABC, Feb. 26, 1988. Co-creator of *Get Smart* television source material.

Marlo Thomas and Friends in Free to Be … A Family. Television educational/variety special; subsequent video release. ABC, Dec. 14, 1988. Performer.

Marlo Thomas and Friends in Free to Be … A Family. Audiorecording. 1988. Vocal performer.

The Fly II. Motion picture; subsequent video release. 1988. Executive producer.

The Nutt House. Television sitcom. NBC, 1988. Co–creator, co-executive producer.

The Nutt House. Television sitcom: pilot episode. NBC, Sept. 20, 1989. Co-writer.

Inside the Comedy Mind. Television interview series. Comedy Central, 1990s. Interview participant.

Look Who's Talking Too. Motion picture; subsequent video release. 1990. Voice-over performer.

The Tracey Ullman Show. Television comedy/variety series. Fox, Feb. 4, 1990. Guest performer.

The Tracey Ullman Show. Television comedy/variety series. "Best of '89–90" compilation episode. Fox, May 26, 1990. Performer in previous *Tracey Ullman Show* television material.

The Best of the Tracey Ullman Show. Video release. 1990. Performer in previous *Tracey Ullman Show* television material.

Mickey's Audition. Live-action/animated theme park motion picture presentation. Disney-MGM Studios, 1990. Performer.

The Big Book of New American Humor: The Best of the Past Twenty-five Years. Nonfiction book edited by William Novak and Moshe Waldoks with Donald Altschiller. 1990. Co-writer of previous material.

Hollywood Stars. Television documentary special. Syndication, 1991. Interview participant.

The Sullivan Years: Comedy Classics. Audiorecording. 1991. Performer, co-writer of previous material.

Life Stinks. Motion picture; subsequent video release. 1991. Co-writer, director, performer, producer, lyricist.

The Fifth Annual American Comedy Awards. Television awards special. ABC, April 3, 1991. Guest performer, presenter.

Today. Television morning news/interview show. NBC, July 22–23, 1991. Interview participant.

The Tonight Show Starring Johnny Carson. Television talk show. NBC, July 24, 1991. Interview participant.

Naked Hollywood. Television documentary special. A&E, July 28, Aug. 4, Aug. 11, Aug. 18, Aug. 25, 1991. Interview participant.

Later with Bob Costas. Television prime-time talk show special. NBC, July 27, 1991. Interview participant.

Later with Bob Costas. Television late-night talk show. NBC, July 29–Aug. 1, 1991. Interview participant.

Today at 40. Television morning news/interview show retrospective. NBC, Jan. 14, 1992. Interview participant.

The Tonight Show Starring Johnny Carson. Television talk show. NBC, May 19, 1992. Interview participant.

The Vagrant. Motion picture; subsequent video release. 1992. Executive producer.

Little Tramp. Stage musical concept album. 1992. Vocal performer.

My Favorite Year. Stage musical. 1992. Executive producer of source motion picture *My Favorite Year.*

Holiday Greetings from the Ed Sullivan Show. Video release. 1992. Performer, co-writer of previous material.

Robin Hood: Men in Tights. Motion picture; subsequent video release. 1993. Co-writer, director, performer, lyricist, producer.

Robin Hood: Men in Tights: Music from the Original Motion Picture Soundtrack. Soundtrack audiorecording. 1993. Lyricist, co-creator of original motion picture source material.

shinbone alley: The 1957 Musical. Original cast audiorecording. 1993. Co-writer of original stage musical.

More of the Best of The Hollywood Palace. Television comedy/variety special. ABC, 1993. Performer, co-writer of earlier material.

Four Decades with Studs Terkel. Audiorecording. 1993. Interview participant in previous radio broadcasts.

The Tonight Show with Jay Leno. Television talk show. NBC, July 28, 1993. Interview participant.

Frasier. Television sitcom: "Miracle on Third or Fourth Street" episode. NBC, Dec. 16, 1993. Guest voice-over performer.

Later with Bob Costas: One Last Time. Television talk show special broadcast. NBC, Feb. 25, 1994. Interview participant in previous material.

The Visitors. Motion picture; subsequent video release. 1994. English voice-over director for dubbed version of French-language motion picture *Les Visiteurs.*

The Little Rascals. Motion picture; subsequent video release. 1994. Performer.

Silence of the Hams. Motion picture; subsequent video release. 1994. Performer.

The Best Disco in Town, Vol. 2. Audiorecording. Performer, co-writer of previous material.

The Complete 2,000 Years with Carl Reiner and Mel Brooks. Audiorecording. 1994. Performer, co-writer of previous material.

It's Alive: The True Story of Frankenstein (a.k.a. The True Story of Frankenstein). Television documentary special; subsequent video release. A&E, Nov. 20, 1994. Interview participant.

Hal Roach: Hollywood's King of Laughter. Television documentary special. The Disney Channel, 1994. Interview participant.

Biography. Television documentary series: "Sid Caesar: Television's Comedy Genius" episode. A&E, 1994. Interview participant.

Your Show of Shows, Vols. 1–2. Video release. 1994. Co-writer of previous material.

Box Office Online. Online magazine: "Mel Brooks Interview" by Ray Greene. 1995. Interview participant.

Biography. Television documentary series: "Carl Reiner: Still Laughing" episode; subsequent video release. A&E, 1995. Interview participant.

Get Smart. Television revival series. Fox, 1995. Co-creator of original *Get Smart* source material.

The Simpsons. Animated television sitcom: "Homer vs. Patty and Selma" episode.

Fox, Feb. 26, 1995. Guest voice-over performer.

Dracula: Dead and Loving It. Motion picture; subsequent video release. 1995. Co-writer, director, performer, producer.

But Seriously: The American Comedy Box, 1915–1994. Audiorecording. 1995. Performer, co-writer of previously released material.

Favorite Moments of the Stars: The 100 Funniest Moments of the 20th Century. Video release. 1995. Performer, co-writer of previous material.

The NewsHour with Jim Lehrer. Television news show: "Happy 100th, George Burns" segment. PBS, Jan. 19, 1996. Interview participant.

Dracula: Dead and Loving It. Original Motion Picture Soundtrack. Audiorecording. 1996. Co-creator of original motion picture source material.

Written By. Magazine: interview. March 1996. Interview participant.

Caesar's Writers. Television special; subsequent video release. PBS, Aug. 19, 1996. Interview participant.

American Dreamers. Television documentary special. TNT, June 19, 1996. Interview participant.

Mad About You. Television sitcom: "The Grant" episode. NBC, Sept. 24, 1996. Guest performer.

Holiday Greetings from The Ed Sullivan Show. Video release. 1996. Co-writer, performer in earlier material.

Mad About You. Television sitcom: "The Penis" episode. NBC, Feb. 11, 1997. Guest performer.

Pretty as a Picture: The Art of David Lynch. Television documentary special; subsequent video release. Bravo, March 14, 1997. Interview participant.

I Am Your Child. Television educational/variety special; subsequent video release. ABC, April 27, 1997. Co-writer, performer of original material.

The Keaton Chronicle. Magazine: "Believing in Make-Believe: An Interview with Mel Brooks" by Dan Lyberger. Autumn 1997. Interview participant.

The New York Times Magazine. Magazine: "Funny is Money" interview. Oct. 1997. Interview participant.

The Tonight Show with Jay Leno. Television talk show. NBC, Oct. 6, 1997. Interview participant.

The Rosie O'Donnell Show. Television talk show. Syndicated, Oct. 8, 1997. Interview participant.

The Charlie Rose Show. Television talk show. PBS, Oct. 9, 1997. Interview participant.

The Late Show with David Letterman. Television talk show. CBS, Oct. 29, 1997. Interview participant.

The Late Late Show with Tom Snyder. Television talk show. CBS, Oct. 29, 1997.

Mad About You. Television sitcom: "Uncle Phil and the Coupons" episode. NBC, Nov. 4, 1997. Guest performer.

"2,000 Year Old Man Chat." Online interview. Internet, Nov. 30, 1997. Interview participant.

The Jewish Journal of Greater L.A. Magazine: "Tummeling Toward the Millennium: The 2,000 Year Old Man is Alive, Well, and Still Doesn't Touch Fast Food—An Interview with Mel Brooks and Carl Reiner" by Diane Arieff Zaga. Dec. 5, 1977. Interview participant.

The 2,000 Year Old Man in the Year 2000. Audiorecording. 1997. Co-writer, performer, producer.

The 2,000 Year Old Man in the Year 2000. Book adaptation of earlier audiorecordings. 1997. Co-writer.

Warner Brothers 75 Years of Film Music. Audiorecording. 1998. Co-writer, performer of previous material.

Fresh Air on Stage and Screen. Audiorecording. 1998. Interview participant in previous radio material.

M*A*S*H, Tootsie, & God: A Tribute to Larry Gelbart. Television tribute special.

PBS, March 7, 1998. Interview participant.

The Fiftieth Annual Emmy Awards. Television awards special. NBC, Sept. 13, 1998. Award recipient.

The Prince of Egypt. Motion picture; subsequent video release. 1998. Vocal performer.

AFI's 100 Years, 100 Movies. Television documentary special; subsequent video release. CBS, June 16, 1998. Interview participant.

AFI's 100 Years, 100 Movies. Expanded television documentary special series. TNT, June 23, 30; July 7, 14, 21, 28; Aug. 4, 11, 18, 25, 1998. Interview participant.

Biography. Television documentary series: "Neil Simon — The People's Playwright" episode; subsequent video release. A&E, Jan. 22, 1999. Interview participant.

Mad About You. Television sitcom episode: "Uncle Phil Goes Back to High School" episode. NBC, March 1, 1999. Guest performer.

Modern Maturity. Magazine: "Brooks and Reiner" interview by Claudia Dreifus. March/April 1999. Interview participant.

"American Online Interview with Mel Brooks." Online interview. Internet, April 10, 1999. Interview participant.

Screw Loose (a.k.a. Svitati). Motion picture; subsequent video release. 1999. Performer.

Voices of Our Time: Five Decades of Studs Terkel. Audiorecording. 1999. Interview participant in previous radio broadcasts.

Forgotten Horrors: The Definitive Edition. Nonfiction book by George E. Turner and Michael H. Price. 1999. Introduction author.

Sex, Lies, & Videovald (Sex, Lies, & Video Violence). Video release. 2002. Actor.

The Late Show with David Letterman. Television talk show. CBS, March 2, 2000. Interview participant.

The Martin Short Show. Television talk/variety show. Syndication, March 22, 2000. Interview participant.

AFI's 100 Years, 100 Laughs. Television documentary special. CBS, June 13, 2000. Interview participant.

Intimate Portrait. Television documentary: "Madeline Kahn" episode. Lifetime, Oct. 2, 2000. Interview participant.

The Sid Caesar Collection, Vols. 1–3. Video release. 2000. Co-writer, interview participant.

The Kennedy Center Presents The Mark Twain Prize Celebrating the Comedy of Carl Reiner. Television awards special. PBS, Feb. 28, 2001. Guest.

60 Minutes. Television newsmagazine series: "Mel Brooks on Broadway" segment. CBS, April 15, 2001. Interview participant.

The Producers. Stage musical based on Brooks' 1968 motion picture *The Producers.* 2001. Co-writer, lyricist, music composer, voice-over performer. 2001.

The Producers: Original Broadway Cast Recording. Original Cast audiorecording. 2001. Lyricist, music composer, voice-over performer.

CBS News Sunday Morning. Television news/arts program: "Producing *The Producers*" segment. CBS, May 13, 2001. Interview participant.

Written By. Magazine: "Great Caesar's Scripts" article. May 2001. Interview participant.

All Things Considered. News/information radio series: "Mel Brooks Discusses His Tony Nomination for *The Producers*" by Robert Siegel. NPR, May 18, 2001.

Hail Sid Caesar! The Golden Age of Comedy. Television documentary special. Showtime, May 26, 2001. Interview participant.

The First Ten Awards: Tonys 2001. Television awards special. PBS, June 3, 2001. Award recipient.

The 55th Annual Tony Awards. Television

awards special. CBS, June 3, 2001. Award recipient.

Showbiz This Weekend. Television entertainment news show. CNN, June 9, 2001. Interview participant.

Great Performances: Recording The Producers. Television documentary series: "Recording the Producers" episode; subsequent video release. PBS, Aug. 8, 2001. Interview participant.

The Producers: The Story Behind the Biggest Hit in Broadway History! How We Did It. Nonfiction book by Mel Brooks and Thomas Meehan. 2001. Co-author.

Backstory. Television documentary series: "*Young Frankenstein*" episode. AMC, Jan. 28, 2002. Interview participant.

Bibliography

"*The ABC Sunday Night Movie: Get Smart, Again!*" Rev. of *Get Smart Again!*, dir. by Gary Nelson. *Variety.* (Feb. 24, 1989). Rpt. in *Variety Television Reviews.* Vol. 16. New York: Garland Publishing, Inc., 1992.

Adler, Bill, and Jeffrey Feinman. *Mel Brooks: The Irreverent Funnyman.* Chicago: Playboy Press, 1976.

Adler, Renata. "*The Producers.*" Rev. of *The Producers,* dir. by Mel Brooks. *The New York Times.* (March 21, 1968). Rpt. in *The New York Times Film Reviews.* Vol. 2. New York: Garland Publishing, Inc., 1970. 3742.

"*All-Star Comedy Hour.*" Rev. of *The Timex All-Star Comedy Hour,* dir. by Coby Ruskin. *Variety.* (April 11, 1962). Rpt. in *Variety Television Reviews.* Vol. 7. New York: Garland Publishing, Inc., 1989.

Allen, Steve. *Funny People.* Briarcliff Manor, NY: Stein and Day, 1981.

"America Online Interview with Mel Brooks." Online. 10 April 1999: http://userwww.service.emory.edu/~mgros/brooks/Interview.html.

"*American Comedy Awards.*" Rev. of *The American Comedy Awards,* dir. by Martin Pasetta, Jr. *Variety.* (May 25, 1988). Rpt. in *Variety Television Reviews.* Vol. 14. New York: Garland Publishing, Inc., 1990.

"*Annie & The Hoods.*" Rev. of *Annie & The Hoods,* dir. by Martin Charnin. *Variety.* (Dec. 4, 1974). Rpt. in *Variety Television Reviews.* Vol. 11. New York: Garland Publishers, Inc., 1989.

"*Annie, the Women in the Life of a Man.*" Rev. of *Annie, the Women in the Life of a Man,* dir. by Walter C. Miller. *Variety.* (Feb. 25, 1970). Rpt. in *Variety Television Reviews.* Vol. 10. New York: Garland Publishers, Inc., 1989.

Ansen, David. "Upstaging the Third Reich." Rev. of *To Be or Not to Be,* dir. by Mel Brooks. *Time.* 19 Dec. 1983: 66.

"*As Caesar Sees It.*" Rev. of *As Caesar Sees It. Variety.* (Jan. 23, 1963). Rpt. in *Variety Television Reviews.* Vol. 8. New York: The New York Times and Arno Press, 1989.

Atkinson, Brooks. "*New Faces of 1952.*" Rev. of *New Faces of 1952,* dir. by John Murray Anderson and John Beal. *The New York Times.* (May 17, 1952). Rpt. in *The New York Times Theater Reviews.* Vol. 6. New York: The New York Times and Arno Press, 1971.

_____. "*New Faces of 1952.*" Rev. of *New Faces of 1952,* dir. by John Murray Anderson and John Beal. *The New York Times.* (May 25, 1952). Rpt. in *The New York Times Theater Reviews.* Vol. 6. New York: The New York Times and Arno Press, 1971.

_____. "*Shinbone Alley.*" Rev. of *shinbone alley,* dir. by John D. Wilson. *The New York Times.* (April 28, 1957). Rpt. in *The New York Times*

Theater Reviews. Vol. 6. New York: The New York Times and Arno Press, 1971.

_____. *"Shinbone Alley."* Rev. of *shinbone alley,* dir. by John D. Wilson. *The New York Times.* (April 15, 1957). Rpt. in *The New York Times Theater Reviews.* Vol. 6. New York: The New York Times and Arno Press, 1971.

"At the Movies." Rev. of *At the Movies,* dir. by Alan Handley. *Variety.* (May 5, 1959). Rpt. in *Variety Television Reviews.* Vol. 6. New York: Garland Publishing, Inc., 1989.

Atlas, Jacoba. "Mel Brooks Interview." *Film Comment.* March–April 1975. Online. 10 April 1999: http://www.ews.uiuc.edu/~yin/Org/MBrooks/interviews/FilmComment.html.

An Audience with Mel Brooks, dir. by Alasdair MacMillan. Perf. Mel Brooks, Ronny Graham, and Jonathan Pryce. 1984. Videocassette. Prism Entertainment, 1984.

Beck, Jerry, and Will Friedwald. *Looney Tunes and Merrie Melodies: A Complete Illustrated Guide to the Warner Bros. Cartoons.* New York: Henry Holt and Company, 1989.

Benjamin, Richard, dir. *My Favorite Year.* Perf. Peter O'Toole, Mark Linn-Baker, Jessica Harper, Joseph Bologna, Bill Macy, and Lainie Kazan. 1982. Videocassette. MGM/UA Home Video, 1989.

Bernard, Hugh. "Silent Movie." Rev. of *Silent Movie,* dir. by Mel Brooks. *Films in Review.* Aug./Sept. 1976: 441.

"Black Bart." Rev. of *Black Bart,* dir. by Robert Butler. *Variety.* (April 9, 1975). Rpt. in *Variety Television Reviews.* Vol. 11. New York: Garland Publishing, Inc., 1989.

Brantley, Ben. "A Scam That'll Knock 'Em Dead." Rev. of *The Producers,* dir. by Susan Stroman. *The New York Times.* 15 April 2001: 16.

Brooks, Mel. *History of the World — Part I.* New York: Warner Books, 1981.

Brooks, Mel, dir. *Blazing Saddles.* Perf. Cleavon Little, Gene Wilder, Harvey Korman, Slim Pickens, Madeline Kahn, Alex Karras, David Huddleston, Liam Dunn, John Hillerman, Claude Ennis Starrett, Jr., and Dom DeLuise. 1974. Videocassette. Warner Home Video, 1991.

_____, dir. *Dracula: Dead and Loving It.* Perf. Leslie Nielsen, Mel Brooks, Peter MacNicol, Steven Weber, Amy Yasbeck, Lysette Anthony, Harvey Korman, and Megan Cavanagh. 1995. Videocassette. Columbia/Tristar Home Video, 1995.

_____, dir. *High Anxiety.* Perf. Mel Brooks, Madeline Kahn, Cloris Leachman, Harvey Korman, Ron Carey, Howard Morris, Dick Van Patten, Jack Riley, Charlie Callas, Ron Clark, and Rudy DeLuca. 1977. Videocassette. Fox Video, 1997.

_____, dir. *History of the World — Part I.* Perf. Mel Brooks, Dom DeLuise, Madeline Kahn, Harvey Korman, Cloris Leachman, Ron Carey, Gregory Hines, Pamela Stephenson, Andreas Voutsinas, Mary-Margaret Humes, Shecky Greene, Sid Caesar, and Spike Milligan. 1981. Videocassette. Fox Video, 1992.

_____, dir. *Life Stinks.* Perf. Mel Brooks, Lesley Ann Warren, Jeffrey Tambor, Howard Morris, Teddy Wilson, Stuart Pankin, and Rudy DeLuca. 1991. Videocassette. MGM/UA Home Video, 1992.

_____, dir. *The Producers.* Perf. Zero Mostel, Gene Wilder, Dick Shawn, Kenneth Mars, Christopher Hewett, Andreas Voutsinas, and Estelle Winwood. 1968. Videocassette. Embassy Home Entertainment, 1987.

_____, dir. *Robin Hood: Men in Tights.* Perf. Cary Elwes, Richard Lewis, Roger Rees, Amy Yasbeck, Dave Chappelle, Isaac Hayes, Tracey Ullman, Megan Cavanagh, Mark Blankfield, Eric Allan Kramer, Matthew Porretta, Dick Van Patten, and Dom DeLuise. 1993. Videocassette. Fox Video, 1993.

_____, dir. *Silent Movie.* Perf. Mel Brooks, Marty Feldman, Dom DeLuise, Bernadette Peters, Sid Caesar, Harold Gould, and Ron Carey. Videocassette. Key Video, 1988.

_____, dir. *Spaceballs.* Perf. Mel Brooks, John Candy, Rick Moranis, Bill Pullman, Daphne Zuniga, Dick Van Patten, and George Wyner. 1987. Videocassette. MGM/UA Home Video, 1988.

_____, dir. *The Twelve Chairs.* Perf. Ron Moody, Frank Langella, Dom DeLuise, and Mel Brooks. 1970. Videocassette. Media Home Entertainment, Inc., 1983.

_____, dir. *Young Frankenstein.* Perf. Gene Wilder, Peter Boyle, Marty Feldman, Cloris Leachman, Teri Garr, Kenneth Mars, Teri Garr, and Gene Hackman. 1974. Videocassette. Key Video, 1988.

Brooks, Mel, and Carl Reiner. *The 2,000 Year Old Man.* New York: Warner Books, 1981.

_____. *The 2,000 Year Old Man in the Year 2000: The Book.* New York: Cliff Street Books, 1997.

Brooks, Tim, and Earle Marsh. *The Complete Directory to Prime Time Network and Cable TV Shows: 1946–Present.* New York: Ballantine, 1995.

Buckley, Michael. "*Blazing Saddles.*" Rev. of *Blazing Saddles,* dir. by Mel Brooks. *Films in Review.* March 1974: 182–3.

_____. "*Spaceballs.*" Rev. of *Spaceballs,* dir. by Mel Brooks. *Films in Review.* Oct. 1987: 491–2.

_____. "*Young Frankenstein.*" Rev. of *Young Frankenstein,* dir. by Mel Brooks. *Films in Review.* Feb. 1975: 120–1.

Canby, Vincent. "*Blazing Saddles.*" Rev. of *Blazing Saddles,* dir. by Mel Brooks. *The New York Times.* (Feb. 8, 1974). Rpt. in *The New York Times Film Reviews.* Vol. 6. New York: Garland Publishing, Inc., 1975. 175.

_____. "*High Anxiety.*" Rev. of *High Anxiety,* dir. by Mel Brooks. *The New York Times.* (Dec. 26, 1977). Rpt. in *The New York Times Film Reviews.* Vol. 7. New York: Garland Publishing, Inc., 1979. 150.

_____. "*Robin Hood: Men in Tights.*" Rev. of *Robin Hood: Men in Tights,* dir. by Mel Brooks. *The New York Times.* (July 28, 1993). Rpt. in *The New York Times Film Reviews.* Vol. 15. New York: Garland Publishing, Inc., 1996, 113–4.

_____. "*Shinbone Alley.*" Rev. of *shinbone alley,* dir. by John D. Wilson. *The New York Times.* (April 8, 1971). Rpt. in *The New York Times Film Reviews.* Vol. 4. New York: Garland Publishing, Inc., 1972. 45.

_____. "*Silent Movie.*" Rev. of *Silent Movie,* dir. by Mel Brooks. *The New York Times.* (July 1, 1976). Rpt. in *The New York Times Film Reviews.* Vol. 6. New York: Garland Publishing, Inc., 1977. 229–30.

_____. "*12 Chairs, A Comedy, at Tower East.*" Rev. of *The Twelve Chairs,* dir. by Mel Brooks. *The New York Times.* (Oct. 29, 1970). Rpt. in *The New York Times Film Reviews.* Vol. 3. New York: Garland Publishing, Inc., 1971. 233.

_____. "*Warsaw Wags.*" Rev. of *To Be or Not to Be,* dir. by Alan Johnson. *The New York Times.* (Dec. 16, 1983). Rpt. in *The New York Times Film Reviews.* Vol. 10. New York: Garland Publishing, Inc., 1988. 160–1.

_____. "*Young Frankenstein.*" Rev. of *Young Frankenstein,* dir. by Mel Brooks. *The New York Times.* (Dec. 16, 1974). Rpt. in *The New York Times Film Reviews.* Vol. 5. New York: Garland Publishing, Inc., 1977. 308.

Cecil, Norman. "*The Producers.*" Rev. of *The Producers,* dir. by Mel Brooks. *Films in Review.* April 1968: 244.

Claro, Christopher, and Julie Klam. *Comedy Central: The Essential Guide to Comedy.* New York: Boulevard Books, 1997.

Claster, Bob. "*Caesar's Hour* Revisited." *Written By.* March 1996. Online. 6 June 2001: http://www.wga.org/WrittenBy//1996/0396/caesar.htm.

"*Colgate Comedy Hour.*" Rev. of *The Colgate-Comedy Hour,* dir. by Gordon Wiles. *Variety.* (May 17, 1967). Rpt. in *Variety Television Reviews.* Vol. 9. New York: Garland Publishing, Inc., 1989.

"Comedy's King Has Found Awards Formula." Rev. of *The Second Annual Comedy Awards,* dir. by John Moffitt. *Variety.* (April 14, 1976). Rpt. in *Variety Television Reviews.* Vol. 11. New York: Garland Publishers, Inc., 1989.

"Composers Net: Hummie Mann." 17 March 2001. http://composersnet.com/mann/bio.html.

Cox, Jay. "Monster Mash." Rev. of *Young Frankenstein,* dir. by Mel Brooks. *Time.* 30 Dec. 1974: 2.

Desser, David, and Lester D. Friedman. *American-Jewish Filmmakers: Traditions and Trends.* Chicago: University of Illinois Press, 1993.

"*Dom DeLuise & Friends.*" Rev. of *Dom DeLuise & Friends,* dir. by Greg Garrison. *Variety.* (Feb. 23, 1983). Rpt. in *Variety Television Reviews.* Vol. 13. New York: Garland Publishing, Inc., 1989.

Ebert, Roger. "*High Anxiety.*" Rev. of *High Anxiety,* dir. by Mel Brooks. *Cinemania 96.* CD-ROM. Microsoft, 1995.

_____. "*History of the World — Part I.*" Rev. of *History of the World — Part I,* dir. by Mel Brooks. *Cinemania 96.* CD-ROM. Microsoft, 1995.

_____. "*Life Stinks.*" *Life Stinks,* dir. by Mel Brooks. *Cinemania 96.* CD-ROM. Microsoft, 1995.

_____. "*Spaceballs.*" Rev. of *Spaceballs,* dir. by Mel Brooks. *Cinemania 96.* CD-ROM. Microsoft, 1995.

_____. "*To Be or Not to Be.*" Rev. of *To Be or Not to Be,* dir. by Mel Brooks. *Cinemania 96.* CD-ROM. Microsoft, 1995.

_____. "*Young Frankenstein.*" Rev. of *Young Frankenstein,* dir. by Mel Brooks. *Cinemania 96.* CD-ROM. Microsoft, 1995.

Edelman, Rob. "*High Anxiety.*" Rev. of *High Anxiety,* dir. by Mel Brooks. *Films in Review.* Feb. 1978: 118.

Firestone, Ross, ed. *Breaking It Up! The Best Routines of The Stand-Up Comics.* New York: Bantam Books, 1975.

Franklin, Joe. *Joe Franklin's Encyclopedia of Comedians.* Secaucus, NJ: Citadel Press, 1979.

Frawley, James, dir. *The Muppet Movie.* Perf. Jim Henson, Frank Oz, Jerry Nelson, Richard Hunt, Dave Goelz, Charles Durning, Austin Pendleton, Edgar Bergan, Milton Berle, Mel Brooks, James Coburn, Dom DeLuise, Elliott Gould, Bob Hope, Madeline

Kahn, Carol Kane, Cloris Leachman, Steve Martin, Richard Pryor, Telly Savalas, Orson Welles, and Paul Williams. 1979. Videocassette. Columbia Tristar Home Video, 1999.

"*Free to Be ... A Family.*" Rev. of *Marlo Thomas and Friends in Free to Be ... A Family,*" dir. by Gary Halvorson. *Variety.* (Dec. 28, 1988). Rpt. in *Variety Television Reviews.* Vol. 14. New York: Garland Publishing, Inc., 1990.

"Funny Is Money." *The New York Times Magazine.* Oct. 1997. Online. 10 April 1999: http://www.ews.uiuc.edu/~yin/Org/MBrooks/interviews/NewYork97.html.

Gardner, Elysa. "Hilarious *Producers* Signals Springtime for Musicals." Rev. of *The Producers,* dir. by Susan Stroman. *USA Today.* 20 April 2001: 1E.

"*Get Smart.*" Rev. of *Get Smart,* dir. by Howard Morris. *Variety.* (Sept. 22, 1965). Rpt. in *Variety Television Reviews.* Vol. 8. New York: Garland Publishing, Inc., 1989.

Gold, Herbert. "Mel Brooks Interview." *The New York Times Magazine.* March 30, 1975. Online. 10 April 1999: http://www.ews.uiuc.edu/~yin/Org/MBrooks/interviews/NewYork Times.html.

Goldberg, Lee. *Unsold Television Pilots; 1955 through 1988.* Jefferson, N.C.: McFarland & Company, Inc., 1990.

Grant, Edmond. "*Robin Hood: Men in Tights.*" Rev. of *Robin Hood: Men in Tights,* dir. by Mel Brooks. *Films in Review.* Sept./Oct. 1993: 338–9.

Green, Joey. *The Get Smart Handbook.* New York: Collier Books, 1993.

Green, Stanley. *Broadway Musicals: Show by Show.* Milwaukee: Hal Leonard Corp., 1996.

Greenspan, Roger. "*Ten from Your Show of Shows.*" Rev. of *Ten from Your Show of Shows,* dir. by Max Liebman. *The New York Times.* (Feb. 24, 1973). Rpt. in *The New York Times Film Reviews.* Vol. 5. New York: Garland Publishing, Inc., 1975. 23.

Greggio, Ezio, dir. *Screw Loose.* Perf. Mel Brooks, Ezio Greggio, Julie Condra, Gianfranco Barra, and Randi Ingerman. 1999. Videocassette. Columbia Tristar Home Video, 2000.

_____, dir. *Silence of the Hams.* Perf. Ezio Greggio, Dom DeLuise, Billy Zane, Joanna Pacula, Charlene Tilton, Martin Balsam, Stuart Pankin, John Astin, Phyllis Diller, Bubba Smith, Larry Storch, Rip Taylor, and Shelley Winters. 1993. Videocassette. CFP Video, 1993.

Guttmacher, Peter. *Legendary Comedies.* New York: MetroBooks, 1996.

Heldenfels, R.D. *Television's Greatest Year: 1954.* New York: Continuum, 1994.

Hinson, Hal. "*Life Stinks.*" Rev. of *Life Stinks,* dir. by Mel Brooks. *The Washington Post.* July 27, 1991. Online. 6 July 2000: http://www.washingtonpost.com/wp-srv/style/longterm/mo.../ lifestinkspg13hinson-a0a6ce.ht.

"*The Hollywood Palace.*" Rev. of *The Hollywood Palace,* dir. by Mel Ferber. *Variety.* (Jan. 15, 1964). Rpt. in *Variety Television Reviews.* Vol. 8. New York: Garland Publishing, Inc., 1989.

Holtzman, William. *Seesaw: A Dual Biography of Anne Bancroft and Mel Brooks.* Garden City, NY: Doubleday & Company, Inc., 1979.

Howard, Jeffrey K., and Dave Neil. "A Word with ... John Morris." *Las Vegas Weekly.* 6 Jan. 1999. http://www.lasvegasweekly.com/departments/01_06_99/film_morris.html.

Howe, Desson. "*Robin Hood: Men in Tights.*" Rev. of *Robin Hood: Men in Tights,* dir. by Mel Brooks. *The Washington Post.* July 30 1993. Online. 10 April 1999: http://www.washingtonpost.com/wp-srv/style/longt.../robinhoodmenintightspg13howe-a0fe4.ht.

"Hummie Mann: Inspired Circus." 19 May 2001. http://www.scorelogue.com/manntalk.html.

"Imogene Coca...." Rev. of *The Imogene Coca Show,* dir. by Ernest D. Glucksman. *Variety.* (Nov. 10, 1954). Rpt. in *Variety Television Reviews.* Vol. 5. New York: Garland Publishing, Inc., 1989.

"Imogene Coca's...." Rev. of *The Imogene Coca Show. Variety.* (Oct. 13, 1954). Rpt. in *Variety Television Reviews.* Vol. 5. New York: Garland Publishing, Inc., 1989.

"*Imogene Coca Show.*" Rev. of *The Imogene Coca Show,* dir. by Marc Daniels. *Variety.* (Oct. 6, 1954). Rpt. in *Variety Television Reviews.* Vol. 5. New York: Garland Publishing, Inc., 1989.

"Internet Movie Database: Mel Brooks." 9 May 2001: http://us.imdb.com/Name?Brooks%2C+Mel.

"Interview with Mel Brooks." *Maclean's.* April 17, 1978. Online. 10 April 1999: http://www.ews.uiuc.edu/~yin/Org/MBrooks/interviews/Maclean1.html.

Isherwood, Charles. "Swing Time for Hitler: *Producers* a Knockout." Rev. of *The Producers,* dir. by Susan Stroman. *Variety.* 23–9 April 2001: 16, 25.

"The Jerry Lewis Show." Rev. of *The Jerry Lewis Show,* dir. by Jack Shea. *Variety.* (Dec. 12, 1958). Rpt. in *Variety Television Reviews.* Vol. 6. New York: Garland Publishing, Inc., 1989.

"Johnny Carson Show." Rev. of *The Tonight Show Starring Johnny Carson,* dir. by Dick Carson. *Variety.* (Oct. 3, 1962). Rpt. in *Variety Television Reviews.* Vol. 7. New York: Garland Publishing, Inc., 1989.

Johnson, Alan, dir. *To Be or Not to Be.* Perf. Mel Brooks, Anne Bancroft, Tim Matheson, Charles Durning, Jose Ferrer, George Gaynes, Christopher Lloyd, George Wyner, Lewis J. Stadlen, Jack Riley, James Haake, Estelle Reiner, and Ronny Graham. 1982. Videocassette. Fox Video, 1993.

Kael, Pauline. *"Blazing Saddles."* Rev. of *Blazing Saddles,* dir. by Mel Brooks. *Cinemania 96.* CD-ROM. Microsoft, 1995.

_____. *"High Anxiety."* Rev. of *High Anxiety,* dir. by Mel Brooks. *Cinemania 96.* CD-ROM. Microsoft, 1995.

_____. *"History of the World — Part I."* Rev. of *History of the World — Part I,* dir. by Mel Brooks. *Cinemania 96.* CD-ROM. Microsoft, 1995.

_____. *"The Producers."* Rev. of *The Producers,* dir. by Mel Brooks. *Cinemania 96.* CD-ROM. Microsoft, 1995.

_____. *"To Be or Not to Be."* Rev. of *To Be or Not to Be,* dir. by Mel Brooks. *Cinemania 96.* CD-ROM. Microsoft, 1995.

_____. *"The Twelve Chairs."* Rev. of *The Twelve Chairs,* dir. by Mel Brooks. *Cinemania 96.* CD-ROM. Microsoft, 1995.

_____. *"Young Frankenstein."* Rev. of *Young Frankenstein,* dir. by Mel Brooks. *Cinemania 96.* CD-ROM. Microsoft, 1995.

Kauffmann, Stanley. "Remake and Reminder." *The New Republic.* 31 Dec. 1983: 24–5.

Kondek, Joshua, ed. "Mel Brooks." *Contemporary Theatre, Film and Television.* Vol. 24. Detroit: Gale Group, Inc., 2000.

Lahr, John. "The Gold Rush." Rev. of *The Producers,* dir. by Susan Stroman. *The New Yorker.* 7 May 2001: 84–86.

Levy, Shawn. *King of Comedy: The Life and Art of Jerry Lewis.* New York: St. Martin's Press, 1996.

Lybarger, Dan. "Believing in Make-Believe: An Interview with Mel Brooks." *The Keaton Chronicle.* Autumn 1997. Online. 10 April 1999: http://userwww.service.emory.edu/ ~mgros/brooks/ Interview2.html.

Maltin, Leonard, ed. *Leonard Maltin's Movie Encyclopedia.* New York: Dutton, 1994.

_____. *"Blazing Saddles."* Rev. of *Blazing Saddles,* dir. by Mel Brooks. *Leonard Maltin's 2001 Movie & Video Guide.* New York: Signet, 2000.

_____. *"Dracula: Dead and Loving It."* Rev. of *Dracula: Dead and Loving It,,* dir. by Mel Brooks. *Leonard Maltin's 2001 Movie & Video Guide.* New York: Signet, 2000.

_____. *"High Anxiety."* Rev. of *High Anxiety,* dir. by Mel Brooks. *Leonard Maltin's 2001 Movie & Video Guide.* New York: Signet, 2000.

_____. *"History of the World — Part I."* Rev. of *History of the World — Part I,* dir. by Mel Brooks. *Leonard Maltin's 2001 Movie & Video Guide.* New York: Signet, 2000.

_____. *"Life Stinks."* Rev. of *Life Stinks,* dir. by Mel Brooks. *Leonard Maltin's 2001 Movie & Video Guide.* New York: Signet, 2000.

_____. *"Look Who's Talking Too."* Rev. of *Look Who's Talking Too,* dir. by Amy Heckerling. *Leonard Maltin's 2001 Movie & Video Guide.* New York: Signet, 2000.

_____. *"The Producers."* Rev. of *The Producers,* dir. by Mel Brooks. *Leonard Maltin's 2001 Movie & Video Guide.* New York: Signet, 2000.

_____. *"Robin Hood: Men in Tights."* Rev. of *Robin Hood: Men in Tights,* dir. by Mel Brooks. *Leonard Maltin's 2001 Movie & Video Guide.* New York: Signet, 2000.

_____. *"Silent Movie."* Rev. of *Silent Movie,* dir. by Mel Brooks. *Leonard Maltin's 2001 Movie & Video Guide.* New York: Signet, 2000.

_____. *"Spaceballs."* Rev. of *Spaceballs,* dir. by Mel Brooks. *Leonard Maltin's 2001 Movie & Video Guide.* New York: Signet, 2000.

_____. *"To Be or Not to Be."* Rev. of *Blazing Saddles,* dir. by Alan Johnson. *Leonard Maltin's 2001 Movie & Video Guide.* New York: Signet, 2000.

_____. *"The Twelve Chairs."* Rev. of *The Twelve Chairs,* dir. by Mel Brooks. *Leonard Maltin's 2001 Movie & Video Guide.* New York: Signet, 2000.

_____. *"Young Frankenstein."* Rev. of *Young Frankenstein,* dir. by Mel Brooks. *Leonard Maltin's 2001 Movie & Video Guide.* New York: Signet, 2000.

"Marlo Thomas and Friends in Free to Be You and Me." Rev. of *Marlo Thomas and Friends in Free to Be ... You and Me."* *Variety.* (March 20, 1974). Rpt. in *Variety Television Reviews.* Vol. 11. New York: Garland Publishing, Inc., 1989.

"Marriage — Handle with Care." Rev. of *Marriage — Handle with Care,* dir. by Jerome

Shaw. *Variety.* (Dec. 4, 1959). Rpt. in *Variety Television Reviews.* Vol. 6. New York: Garland Publishing, Inc., 1989.

Maslin, Janet. "*Dracula: Dead and Loving It.*" Rev. of *Dracula: Dead and Loving It,* dir. by Mel Brooks. *The New York Times.* (Dec. 22, 1975). Rpt. in *The New York Times Film Reviews.* Vol. 16. New York: Garland Publishing, Inc., 1998. 190.

_____. "From Time Immemorial." Rev. of *History of the World — Part I,* dir. by Mel Brooks. *The New York Times.* (June 12, 1981). Rpt. in *The New York Times Film Reviews.* Vol. 9. New York: Garland Publishing, Inc., 1984. 70.

_____. "*Life Stinks.*" Rev. of *Life Stinks,* dir. by Mel Brooks. *The New York Times.* (July 26, 1991). Rpt. in *The New York Times Film Reviews.* Vol. 14. New York: Garland Publishing, Inc., 1993. 138–9.

_____. "Sci-fi Sendup." Rev. of *Spaceballs,* dir. by Mel Brooks. *The New York Times.* (June 24, 1987). Rpt. in *The New York Times Film Reviews.* Vol. 13. New York: Garland Publishing, Inc., 1990. 86.

McCrohan, Donna. *The Life & Times of Maxwell Smart.* New York: St. Martin's Press, 1988.

_____. *The Second City: A Backstage History of Comedy's Hottest Troupe.* New York: Perigee Books, 1987.

"Mel Brooks." *NBC News Archives.* Online. http://ebseg?view=NBC&TemplateName= hitlist.tmpl&operator=or&query=Mel+ Brooks

"The Mel Brooks Humor Site." 27 May 2001. http://www.tmbhs.com/tmbhs/tvappear-ancefilmology.asp.

Morton, Alan. "*The Nutt House:* An Episode Guide." http://www.xnet.com/~djk/main_ page.shtml.

_____. "*When Things Were Rotten:* An Episode Guide." http://www.xnet.com/~djk/main_ page.shtml.

"*Naked Hollywood.*" Rev. of *Naked Hollywood,* dir. by Margy Kinmonth. *Variety.* (July 26, 1991). Rpt. in *Variety Television Reviews.* Vol. 17. New York: Garland Publishing, Inc., 1994.

"*New Faces.*" Rev. of *New Faces,* dir. by Harry Horner. *The New York Times.* (Feb. 20, 1954). Rpt. in *The New York Times Film Reviews.* Vol. 1. New York: Garland Publishing, Inc., 1970.

"*New Les Crane Show.*" Rev. of *The New Les Crane Show,* dir. by Barry Shear. *Variety.*

(Aug. 5, 1964). Rpt. in *Variety Television Reviews.* Vol. 8. New York: Garland Publishing, Inc., 1964.

Nightcap: Conversations on the Arts and Letters." Rev. of *Nightcap: Conversations on the Arts and Letters with Studs Terkel and Calvin Trillin. Variety.* (Nov. 9, 1983). Rpt. in *Variety Television Reviews.* Vol. 13. New York: Garland Publishing, Inc., 1989.

"*The Nutt House.*" Rev. of *The Nutt House,* dir. by Gary Nelson. *Variety.* (Sept. 20, 1989). Rpt. in *Variety Television Reviews.* Vol. 17. New York: Garland Publishing, Inc., 1992.

O'Neil, Thomas. *The Emmys: The Ultimate, Unofficial Guide to the Battle of TV's Best Shows and Greatest Stars.* New York: Perigee, 1992.

_____. *The Grammys: For the Record.* New York: Penguin, 1993.

"*Open End.*" Rev. of *Open End. Variety.* (March 25, 1964). Rpt. in *Variety Television Reviews.* Vol. 8. New York: Garland Publishing, Inc., 1989.

"*The Play of the Week.*" Rev. of *The Play of the Week: archy and mehitabel,* dir. by Bob Blum. *Variety.* (June 22, 1960). Rpt. in *Variety Television Reviews.* Vol. 7. New York: Garland Publishing, Inc., 1989.

"*Polly Bergen Show.*" Rev. of *The Polly Bergen Show,* dir. by Bill Colleran. *Variety.* (Oct. 9, 1957). Rpt. in *Variety Television Reviews.* Vol. 6. New York: Garland Publishing, Inc., 1989.

Richmon, Ray. *The Simpsons: A Complete Guide to Our Favorite Family.* New York: HarperPerennial, 1997.

Sackett, Susan. *The Hollywood Reporter Book of Box Office Hits.* New York: Billboard, 1990.

Sennett, Ted. *Laughing in the Dark: Movie Comedy from Groucho to Woody.* New York: St. Martin's Press, 1992.

Shalit, Gene, ed. *Laughing Matters: A Celebration of American Humor.* New York: Ballantine, 1987.

Sheward, David. *It's a Hit: The Back Stage Book of Longest-Running Broadway Shows, 1984 to the Present.* New York: Back Stage Books, 1994.

"*Sid Caesar-Imogene Coca-Carl Reiner-Howard Morris Special.*" Rev. of *The Sid Caesar, Imogene Coca, Carl Reiner, Howard Morris Special,* dir. by Bill Hobin. *Variety.* (April 12, 1967). Rpt. in *Variety Television Reviews.* Vol. 9. New York: Garland Publishing, Inc., 1989.

"*Sid Caesar Invites You.*" Rev. of *Sid Caesar Invites You,* dir. by Frank Bunetta. *Variety.* (Jan. 29, 1958). Rpt. in *Variety Television*

Reviews. Vol. 6. New York: Garland Publishing, Inc., 1989.

Siegel, Larry. "Mel Brooks Interview." *Playboy.* 1966. Online. 10 April 1999. http:/www. ews.uiuc.edu/~yin/Org/MBrooks/interviews/Playboy1966.html.

____. "Mel Brooks Interview." *Playboy.* 1977. Online. 10 April 1999. http://www.ews. uiuc.edu/~yin/Org/MBrooks/interviews/Playboy1975.html.

Siegel, Robert. "Interview: Mel Brooks Discusses His Tony Nomination for *The Producers.*" *All Things Considered,* National Public Radio. Online. 18 May 2001: http://www.kyvl.org:8000/WebZ/FETCH?sessionid=01-36821-111303743&recno=3&results.

Sinyard, Neil. *The Films of Mel Brooks.* New York: Exeter, 1987.

Smith, Dave. *Disney A to Z: The Official Encyclopedia.* New York: Hyperion, 1996.

Smurthwaite, Nick and Paul Gelder. *Mel Brooks and the Spoof Movie.* New York: Proteus Books, 1982.

Spheeris, Penelope, dir. *The Little Rascals.* Perf. Travis Tedford, Bug Hall, Brittany Ashton Holmes, Kevin Jamal Woods, Jordan Warkol, Zachary Mabry, Ross Elliot Bagley, Blake McIver Ewing, Sam Saletta, Blake Jeremy Collins, Courtland Mead, Mel Brooks, Whoopi Goldberg, Daryl Hannah, Reba McIntire, Lea Thompson, and George Wendt. 1994. Videocassette. MCA/Universal Home Video 1998.

Spreng, Patrick. *Everything Rosie: The Ultimate Guide for Rosie O'Donnell Fans.* Secaucus, NJ: Birch Lane Press, 1998.

Taubman, Howard. "Musical with Bolger at Winter Garden." Rev. of *All-American,* dir. by Joshua Logan. *The New York Times.* (March 20, 1962). Rpt. in *The New York Times Theater Reviews.* Vol. 2. New York: New York Times and Arno Press, 1971.

"Tele Follow-up Comment." Rev. of *Your Show of Shows,* dir. by Max Liebman. *Variety.* (June 16, 1954). Rpt. in *Variety Television Reviews.* Vol. 5. New York: Garland Publishing, Inc., 1989.

"*The Television Academy Hall of Fame.*" Rev. of *The Television Academy Hall of Fame,* dir. by Dwight Hemion. *Variety.* (May 1, 1985). Rpt. in *Variety Television Reviews.* Vol. 13. New York: Garland Publishing, Inc., 1989.

Thomas, Dave, Robert Crane, and Susan Carney. *SCTV: Behind the Scenes.* Toronto: McClelland & Stewart, 1996.

"*Tiptoe Through TV.*" Rev. of *Tiptoe Through TV,* dir. by Jerome Shaw. *Variety.* (May 11, 1960). Rpt. in *Variety Television Reviews.* Vol. 7. New York: Garland Publishing, Inc., 1989.

Took, Barry. *Comedy Greats: A Celebration of Comic Genius Past and Present.* Wellingborough, England, 1989.

"*The 2,000-Year-Old Man.*" Rev. of *The 2,000 Year Old Man,* dir. by Leo Salkin. *Variety.* (Jan. 15, 1975). Rpt. in *Variety Television Reviews.* Vol. 11. New York: Garland Publishing, Inc., 1989.

"*Variety — World of Show Biz.*" Rev. of *Variety — World of Show Biz,* dir. by Jerome Shaw. *Variety.* (June 8, 1960). Rpt. in *Variety Television Reviews.* Vol. 7. New York: Garland Publishing, Inc., 1989.

Waldron, Vince. *The Official Dick Van Dyke Show Book: The Definitive History and Ultimate Viewer's Guide to Television's Most Enduring Comedy.* New York: Hyperion, 1994.

Weissman, Ginny, and Coyne Steven Sanders. *The Dick Van Dyke Show: Anatomy of a Classic.* New York: St. Martin's Press, 1983.

"*When Things Were Rotten.*" Rev. of *When things Were Rotten,* dir. by Jerry Paris. *Variety.* (Sept. 17, 1975). Rpt. in *Variety Television Reviews.* Vol. 11. New York: Garland Publishing, Inc., 1989.

Yacowar, Maurice. *Method in Madness: The Comic Art of Mel Brooks.* New York: St. Martin's Press, 1981.

Zaga, Diane Arieff. "Tummeling Toward the Millennium: The 2,000 Year Old Man Is Alive, Well, and Still Doesn't Touch Fried Food — An Interview with Mel Brooks and Carl Reiner." *The Jewish Journal of Greater LA.* Dec. 5, 1997. Online. 10 April 1999: http://userwww.service.emory.edu/ ~mgros/brooks/Interview3.html.

Zimmerman, Paul D. "Babbling Brooks." Rev. of *Young Frankenstein,* dir. by Mel Brooks. *Newsweek.* 23 Dec. 1974: 79.

Index

243